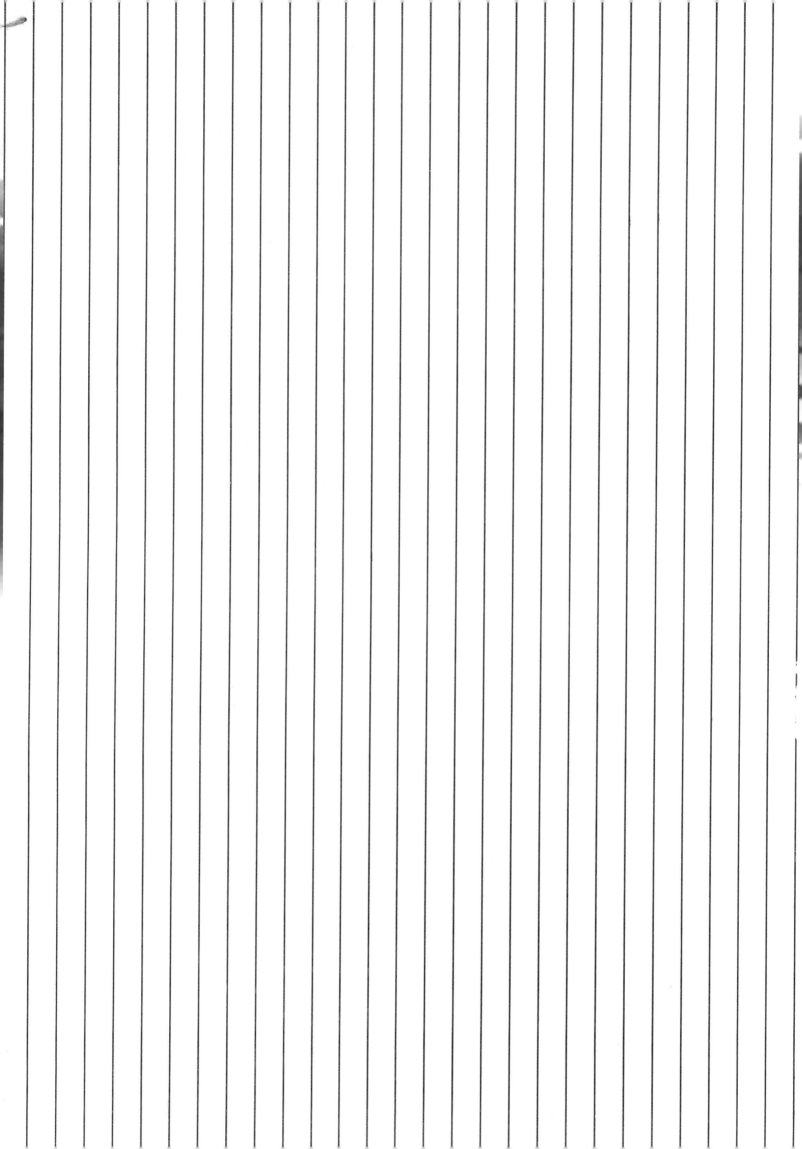

Baseball

By Donald Honig

NONFICTION
Baseball When the Grass Was Real
Baseball Between the Lines
The Man in the Dugout
The October Heroes
The Image of Their Greatness (with Lawrence Ritter)
The 100 Greatest Baseball Players of All Time (with Lawrence Ritter)
The Brooklyn Dodgers: An Illustrated Tribute
The New York Yankees: An Illustrated History
Baseball's 10 Greatest Teams
The Los Angeles Dodgers: The First Quarter Century
The National League: An Illustrated History
The American League: An Illustrated History
The Boston Red Sox: An Illustrated Tribute
Baseball America
The New York Mets: The First Quarter Century
The World Series: An Illustrated History
Baseball in the '50s
The All-Star Game: An Illustrated History
Mays, Mantle, Snider: A Celebration
The Greatest Pitchers of All Time
The Greatest First Basemen of All Time
Baseball in the '30s
The Donald Honig Reader
Baseball: The Illustrated History of America's Game

FICTION
Sidewalk Caesar
Walk Like a Man
The Americans
Divide the Night
No Song to Sing
Judgment Night
The Love Thief
The Severith Style
Illusions
I Should Have Sold Petunias
The Last Great Season
Marching Home

DONALD

HONIG

Baseball

THE

ILLUSTRATED

HISTORY

OF

AMERICA'S

GAME

CROWN PUBLISHERS, INC. · NEW YORK

Published by Crown Publishers, Inc., 201 East 50th Street,
New York, New York 10022

CROWN is a trademark of Crown Publishers, Inc.

Manufactured in the United States of America

Design by Ken Sansone and Peggy Goddard

Library of Congress Cataloging-in-Publication Data

Honig, Donald.
Baseball: an illustrated history of America's game/
by Donald Honig.
p.   cm.
Includes index.
1. Baseball—United States—History—Chronology.
2. Baseball—United States—History—Pictorial works.
I. Title.
GV863.A1H64   1989   89-1223
796.357'0973—dc19   CIP

ISBN 0-517-57295-8
1   3   5   7   9   10   8   6   4   2
First Edition

For my daughter, Cathy

C O N T E N T S

ACKNOWLEDGMENTS

I am deeply indebted to a great number of people for their generous assistance in photo research and in gathering the photographs reproduced in this book. Special thanks are due Michael P. Aronstein, president of Card Memorabilia Associates, Ltd.; Patricia Kelly of the National Baseball Hall of Fame and Museum in Cooperstown, New York; Jon Braude of the Cincinnati Reds public relations office; Richard Cohen of Sports Bookshelf, Inc.; David Szen, publisher of *Yankees Magazine;* Kip Ingle, director of publicity for the St. Louis Cardinals; Julie Wagner of the Baltimore Orioles public relations office; and Lawrence Cancro, director of marketing for the Boston Red Sox.

The following photographs are the work of Nancy Hogue: pages 273 (top left), 275 (top right), 284 (top left, top right), 285 (top center right), 287 (top left, top center), 288 (top left, top right, bottom right), 290 (top right, center left), 291 (top left, top center, center right, bottom left), 292 (top right, bottom left), 293 (center right), 294 (top left, bottom left), 295 (bottom), 296 (bottom), 297, 305 (top), 307, 318 (2 top left, center left), 319 (center, bottom right), 322 (top left, top right, bottom left), 325 (top left). A special thanks to W. F. Schildman and the Cincinnati Reds for the photo of Pete Rose breaking Ty Cobb's career record for hits.

For their good advice, wise counsel, and steady encouragement, I am grateful to these keen students of baseball history: David Markson, Lawrence Ritter, Stanley Honig, Andrew Aronstein, Douglas Mulcahy, Jeffrey Neuman, Louis Kiefer, and Thomas Brookman. And a final word of gratitude to my editor, Erica Marcus, for her patience, good humor, and editorial acumen.

Baseball

Wee Willie Keeler

This is what we have been told: Abner Doubleday invented baseball in Cooperstown, New York, in 1839.

It's an amiable myth—no one believes it, nor does anyone attack it with particular fervor, for this is a myth that sounds right and feels comfortable nestling among the lighter harvests of the imagination. An institution as nationally involving as baseball ought to have a documented beginning, no matter how artful. And if Cooperstown was not the cradle of baseball, well, then it looks like it should have been. For like the game itself, the upstate New York village on the shores of Lake Otsego seems to depict and embody something timelessly American.

Abner Doubleday, it has been written, "didn't know a baseball from a kumquat." Nevertheless, the man who did not invent baseball did make something of a name for himself in another field of endeavor, where the competition was a bit more lethal. A native of Ballston Spa, New York, Doubleday graduated from West Point in 1842 and went on to serve his country faithfully but obscurely until 1861. In the spring of that year, Major Doubleday was in command of the garrison at Fort Sumter, South Carolina, when it was fired upon by Confederate shore batteries. Doubleday is said to have aimed the first cannon to respond to the attack, and the Civil War had begun. He later served (as a breveted general) at Second Bull Run, Antietam, Fredericksburg, and Gettysburg. He retired in 1873 and died in New Jersey in 1893 at the age of seventy-three. As far as anyone knows, he never uttered the word *baseball*.

It wasn't until 1907, fourteen years after his death, that Doubleday was officially credited with having been the sole begetter of baseball. This exercise in American mythology was the conclusion of the Mills Commission, a panel of seven distinguished gentlemen of impeccable pedigree, organized at the behest of Albert Spalding to investigate and determine the origins of baseball. (Spalding was one of the game's more impressive pioneer figures, a star pitcher in the 1870s and later founder of the sporting goods firm that still bears his name.)

The Commission included A. G. Mills, a former president of the National League; Arthur P. Gorman, a former United States Senator from Maryland; and Morgan G. Bulkeley, a former governor of Connecticut and one-time National League president. These estimable gentlemen and their colleagues sifted through the records and came to the following conclusions:

That Base Ball had its origins in the United States.

Abner Doubleday

That the first scheme for playing it, according to the best evidence obtainable to date, was devised by Abner Doubleday, at Cooperstown, New York, in 1839.

Part of the "evidence" was "a circumstantial statement by a reputable gentleman, according to which the first known diagram of the diamond, indicating positions for the players was drawn by Abner Doubleday in Cooperstown, New York, in 1839." In the event someone might question the evidence, which had all the weight of a flea's eyelash, the report pointed out "how the orderly mind of the embryo West Pointer would devise a scheme for limiting the contestants on each side and alloting them to field positions, each with a certain amount of territory. . . ." Ergo, there were military connotations to baseball's diagrammatic configurations.

There was an evident jingoist streak in the Mills Commission, and Spalding, whose hand guided the commission's deliberations, was anxious to apply the "Made in America" stamp to the game and thus foreclose any future claimants.

No one, of course, invented baseball. Henry Chadwick (1824–1908), one of the game's significant early figures, maintained that American baseball evolved out of an English game called *rounders*. Some of the basics of America's game were indeed present in the English version, such as batting at a thrown ball and running to a base. Since there seems not to have been any great English passion associated with rounders, the game remained fairly static, while America's incremental love affair with

baseball forced constant tinkering and refining of the game until it had been shaped to perfection.

Chadwick, who was born in England and came to America with his parents at the age of thirteen, was probably the first baseball junkie. Fascinated by the game, he began writing about it in the 1850s (it was he who devised that marvel of condensed information known as the box score) and remained the sport's preeminent chronicler until his death.

In its early, awkward stirrings up from the mud flats of its own creation, baseball as played in the 1840s bears more than a passing resemblance to today's game, such as three strikes and out, and out on a caught fly ball. Another way of putting a man out, however, has long since vanished. Back in those rudimentary days a fielder picked up a batted ball and threw it at the runner; if the runner was hit with the ball he was out. This was called *plugging*. (Obviously the ball was much softer then.)

The man who began changing the rules of the game was Alexander Cartwright (1820–1892). In 1845, the New York–born Cartwright, an engineer by training, organized the first ball club, the Knickerbockers. On June 19, 1846, the Knickerbockers and another team, the New York Nine, played the first game between two organized teams.

Henry Chadwick

The site was the Elysian Fields in Hoboken, New Jersey. With Cartwright acting as umpire, the New York Nine won 23–1.

This historic game was played under rules newly formulated by Cartwright and it was under these rules that baseball began assuming recognizable shape. There were nine-man teams, plugging had been eliminated, the bases were flat (they had been posts), and most significant of all, a diamond-shaped infield was laid out with bases ninety feet apart.

"Ninety feet between bases is the nearest to perfection that man has yet achieved," Red Smith has written. That magical distance has remained unchanged since 1845. After experimenting with cleanly handled ground balls, Cartwright decided that ninety feet was the point where a runner and the throw would both arrive with the greatest degree of simultaneity, with the throw usually beating the runner by a split second. It has never changed, nor have the checks and balances—as runners became faster, so did infielders adjust, compensating with increased agility and stronger throwing arms.

Under Cartwright's formulations, baseball became a game of swifter action and greater excitement. By the late 1850s there were more than two dozen organized ball clubs in the New York area. It was all still amateur ball then, considered a "gentleman's" game, played for relaxation by the city's young dandies.

Until the development and evolution of baseball, there had been no team sports in America. Baseball had a catalyzing effect, bringing people together, first in teams and then in the crowds that gathered around the unfenced grounds to watch the games. Something about the new game—its tempo, its balance, its potential for individual excellence amid team unity—was deeply appealing to those early spectators. As the game's popularity spread, more and more young men began playing it, ending the days of baseball as a purely social indulgence, raising the caliber of play, and beginning its history as a sport with considerable competitive verve.

When the Civil War broke out in 1861, the swelling ranks of the Union Army included many men who had played baseball, and throughout the course of the war, during the long respites between battles, the game was played in many encampments. Because of the huge troop concentrations, the game was being introduced to multitudes of men from all over the country (a game played on Christmas Day 1862, at Hilton Head, South Carolina, was watched by a crowd estimated at forty thousand), and after the war they returned to their cities and towns and villages and with them came the new game.

In retrospect, baseball's quick acceptance was a phenomenon. Those who even today wonder about the mystique of baseball might look back to the 1860s and see it spreading, informally and irresistibly, across the land, something so indigenously American in appeal it was almost as if the nation had been waiting for its arrival, like some marvelous gift to be cherished and enjoyed.

Professional baseball—played by salaried ballplayers in front of paying customers—began in 1869 with the formation of the Cincinnati Red Stockings. They were owned by the man called by some "the father of professional baseball," Harry Wright (1835–1895). The English-born Wright, who came to America as a boy, was originally a professional cricket player in New York and New Jersey, but gradually turned to the new game.

After moving to Cincinnati, Wright organized the first openly professional baseball team. One of the team's unique features was that only one of its players came from Cincinnati—the rest had been hired away from other teams in other cities. Soon to become the norm, this was then a novelty; hitherto, teams had been made up exclusively of players who lived in the cities they represented.

The star of the Cincinnati Red Stockings was Harry Wright's younger brother George (1847–1937). Born in Yonkers, New York, George Wright was America's first baseball superstar. He was a shortstop of such compelling ability that for years the name George Wright was virtually synonymous with the position. There is no way of knowing just how good a ballplayer he was, of course, but there is no question that he was an innovator; at a time when most players showed little mobility or imagination in defensive play, George ranged far and covered a lot of ground.

Harry Wright designed the team's uniform—blouses, knee-length pants, and stockings (red, of course), which is still pretty much the upholstery today. He then took his club of ten men (nine regulars and one substitute) on a tour of cities large and small, from San Francisco to Omaha and Chicago and Cleveland, and east to Philadelphia, Washington, New York, and Boston, playing all comers. Sometimes they pummeled the hapless locals by scores like 103–8 and 80–5; some games were much tighter. But whatever the score, the boys from Cincinnati were always on top. The Red Stockings intrigued sporting America and aroused their native town by going undefeated in 57 games (during which George Wright reportedly hit 59 home runs and batted over .500, for whatever those statistics are worth).

In 1871, the National Association of Professional Baseball Players, forerunner of the National League, was formed. The charter members were Boston (where the Wrights had moved, along with some of their Cincinnati players), Chicago, Cleveland, New York, Philadelphia, Washington, Troy, Fort Wayne (Indiana), and Rockford (Illinois).

The National Association stayed in business for five years, for four of those years dominated by the Boston Red Stockings, who in 1875 ran away with the championship with a 71–8 record. The club's star pitcher was Albert

Albert Spalding

Harry Wright

William Hulbert

Spalding, who in 1874 and 1875 had won-lost records of 52–18 and 57–5.

The National Association was an awkward first step, and it soon crumbled under the weight of various factors, most notably drunkenness on the field, bribery, corruption (betting on games was common among the players), and a general rowdyism that made the game unpalatable to many spectators.

Early in 1876, William Hulbert, president of the Chicago club, got together with Spalding. They agreed that baseball had a bright future if properly conducted and supervised, and decided to organize a new league—the National League. On February 2, 1876, the new circuit officially came into existence, with Morgan Bulkeley its first president, though Hulbert and Spalding were the league's strongmen.

The tough-minded founders of the National League knew there was only one formula for survival—strict rules and strict enforcement. No liquor was to be sold at the park. Players were to appear on the field sober (that it

was felt necessary to have this rule is telltale). Players were forbidden to bet on games. Written contracts were to be respected by the league's teams (meaning there would be no pirating of somebody else's players).

The original members of the eight-team league were Chicago, St. Louis, Louisville, and Cincinnati in the west; Boston, New York, Philadelphia, and Hartford in the east. Teams came and went over the next several decades, and at one time or another the National League was represented by teams in Providence, Milwaukee, Buffalo, Indianapolis, Troy, Syracuse, Cleveland, Worcester, Detroit, Baltimore, Washington, Columbus (Ohio), and Kansas City. But whoever came or went, the league itself remained solidly established, thanks to the stern and uncompromising stewardship of its founders.

The first people to learn that the new league's rules were not to be flouted were the owners of the New York and Philadelphia clubs. In 1876 they decided not to play out their schedule (of about 70 games) and canceled their final western trips. Summoned to league headquarters, they expected to be fined and lectured; instead, to their astonishment, both clubs were booted out of the league. Hulbert had elected to take this action, losing two prized cities rather than see his rules finessed. (Both cities were readmitted six years later.)

Hulbert took over the presidency in 1877 and ran the league with an iron hand until his death in 1882.

Then, as now, baseball was highlighted by the exploits of its star players. Most of those stars are now names linked to a remote era and exclusive to the conjuring of historians. But in their time they stood large and

Cap Anson

Charles Radbourne

were robust in the imagination of small boys the land over.

The greatest of these players from baseball's formative years was Chicago's Adrian ("Cap") Anson, who played from 1876 through 1897, was the first to amass 3,000 hits (3,041), and who, just before his death in 1922 at the age of sixty-nine, struck a familiar theme when he said that the stars of the moment (Ruth, Cobb, Sisler, Hornsby, etc.) could not measure up to the stars of his day. Anson's Chicago White Stockings won the first National League pennant with a 52–14 record, with ace pitcher Al Spalding, pitching from the then-regulation 45-foot distance, racking up a 47–13 record (most clubs carried just two pitchers).

The National League's slow, steady success did not go unnoticed, and in 1882 another league, the American Association, was formed. The new outfit, which remained in operation until 1891, gave the older circuit some sharp competition. It cut ticket prices from fifty to twenty-five cents and permitted Sunday games (forbidden in the National League). The newcomers also raided National League rosters for players.

The competing leagues came to an accommodation in 1883, the most important article of agreement being a promise not to try and lasso any of the other's players. In 1884 there was enough amity between the two leagues for a postseason championship series between their respective pennant winners. In this best-of-five matchup, a forerunner of the World Series, the National League's Providence Grays took the American Association's New York Metropolitans in three straight.

The winning pitcher in each game was a twenty-nine-

year-old right-hander named Charles Radbourn, known as "Old Hoss." During that 1884 season Charlie rang up a resounding 60–12 record, pitching 679 innings, starting 73 games and completing all of them. The reason Radbourn pitched so many of his club's 112 games was the early-season defection of Providence's other pitcher Charlie Sweeney to the Union Association, a one-year confection that had franchises dropping in and out all summer. So Radbourn agreed to pitch the rest of the way, and he did, frequently with a sore arm. Charlie was quite a performer that year, but his heroics were not without cost—he was never the same pitcher after 1884.

Other notable players of the time included first baseman Dan Brouthers, a four-time National League batting champion; first baseman Roger Connor, whose 136 lifetime home runs were not surpassed until the coming of Babe Ruth; Buck Ewing, widely accorded the distinction as the nineteenth century's greatest catcher; outfielder Pete Browning, another thunderous hitter; and pitchers Tim Keefe, Mickey Welch, and Pud Galvin.

The most popular player of the 1880s was Chicago (later Boston) outfielder Mike ("King") Kelly. This handsome, hard-playing, hard-drinking fellow apparently had charisma to spare. He was master of an innovative slide (contemporary descriptions make it sound like a hook slide) that he executed with such dramatic flair it became the inspiration for a popular song, "Slide, Kelly, Slide!", which fans would sing whenever Mike got to first base. Kelly, who spent lavishly in saloons and at race tracks, was in 1887 sold by Chicago to Boston for $10,000, a sum then so staggering that newspapers felt constrained to

The Polo Grounds in 1886, then located at Fifth Avenue and 110th Street. Note how far behind the catcher the umpire is positioned.

reproduce in their pages the sales agreement to convince an incredulous public. Kelly's accelerated life-style caught up to him in 1894, when he died of pneumonia at the age of thirty-six.

In 1890, another one-year barnacle adhered itself to the flanks of the National League and American Association. This was the Players League, formed by ballplayers who had become disgruntled by the monopolistic practices of the established leagues, which included salary caps, the reserve clause, unreasonable fines, and other objectionable practices.

The Players League succeeded in siphoning off some outstanding talent, including Brouthers, Connor, Ewing, Radbourn, Keefe, and others. But the Players was one league too many, and its existence put a serious financial dent in the American Association, which folded after the 1891 season, leaving the National League the sole employer of America's top baseball players.

The surviving National League emerged stronger than ever, expanding to twelve teams in 1892. The six eastern representatives were Boston, Brooklyn, Philadelphia, Baltimore, New York, and Washington. In the west were Chicago, Pittsburgh, Louisville, Cincinnati, St. Louis, and Cleveland.

Showing the gritty ethics of any survivor, the league reduced rosters to thirteen players and forced salary cuts. Having nowhere else to go, the players damned it and bore it anyway.

In the 1890s, the National League was dominated by two teams, the Boston Beaneaters and the Baltimore Orioles, who between them won every pennant from 1891 through 1898. The Beaneaters, who won in 1891, 1892, 1893, 1897, and 1898, fielded some of the waning century's great players, including pitchers John Clarkson and Kid Nichols, third baseman Jimmy Collins, and outfielders Tommy McCarthy, Billy Hamilton, and Hugh Duffy. It was Duffy who in 1894 achieved the highest batting average ever in the major leagues, .438.

Although the Beaneaters won five pennants in the 1890s to the Orioles' three, it was the latter that became the team of legend, baseball's first "greatest team of all time."

These were the Orioles of John McGraw, Wee Willie Keeler, Hugh Jennings, Joe Kelley, and Wilbert Robinson, a gang of Gay Nineties marauders whose grit and style became synonymous with a way of baseball life—the "Old Oriole spirit," which allegedly impelled men to ignore cuts and bruises and broken bones and continue playing.

Managed by "Foxy" Ned Hanlon, they took a lively but crude game and brought to it tactics and strategy more daring and sophisticated than any previously seen. Hanlon and his feisty band of Orioles made baseball more of a team sport than it had ever been before. They pioneered in relays and cut-offs and they perfected the hit-and-run, with Keeler (hitting) and McGraw (running) the most skilled proponents.

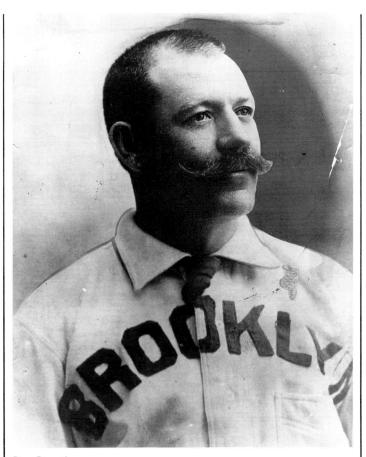

Dan Brouthers

The core of the Baltimore Orioles in the 1890s. Left to right: Willie Keeler, Hugh Jennings, groundskeeper, Joe Kelley, John McGraw.

Amos Rusie

McGraw, of course, went on to become a stormy celebrity as manager of the New York Giants from 1902 to 1932, while Keeler remains one of the few nineteenth-century players to leave behind his own mystique, built partially upon Willie's succinct explanation of his uncanny way with a base hit: "I hit 'em where they ain't." A 44-game hitting streak in 1897 and a .432 batting average that same year have also helped keep Willie's memory green.

The most exciting pitcher of the 1890s was New York's Amos Rusie, also known as "the Hoosier Thunderbolt." The husky right-hander was the fastest pitcher of the day. Rusie, in fact, threw so hard that he was the reason for one of baseball's most crucial rule changes. When Rusie broke in, in 1889, the distance from pitcher to batter was fifty feet, but the Indianan's speed was so great that it was deemed unfair to batters to have to face him from that neighborly distance (and probably dangerous, too; Amos generally walked over 200 men a year, meaning that those thunderbolts exploded just about anywhere). So in 1893 the pitcher's box was moved back to its current sixty feet, six inches (those extra six inches derived from a mismeasurement). The impact of this change was felt immediately. In 1892, the last year of the fifty-foot distance, the National League batted a collective .245; in the following two years the league batting average jumped to .280 and then .309.

For long-term efficiency, nobody came close to Denton True ("Cy") Young, possessor of a high-voltage fast-ball (though by common agreement not in Rusie's class), an excellent curve, good control, and the most tireless arm in baseball history. Cy worked for Cleveland and St. Louis in the 1890s, winning over 30 three times, and then for Boston and Cleveland during the first decade of the twentieth century. When he finally retired at the age of forty-four in 1911, he had racked up his record 511 wins, an incomparable accomplishment that would one day earn him the honor of having baseball's most prestigious pitching award named for him.

Those early players, playing for clubs that carried many fewer players than they do today, had to be tough and durable. Any injury less than a broken bone was expected to be tolerated. Cap Anson derided any player begging off because of pain or injury as "unmanly." The same kind of callousness existed in baseball's executive suites.

The Polo Grounds in 1890.

Enjoying an unchallenged monopoly, the National League owners exercised it in traditional fashion, most harshly by imposing a salary ceiling ($2,400 a year) and arbitrarily cutting salaries whenever they felt like it.

The autocrats who so high-handedly invoke this sort of power generally believe themselves invulnerable. But by the middle 1890s there was a fox loose in their hen coop, one as tough and as wily as they were. His name was Byron Bancroft Johnson, known as Ban. Originally a sportswriter, the Ohio-born Johnson became in 1893 president of the Western League, which he soon built into the strongest of the minor leagues. For Ban, this was but a carefully planned first step, for the man's ego was too capacious and his ambitions too vast to ever accommodate minor league status.

From the very beginning it was Johnson's aim to build a competitor for the National League. His chief confidant was Charles Comiskey, former first baseman for St. Louis of the defunct American Association, currently manager of Cincinnati in the National League, and future owner of the Chicago White Sox. Managing the Milwaukee club in Ban's Western League was Connie Mack, who had impressed Johnson as possessing the integrity and dignity that would be needed to give a new league credibility.

In 1900, the Western League changed its name to the American League and at the same time placed teams in several eastern cities. The National League owners were outraged, but that was nothing compared to their reaction when in 1901 Johnson declared his circuit a major league and began enticing the opposition's stars with that infallible old elixir—money. Among the notables who allowed themselves to be seduced were ace pitchers Cy Young and Joe McGinnity, infielders John McGraw, Nap Lajoie, and Jimmy Collins, and outfielder Ed Delahanty. They were joined over the next several years by shortstop Bobby Wallace (so dominant at the position at the time that he was known as "Mr. Shortstop"), outfielders Willie Keeler and Jesse Burkett, and pitchers Jack Chesbro and Wild Bill Donovan. Every one of these men was a star and their defections were serious blows to the National League.

Johnson's eight original American League teams were Chicago, Detroit, Cleveland, and Milwaukee in the west, and Washington, Baltimore, Boston, and Philadelphia in the east. In 1902, St. Louis replaced Milwaukee and in 1903 Johnson achieved a long-sought goal when New York entered the league, replacing Baltimore.

The National League in 1901 was already fixed in the eight-team alignment that would remain intact until 1953: New York, Brooklyn, Boston, and Philadelphia in the east, and Cincinnati, Chicago, Pittsburgh, and St. Louis in the west.

Those early years were marked by name-calling, threats, fist-shaking, suits, and countersuits, with some players jumping back and forth between the leagues. Johnson, as tough and determined as his opponents, held his ground, as well he might, for his new operation was succeeding. In three of the cities where he had audaciously placed teams in head-to-head competition with National League clubs—Boston, Philadelphia, and Chicago—the newcomers were outdrawing them by healthy margins.

By 1903, the National League realized that continued

A baseball game in progress at Boston's South End Grounds in the early 1890s.

Ban Johnson

Cy Young in the 1890s.

Pittsburgh manager Connie Mack in 1895.

Ed Delahanty

warfare with the adamant Johnson and his new league would prove ruinous, and a grudging agreement was struck. Rosters would no longer be raided, contracts would be honored, and the National League even agreed to a postseason series between the leagues' respective pennant winners to determine a champion. A World Series. (For Johnson, this was the ultimate admission of parity.)

For most people, baseball's modern era begins in 1901, with the formation of the two-league structure. Not only is it by coincidence chronologically ideal, but it is the structure that remains unshaken to this day, the only vibrations being caused by the two-year intrusion of the Federal League in 1914–15, a failed attempt to establish a third major league.

After decades of successes and failures, of bickering and infighting, major league baseball was firmly and permanently organized.

Ty Cobb

1901

Grudgingly or not, inharmoniously or not, like two hemispheres of equal shape and weight, the National and American leagues in 1901 came together, clamped shut, adhered, and created the world of major league baseball.

The leagues each played a 140-game schedule during the first three years of their uneasy coexistence. The first American League champion was the Chicago White Sox, whose manager was also the team's star pitcher—Clark Griffith, with a 24–7 record. (The Griffith name would remain prominent in American League circles throughout most of the century, until Clark's son Calvin divested himself of ownership of the Minnesota Twins in the 1980s.) Other patriarchal names at work in the league were Connie Mack, beginning a fifty-year reign as manager of the Philadelphia Athletics, and John McGraw, managing the Baltimore Orioles, though a year later he would be taking over the New York Giants and beginning his own historic managerial tenure.

Four games behind the White Sox were the Boston Pilgrims (soon to become the Red Sox), who had the league's top winner in thirty-four-year-old Cy Young, who had a 33–10 record. Some sourgrapes National Leaguers, smarting over the loss of baseball's best pitcher to the new league, claimed that Cy was over the hill and racked up his sterling record only because he was pitching against "minor league" opposition. The old boy spent the better part of the decade proving them wrong.

Other 20-game winners in that long-ago first season of the American League were Chicago's Roy Patterson (20–16), Detroit's Roscoe Miller (23–13), Philadelphia's Chick Fraser (22–16), and Baltimore's Joe McGinnity (26–19).

The new league's most dominant hitter was Philadelphia's Nap Lajoie, who the year before had been playing for Philadelphia's National League entry. Connie Mack's second baseman won the Triple Crown with a .422 batting average (still the all-time league high), 14 home runs, and 125 runs batted in. Nap also led with 145 runs scored, 229 hits, 48 doubles, and a .635 slugging average. If there had been an MVP Award then, there is no question where the trophy would have gone. Lajoie's 76-point margin over runner-up Buck Freeman of Boston, who batted .346, is the largest ever for a batting champion.

An interesting sidebar to Lajoie's batting average is that it was originally logged in at .405, a figure that remained in the books for nearly a half century, until some

1901–All for the Better 1909

later research uncovered nine uncredited hits for Nap. This tells us two things: how untidy turn-of-the-century record keeping was, and how cavalier Lajoie was about counting his base hits.

The 1901 National League pennant was won by Fred Clarke's Pittsburgh Pirates, by a 7½-game margin over the Phillies. The star of the club, along with right-handers Deacon Phillippe (22–12) and Jack Chesbro (21–10) was that star of stars, the twenty-seven-year-old Honus Wagner. Honus, who anticipated the arcane wisdom of Yogi Berra by once saying, "There ain't much to being a ballplayer—if you're a ballplayer," batted .353 while driving in a league-high 126 runs and stealing the most bases (49). The greatest shortstop of all time was still showing off his versatility, dividing his time in the outfield, at third base,

as well as at the position he was to make uniquely his own.

The league's top hitter was St. Louis's Jesse Burkett with a .382 average. No surprise here; while playing for Cleveland, Jesse (known as "the Crab" because of a testy disposition) had led the league with .423 in 1895 and .410 in 1896.

The home run champion was Cincinnati's Sam Crawford (soon to jump to Detroit in the American League) with 16. Old timers said that Sam was the most powerful hitter of the dead-ball era, and if Sam couldn't set home run records with the lifeless ball, he did the next best thing: his 312 lifetime triples are the major league record.

Brooklyn's Wild Bill Donovan was the best of the league's eight 20-game winners with a 25–15 record. Other 20-game winners included Philadelphia's Al Orth (20–12) and Red Donahue (21–13), St. Louis's Jack Harper (23–13), Cincinnati's Noodles Hahn (22–19), and New York's Christy Mathewson (20–17).

The Boston Braves set a record for pitching economy, using just five pitchers all season (the Red Sox tied this in 1904), and if you forget Bob Lawson, who appeared in just six games, it meant that all of the club's 140 games were worked by right-handers Kid Nichols, Vic Willis, Bill Dinneen, and Togie Pittinger. These indefatigable fellows started 136 games between them and completed 124. With small pitching staffs the norm and relief pitching virtually unheard of, the complete game was an everyday statistic. The Chicago Cubs staff completed 131 of 140 starts that year.

On June 9, the Giants set a one-game major league record when they assaulted Cincinnati pitching with a 31-hit attack, winning by a score of 25–13. A month later, on July 15, the Giants' twenty-two-year-old Mathewson showed how it could all be done more efficiently and less frantically when he no-hit the Cardinals, 5–0. The handsome, regally aloof young pitcher would soon become the pride of New York and of all baseball, on his way to the achievements that would find summation in the last line of his Hall of Fame plaque: "Matty was master of them all."

Nap Lajoie

Jesse Burkett

Sam Crawford

1902

Connie Mack won the first of his nine pennants in 1902, his Philadelphia Athletics finishing five games ahead of St. Louis (which had replaced the Milwaukee franchise). Connie's club featured six .300 hitters, including Socks Seybold, who hit a league-leading 16 home runs, which stood as the American League record until 1919. On the mound, Connie had two of the greatest left-handers of all time, Rube Waddell (24–7) and Eddie Plank (20–15), a couple of prodigious winners who were antithetical in every way. Rube was gregarious, fun-loving, eccentric; Eddie was reserved, poker-faced, a loner; Rube threw whistling fast balls; Eddie was a wily control pitcher.

Waddell was spectacular during the American League's early years. Beginning in 1902, he led in strikeouts for six successive years. He also set a major-league record for a good month's work when he won ten games that July.

Boston's Cy Young remained the league's dominant pitcher with a 32–11 record, completing 41 of his 43 starts. Cy's teammate Bill Dinneen had a break-even 21–21 record, while other big winners were St. Louis's Red Donahue (22–11) and Jack Powell (22–17), and Chicago's Roy Patterson (19–14). Chicago's Jim (Nixey) Callahan pitched the American League's first no-hitter, stifling the Tigers on September 20, 3–0.

The league's leading hitter, with a .376 batting average, was Washington's Ed Delahanty, who had jumped from the Philadelphia Phillies. In 1902, players were still following the winding greenback trail between the leagues. The National League continued to assert the validity of their contracts in various state courts. The Pennsylvania Supreme Court had ruled that the Athletics' Nap Lajoie still belonged to the Philadelphia Phillies and ordered him back to that club, citing the reserve clause in Nap's Phillies contract. Since the ruling applied only in Pennsylvania (the other state courts that held hearings on the matter ruled against the reserve clause), the crafty Ban Johnson, unwilling to lose one of his league's top stars, finessed the ruling by transferring Nap to the Cleveland Indians. It meant that Lajoie had to skip the games in Philadelphia, but Johnson had once more outflanked the National League.

Fred Clarke's Pittsburgh Pirates took a second straight pennant in 1902 and in the process made a shambles of the National League race, winning 103 games (out of 139) and setting an all-time record by finishing 27½ games ahead of second-place Brooklyn.

The Pirates led the league in every offensive category—runs, hits, doubles, triples, home runs, runs batted in, stolen bases, batting average, and slugging. The club had three 20-game winners in spitballer Jack Chesbro (28–

Rube Waddell

6, and soon to jump to the American League), lefty Jesse Tannehill (20–6, and also on his way to the American League), and Deacon Phillippe (20–9).

The Pirates also ran away with most of the individual hitting honors, with Ginger Beaumont leading in batting (.357) and hits (194), Tommy Leach leading in home runs with a modest six, and Honus Wagner leading in just about everything else: runs (105), doubles (33), runs batted in (91), stolen bases (42), and slugging (.467). Honus was still playing all over the field, dividing his time between shortstop, first base, and the outfield.

A new era of National League history began on July 19 when John McGraw took over as manager of the New York Giants. The twenty-nine-year-old McGraw had been running afoul of Ban Johnson's edict against umpire baiting, a favorite McGraw tactic. Tempers erupted on both sides in July, and Johnson suspended the sulphurous Baltimore skipper for an indefinite period. This led to a most devious sequence of events.

McGraw plotted with John T. Brush, owner of the Cincinnati Reds and Chairman of the National League Executive Committee, to have Brush buy the Orioles. The apopleptic Ban Johnson suddenly found the enemy in his

Ginger Beaumont

own living room, and soon the enemy departed with most of the furniture.

Conspiring with McGraw, Brush quickly released John J. along with star pitcher Joe McGinnity, first baseman Dan McGann, catcher Roger Bresnahan, and outfielders Cy Seymour and Joe Kelley. McGraw, McGinnity, Bresnahan, and McGann immediately joined the New York Giants, with McGraw as manager. A year later Brush bought the Giants. Thus the ethics and chicanery of turn-of-the-century baseball.

Wearying of such high-handed maneuvering, which they realized could totally unravel their game, the two leagues held peace talks during the winter of 1902, coming to agreement in January 1903. The leagues agreed to operate on parity, honor each other's contracts, and leave all contested players in place (a large concession on the part of the National League, which had suffered most of the defections). Another article of the treaty allowed the American League to transfer the depleted Baltimore club to New York, a move which incensed McGraw. And so out of turmoil and peacemaking came the New York Highlanders, soon to be known as the Yankees.

The two-year war between the leagues was over, and major league baseball was now stabilized. Beginning in 1903, all sixteen of the big-league franchises were to remain in place for the next half century.

Roger Bresnahan

1903

Baseball's historical calendar is sequined with glittering "firsts," "mosts," "leasts," "longests," etc., but no year in the twentieth century occasioned an event as illustrious as 1903: the first World Series. The Series evolved out of the recent truce that had been established between the leagues and because a pair of runaway pennant races had given the respective club owners something else to think about late in the summer.

With Pittsburgh in the National League and Boston in the American winning their pennants rather handily, the respective club owners, Barney Dreyfus and Henry Killilea, agreed to a nine-game postseason series to determine the "world's champion." In giving his blessing to the match, Ban Johnson, realizing what an opportunity this was for his still-fledgling league, sternly told Killilea: "You must beat them."

Boston had followed the tireless thirty-six-year-old arm of Cy Young to its first pennant. With Cy checking in at 28–9, Long Tom Hughes 20–7, and Bill Dinneen 21–13, Boston had little trouble, winning by 14½ games. Boston's infield was anchored by third baseman–manager Jimmy Collins, generally regarded the preeminent man at the position until the arrival of Pie Traynor in the 1920s. Jimmy was a solid hitter (.294 lifetime), but it was his defensive prowess that left the sharpest memories, particularly his ability to swoop in on bunts and turn them into outs—an invaluable skill in that era, when bunting for base hits was common practice.

Boston first baseman Buck Freeman led in home runs (13) and runs batted in (104), while Cleveland's Nap Lajoie hit .355 to take the batting title. That master of the three-base hit, Sam Crawford, who had jumped from Cincinnati to Detroit before the leagues agreed to remove the trampoline, banged out 25 of them, second-highest single-season total in American League history.

Connie Mack's left-handed tandem were 20-game winners for the second year in a row, Eddie Plank coming in at 23–16 and Rube Waddell at 21–16, with Rube fanning 302 batters, a phenomenal number for that contact-hitting era (the next highest was Wild Bill Donovan's 187). There were two other 20-game winners in the league—New York's Jack Chesbro and St. Louis's Willie Sudhoff, each 21–15.

The question of who was the league's best hitter, Lajoie or Delahanty, stopped being asked on July 2. Delahanty, doing battle with alcoholism, had left the Washington club in Detroit and was returning East. He was known to have boarded a New York Central train, and while crossing the bridge over Niagara Falls sometime during the night, Big Ed fell to his death into the waters below. His body was recovered two days later. What caused Ed's fatal plunge remains eternally unanswered. He might have gotten in a brawl and been chucked out, or he might have committed suicide. One version of the story has him being put off the train in Buffalo for being belligerently drunk and then running after it, losing his footing and dropping into the river, where the tides carried him over the Falls. Thirty-five years old at the time of his death, Delahanty (one of five brothers to play in the major leagues) left behind a lifetime batting average of .345.

Despite having lost ace pitchers Jack Chesbro and Jesse Tannehill to the American League, Fred Clarke's Pirates won their third straight pennant, with Sam Leever (25–7) and Deacon Phillippe (24–7) heading the staff. Honus Wagner, spending most of his time at shortstop now—a planet finally in proper orbit—won his second batting title with a .355 average (he had won in 1900 with

BELOW: Deacon Phillippe

The infield of the Boston Pilgrims in the early days of the century. Left to right: third baseman Jimmy Collins, shortstop Fred Parent, second baseman Hobe Ferris, first baseman Buck Freeman.

Bill Dinneen

1904

The New York Highlanders did not win their first pennant in 1904, but it was hardly the fault of their ace, spitballer Jack Chesbro. The thirty-year-old right-hander set a modern record with 41 wins, against just 12 defeats. Jack started 51 games and completed 48 (both major league records), pitched 455 innings, fanned 239, had six shutouts, logged a 1.82 earned run average—and is chiefly remembered today for throwing a wild pitch on the last day of the season.

The New Yorkers were a game-and-a-half behind Boston on the last day, with the clubs playing a doubleheader at New York's Hilltop Park. With the score two-all in the top of the ninth of the opener, Boston had a man on third with two out when Chesbro let fly one of history's most celebrated wild pitches, allowing home the run that beat New York, 3–2, and gave Boston its second straight pennant.

For the second year in a row the Pilgrims had three 20-game winners: Cy Young (26–16, with 10 shutouts), Bill Dinneen (23–14), and Jesse Tannehill (21–11). Young was beginning to slow down now, but with the utmost grace, for on May 5, he pitched a perfect game against Rube Waddell and the Athletics, winning by a 3–0 score. On August 17, Tannehill no-hit Chicago by a 6–0 score.

All told, there were nine pitchers with 20 or more wins in the American League that year. Connie Mack's brace of southpaw aces, Waddell and Plank, were again among them, Eddie at 26–16 and Rube at 25–19, with Rube fanning a remarkable 349 batters, which remained the major league record until 1965 and the American League record until 1973. Other 20-game winners included New York's Jack Powell (23–19), Cleveland's Bill Bernhard (23–13), and Chicago's Frank Owen (21–15). There was also a less gaudy side to American League pitching that year—Washington's Jack Townsend set the league high for losses with 26 (against just 5 wins).

With all of the tight-fisted pitching in the league, Nap Lajoie's top average of .381 was impressive. The Cleveland second baseman also led in hits (211), doubles (50), and runs batted in (102). Philadelphia first baseman Harry Davis was the home run leader with 10, which is pretty thin soup compared to later days, but still, nobody else in the league had more than seven.

In the National League, John McGraw won the first of his ten pennants. The Giants, whose 106 wins gave them an easy 13-game margin over the Cubs, ran off a midseason 18-game winning streak, which threw up a lot of dust in the faces of their pursuers.

McGraw's well-drilled, highly disciplined club earned their title with good defense, basepath aggressiveness (283 stolen bases), and the superb pitching of Joe Mc-

.381), while skipper Clarke shadowed him with .351. In first place from June 19 on, the Pirates finished 6½ games ahead of New York.

Brooklyn's Jimmy Sheckard led the league in two seemingly incompatible categories—home runs (9) and stolen bases (67). The only other National Leaguer to do this was Philadelphia's Chuck Klein in 1932.

While Pittsburgh's pennant winners had two 20-game winners, John McGraw's second-place Giants showed a couple of 30-gamers in Joe McGinnity (31–20) and Christy Mathewson (30–13). This was the year that Joe earned his "Iron Man" nickname by pitching and winning three doubleheaders in the month of August—on August 1 against Boston, August 8 against Brooklyn, and August 31 against Philadelphia. Joe pitched a National League record 434 innings that year. Nevertheless, Mathewson was the ace, with a .698 winning percentage to Joe's .608. Matty fanned 267 batters, a league record that stood until 1961, when Sandy Koufax struck out 269.

Third-place Chicago had a pair of big winners in Jack Taylor (21–14) and rookie left-hander Jake Weimer (21–9), while Cincinnati's Noodles Hahn (22–12) and Brooklyn's Oscar Jones (20–16) and Henry Schmidt (21–13) also won big. For Henry it was a most curious career—that was his one and only year in the big leagues. Philadelphia's Chick Fraser pitched 1903's only no-hitter, stopping the Cubs cold on September 18 in a 10–0 victory.

The first World Series commenced on October 1, in Boston. Pittsburgh got off to a 3–1 lead in games and seemed on the way to validating the National League's assumptions of superiority. Boston, however, turned it right around and took four in a row, winning the title five games to three, establishing then and forever American League parity. Bill Dinneen won three of four decisions for Boston, while Pittsburgh's Deacon Phillippe was heroic in defeat, starting five times, winning three and losing two.

Ginnity (35–8) and Christy Mathewson (33–12). This early version of New York M&M splendor (anticipating Mantle and Maris in 1961) were backed up by Dummy Taylor, who was 21–15, giving the trio 89 of New York's 106 victories.

Three-time champion Pittsburgh dropped to fourth place, as Honus Wagner took his third batting crown and second in a row with a .349 average.

St. Louis Cardinals right-hander Jack Taylor, with a 21–19 ledger, set a record for consecutive complete games in a season when he went the distance in all 39 of his starts. For the durable Taylor, this was business as usual—from 1902 through 1905 he completed all 139 of his starts. (If there had been relief pitching then as we know it today, Jack might well have been picketed by his own bullpen.)

Other 20-game winners that year were Chicago's Jake Weimer (20–14), Cincinnati's Jack Harper (23–9), and St. Louis's Kid Nichols (21–13).

Outfielder Harry Lumley brought sixth-place Brooklyn what little glory they enjoyed when he led the league with 18 triples and 9 home runs. It would not be until 1955, when Willie Mays did it, that anyone was again at the top in both of these categories in the same year.

Thanks to the orneriness of John McGraw (still nursing his grudge against Ban Johnson) and Giants owner John Brush, there was no World Series played that year. According to Brush, there was nothing in the league constitution that required its champion to submit "to a contest with a victorious club in a minor league." It was one of the final broadsides fired between the two leagues. Newspaper criticism of this stand was withering, the public felt deprived, and so did the Giants players, who were losing out on some postseason money. Accordingly, during the off-season, agreement was reached to make the World Series an annual affair, with a best-of-seven series determining the champion. Most of the rules governing the playing and financial arrangements of the series were, ironically, proposed by John Brush.

Jack Chesbro

Jack Taylor

1905

The American League experienced a year of feeble hitting in 1905, with only two regulars batting over .300—Cleveland's Elmer Flick, the league leader at .306, and New York's veteran Willie Keeler, .302. (Nap Lajoie batted .329, but played only 65 games because of a mid-season injury.)

There were nine 20-game winners in the league, with Connie Mack's pennant-winning Athletics having three of them. For the fourth year in succession Connie's southpaw aces, Rube Waddell and Eddie Plank, each won handsomely, Rube 26–11 and Eddie 25–12, followed by young right-hander Andy Coakley's 20–7.

The A's big hitter was first baseman Harry Davis, who led in home runs (8) for the second year in a row, and in runs batted in with 83.

The second-place White Sox, finishing just two games behind, had 20-game winners in Frank Owen (21–13) and left-hander Nick Altrock (22–12). With four regulars batting .201 or under, it was the pitching staff's 1.99 earned run average that kept the Sox in the race until the season's final days.

The league's highest team ERA was sixth-place New York's 2.92, where Jack Chesbro dropped from 41 wins to a more reasonable 19.

There were three no-hitters in the league—the Athletics' Weldon Henley (just 4–12 for the season), 6–0, over the Browns on July 22, the White Sox' Frank Smith, 15–0, over Detroit on September 6, and the Red Sox' Bill Dinneen, 2–0, over the White Sox on September 27.

The twin pitching effort of the year occurred on July 4, when Waddell outlasted Cy Young in a 20-inning trial of aces, Rube winning it, 4–2. The thirty-eight-year-old Young did not walk a man, which was perfectly in character—in 320 innings that season he walked only 30. Cy was on the downhill side now; with a record of 18–19, it was the first time since 1890 that he had not been a 20-game winner.

Detroit had a pair of 20-game winners in left-hander Ed Killian (23–14) and George Mullin (21–21), Boston's Jesse Tannehill was 22–9, and Cleveland's Addie Joss was 20–12.

Late in August, baseball's most glittering and controversial career began. The Tigers had purchased the contract of eighteen-year-old Tyrus Raymond Cobb from the Augusta club of the South Atlantic League. The opening salvo was fired on August 30, when the youngster doubled off of New York's Chesbro for the first of his 4,191 hits. Playing with an intensity that for a quarter of a century would never slacken ("His every time at bat was like a crusade," a teammate said), the new recruit played in 41 games and batted .240. He would retire 23 years later with a lifetime batting average of .367.

Harry Davis

Vic Willis

ABOVE: Three Finger Brown. BELOW: John McGraw (left) and Joe McGinnity.

In the National League, it was McGraw and his Giants for the second year in a row. John J. had a .356 hitter in Turkey Mike Donlin, but the team's strength lay in the élan of its speed (291 stolen bases) and the mastery of its pitchers. Christy Mathewson was a 30-game winner for the third year in a row (31–8), including a 1–0 no-hitter over the Cubs on June 13. Joe McGinnity was 21–15 and Leon Ames 22–8.

Pittsburgh finished second, 9 games behind the Giants, despite Honus Wagner's .363 batting average. Wagner's lusty hitting earned him only second-spot honors in the batting race to Cincinnati's Cy Seymour, who was the league's dominant hitter that year. Seymour (a 25-game-winning pitcher with the Giants in the late 1890s) batted a career-high .377 and also led in runs batted in (121), hits (219), doubles (40), and triples (21). Cy's eight home runs left him one short of a tie for the lead with teammate Fred Odwell, which also would have meant a Triple Crown.

It was a frustrating season for Boston right-hander Vic Willis. Frequently mentioned in the 1980s as a Hall of Fame candidate, Willis had been a four-time 20-game winner for Boston, and soon would be a four-time 20-game winner for Pittsburgh; but in 1905, in spite of pitching reasonably good ball, Vic was sabotaged by his teammates (who batted .234 while idling through a 51–103 season) into losing a major league record 29 games (against 11 wins).

Deacon Phillippe was 22–13 for Pittsburgh, Togie Pittinger 23–14 for Philadelphia, Bob Ewing 20–11 for Cincinnati, and left-hander Irv Young 20–21 for Boston. Young, who completed 41 of 42 starts, was a rookie who was dubbed "Cy the Second" by some sportswriters, but he remained pretty much "Irv the First."

The 1905 World Series, won by the Giants in five games, was the "Series of Shutouts," with every game a blanking. It was the World Series upon which Christy Mathewson affixed once and for all his seal of greatness. McGraw's ace mesmerized the Athletics in games 1, 3, and 5, all in the space of six days, allowing Connie Mack's American League champs no runs, 14 hits, and just one base on balls in 27 innings. McGinnity shut out the A's in game 4, while Chief Bender blanked the Giants in game 2 for his club's only win.

1906

They batted .228 (lowest in the American League) and hit just seven home runs (lowest in the American League), but still won the pennant, by three games over New York. They were the Chicago White Sox of 1906, managed by outfielder Fielder Jones (his real name), and they are one of major league baseball's few individual teams to have earned a descriptive nickname: "the Hitless Wonders."

In fourth place in early August, the Sox suddenly found a fast lane and went on a 19-game winning streak (still the American League record), passed Cleveland and Philadelphia and outwrestled the Yankees in the season's final week.

A .228-hitting pennant winner implies strong pitching, and the White Sox had it. Frank Owen was 22–13, Nick Altrock 20–13, Doc White (a practicing dentist) 18–6, and young spitballer Ed Walsh 17–13, garnished with ten shutouts.

The second-place Yankees (managed by Clark Griffith) featured young first baseman Hal Chase, a .323 batter whose dazzling glovework around the bag was quickly making him one of the league's top drawing cards. New York also had a 27-game winner in Al Orth and a 24-gamer in Jack Chesbro, but it wasn't enough to prevent the White Sox from going on to fulfill their unlikely destiny.

Cleveland had three 20-game winners in Bob Rhoades (22–10), Addie Joss (21–9), and Otto Hess (20–17), in addition to Nap Lajoie and his .355 batting average. Nap, however, was aced out of the batting title by St. Louis's George Stone, who hit .358. The coming man, Detroit's nineteen-year-old Ty Cobb, batted .320 in his first full season, which was as low as he would hit for the next 22 years. Cobb's Tiger teammate George Mullin was 21–18. The A's' Harry Davis led in home runs (12) for the third straight year and runs batted in (96) for the second straight year.

While the White Sox illuminated the season with their 19-game winning streak, the Red Sox went dimly in the other direction in May with a 20-game losing streak. Losers of 105 games, Boston's dismal last-place season was embodied in the 2–21 record of right-hander Joe Harris. But the luckless Harris could not be accused of not trying; on September 1, he went 24 innings against Philadelphia's Jack Coombs before losing, 4–1. (This was the American League's longest game by innings, tied in 1945 by the Athletics and Tigers.)

It was an all-Chicago year in major league baseball, with Frank Chance's Cubs winning the National League pennant in record-making style, winning 116 games, still baseball's all-time high.

Chance's pitching staff, which logged a collective 1.76 earned run average, was topped by Mordecai ("Three Finger") Brown, a twenty-nine-year-old right-hander who made a leap to stardom that year with a 26–6 record and National League all-time low 1.04 ERA, built upon nine shutouts. Brown, who gained his nickname from a childhood accident in which he lost a finger, was for the next few years Christy Mathewson's only bona fide rival as the league's top pitcher, and indeed beat Matty 14 of the 26 times they went to a decision against one another.

Following Brown in the rotation was rookie left-hander Jack Pfiester (20–8, 1.56 ERA), Ed Reulbach (19–4, 1.65), and Carl Lundgren (17–6, 2.21).

This was the team of Tinker to Evers to Chance, a flashy infield combine adept at picking up all those ground balls the parsimonious staff was delivering. At third base was Harry Steinfeldt, who led the team with a .327 average and the league with 83 RBIs and 176 hits. Johnny Kling, regarded as one of the best catchers of the day, batted .312, while skipper Chance batted .319 and led the league with 57 stolen bases.

Hoping for a third successive pennant, John McGraw had to swallow a second-place finish, 20 games behind the runaway Cubs, despite 27 wins by Joe McGinnity (his last big season) and 22 from Mathewson.

The batting title went back to familiar hands, Honus Wagner winning for the fourth time with a .339 average. Brooklyn first baseman Tim Jordan became the first National Leaguer in five years to reach double figures in home runs, hitting a loud-for-the-time 12.

On August 13, Jack Taylor, the pitcher who set records by finishing what he started, was finally knocked out of a game, in the third inning by Brooklyn. For Taylor, the early departure ended a string of 188 consecutive complete games, dating back to 1901. Working for the Cubs and Cardinals, Taylor was 20–12. Other 20-game winners were Pittsburgh's Vic Willis (22–13) and Sam Leever (22–7), and Cincinnati's Jake Weimer (20–14).

The National League saw two no-hitters that season: Philadelphia's Johnny Lush winning 6–0 over Brooklyn on May 1, and Brooklyn's Mal Eason 2–0 over St. Louis on July 20. On August 1, Brooklyn's Harry McIntyre pitched 10 hitless innings against Pittsburgh, gave up a hit in the 11th and finally lost in 13, 1–0.

The all-Chicago World Series began with the Cubs as heavy favorites. But it was to be the year of the Hitless Wonders, who stunned their West Side neighbors by winning the championship in six games.

1907

In 1907 the most piercing ballplayer of all time went on his first genuine rampage through the American League. "The rebel yell incarnate," as a later writer called him, Ty Cobb, all of twenty years old, batted .350 to win the first of his twelve batting titles, led with 212 hits, 116 runs batted in, 49 stolen bases, and a .473 slugging average. This performance was the cutting edge of Detroit's first successful pennant race, which the Tigers won by 1½ games over the Athletics.

Hughie Jennings's Tigers had the league's most potent batting entry in Cobb and Sam Crawford, who batted .323, second to Ty. Detroit also had four big winners in Wild Bill Donovan (25–4), Ed Killian (25–13), George Mullin (20–20), and Ed Siever (18–11).

The A's had 20-game winners in Eddie Plank (24–16) and young Jimmy Dygert (21–8, his only big season). Rube Waddell was 19–13 and with 232 strikeouts led the league for the sixth straight year. Rube, however, suffered a late-season slump that probably cost the club the pennant; in addition, Connie Mack was tiring of Rube's antics and eccentricities (which included disappearing for a few days to go fishing) and after the season sold him to the Browns.

Connie's first baseman Harry Davis banged out eight home runs; not a resounding number, but enough to give Harry the home run title for the fourth straight year; and anyway, nobody else in the league hit more than five.

The third-place White Sox had three 20-game winners in Doc White (27–13), Ed Walsh (24–18, while pitching a monstrous 422 innings), and Frank Smith (23–10). The Sox staff had the league's best ERA, 2.22, but this time Fielder Jones's Hitless Wonders achieved no miracles with their .237 team batting average and six home runs.

Cleveland's gifted right-hander Addie Joss, who featured a spin-around delivery, à la Luis Tiant, tied White for the most wins with 27.

At the age of forty, Cy Young's setting sun gave off a proud glow with a 22–15 record. And even as the noblest pitcher of them all was fading, the league was breaking in some new royal bloods—Eddie Collins got into a few games with the Athletics, Tris Speaker a handful with the Red Sox, and nineteen-year-old speedballer Walter Johnson with the Senators. Signed from the amateur ranks in Idaho late in the season, Walter came East, won his first game on August 7 and though finishing with a 5–9 record, he had a 1.87 ERA and had batters muttering about what Ty Cobb described as "the fastest pitch I've ever seen."

Frank Chance's Cubs won nine fewer games in 1907 than the year before, but 107 wins were enough to put them 17 ahead of second-place Pittsburgh. Again, the Cubs built their success on a foundation of pitching, led by

Orval Overall (23–8), Three Finger Brown (20–6), Carl Lundgren (18–7), and Ed Reulbach (17–4), each of whom had an ERA under two, while 15-game winner Jack Pfiester had the lowest in the league, 1.15.

In a league that batted .243 as a whole and had only four .300 hitters, Honus Wagner demonstrated his superiority by batting .350 and winning his fifth batting title. Vic Willis (22–11) and Lefty Leifield (20–16) were Pittsburgh's biggest winners. Other leading pitchers were Philadelphia's Tully Sparks (22–8) and New York's Christy Mathewson (24–13).

In May, Pittsburgh manager Fred Clarke objected to the new equipment donned by Giants catcher Roger Bresnahan—shin guards—claiming they were illegal, and protested the game. League president Harry Pulliam ruled against Clarke, and Bresnahan's sensible innovation soon became *de rigueur* for all catchers.

Both of the major leagues' no-hitters that year were delivered in the National League. Boston's Francis (Big Jeff) Pfeffer, just 6–8 on the year, stopped Cincinnati, 6–0, on May 8; and on September 20, Pittsburgh's Nick Maddox throttled Brooklyn, 2–1. In that same game, Brooklyn's Elmer Stricklett allowed just two hits, both by Fred Clarke, neither of which figured in the scoring.

In the World Series, it was all Chicago. After an opening game that ended in a 12-inning tie, the Cubs swept the Tigers in the next four, with Pfiester, Reulbach, Overall, and Brown each winning. The tight-fisted Cubs pitchers gave the Tigers a dose of what the National League had been up against all season long—logging a composite 0.75 ERA for the Series.

Fred Clarke

Fred Merkle

1908

One of the most tumultuous years in baseball history, 1908 featured a pair of finespun pennant races, some truly heroic individual performances, and the game's most celebrated moment of mental omission.

In the American League, Detroit won a grimly contested three-way race with Cleveland and Chicago, finishing a half game ahead of the Indians and 1½ ahead of the White Sox. (The Tigers were 90–63 to the Indians' 90–64. In those years, unplayed games that had a bearing on the pennant race did not have to be made up.)

Detroit's Ty Cobb won his second straight batting title with a .324 average, with teammate Sam Crawford (the home run leader with seven) batting .311. Along with Boston's Doc Gessler, who batted .308, they were the league's only .300 hitters that year—the American League batted just .239. Detroit's .264-hitting team must have seemed awesome that year, the next-highest team average being Boston's .246.

Tiger skipper Hughie Jennings got a brilliant rookie season out of Ed Summers, who broke in with a 24–12 record. Wild Bill Donovan was the club's next biggest winner at 18–7.

Second-place Cleveland was led by Addie Joss, who was 24–11 with the league's lowest earned run average, 1.16. Addie was one of 13 pitchers who had ERAs under 2.00 in that year of feathery hitting.

Joss participated in one of history's great pitching duels at the end of the season. With Cleveland and Chicago in a virtual second-place tie, a short breath out of first place, Joss and Chicago's Ed Walsh opposed each other on October 2. Walsh pitched a four-hitter and fanned 15; Joss, however, pitched a perfect game, winning 1–0. Considering that the season's full weight was riding on every pitch, the game remains one of baseball's classics.

Walsh's season was nothing less than Herculean. The Chicago spitballer won a prodigious 40 games, losing 15, and pitching a major league record 464 innings. For this mountain of work he had a remarkably low 1.42 ERA, abetted by 11 shutouts. Ed's favorite targets that year were the Yankees and Red Sox, whom he beat nine times each. Walsh's record is even more amazing when one considers that his teammates batted just .224, tapping out an all-time low three home runs, one of which was hit by Walsh himself.

Young Walter Johnson, in his first full season, was 14–14 for the seventh-place Washington Senators. Walter, however, turned in his first bit of overachievement when he pitched three straight shutouts against the Yankees on September 4, 5, and 7.

Despite the paucity of hitting, there were only four 20-game winners in the league that year—Summers, Joss, Walsh, and Boston's forty-one-year-old Cy Young, who with a 21–11 record turned in his sixteenth and final 20-win season. Cy even pitched his third no-hitter, nailing the Yankees 8–0 on June 30. Only a walk to New York's leadoff batter (who was quickly caught stealing) prevented Young from achieving his second perfect game.

There were two other no-hitters this year—Cleveland's Bob Rhoads, 2–1, over Boston on September 18, and on September 20, Chicago's Frank Smith pitched the second no-hitter of his career, 1–0, over Philadelphia, the run coming in the bottom of the ninth.

National League hitting in 1908 was just as feeble as American League, the Nationals posting the same .239 average as their brethren, a mark which remains the lowest in its history. Frank Chance's Chicago Cubs made it three pennants in a row, but after winning by margins of 20 and 17 games, the Cubs had to beat the Giants in a make-up game after both clubs finished the season with identical 98–55 records.

The game that had to be made up, the September 23 game between New York and Chicago at the Polo Grounds, was one of the most controversial in baseball history. The clubs were tied 1–1 in the bottom of the ninth. With two out and Moose McCormick on third and nineteen-year-old rookie Fred Merkle on first, the Giants' Al Bridwell singled to center. The game-winning hit . . . but not quite. McCormick came across the plate, but Merkle ran halfway to second and then sprinted for the Giants'

Ed Walsh

clubhouse in center field, never touching the bag, as he was supposed to. Merkle's omission was common practice in those days; it was an appeal play that was seldom appealed.

Cubs second baseman Johnny Evers spotted the oversight, however, and called for the ball, for Merkle was now vulnerable to a force play, which would nullify the run. One story has the Giants' Joe McGinnity, seeing what Evers was up to, getting hold of the ball and throwing it into the crowd. Somehow, Evers got his hands on a baseball—either the game ball or another one—and stepped on second. Abiding by the rules, umpire Hank O'Day called Merkle out, erasing McCormick's run. The inning was over, the score still tied.

A jubilant New York crowd had overrun the field, however, and play could not be continued. Protests and accusations raged back and forth, but league president Harry Pulliam upheld O'Day's decision. The game was ruled a tie. The significance of this grew day by day as the two clubs fought down to the closing days and ended in a tie.

The make-up game (it was not a playoff) was played in New York on October 5, before a record crowd of some thirty-five thousand, and a very hostile, anti-Chicago crowd it was. Feelings were so intense that the Cubs had to be spirited in and out of New York under police protection. Nevertheless, the gritty Cubs, behind Three Finger Brown, beat Mathewson and the Giants, 4–2, to win the pennant.

Brown had his greatest season in 1908, posting a 29–9 record, followed by Ed Reulbach's 24–7. Reulbach also turned in baseball's most impeccable iron-man performance on September 26, when he beat the Dodgers 5–0 and 3–0, pitching all 18 innings of the doubleheader. It remains the only doubleheader shutout ever pitched.

Like Brown, Mathewson had his biggest season in 1908, with a 37–11 record, the most games ever won in a season by a National League pitcher. Giants left-hander Hooks Wiltse was 23–14, while three other league pitchers also won 23 games—Vic Willis (23–11) and Nick Maddox (23–8) for the Pirates, and George McQuillan (23–17) for the Phillies.

Wiltse and Brooklyn's gifted left-hander Nap Rucker pitched no-hitters this year, Hooks going ten hitless innings on July 4 to beat the Phillies, 1–0, and Nap throttling the Braves, 6–0, on September 5.

Honus Wagner won batting title number six with a .354 average, also leading with 109 RBIs, 201 hits, 39 doubles, 19 triples, a .542 slugging percentage, and 53 stolen bases. Brooklyn's Tim Jordan was the home run champ with an even dozen.

In the World Series, it was Chicago again over Detroit, this time in five games, with Brown and Orval Overall winning two apiece.

1909

Ty Cobb was getting better and better. In 1909, the twenty-two-year-old Georgian, playing with a fury and an intensity that opponents and even some teammates found terrifying, won the Triple Crown with his third straight batting title (.377), nine home runs, and 107 runs batted in. These gaudy numbers led Hughie Jennings's team to their third successive pennant, 3½ games ahead of a resurgent Philadelphia club that had finished sixth the year before.

Detroit featured three big winners, headed by ace George Mullin (29–8), Ed Willett (21–10), and Ed Summers (19–9).

Connie Mack's A's benefitted from an influx of shimmering new talent, led by second baseman Eddie Collins, whose .346 batting average was second to Cobb's, and third baseman Frank Baker, who led the league with 19 triples in his first season. Connie also had a gifted new pitcher in twenty-two-year-old left-hander Harry Krause, who was 18–8 with a league-low 1.39 ERA. Unfortunately, an arm injury soon cost Krause the opportunity to build on this early brilliance.

Another sparkling young talent was Boston's twenty-one-year-old center fielder Tris Speaker, who batted .309 in his first full season.

Reflecting the previous year's terrific work load, Chicago's Ed Walsh dropped from 40–15 to 15–11, but still with enough on his spitter to turn in eight shutouts. Teammate Frank Smith was 25–17.

Washington's Walter Johnson experienced what some people might describe as a character-building season. Pitching for a club that batted a noiseless .223, scored the fewest runs of any team in American League history (380), and was shut out a league record 30 times, Walter labored through a 13–25 season, absorbing 10 of those shutouts personally.

Walter's teammate, rookie right-hander Bob Groom, suffered even worse agonies with a 7–26 record (the league mark for losses in a season), including a major league record 19 losses in a row.

Cleveland shortstop Neal Ball executed the American League's first unassisted triple play, retiring three Boston players at once on July 19.

Playing in their newly opened Forbes Field, a triple-decked steel-girdered ball park, the Pirates won 110 games, beating back the Cubs' try for a fourth straight pennant. Chicago won 104 games (most ever for a second-place team), but it wasn't enough.

Fred Clarke's Pirates had Howie Camnitz (25–6), Vic Willis (22–11), and Lefty Leifield (19–8) heading a strong mound corps, and siege-gun Honus Wagner at short again proving how much better he was than anyone else. Honus

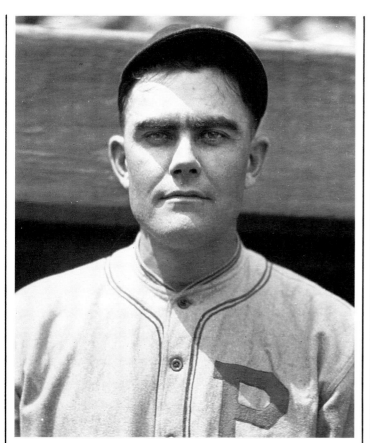

Babe Adams

Christy Mathewson

Ed Delahanty

Frank "Noodles" Hahn, Cincinnati's 20-game-winning left-hander who starred around the turn of the century.

George Davis, a big leaguer from 1890 through 1909, most of it as a shortstop. He managed the Giants in 1900–01 and was replaced by McGraw.

Chief Bender, for years one of Connie Mack's aces. The Chief pitched for Connie from 1903–14, then put in a couple of years with the Phillies. Lifetime major league record: 206–111.

won his fourth straight batting title and sixth overall, batting .339. Honus also led in doubles for the eighth time (the National League record) and RBIs (100).

Three Finger Brown followed his 29–9 season with another almost as good, 27–9. Teammate Orval Overall was 20–11. For McGraw's Giants, buried in third place under that shower of Pirates and Cubs victories, Christy Mathewson continued on the road to Valhalla with a 25–6 record and league-low 1.14 ERA. Giant lefty Hooks Wiltse was 20–11, while another Giant pitcher, Leon Ames, earned the "too bad" award for the year on opening day, April 15. Ames pitched 9⅓ innings of no-hit ball against Brooklyn before losing in 13, 3–0. Another Giant, outfielder Red Murray, was the home run leader with seven.

In mid-August, the Phillies had imposed upon them one of baseball's more passive records—they were rained out for ten straight days.

There was a notable "first" during the season, occurring on September 16 in Chicago, when William H. Taft became the first president of the United States to attend a baseball game.

The Pirates handed the Tigers a third straight World Series loss, edging them in seven. Pittsburgh's hero was rookie pitcher Babe Adams (12–3 for the season), who won three games while star pitchers Camnitz, Willis, and Leifield were being bumped around by Detroit. In their only head-to-head confrontation, Wagner outhit Cobb, .333 to .231. Ty would play another 19 years, but never again appeared in a World Series.

Cy Young. He pitched for 22 years and claimed he never had a sore arm, though he conceded that occasionally it got "tired."

Eddie Plank. They called him "Gettysburg Eddie," because he was born there, went to school there, and in the off-season worked as a tour guide on the battlefield. In his spare time he won 306 big-league games.

The Pirates in their rather ramshackle dugout at Boston's Huntington Grounds Park during the 1903 World Series.

Long Tom Hughes, who pitched for five teams from 1900–13. He was 20–7 for Boston (A.L.) in 1903, his best year, and 131–174 for his career.

Dan McGann, big-leaguer from 1895–1908, and first baseman on McGraw's pennant winners in 1904–05. It seems Dan wanted to be photographed in his best cap.

Standees ring the outfield during the first World Series game ever played, at Boston's Huntington Grounds Park on October 1, 1903.

Bobby Wallace. He played in the bigs for 25 years (1894–1918). For a while he was known as "Mr. Shortstop." But that was before Wagner.

Danny Murphy, a second baseman and outfielder from 1900–13, most of it spent with the Philadelphia Athletics. His lifetime batting average is .288.

Sam Leever, Pittsburgh's ace right-hander during the century's first decade. He was a 25-game winner in 1903, 193–101 lifetime.

Outfielder Harry Lumley, a Dodger mainstay from 1904–10, during which he compiled a .274 batting average.

Elmer Flick, an outfielder who starred for the Phillies, A's, and Indians from 1898–1910. In 1900 he batted .378 and finished second to Wagner; in 1905 he batted .306 and won the American League batting title. "You can't figure it," he said.

At 5 feet 4½ inches, Willie Keeler was one of the smallest men in baseball history, but his lifetime average is one of the highest—.345. Willie played from 1892–1910.

A well-dressed crowd departing the Boston Pilgrim's Huntington Avenue Grounds ball park after a 1903 game.

Nap Lajoie, one of baseball's all-time great second basemen. His lifetime average is .339. He played from 1896–1916.

Jack Chesbro, who had a 41–12 superman season for the Yankees in 1904. Jack pitched from 1899–1909, compiling a 198–132 record.

Jimmy Sheckard, a big-league outfielder from 1897–1913.
Lifetime average: .275.

Third baseman–manager Jimmy Collins raising Boston's 1903
World Championship flag in the spring of 1904.

James "Nixey" Callahan. He pitched and played outfield for the
Cubs and White Sox from 1897–1905, retired for five years, then
came back in 1911 and put in a couple of years in the outfield
for the White Sox, whom he later managed to a pennant in 1917.
Nixey was a .273 hitter and 99–73 pitcher.

Clark Griffith when he was managing the Yankees in 1904.
A right-handed pitcher, Griff's heyday years were with Chicago
in the 1890s. He pitched from 1891–1914, retiring with a
240–141 record.

Tommy Leach, who primarily played third base and outfield in the National League from 1898–1915 and 1918, most of the time for Pittsburgh. He batted .269 lifetime.

Baseball at the Polo Grounds in the early days of the century.

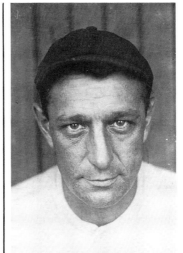

Art Devlin, a big leaguer from 1904–13, most of it spent as McGraw's third baseman. His lifetime average is .269.

Turkey Mike Donlin, seen here sharing a baseball with Broadway producer Daniel Frohman. Mike, who played with six different teams from 1899–1914 and batted .333, left baseball to go into vaudeville and eventually on to Hollywood to make movies. Many of his contemporaries felt that if the stagestruck Mike had taken baseball more seriously he could have been one of its greatest stars.

Patsy Dougherty, American League outfielder from 1902–11. He was a lifetime .284 hitter.

Fielder Jones, outfielder-manager of the "Hitless Wonders," the world champion 1906 Chicago White Sox. Jones played from 1896–1908 and batted .285.

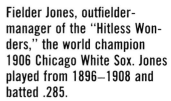

Nineteen-year-old Ty Cobb in 1906, his first full season in the major leagues.

Cy Seymour, who played from 1896–1910 and 1913, first as a pitcher, then as an out-fielder. He won the batting championship with the Reds in 1905, batting .377, by far his best year. Overall, he hit .303. Pitching for the Giants in the late 1890s, Cy was 63–54.

Nick Altrock, a 20-game winner for the White Sox in 1905 and 1906. Always a colorful character, Nick later teamed with baseball's "Clown Prince" Al Schacht in a slapstick pregame entertainment act. Nick's lifetime record was 82–75.

Hal Chase, perhaps baseball's greatest defensive first baseman and surely its most devious character. He played from 1905–19, when he was booted from organized ball under suspicion of throwing games.

Doc White, a superb lefthander who pitched for the Phillies and White Sox from 1901–13, running up a 190–157 career record.

Shortstop Joe Tinker, front man on the most famous double play combination of all time. Joe played from 1902–13, all but the last year with the Cubs, before jumping to the Federal League. He batted .264 lifetime.

Roy Hartzell (left) and George Stone of the St. Louis Browns in a pregame warmup. Stone was the American League batting champion in 1906.

Johnny Kling, who caught those marvelous pitchers on the Cub pennant winners of 1906–08 and 1910. A 13-year major leaguer, he batted .272.

Cubs first baseman and manager Frank Chance, who played from 1898–1914, batting .297.

Ed Reulbach, the Cubs' hard-to-beat right-hander, who led National League pitchers in winning percentage for three straight years (1906–08). His big-league record is 161–95.

Ed Killian, one of Detroit's star pitchers in the century's first decade. Lifetime record: 102–78.

Davy Jones, who played outfield for Detroit's 1907, '08, and '09 pennant winners. A 12-year big leaguer, he batted .269 lifetime.

BELOW: George Stovall, who played first base for the Indians and Browns from 1904–13. A spirited player whose nickname was "Firebrand," George left with a .266 lifetime average.

Harry Steinfeldt, the third baseman on the Tinker-Evers-Chance infield. Harry was a big leaguer from 1898–1911, batting .268.

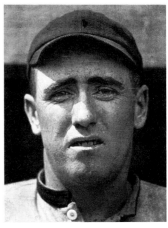

Donie Bush, a big-league shortstop from 1908–23, most of those years spent with the Detroit Tigers. He batted .250 lifetime.

Dodger catcher Bill Bergen, the weakest hitter in major league history. Bill played from 1901–11, getting into 947 games and batting a lifetime .170. Either Bill was a remarkably gifted defensive catcher, or else he knew where all the bodies were buried.

Cubs right-hander Orval Overall. He was 106–71 over a short but snappy seven-year career.

Jack Pfiester, a 20-game winner for the Cubs in 1906. Lifetime he was 71–44.

Second baseman Johnny Evers, regarded as one of the shrewdest players of his time. Johnny batted .270 over a career that ran from 1902–17.

Frank Chance barreling around third and heading home, ignoring what seems to be the third-base coach's attempt to stop him.

It's a sunny May 30, 1907, at the Polo Grounds and the early arrivals are taking in the infield workout.

Wild Bill Donovan, who pitched in the big leagues for 18 years (186–139) and later managed the Yankees from 1915–17.

Right-hander George Mullin, Detroit's ace from 1902–12. He was 212–184 lifetime, with a 29–8 season in 1909.

Brooklyn first baseman Tim Jordan, the National League home run leader in 1906 and again in 1908.

Brooklyn's talented southpaw Nap Rucker. Nap pitched from 1907–16, leaving with a 134–134 record.

Probably the most famous of all baseball pictures. A snarling Ty Cobb is sliding into a third base gingerly defended by New York's Jimmy Austin. The picture was taken in 1909.

Six-time 20-game winner Jesse Tannehill (right), seen here with Washington in 1909, pitched in the big leagues in 1894, from 1897–1909, and in 1911, winning 197 and losing 116.

Right-hander Ed Summers, who pitched for Detroit from 1908–12, posting a 68–45 record before a sore arm ended his career.

Outfielder Frank "Wildfire" Schulte, who played for 15 years (1904–18), most of that time for the Cubs. Lifetime average: .270.

Herman "Germany" Schaefer, a blithe spirit, who played second base on Detroit's 1907–08 pennant winners. Schaefer is remembered as the man who stole first base. One day, he was on first and a teammate on third. Germany broke for second, hoping to draw a throw that would enable the man on third to come home. The catcher, however, did not throw. On the next pitch, Germany ran back to first, still hoping to draw a throw. Again the catcher did not bite, and Schaefer had accomplished what baseball lore says you cannot do—steal first base.

Christy Mathewson

Addie Joss (left) and Ed Walsh.

John McGraw

Leon "Red" Ames pitched in the National League from 1903–19, compiling a 183–167 record.

Larry Doyle. "Laughing Larry" played second base in the National League from 1907–20, all but one year with the Giants. He was the batting champion in 1915 (.320). Lifetime he checks in at .290.

Walter Johnson

Frank "Home Run" Baker. He played third base for the A's from 1908–14 and for the Yankees from 1916–19 and 1921–22. Lifetime average: .307.

Miller Huggins, the future Yankee manager, seen here as a Cincinnati Reds second baseman in 1908. Huggins's playing career extended from 1904–16. Lifetime average: .265.

Dick Hoblitzell, first baseman for the Reds and Red Sox from 1908–18, compiling a .278 lifetime average.

Arthur "Bugs" Raymond, a talented 18-game winner for the Giants in 1909, but a man whose weakness for booze soon drove him from the big leagues. He died of alcoholism in 1912 at the age of 30. His lifetime record is 45–57.

Hooks Wiltse, a steady winner for McGraw from 1904–14. Hooks was 136–85 lifetime.

Norman "Kid" Elberfeld, big-league shortstop for six teams from 1898–99, 1901–11, and 1914. His career average is .271.

Lefty Leifield, Pittsburgh ace during the first decade of the century. Lefty was 124–96 over his career.

Ed Konetchy, who played first base for five National League teams between 1907 and 1921. Ed is seen here working out at the Polo Grounds in 1908. The player behind him is Red Murray. Konetchy was a lifetime .278 hitter.

Cleveland shortstop Neal Ball, who in 1909 pulled the major leagues' first unassisted triple play. Neal played from 1907–13, with a lifetime average of .251.

Eddie Collins, in the opinion of many the greatest of all second basemen. Over his 25-year career (1906–30), divided between the A's and White Sox, Collins batted .333.

Harry Krause, Connie Mack's fine young left-hander, whose career was aborted by a sore arm. Harry pitched from 1908–12 and left behind a 37–26 record.

The Giants' Moose McCormick is churning up the real estate, but Phillies third baseman Eddie Grant is tagging him out. Grant, who enlisted in the army at the outbreak of World War I, was killed in the battle of the Argonne Forest in France in 1918.

It's August 24, 1909, the Tigers versus the Athletics. Cobb is trying to steal third (during an intentional walk to Sam Crawford) and Frank Baker, with the ball in his bare hand, is making the tag. Cobb's spikes cut Baker's hand and forearm, leading the A's to demand Ty's expulsion for deliberately spiking Baker. The umpires didn't buy it.

Right-hander Bob Groom, who was 7–26 in his rookie year, but survived to become a 24-game winner a few years later. Groom pitched for three major league clubs between 1909 and 1918, with a career record of 95–119.

Right-hander Howie Camnitz, who pitched for the Pirates in 1904 and from 1906–13. A three-time 20-game winner, he had a lifetime mark of 119–86.

John "Dots" Miller, first baseman, second baseman, and occasional shortstop and third baseman for the Pirates, Cards, and Phillies between 1909 and 1921. He was a .263 lifetime hitter.

ABOVE AND LEFT: There are just a handful of candidates for Greatest Ballplayer of All Time. Here's one of them: Honus Wagner.

Christy Mathewson

1910 President William H. Taft launched a tradition when he opened the 1910 season in Washington by throwing out the ceremonial first ball and adding a new dimension to the art of politics. The president saw Walter Johnson fire a one-hitter against the Athletics. Things grew progressively better for Connie Mack's club, however, and at the end of the season they had won the pennant by a comfortable 14½ games over the Yankees.

Connie had a big winner that year in right-hander Jack Coombs, who rang up a 31–9 record, including 13 shutouts, still the league record. Along with Coombs, Chief Bender had his best season with a 23–5 mark, giving Connie two pitchers with a combined 54–14 won-lost record.

Second baseman Eddie Collins led the A's with a .322 batting average and the league with 81 stolen bases. But as was fast becoming the custom, the batting title went for the fourth straight year to Ty Cobb, though this time Tyrus had quite a scare—nosing out Nap Lajoie, .385 to .384. Detroit's hopes for a fourth pennant in a row withered when ace pitchers Ed Willett and Ed Summers slumped after their fine 1909 seasons, though George Mullin was 21–12.

The Yankees made second place largely on the 26–6 record compiled by rookie right-hander Russ Ford. The most ironic set of pitching statistics was juxtaposed by Chicago's Ed Walsh. The great spitballer was 18–20, with a 1.27 ERA, leading the league in both losses and ERA, the former being the consequence of Chicago's .212 team batting average, lowest in major league history.

Walter Johnson, who had lost 25 games the year before, turned it around in 1910 with 25 wins, the first of 7 consecutive seasons of 25 or more victories and 10 straight 20-game seasons overall. The twenty-two-year-old Washington speedballer also led with 313 strikeouts, the first of 12 strikeout titles he would earn. Until Bob Feller did it in 1946, Rube Waddell and Johnson were the only big-league pitchers to amass as many as 300 strikeouts in a season.

Despite a sore arm that held him to a 5–5 season, Cleveland's Addie Joss pitched a no-hitter against the White Sox on April 20, winning 1–0. On May 12, Chief Bender put Cleveland on the short end of a no-hitter when he smothered them, 4–0. Cleveland was involved in another superb pitching effort on August 30, when New York's Tom Hughes no-hit them for nine innings, but the Indians' George Kahler kept delivering shutout innings and Cleveland won it in 11, 5–0.

1910–Heading for Scandal 1919

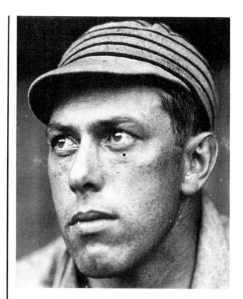

Jack Coombs

Cy Young, pitching for Cleveland now, scored his landmark 500th victory on July 19. At the age of forty-three, Cy was 7–10 for the year. The most spectacular dual pitching exploit of the season came on August 4, when Coombs and Walsh faced each other for 16 scoreless innings, the game ending in a 0–0 tie, Coombs fanning 18 and allowing just three hits.

Boston first baseman Jake Stahl was the home run leader with 10.

Tinker, Evers, and Chance and their teammates made it four pennants in five years as Frank Chance's Cubs won it easily in the National League, outpacing the Giants by 13 games. Three Finger Brown once again headed up the pitching with a 25–13 record, backed by rookie right-hander Leonard ("King") Cole, who was 20–4. Outfielder Frank ("Wildfire") Schulte hit 10 homers, tying him with Boston's Fred Beck for the lead. The league overall set a new home run record with 214, thanks largely to a new cork-center baseball it introduced that year. The league batting average also jumped, from .244 to .256.

Once again Christy Mathewson won prodigiously for the Giants, compiling a 27–9 record. The league's other 20-game winner was Philadelphia's Earl Moore, 22–15.

Honus Wagner was dethroned as batting champion after four years and supplanted by Philadelphia's Sherrod Magee, a seven-year veteran who had the year of his life with a .331 batting average and league-leading 123 runs batted in. Honus batted .320.

Despite Babe Adams's 18–9 record, Pittsburgh's failure to repeat was due primarily to pitching problems. Howie Camnitz dropped from 25–6 to 12–13 and Nick Maddox from 13–8 to 2–3, while 20-game winner Vic Willis had been sold to the Cardinals.

In the World Series, the heavily favored Athletics made the oddsmakers look good, defeating the Cubs in five games. Jack Coombs won three games for the A's.

1911

He had played a few games for the Athletics in 1908 and 1909, and then got into 20 games for the Indians in 1910. In 1911 he became a regular in the Indians' outfield and Joe Jackson (known quaintly as "Shoeless Joe" for, among other things, his homey unsophistication) exploded with 233 hits and a .408 batting average. Unfortunately for Joe, not even that illustrious figure was good enough for the batting title; for this was the year that Ty Cobb snarled, stroked, and sped his way to a .420 average. In this, his greatest season, Ty achieved personal highs in hits (248), doubles (47), triples (24), runs (147), and runs batted in (144, an incredible amount for that era). For Cobb, it was now five batting titles in a row. Teammate Sam Crawford also turned in his greatest season, batting .378, with 217 hits.

Despite that premier hitting, neither Cleveland nor Detroit finished first. For the second year in a row it was Connie Mack and his Philadelphia Athletics in a runaway, 13½ games over Detroit. Connie now had his famous "$100,000 infield" in place (the dollar figure referred to the value Connie placed upon them, which was considerable for the time): Stuffy McInnis at first, Eddie Collins (a .365 hitter that year) at second, Jack Barry at short, and Frank Baker at third. Baker led with 11 home runs and batted .334. This Athletics team batted .296, major league baseball's best until 1920.

On the mound, Mack had Jack Coombs following his 31–9 season with an almost equally handsome 28–12. Eddie Plank was 23–8 and Chief Bender 17–5.

With the American League having adapted the slightly livelier ball already in use in the National League, averages were decisively higher, the eight-team circuit jumping from .243 in 1910 to .273 in 1911.

Chicago's Ed Walsh had a big year with a 27–18 record, Walter Johnson was 25–13 for his seventh-place Senators, hard-throwing young Smoky Joe Wood was 23–17 for the Red Sox, Cleveland's rookie southpaw Vean Gregg was 23–7, and New York's Russ Ford 22–11. Both Wood and Walsh pitched no-hitters, Wood, 5–0, against the Browns on July 29, and Walsh, 5–0, over the Red Sox on August 27. Walsh also had the satisfaction of stopping Ty Cobb's 40-game hitting streak on July 14.

Cleveland's gifted right-hander Addie Joss died suddenly on April 14, two days after his thirty-first birthday. Joss's death was attributed to spinal meningitis. The 1.88 lifetime ERA achieved by Addie is the second lowest in history to Walsh's 1.82.

As the American League introduced a rookie hitter of great proportions in Joe Jackson, so did the National League unveil a pitcher of similar stature in Grover Cleveland Alexander. The Phillies' twenty-four-year-old new-

Shibe Park's right-field fence, about 1911. Note the freeloaders watching from the rooftops across the street.

comer, a freckle-faced farmboy from Nebraska, broke in with a 28–13 record and 227 strikeouts, setting rookie records for both victories and whiffs.

Winning 20 of their last 24, McGraw's Giants out-legged the Cubs in September, finishing the season with a 7½-game margin. The Giants got their usual fine season

Grover Cleveland Alexander

out of Christy Mathewson (26–13), and a surprising 24–7 from young left-hander Rube Marquard. Dubbed "the $11,000 lemon" for the price McGraw had paid a minor-league club for him and for Rube's hitherto uninspired pitching, Marquard rose to stardom in 1911, adding a league-high 237 strikeouts to his 24 wins.

John J. really turned his rabbits loose that year, the Giants stealing the all-time major league record of 347 bases, with five men having 38 or more, topped by Josh DeVore's 61.

The Cubs got Three Finger Brown's last big season (21–11), and a remarkable (for the day) 21 home runs from Wildfire Schulte, a new major league record. The Cubs' Jimmy Sheckard drew 147 walks, which remained tops in the league until 1945, when Brooklyn's Ed Stanky drew 148.

Pittsburgh's thirty-seven-year-old Honus Wagner won his eighth and final batting crown with a .334 average, nosing out Boston's Doc Miller by one point. Cincinnati speedboy Bob Bescher led the league in stolen bases for the third year in a row, his 81 thefts standing as the league record until Maury Wills's landmark 104 in 1962.

Other 20-game winners included Pittsburgh's Babe Adams (22–12) and Howie Camnitz (20–15), St. Louis's Bob Harmon (23–16), and Brooklyn's Nap Rucker (22–18).

On September 22, forty-four-year-old Cy Young, pitching for the Boston Braves now (he was a midseason waiver acquisition from Cleveland) beat the Pirates, 1–0, for his 511th and final major league victory.

In the World Series, the Athletics won their second straight title, beating the Giants in six games. It was in this Series that Frank Baker hit two pivotal home runs, which earned him baseball's most prestigious nickname: "Home Run."

1912

They called right-hander Joe Wood "Smoky" for the heat generated by his fastball, and in 1912 it burned with a particular blazing light as the Red Sox pitcher hurled himself to a 34–5 record and the team to a pennant in the club's first season in its new home, Fenway Park. The twenty-two-year-old Wood struck out 258 batters and pitched 10 shutouts. Boston, which won by 14 games over second-place Washington, had two other big winners in Hugh Bedient (20–9) and Buck O'Brien (20–13).

Boston's stellar outfield of Tris Speaker, Harry Hooper, and Duffy Lewis was considered the finest defensive unit of its time. Speaker, with a .383 batting average, was the club's top hitter. That snow-capped figure, however, placed him no better than third in the league batting race as Ty Cobb put together another sizzling season with a .410 average, which beat out Joe Jackson's .395. In his two big-league seasons Jackson had batted .408 and .395 and not won anything.

Jake Stahl's Red Sox won 105 games, which remained the league record until the unleashing of the 1927 Yankees.

Walter Johnson's 32–12 record helped lift his Washington club to unaccustomed heights, and despite the sharper hitting general throughout the league, Johnson fanned 303 and posted a 1.39 ERA; he and Wood (1.91) were the only pitchers to finish with ERAs under 2.00. Also, they each had American League–record 16-game winning streaks in the course of the season; Johnson setting the standard first, Wood tying him later.

Connie Mack's A's, thwarted in their try for a third straight pennant, got a big 26–6 season out of Eddie Plank, while Jack Coombs was 21–10. Frank Baker had a solid summer of hitting, batting .347 and leading the league with 10 homers (tied by Speaker) and 133 RBIs.

While he didn't win the batting title, Jackson did set a league record with 26 triples, and Washington's Clyde (Deerfoot) Milan stole 88 bases, which also was a new league mark. For single-game larceny, Eddie Collins set still another league record, stealing six bases in a game, which he did twice, on September 11 and 22.

Washington's Bob Groom was 24–13, Chicago's Ed Walsh was 27–17, and Cleveland's Vean Gregg 20–13. On July 4, Detroit's George Mullin no-hit the Browns, 7–0, and on August 30 the Browns retaliated in kind when Earl Hamilton no-hit Detroit, 5–1.

John McGraw's Giants were once more the class of the National League, taking the pennant by 10 games over Pittsburgh. The Giants jumped out to an early lead, thanks primarily to the spectacular pitching of Rube Marquard, who opened the season with an all-time record 19-game winning streak. Rube finished up at 26–11, with Mathewson 23–12, and rookie spitballer Jeff Tesreau 17–7. On June 13, Mathewson beat the Cubs, 3–2, for his 300th career victory.

The Giants had six men with over 30 steals apiece and a team total of 319. McGraw also had the league's best hitting—.286—with Chief Meyers topping the club with .358, still the National League high for catchers. Second baseman Larry Doyle, a blithe spirit known as "Laughing Larry" and remembered for the lovely line, "It's great to be young and a Giant," batted .330.

Second-place Pittsburgh had 20-game winners in Claude Hendrix (24–9) and Howie Camnitz (22–12) and wrung one more solid season from its thirty-eight-year-old icon Honus Wagner, who batted .324. But it was another Pirate who set one of baseball's more enduring records, outfielder Owen Wilson hitting a remarkable 36 triples. Wilson must have had an uncanny knack for hitting into Forbes Field's roomy gaps that summer—the same summer that Joe Jackson set the American League record with 26 triples.

The loudest batting noise in the league in the year 1912 came from Chicago, where third baseman Heinie Zimmerman became the first National Leaguer to win a Triple Crown, doing it with 14 home runs, 103 runs batted in, and a .372 batting average. Heinie also led with 207

Smoky Joe Wood

Smoky Joe Wood (left) and Christy Mathewson posing during the 1912 World Series.

hits and 41 doubles in what was by far the biggest year of his career. The Cubs also continued to display good fortune in finding winning pitchers; rookie right-hander Larry Cheney broke in with a 26–10 record, replacing the aging Three Finger Brown as the ace of the staff.

Tesreau pitched the league's only no-hitter of 1912, stopping the Phillies, 3–0, on September 6. The big spitballer was fully on his game that day, one writer describing his deliveries as "having lots of sop and speed and spin."

The World Series went to the Red Sox, four games to three (there was also a tie game). Joe Wood—it was his year, no question—won three games, including the finale, which featured Giants center fielder Fred Snodgrass's famous muff of a fly ball, enabling the Sox to score two runs in the bottom of the 10th and come from behind to win, 3–2.

Vean Gregg

1913

If Walter Johnson proved anything in 1913, it was that one man by himself couldn't pitch his team to a pennant. Walter had what is arguably the single greatest season any pitcher ever had—a 36–7 record, 1.09 ERA, 243 strikeouts, 11 shutouts, and, early in the season, 55⅔ consecutive scoreless innings, a major league record that stood until 1968. But all that this outpouring of individual heroics earned the Washington Senators was second place, 6½ games behind.

The American League pennant winners, for the third time in four years, were the Philadelphia Athletics. Three members of Connie Mack's $100,000 infield hit .320 or better—Stuffy McInnis (.326), Eddie Collins (.345), and Frank Baker (.336), with Baker leading the league with 12 home runs and 126 runs batted in. Though Mack's pitching was hurt by the loss of ace Jack Coombs to illness, the slack was picked up by Chief Bender (21–10) and the veteran Eddie Plank (18–10). Connie was also bringing along some exceptional young mound talent in Bullet Joe Bush, Bob Shawkey, and Herb Pennock, all of whom were destined to have their greatest seasons for the Yankees in the 1920s.

Cleveland's Joe Jackson hit .373, but still wasn't close to a batting title, as Ty Cobb checked in at .390, giving Tyrus a five-year average of .397. It was the Tiger star's seventh title in a row.

Boston's failure to repeat was attributed in large part to an April injury to their sparkling young right-hander Joe Wood. Playing a bunt on the wet grass, Wood slipped and fell, hurting his thumb; this led later to a shoulder injury, and the phenomenon of 1912 dropped from 34–5 to 11–5. He was never the same again, taking a career from the brightest sunlight and leaving it in the shadows of what might have been.

There were four other 20-game winners this year: Cleveland's Cy Falkenberg (23–10) and Vean Gregg (20–13), and Chicago's rookie left-hander Reb Russell (22–16) and Jim Scott (20–20). For Gregg it was three 20-game seasons in three years; an injury the following year, however, ended this upward spiral to greatness.

In the National League, John McGraw's Giants easily made it three in a row, finishing 12½ games ahead of second-place Philadelphia. McGraw had a trio of 20-game winners in Christy Mathewson (25–11), Rube Marquard (23–10) and Jeff Tesreau (22–13). Mathewson's 2.06 ERA gave him the lead for the fifth time, a league record he shares with Grover Cleveland Alexander and Sandy Koufax.

The Phillies received a 27–12 season from right-hander Tom Seaton and a 22–8 effort from Alexander. The club also got some good hitting from Gavvy Cravath, who took advantage of the modest dimensions of Baker Bowl (Philadelphia's home park) to bang out 19 home runs and drive in 128 runs—both good enough to lead the league. Brooklyn first baseman Jake Daubert was the batting champion with a .350 average.

Chicago's Larry Cheney followed up his big 26–10 rookie year with a 21–14 mark, one of his wins a September 14 shutout of the Giants in which he allowed 14 hits, a National League record for most hits allowed in a shutout. Pittsburgh's Babe Adams was 21–10.

Honus Wagner batted an even .300, the 17th consecutive, and last, .300 season for Honus, who was approaching his fortieth birthday. Wagner's teammate, outfielder Max Carey, led the league with 61 stolen bases, the first of ten times Max would lead in this category over the next 13 years. Carey remained, until the coming of Maury Wills and Lou Brock in the 1960s, the National League's most prolific base stealer.

For the third year in a row, the Giants got the thin end of the World Series stick, losing to the Athletics in five games.

Babe Adams

1914

Like a ghost from the bad old days of upstart leagues, broken contracts, and peripatetic players, a brand-new, self-proclaimed major league hatched itself in 1914. This was the Federal League, a foredoomed, two-year aberration on the big-league scene.

The Feds came in with high hopes and fluttering checkbooks. They established teams in Buffalo, Brooklyn, Baltimore, Pittsburgh, St. Louis, Kansas City, Chicago, and Indianapolis. This gave New York four teams and St. Louis and Chicago three apiece, which was like putting an extra hand on the udder and expecting more milk.

It couldn't last, nor did it, the Federals stacking their bats after the 1915 season. (One thing that did last from the Federal League adventure was Wrigley Field. Built for the Chicago entry, it was taken over by the Cubs after the new league folded.) But while they were in business, they stirred up some old dust, luring established major leaguers into their camp and forcing their opposing numbers to raise salaries to keep restless stars on the reservation.

Some big names did jump to the new league, though many of them were past their prime. Among those who soaked one last big payday out of the Feds were George Mullin, Three Finger Brown, Joe Tinker, Howie Camnitz, Ed Reulbach, and Eddie Plank. Hal Chase, baseball's shadiest character (who would eventually be banned from organized ball for throwing games), always on the lookout for some fresh green, went, as did the Phillies' 27-game winner Tom Seaton. But the game's biggest names, like Ty Cobb, Tris Speaker, and Walter Johnson, remained with their clubs, their loyalties buttressed by salary increases.

Ignoring the intruders as best they could, the established major leagues went about their pennant races in the summer of 1914, as a world war was breaking out in Europe. Connie Mack's Athletics remained the class of the league, winning for the fourth time in five years, finishing 8½ games ahead of Boston. Home Run Baker, living up to his illustrious nickname, hit 9 home runs to lead the league for the fourth year in a row, duplicating what teammate Harry Davis had done from 1904 through 1907. With the home run titles won by Nap Lajoie in 1901 and Socks Seybold in 1902, it gave the A's ten of the league's first 14 home run champions.

For the first time in history, a club won the pennant without a 20-game winner, Chief Bender (17–3) and Joe Bush (16–12) being Mack's top winners. Instead of the big man at the top, the A's had seven pitchers winning in double figures. Eddie Collins and his .344 batting average led the club's attack.

Second-place Boston had a big winner in left-hander Ray Collins (20–13), while lefty Dutch Leonard was 19–5 and posted the lowest ERA ever for a pitcher with 200 or

Brooklyn's Ebbets Field in 1914, one year after it opened.

more innings—1.01. The Red Sox were also responsible for attaching a historical footnote to the 1914 season when in July they purchased nineteen-year-old Babe Ruth from the Baltimore club of the International League. The youngster broke in with a 2–1 record. Manager Bill Carrigan liked Ruth's fastball and also, he said, was impressed with the way the young man swung the bat.

Walter Johnson dropped from his pinnacle 36–7 season to a barely less prodigious 28–18, which included 9 shutouts and a 1.72 ERA. For this hardly discernible fall from grace, owner Clark Griffith wanted to cut Walter's salary, but when Walter whispered "Federal League" to him, Griff relented.

In Detroit, Ty Cobb extended his copyright on the batting title for one more year—the eighth straight—with a .368 average. Cobb's teammate Sam Crawford tied Joe Jackson's league record with 26 triples, and Tiger left-hander Harry Coveleski was 22–12. In Chicago, big Ed Walsh was paying the toll of thousands of innings of concentrated work with a dead arm that held him to a 2–3 record.

Walsh's teammate, right-hander Jim Scott, earned the league's hard-luck award of the year on May 14 when he pitched nine hitless innings against Washington, only to lose on two hits in the tenth, 1–0. A few weeks later, another White Sox right-hander had better luck—Joe Benz no-hit Cleveland, 1–0, on May 31.

At season's end, on September 27, Cleveland's Nap Lajoie rapped out his 3,000th career hit, making him the twentieth century's second player—Honus Wagner was the first—to amass that total.

On July 4, the Boston Braves were occupying the National League cellar, 15 games out of first place. As late as July 18, they were still last. But then George Stallings's club began winning. By August 12 they were second; on September 2 they bobbed into first place. They took over the top spot for keeps on September 8 and never stopped charging ahead, winning 34 of their last 44 games and finishing the season 10½ games ahead of the Giants.

The 1914 Braves were baseball's first "miracle" team, though outside of former Cub Johnny Evers at second and slick-fielding young Rabbit Maranville at short, they were a club of no particular distinction, except they did have three strong starters who pitched superbly coming down the stretch: Dick Rudolph (27–10), Bill James (26–7), and Lefty Tyler (16–14).

The Giants got strong seasons from Jeff Tesreau (26–10) and Christy Mathewson (24–13—his 12th consecutive, 13th overall, and final 20-game season), but saw their third ace, Rube Marquard, slump to 12–22.

The fourth-place Cubs had a pair of 20-game winners in left-hander Jim (Hippo) Vaughn (21–13) and Larry Cheney (20–18), as did the sixth-place Phillies with Erskine Mayer (21–19) and the man who was on the brink of replacing Mathewson as the league's premier pitcher, Grover Cleveland Alexander (27–15). Brooklyn's Jeff Pfeffer was 23–12.

The Phillies' Gavvy Cravath again hit 19 home runs to lead the league and Brooklyn's Jake Daubert won the batting title for the second straight year with a .329 average. On June 9, Honus Wagner became the first player in modern baseball history to accumulate 3,000 hits. On September 9, George Davis, one of Boston's lesser-known pitchers (3–3 for the year), no-hit the Phillies, 7–0.

In the World Series, the Braves uncorked one more miracle when they swept the highly favored Athletics in four, Rudolph and James each winning two for Boston.

1915

After winning four pennants in five years, Connie Mack and his Athletics went clear over the precipice and finished last, and continued to finish last until 1922—seven straight years. Connie's great team had come apart all at once: ace pitchers Eddie Plank and Chief Bender had jumped to the Federal League, Frank Baker had retired to his Maryland farm (he would be back after a year, with the Yankees), while financial considerations forced Connie to sell Eddie Collins, Jack Barry, Bob Shawkey, and Herb Pennock.

With the once-dominant A's no longer a factor, the battle for the pennant was between Boston and Detroit, with the Red Sox winning by 2½ games. The difference was Boston's deeper pitching staff, with Rube Foster and Ernie Shore logging 19–8 records and young Babe Ruth going 18–8 in his first full season.

Detroit had Ty Cobb taking his ninth consecutive batting title with a .369 average and setting a new major league record with 96 stolen bases. Hooks Dauss (24–13) and Harry Coveleski (22–13) each won big for the Tigers. The third-place White Sox had a pair of 24-game winners in Jim Scott and Red Faber, and Walter Johnson continued his relentless high-style pitching, winning 27 for the fourth-place Senators, making it six years in a row of 25 or more for Walter.

On May 6, a bit of history went unobtrusively into the books when Ruth belted his first major league home run, connecting off the Yankees' Jack Warhop at the Polo Grounds, then the Yankees' home field. Still a full-time pitcher, Ruth hit four home runs (the league leader, Braggo Roth, had but seven) and batted .315.

As the Athletics dropped, so did the Phillies rise, Philadelphia's National League entry soaring from sixth place in 1914 to take their first pennant. Grover Cleveland Alexander rose to greatness this year, winning 31 and losing just 10, pitching 12 shutouts and leading the league with a 1.22 ERA, a remarkable statistic when one considers he was pitching in Baker Bowl, a ball park of intimate dimensions. Erskine Mayer (21–15) was the club's other big winner, as manager Pat Moran brought his club home seven games ahead of Boston. Gavvy Cravath established a modern major league record with 24 home runs and led with 115 runs batted in.

The Braves put on another late-season charge in an attempt to produce a second "miracle," but this time came up short, due in part to pitcher Bill James's sore arm and Johnny Evers's injury. Only Dick Rudolph (22–19) won big for the defending champs.

Young right-hander Al Mamaux was 21–8 for Pittsburgh, where the forty-one-year-old Honus Wagner put in a full season at shortstop and batted .274. The Cubs' left-handed ace Hippo Vaughn was 20–12. Hippo's teammate, right-hander George "Zip" Zabel, turned in a record outing against the Dodgers on June 17. Called into the game with two out in the first inning, Zabel continued pitching until the Cubs had won the game, 4–3, in the 19th inning. It remains the longest relief stint in major league history.

The Giants had the league's top hitter in second baseman Larry Doyle, whose .320 average was, and still is, the lowest figure for a National League batting leader. And

New York Giants manager John McGraw (left) and Philadelphia Phillies manager Pat Moran.

Harry Coveleski

Gavvy Cravath (left) and Tris Speaker giving each other five during the 1915 World Series.

Doyle was about all the Giants had in 1915 as, much to the embarrassment of John McGraw, the team sank to its one and only last-place finish in McGraw's 31-year tenure as manager of the club. Assuaging the sting somewhat was the fact that the club's 69 wins and .454 percentage were the highest ever for a cellar dweller.

Contributing to the Giants' woeful season was the sudden collapse of Christy Mathewson—after 12 consecutive seasons of 22 or more wins, Matty fell to an 8–14 record. At the age of thirty-five, the man many still feel was the greatest of all pitchers was through. McGraw also soured on Rube Marquard, waiving him to the Dodgers at the end of August after Rube had gone a shaky 9–8. The season had begun well for the big left-hander; on April 15, he no-hit the Dodgers, 2–0. The league's other no-hitter was crafted by the Cubs' Jimmy Lavender, 2–0, over the Giants on August 31.

Honus Wagner's successor as the league's top player broke in that year. His name was Rogers Hornsby, a nineteen-year-old shortstop, who got into 18 games with the Cardinals and batted .246.

After Alexander beat the Red Sox in the opening game of the World Series, the Red Sox came back and took the next four in a row, (three of them by 2–1 scores), behind the tough pitching of Foster, Shore, and Dutch Leonard.

1916

The Red Sox proved something or other in 1916; unable to agree on a contract with their star player Tris Speaker, the Sox dealt him to Cleveland just before the season opened. Tris batted .386 for the Indians, while the Red Sox won the pennant without him, by two games over the White Sox.

Bill Carrigan's club had the league's best pitching, most notably in twenty-one-year-old Babe Ruth, who was 23–12 and had a league-leading 1.75 ERA and nine shutouts (the league mark for southpaws, tied by Ron Guidry in 1978). Behind Ruth was Dutch Leonard (18–12), and submarine-balling Carl Mays (18–13).

The White Sox had three .300 hitters, including Joe Jackson with a .341 average, but this couldn't compensate for some pitching deficiencies, particularly in Jim Scott and Red Faber, who fell from a combined 48 wins in 1915 to 24 in 1916.

Tris Speaker's batting average was not only impressive, it was also good enough to dethrone Ty Cobb as the league's batting champion after nine straight years. Ty batted .371, but all it earned him was second spot. New York first baseman Wally Pipp was the home run leader with 12, making Wally the first Yankee to lead in one-way tickets.

With their great veteran Sam Crawford near the end of the trail now (he retired the next year), the Tigers began breaking in a young outfielder named Harry Heilmann, who in time would rank with the greatest of hitters. The twenty-one-year-old batted .282 in 1916.

Harry Coveleski (21–11) was a 20-game winner for the third year in a row for the Tigers (a sore arm would soon wash him out of the major leagues) and Bob Shawkey was 24–14 for the Yankees. Walter Johnson, always an inspiring example of a man transcending his environment, was 25–20 for a seventh-place Washington club, giving him seven straight years of 25 or more wins.

The St. Louis Browns had a new first baseman, twenty-three-year-old George Sisler, breaking in modestly at .305. Like Ruth, Sisler had broken into the majors as a left-handed pitcher, but like Ruth, his destiny lay at home plate rather than 60 feet 6 inches away.

For Connie Mack's Athletics, it was a season of pure anguish. The A's lost 117 games, the American League record. Their season included a 20-game losing streak, and a couple of pitchers named Jack Nabors and Tom Sheehan were 1–20 and 1–16, respectively.

There were three no-hitters in the American League that year: Boston's Rube Foster, 2–0, over the Yankees on June 21; Philadelphia's Joe Bush, 5–0, over Cleveland on August 26; and Dutch Leonard, 4–0, over St. Louis on August 30.

Jack Nabors. His lifetime record is 1–25.

For the third year in a row there was a first-time winner in the National League. Following the examples of the 1914 Braves and 1915 Phillies, Wilbert Robinson's Brooklyn Dodgers won their first pennant in 1916.

This first of many Dodger pennant winners had two solid .300 stickers in the lineup—first baseman Jake Daubert at .316 and outfielder Zack Wheat at .312. Also on the squad was outfielder Casey Stengel, a five-year veteran, and even in those days something of a singular spirit. At the outset of the World Series with the highly favored Red Sox, Stengel reportedly approached some of the Boston players and asked them what they thought Brooklyn's losing share would come to.

The Dodgers had a corps of veteran pitchers, including Rube Marquard (13–6), former Athletics ace Jack Coombs (13–8), former Cub Larry Cheney (18–12), and the big winner, Jeff Pfeffer, who was 25–11.

The Braves and Phillies, chasing the Dodgers right to the end, finished second and third, respectively, the Phillies 2½ games out, the Braves 4. Grover Cleveland Alexander was 33–12 for the Phillies, with a league-leading 1.55 ERA and major league record 16 shutouts, nine of which were pitched in Baker Bowl. Left-hander Eppa Rixey was 22–10 and Al Demaree 19–14. They were the league's top starting rotation, but received little help from the rest of the staff.

The Braves had some good pitching of their own, topped by Dick Rudolph's 19–12, but the club was undone by its .233 batting average, lowest in the league. Al Mamaux was 21–15 for the Pirates.

Giving his club a healthy shaking out, McGraw lifted the Giants from the cellar up to fourth place (eastern clubs occupied the entire first division). He got rid of first baseman Fred Merkle, second baseman Larry Doyle, and

catcher Chief Meyers, while allowing Christy Mathewson to go to Cincinnati in midseason to assume the manager's job. Mathewson, who was just 3–4 with the Giants, pitched one final game for the Reds. It was on September 4 and it was a prearranged match with his old rival Three Finger Brown, now spooning out his last days as an active player with the Cubs. The two former grandmasters staggered through a tough afternoon, with Matty finally winning it by a 10–8 score, giving up 15 hits. It was his 373rd and final major league victory.

For the Giants, it was a season highlighted by two prodigious winning streaks; the club, in fact, took half of its 86 wins in these two streaks. The first, early in the season, was a run of 17 straight wins, all on the road; the second was a major league record setter—a mammoth 26-game win streak in September, all at home. Ironically, this victory extravaganza began with the team in fourth place and ended with them in the same spot.

Hal Chase, who signed with Cincinnati after the dissolution of the Federal League, led the National League with a .339 average. The Cardinals discovered they had a live bat in young Rogers Hornsby, who hit .313 in his first full season. The man who was to become the game's greatest second baseman, divided his playing time between third base, shortstop, and a handful of games at first base.

On June 16, Boston's Tom Hughes pitched the league's only no-hitter of 1916, 2–0, over Pittsburgh.

In the World Series, the Red Sox showed that Stengel had taken a pretty realistic view of things, the Sox dropping the Dodgers in five games. In game 2, Ruth outdueled Brooklyn's Sherry Smith in 14 innings, 2–1, with Babe shutting out the Dodgers over the final 13, beginning a string of scoreless innings that would lead to a new Series record.

Hal Chase

1917

The Chicago White Sox, two years away from being a team of infamy, won their third American League pennant in 1917, under skipper Pants Rowland, who in three years at the wheel had finished third, second, and now first. Eddie Cicotte was Rowland's ace with a 28–12 record and 1.53 ERA, lowest in the league, while Lefty Williams was 17–8. Outfielder Happy Felsch led the club with a .308 average, with Joe Jackson batting an uncharacteristically low .301.

Boston, world champs two years running, finished second, nine games out, despite Babe Ruth's 24–13 record and a 22–9 season from Carl Mays. Ruth batted .325 and the club was becoming more and more intrigued by his hitting. Cleveland had 23–13 and 19–14 seasons, respectively, from spitballers Jim Bagby and Stanley Coveleski, but little help after that. Tris Speaker batted .352 for the Indians and George Sisler .353 for the Browns, but both had to be content with runner-up positions as Ty Cobb reestablished a tradition—winning his 10th batting title in 11 years with a .383 average, his season including a 35-game hitting streak. The league as a whole, caught in a rut of sorts, batted .248 for the fourth straight year.

Walter Johnson remained faithful to his own standards of excellence, going 23–16 for his fifth-place Senators and leading the league for the sixth straight time with 188 strikeouts.

It was a banner year for no-hitters in the American League, with five of these notable efforts being turned in. Cicotte pitched one for the White Sox over the Browns on April 14, winning 11–0; the Yankees' George Mogridge stopped the Red Sox, 2–1, on April 24; and on May 5 and May 6 a pair of Browns pitchers hurled no-hitters on successive days against the White Sox, with Ernie Koob winning, 1–0, and Bob Groom getting the victory the following day, 3–0. On June 23, Boston's Ernie Shore received credit for a perfect game after he had taken the mound in the top of the first inning with a man on first and nobody out—Babe Ruth, the starting pitcher, had been ejected for arguing with the umpire after walking the first batter. The runner was promptly caught stealing, and Shore went on to retire the next 26 batters in a row, notching a perfect game.

It took John McGraw just two years to get back on top; after finishing last in 1915, McGraw and his rebuilt Giants took the pennant in 1917, winning by 10 games over the Phillies. Southpaw Ferdie Schupp led the starters with a 21–7 record, followed by another left-hander, Slim Sallee, who was 18–7, and Pol Perritt, who was 17–7. McGraw got .300 seasons out of outfielders Benny Kauff, who had starred in the defunct Federal League, and base-stealing sparkplug George Burns.

Ernie Shore

Grover Cleveland Alexander made it three 30-win seasons in a row with a 30–13 record, taking his third straight ERA title with a 1.86 mark, and also led in shutouts for the third straight time with 8, giving him 36 shutouts over the last three years. The great Phillies right-hander couldn't do it alone, however; he had little help from the rest of the staff—number two starter Eppa Rixey was 16–21. Gavvy Cravath was again the home run champ with 12, tying the Giants' Dave Robertson.

In St. Louis, young Rogers Hornsby continued flexing his muscles, batting .327 and leading the league with a .484 slugging average. Hornsby was a shortstop then, playing 144 games at the position. For another shortstop it was the final stacking of the bats. The forty-three-year-old Honus Wagner—actually playing the bulk of his games at first base—retired after batting .265 in his 21st and final season. "The bases seemed to be getting further apart," Honus said, "while the mound seemed to be getting closer. I figured it was time to go."

The batting champion was Cincinnati's Edd Roush, with a .341 average. Twenty-game winners included Cincinnati's Fred Toney (24–16) and Pete Schneider (20–19), and Chicago's Hippo Vaughn (23–13). On May 2, Toney and Vaughn engaged in one of baseball's memorable pitching duels. For the only time in history, two men pitched nine hitless innings in the same game. Then in the top of the tenth Vaughn gave up two hits and a run; Toney held firm in the bottom of the inning and won baseball's only double no-hitter, 1–0.

Red Faber

Toney hit the record books again on July 1, when he pitched and won both ends of a doubleheader against the Pirates, 4–1 and 5–1, allowing just three hits in each game, setting a record for fewest hits allowed by one pitcher in a doubleheader. Alexander also pitched a doubleheader victory for the Phillies on September 3, the second time he had done this.

John McGraw's luck in World Series play continued to be on the sour side as his Giants lost to the White Sox in six games, despite Dave Roberston's 11 hits and .500 batting average. Chicago's star was Red Faber, who won three games.

Hank Gowdy

1918

By the time the 1918 season was underway the United States was entering its second year of war. The war had barely intruded upon the big leagues in 1917, but a year later its reality was felt. Many players went off to military service, and when the provost general promulgated a "work or fight" order, other players (including Joe Jackson) opted for work in industries associated with the war effort (baseball having been declared a nonessential industry). Also, by decree of the secretary of war, the season ended on September 2, with special dispensation given for the playing of the World Series.

Among the players who spent all or part of the 1918 season in the military were the Red Sox' Dutch Leonard, Jack Barry, Duffy Lewis, and Herb Pennock; the Senators' Sam Rice; the Yankees' Wally Pipp and Bob Shawkey; the White Sox' Eddie Collins and Red Faber; the Tigers' Harry Heilmann; the Cubs' Grover Cleveland Alexander; the Giants' George Kelly, Rube Benton, and Jesse Barnes; Pittsburgh's Casey Stengel; Brooklyn's Jeff Pfeffer; Boston's Rabbit Maranville and Hank Gowdy (who had been the first to enlist); and many others.

In the American League, skipper Ed Barrow led the Red Sox to their third pennant in four years. The Red Sox, always deep in quality pitching in those years, had Carl Mays (21–13), Sam Jones (16–5), Joe Bush (15–15), and Babe Ruth (13–7) heading the staff. Ruth, as his record indicates, was now pitching less and playing more; getting time in the outfield and at first base, the young slugger batted .300, led in slugging with a .555 percentage, and tied the Athletics' Tilly Walker for the lead in home runs with 11, the first of his 12 home run crowns. As an indication of the impact Ruth was beginning to have, the Red Sox as a team hit just 15 homers, 11 of them by Ruth.

Cleveland finished just 2½ games behind, with Stanley Coveleski putting up a 22–13 record. The Indians were handicapped when their star hitter Tris Speaker was suspended for the balance of the season after assaulting an umpire on August 28 after a dispute at home plate.

With a 23–13 record, Walter Johnson pitched the Senators into third place, four games out. Walter's 1.27 ERA was the league's best, and it was built upon the kind of effort he put out on May 15—a 1–0, 18-inning shutout, the longest shutout victory in major league history, and one of his 38 career 1–0 wins.

The league's other 20-game winner came from a most unexpected source—the last-place Athletics, for whom rookie Scott Perry was 21–19.

For the 11th time in the last 12 years the batting champion was Ty Cobb, with a .382 average.

On June 3, Boston's Dutch Leonard pitched his second no-hitter, stopping the Tigers, 5–0. Shortly after, Leonard went off to war.

In the National League, the Cubs were back on top for the first time since 1910, thanks primarily to the league's best pitching: Hippo Vaughn (22–10), Claude Hendrix (19–7), and Lefty Tyler (19–9), with Vaughn and Tyler each delivering eight shutouts.

The Cubs broke in a top-notch rookie shortstop in Charlie Hollocher, who batted .316 and led with 161 hits. Injuries were to abort Hollocher's career in 1924, forcing his retirement at the age of twenty-eight, leaving him somewhat dimly sketched in the mists of history, though Burleigh Grimes was to describe him years later as "one of the greatest shortstops of all time."

McGraw's Giants finished 10½ games behind, with John J. introducing rookie outfielder Ross Youngs to the National League. Youngs batted .302 in his maiden voyage. Like Hollocher, he was to have a superb career shortened, in Youngs's case by an illness which forced his retirement in 1926 and caused his death a year later. He left behind a .322 lifetime batting average and a Pete Rose–type of reputation for nonstop hustle.

Cincinnati's defending batting champion Edd Roush had another good year, hitting .333, but lost out to Brooklyn's fine veteran Zack Wheat, who checked in at the end with .335. The Phillies' Gavvy Cravath led in home runs for the fifth time with just eight, lowest for a league leader since Red Murray's seven in 1909.

In a World Series of tightly pitched games (no one scored more than three runs in any single game), the Red Sox won their fifth championship in five tries, with Ruth and Mays winning two apiece. The Babe pitched a 1–0 shutout in the opener, and then wasn't scored upon until the eighth inning of his next start, giving him a World Series record of 29⅔ consecutive scoreless innings, dating back to 1916. The record was broken by Whitey Ford in 1961.

1919

In 1919 the war was over and everything was back to normal—or so the naively unsuspecting thought.

Looking back, the year was one of those significant lines of division, clearly delineating the end of one era and the arrival of another. It was the end of the dead-ball era, the beginning of the end of corruption in baseball—betting on games by players and the consequent ramifications had been going on for decades—and behind the new curtain about to rise was a gaudily crowded stage, the 1920s, which would offer the abolition of the spitball and other trick deliveries, the introduction of the lively ball, and the flowering of baseball's most gargantuan figure, Babe Ruth, who would change the game forever.

The big-league club owners, never a particularly astute band of executives, began the season with a typically benighted perspective. For some reason they assumed that there would be a lessening of interest in baseball in the immediate postwar world and so they reduced the playing schedules from 154 to 140 games. They were proven wrong, and by wide margins—attendance not only jumped from the previous season, but in some cases the 1918 figures were tripled.

Kid Gleason's Chicago White Sox won a hard-fought pennant race, edging out Cleveland by 3½ games. Joe Jackson, whom many old-timers insisted was a better hitter than either Cobb or Ruth, batted .351 to lead the way for the White Sox. Gleason had a pair of big winners in Eddie Cicotte (29–7) and Lefty Williams (23–11).

Second-place Cleveland got another big season from Stanley Coveleski, who was 24–12. Cleveland right-hander Ray Caldwell, a late-season acquisition from the Red Sox, pitched the league's only no-hitter, stopping the Yankees on September 10, 3–0. A few weeks before, Caldwell had been struck by lightning and knocked unconscious, leading one whimsical writer to comment on the "high-voltage" performance Ray turned in against the Yankees.

Ty Cobb won his 12th and last batting title with an average of .384 (note the almost diabolic consistency of Cobb's league-leading batting averages in 1917, 1918, and 1919: .383, .382, .384). Nevertheless, the era of Ty Cobb, of bunting and stealing, of nagging runs out of the opposition, was coming to a close, with the dirge for this style of play being orchestrated by the booming bat of Babe Ruth, now a full-time outfielder for the Red Sox hitting a record-smashing 29 home runs and captivating fans everywhere, as well as enchanting his Boston teammates, who collectively hit all of four homers that year, three of them by Harry Hooper.

Other 20-game winners that year included New York's Bob Shawkey (20–11), Detroit's George (Hooks) Dauss (21–9), St. Louis's Allen Sothoron (20–13), and

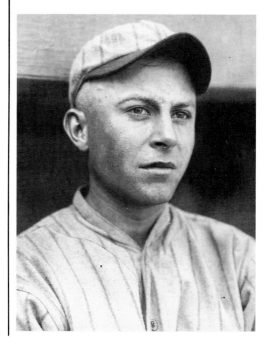

Charlie Hollocher

Babe Ruth pitching . . .

. . . and hitting.

Washington's inevitable Walter Johnson (20–14), whose 1.49 ERA was by far the league's best and whose 147 strikeouts led for the eighth year in a row.

Connie Mack's capsized Athletics were still fathoms-deep in last place, losing 104 games. It was now five straight years in the nether regions for Connie, and some Philadelphia papers were calling for him to sell the club and get out of town. Connie paid no heed.

In the National League, Pat Moran's Cincinnati Reds won their first pennant, thanks to a strong array of pitching: Slim Sallee (21–7), Hod Eller (20–9), Dutch Ruether (19–6), plus winning seasons from Ray Fisher, Jimmy Ring, and Dolf Luque, who was Cuba's first substantial gift to the big leagues. Center fielder Edd Roush won his second batting title with a .321 average, three points better than the Cardinals' Rogers Hornsby, who was about to become a living nightmare for National League pitchers.

John McGraw's Giants came in second, nine games off the mark, despite having the league's biggest winner in Jesse Barnes (25–9) and .300 seasons from Ross Youngs and George Burns. McGraw got singed when he took a chance and signed Hal Chase, whose reputation was by now distinctly malodorous. (In 1917 Hal had been accused by his Cincinnati manager, Christy Mathewson, of throwing games, but beat the rap.) In August, McGraw, after seeing some things he didn't like, quietly let his brilliant but warped first baseman go, along with third baseman Heinie Zimmerman. No accusations were made, but the implications were obvious. Neither man ever returned to organized ball.

Chicago got a 21–14 season from Hippo Vaughn and a 16–11 mark from Grover Cleveland Alexander, back from France where he had suffered shell shock in an artillery bombardment and was already teetering into epilepsy and alcoholism. Alex still had a steady hand on the mound, however, spinning nine shutouts and recording the league's lowest ERA (1.72).

Philadelphia's Gavvy Cravath took his sixth and final home run title with 12, despite playing in just 83 games as his career was coming to a close.

Cincinnati's Hod Eller pitched the league's only no-hitter, throwing the noose around the Cardinals on May 11, 6–0.

With the World Series expanded to a best-of-nine format, the underdog Reds beat the White Sox in eight games (Lefty Williams losing three times) amid swirling rumors of a fix. The rumors would continue to fester throughout the 1920 season, finally erupting to full public disclosure the following September.

A scandal of another sort was already reaching full height by the end of the year. Boston Red Sox owner Harry Frazee, whose true passion was producing Broadway shows, most of which were turkeys, was constantly in need of ready cash, a generous supply of which was in the possession of Jacob Ruppert, who was anxious to build his New York Yankees into a winner. During the 1919 season, Frazee sold the Yankees pitcher Carl Mays; in coming years the Yankees would buy from the Red Sox pitchers Joe Bush, Sam Jones, Herb Pennock, and Waite Hoyt, plus catcher Wally Schang, shortstop Everett Scott, and third baseman Joe Dugan. At the end of 1919, however, Frazee broke the hearts of New England when he did the unforgivable and sold Babe Ruth to the Yankees for around $125,000 (*and* a $300,000 loan). It remains the most pivotal transaction in baseball history; it was the beginning of the Yankees dynasty, the greatest winning tradition ever seen in any sport. With the aplomb of an indicted politico, Frazee said of the Ruth deal, "This transaction will help the Red Sox." (From 1922 through 1930, the Red Sox finished last eight times.)

Jack Barry. Shortstop on Connie Mack's "$100,000 infield," Barry played for the A's and Red Sox from 1908–19. Esteemed more for his glove than his bat, he was a lifetime .243 hitter.

Stuffy McInnis, first baseman on the "$100,00 infield." A superb fielder and a steady hitter, Stuffy played from 1909–27 and had a .308 career average.

Harry Frazee

Eddie Collins

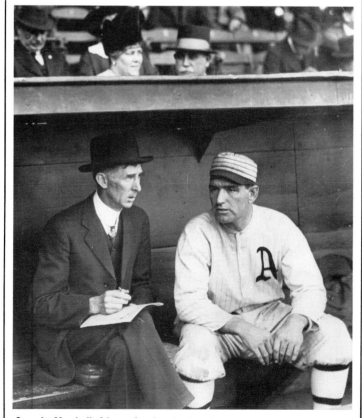

Connie Mack (left) conferring in the dugout with catcher Ira Thomas. Thomas caught for Connie's 1910–11 pennant winners.

Rube Oldring, an outfielder for the Athletics from 1906–15. A 13-year major leaguer, Rube was a .270 lifetime hitter.

Ty Cobb storming into third. Jack Barry is defending the bag.

Yankee pitcher Russ Ford, who broke in with a 26–6 record in 1910 but never came close to repeating that success. After four years with the Yankees and a 73–56 record, he jumped to the Federal League.

Third baseman Jimmy Austin, who came to the majors with the Yankees in 1909 and then went on to play many years with the St. Louis Browns, retiring with a .246 batting average.

Jimmy Archer caught in the big leagues in 1904, 1907, and from 1909–18, most of the time for the Cubs. Lifetime average: .250.

Sam Crawford, one of the mightiest hitters of the dead-ball era. Playing from 1899–1917, most of it with Detroit, Sam collected 2,964 hits and had a .309 batting average.

Nap Lajoie. One of the great players in major league history, Nap plied his trade from 1896–1916, retiring with 3,251 hits and a lifetime average of .339.

Ty Cobb

Josh DeVore, an outfielder who played for the Giants pennant winners in 1911–12 and then for three other clubs in a seven-year career, batting .277. Josh is shown here obliging the photographer at the Polo Grounds in 1912.

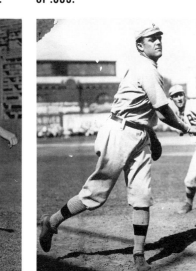

Leonard "King" Cole. He broke in with 20–4 and 18–7 seasons for the Cubs in 1910–11, then faded quickly. Cole was pitching for the Yankees when he died after the 1915 season at the age of twenty-nine.

A big-league pitcher from 1901–13, Earl Moore had his best years with the Indians and Phillies. Lifetime record: 151–139.

LEFT: Burt Shotton, a speedy outfielder with the Browns, Senators, and Cardinals from 1909 to 1923. A .270 lifetime hitter, Shotton later managed the Brooklyn Dodgers to pennants in 1947 and 1949.

RIGHT: Ping Bodie, an outfielder who played for three American League clubs between 1911 and 1921, batting .275.

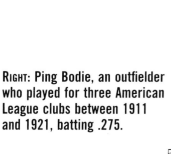

A couple of runs scoring at the Polo Grounds, circa 1910. Why isn't the pitcher backing up home plate?

Dode Paskert swinging and missing. An outfielder, Paskert played for three National League clubs from 1907–21, leaving behind a .268 batting average.

Hans Lobert, an infielder with five National League teams from 1903–17. His lifetime average is .274.

John McGraw

Remembered today chiefly for a costly error in the 1912 World Series, Fred Snodgrass was an excellent outfielder for the Giants and Braves from 1908–16. Lifetime average: .275.

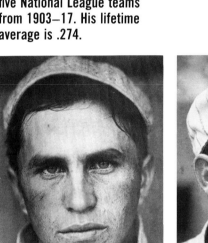

Harry Hooper, who played right field in the great Red Sox outfield of Lewis-Speaker-Hooper. Harry played from 1909–25, the first 12 years with the Red Sox and then finishing up with the White Sox. He batted .281 for his career.

Larry Doyle

Chief Meyers, who caught for McGraw's pennant winners in 1911, 1912, and 1913. The Chief played for three clubs between 1909–17, batting .291.

Fleet-footed outfielder Red Murray, another member of McGraw's 1911–13 pennant winners. Red played for three clubs from 1906–17. Lifetime average: .270.

Rube Marquard, big leaguer from 1908–25, clocking a 201–177 record. He pitched for the Giants, Dodgers, Reds, and Braves.

Infielder Buck Herzog, who played for four National League clubs from 1908–20, batting .259. Disliking him personally but admiring Buck's versatility, McGraw traded him three times and reacquired him twice.

Duffy Lewis, left fielder on the Red Sox pennant winners of 1912, 1915–16. Duffy played for three American League clubs from 1910–17 and 1919–21, batting .284. "Duffy was terrific in the pinch," said Joe Wood.

Rookie right-hander Grover Cleveland Alexander in 1911.

BELOW: Outfielder Max Carey, who played from 1910–29, almost all of it for the Pirates. Max finished up with the Dodgers, whom he managed in 1932–33. He led the league in stolen bases ten times. The fleet-footed switch hitter stole 738 bases in his career and batted .285.

Otis "Doc" Crandall, right-handed pitcher on McGraw's 1911–13 pennant winners. Doc, who jumped to the Federal League in 1914, pitched in the big leagues for eight years, compiling a 68–38 record.

Right-hander Jeff Tesreau pitched for the Giants from 1912–18, ringing up a solid 119–72 record.

Art Fletcher, McGraw's shortstop from 1909–20, finishing up with the Phillies in 1920 and 1922. Lifetime average: .277.

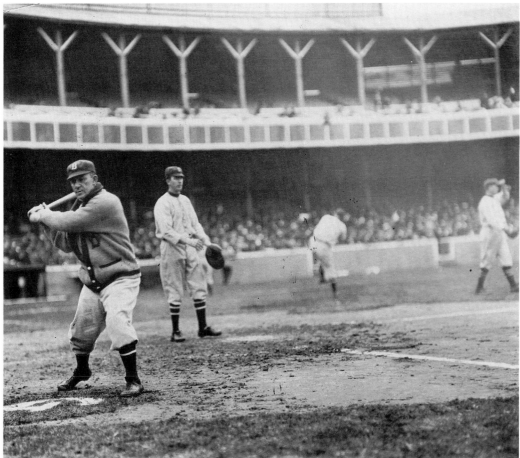

Larry Gardner, third baseman for the Red Sox, A's, and Indians from 1908–24. Five times a .300 hitter, Larry compiled a .289 average overall.

Dodger manager Bill Dahlen putting his boys through a pregame drill in 1911 (managers worked harder in those days). Bill was a longtime National League shortstop, playing for four clubs from 1891–1911, batting .274.

Larry Cheney, who broke in with three 20-game-winning seasons with the Cubs, pitched from 1911–19 with a 116–100 record.

Tris Speaker. He is still the center fielder on many all-time all-star teams. He played from 1907–28, dividing his prime years between the Red Sox and Indians. His 3,515 hits earned him a .344 lifetime batting average, and his 793 career doubles remain the big-league record.

Washington outfielder Clyde Milan, who played from 1907–22, batting .285. A blur on the basepaths, he stole 88 bases in 1912 and was known as "Deerfoot."

Walter Johnson

Jean Dubuc, a nine-year major leaguer who had his best years with Detroit just before World War I. The right-hander's lifetime record is 86–76.

Pittsburgh's Owen Wilson, the man who hit 36 triples in 1912, the all-time record. He played from 1908–16, batting .269.

Big Ed Walsh (center) embracing fellow White Sox pitchers Jim Scott (left) and Eddie Cicotte.

RIGHT: Heinie Zimmerman, third baseman for the Cubs and Giants from 1907–19, when he was edged out of baseball under suspicion of conspiring to throw games. He led the league with a .372 batting average in 1912 and batted .295 overall.

LEFT: Right-hander Bullet Joe Bush, who had a long career (1912–28) pitching for seven teams in both leagues. He is shown here with the Athletics in 1916. Lifetime record: 194–183.

The usually astute Connie Mack had young Stanley Coveleski on the A's in 1912 but let him get away. Stanley resurfaced four years later and began a brilliant career with Cleveland.

Chief Meyers (left) and Jim Thorpe in 1913. Thorpe, the dazzling star of the 1912 Olympic Games, played big-league ball with the Giants, Reds, and Braves from 1913–15 and 1917–19, with indifferent success. Never a regular, he had a .252 lifetime average.

The Phillies' Sherwood Magee coming home after hitting a home run at Baker Bowl. A solid outfielder, Magee played from 1904–19, spending his prime years with the Phillies, for whom he was a batting champion in 1910. Four times the league RBI leader, he batted .291 for his career.

LEFT: George Burns, National League outfielder from 1911–25, most of it spent with the Giants, for whom he was a prolific base stealer. Burns, who led the league in runs scored five times, was a .287 career batter.

RIGHT: Outfielder Bob Bescher was one of the National League's outstanding base stealers throughout much of his career (1908–18). Playing for Cincinnati, he led the league in steals from 1909–12. He was a .258 lifetime batter.

Frank Baker taking his rips in the 1913 World Series. The catcher is the Giants' Larry McLean.

One of the top first basemen of his era, Jake Daubert played with the Dodgers and Reds from 1910–24. Ten times a .300 hitter, he led the National League in batting in 1913 and 1914 while playing for the Dodgers. A .303 lifetime hitter, Jake died suddenly after the 1924 season at the age of forty.

Honus Wagner

Right-hander Tom Seaton, the Phillies' 27-game winner in 1913 who jumped to the Brooklyn club in the Federal League. After the Feds folded, Seaton rejoined the National League with the Cubs but was not the same pitcher. His National League history was 54–34. (One of the reasons the Federal League folded is that they didn't know how to spell *Brooklyn*.)

Bobby Veach, one of those good-hitting outfielders the Tigers always seemed to come up with. Veach, who played from 1912–25, spent all but the last two years with Detroit, led in RBIs three times, and batted .310 overall.

RIGHT: Walter Johnson

Second baseman Del Pratt played for four American League clubs from 1912–24. Six times a .300 hitter, he retired with a .292 lifetime average.

One of the top shortstops of his time, Roger Peckinpaugh's long career (1910–27) was spent with four teams, most prominently the Yankees and the Senators. Lifetime average: .259.

George "Hooks" Dauss, who pitched for Detroit from 1912–26. Lifetime record: 221–183.

Hank Gowdy, catcher for the "Miracle Braves" of 1914. Hank came up in 1910 with the Giants and caught for 17 years, mostly for the Braves, before retiring with a .270 batting average. Hank stunned everybody by batting .545 in Boston's four-game sweep of the Athletics in the 1914 Series.

Christy Mathewson

BELOW: Bill Doak, a right-handed pitcher known as "Spittin' Bill" because he threw a wet one (it was legal then). A Cardinal ace around the time of the First World War, Bill came up in 1912 and pitched for three teams until 1929. He was the ERA leader in 1914 and 1921. Lifetime record: 170–157.

Rabbit Maranville, who played shortstop in the National League for 23 years (1912–33, 1935) with five teams. Known as an impish practical joker, Rabbit batted .258 lifetime.

ABOVE: Bill Carrigan, catcher for the pennant-winning 1912 Red Sox and catcher-manager for the 1915–16 winners, after which he retired at thirty-three. Bill's career began in 1906, then ran from 1908–16, with a .257 batting average.

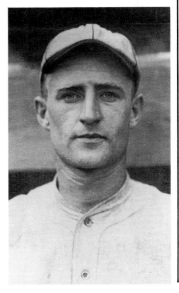

Some cloud-of-dust action from the 1914 World Series. It's the bottom of the first inning of the opening game. The Athletics' Eddie Murphy, who was on second base, tried to tag up and go to third on Frank Baker's pop foul to first baseman Butch Schmidt, but Butch fired to third baseman Charlie Deal, who slapped on the tag. Notice three alert Braves backing up the play.

George "Lefty" Tyler, southpaw ace of the 1914 Braves. He pitched for the Braves and Cubs from 1910–21, with a 127–119 record.

Dick Rudolph, a 27-game winner for the 1914 Braves. He came up with the Giants in 1910 and pitched for 13 years, 11 with Boston, compiling a 122–108 record.

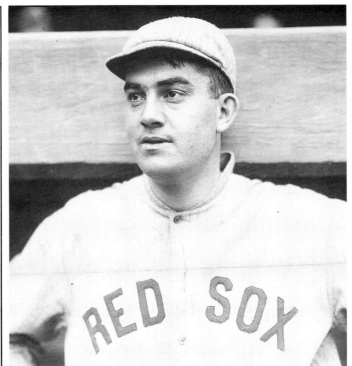

Eppa Rixey had one of the longest pitching careers in National League history— 1912–17 and 1919–33. Working for the Phillies and Reds, he posted a 266–251 record.

Erskine Mayer, who had a couple of 21-game-winning seasons for the Phillies in 1914 and 1915. He pitched for three clubs from 1912–19, putting together a 91–70 record.

Red Sox southpaw Ray Collins, who put together an 84–62 career pitching from 1909–15.

Bill James, part of the "Miracle Braves" trio of aces in 1914. The pennant year was Bill's only big season (he was 26–7), a sore arm aborting a career that ran from 1913–16, leaving him with just a 37–21 record.

Dave Bancroft, superb shortstop for four National League clubs from 1915–30. He played for pennant winners in Philadelphia in 1915 and New York in 1921–23. Lifetime average: .279.

Braves Field in 1915. Beyond is the Charles River.

Honus Wagner

Carl Mays, who employed his submarine-style delivery in both leagues from 1915–29. Pitching for four teams, the five-time 20-game winner was 208–126 lifetime.

Ty Cobb on the go, as ever.

Al Mamaux, who pitched for the Pirates and Dodgers from 1913–23, finishing with the Yankees the next year. He was 76–67 lifetime.

BELOW: Zack Wheat, the long-time Dodger favorite; he played for Brooklyn from 1909–26, finishing up with the Athletics a year later. A batting champion in 1918, he was a .300 hitter 13 times and batted .317 lifetime.

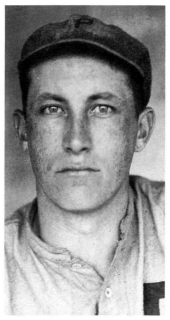

Fred Luderus, first baseman on the 1915 Phillies pennant winners. Fred was in the National League from 1909–20, batting .277.

Grover Cleveland Alexander

RIGHT: Left-hander Dutch Leonard, who came up with the Red Sox in 1913 and later pitched for the Tigers, retiring in 1925. His 1.01 ERA in 1914 is the lowest in baseball history. His career record is 139–112.

Six-time National League home run leader Gavvy Cravath. He played for 11 years, retiring in 1920 with a .287 average.

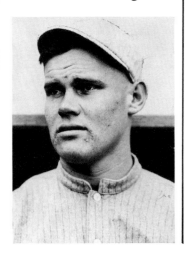

Casey Stengel, shown here standing in Ebbets Field's right field in 1915. Casey began his long career in baseball with the Dodgers in 1912 and played for four other National League teams until 1925, when he retired. His lifetime average is .284. He later managed the Dodgers, Braves, Yankees, and Mets.

Here's Stengel being tagged out on an attempted steal of third. The man who has him blocked way off the bag is the Phillies' Hans Lobert.

Jeff Pfeffer, big, hard-throwing 25-game-winning ace of the 1916 Dodger pennant winners. He pitched for three National League teams in 1911 and from 1913–24, with a 158–112 record.

Shortstop Ivy Olson, who came to the majors with Cleveland in 1911 and who had his most productive years with Brooklyn from 1916 through 1924. Lifetime average: .258.

Former Athletics ace Jack Coombs, shown here getting ready for a game with the Dodgers, for whom he pitched from 1915–18. "Colby Jack" pitched from 1906–18 and in 1920, with a 159–110 record, including a perfect 5–0 mark in World Series play.

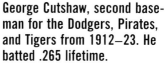

George Cutshaw, second baseman for the Dodgers, Pirates, and Tigers from 1912–23. He batted .265 lifetime.

LEFT: George Sisler joined the Browns as a left-handed pitcher in 1915, but his sterling bat soon made him a first baseman. He played for the Browns until 1928, then briefly for Washington and finally for the Braves until 1930. Twice a .400 hitter, he retired with a .340 lifetime average.

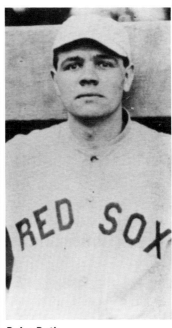

Babe Ruth

RIGHT: Right-hander Fred Toney's name will always be linked with Hippo Vaughn's. Toney came up to the majors in 1911 and pitched until 1923, having his best years with the Reds and Giants. He had a career mark of 137–102.

Frank Baker, who retired from the A's in 1914, then came back in 1916 and played six years for the Yankees.

Ferdie Schupp, who came up with the Giants in 1913 and later pitched for three other teams, retiring in 1922 with a 61–39 record.

George Burns, who played first base in the majors from 1914 to 1929 and was one of the steadiest players of his era. Playing for five American League teams, he batted over .300 eight times and had a .307 lifetime average.

Rube Benton, who pitched for the Reds and Giants from 1910–25, posting a 156–145 record.

Burleigh Grimes, shown here when he was a rookie pitcher for the Pirates in 1916. He was employed by every National League team except the Phillies and Reds before he retired in 1934, having compiled a 270–212 record.

Clarence "Tilly" Walker. He roamed the American League outfields with four different teams from 1911–23, batting .281.

Jim "Hippo" Vaughn, one of the premier pitchers of his time. Jim came to the majors in 1908 and retired in 1921, having his best years with the Cubs, for whom he was a 20-game winner five times. Vaughn is best remembered for the double no-hitter he pitched with Fred Toney in 1917. Lifetime he was 178–136.

Rogers Hornsby in 1917, his second full year in the majors.

Billy Southworth came to the big leagues in 1913 and played the outfield for five teams before retiring in 1929 with a lifetime average of .297. Later, he was a highly sucessful pennant-winning manager in the 1940s with the Cardinals and Braves.

Ray Schalk, big-league catcher from 1912–29, all but the last year spent with the White Sox. A gifted receiver, Ray batted .253 across his 18-year career.

Ty Cobb

Chick Gandil, first baseman and alleged ringleader of the 1919 Chicago "Black Sox." Chick came to the major leagues in 1910 and played until 1919. Sensing the conspiracy was going to unravel, he did not report in 1920. He was a .277 hitter.

LEFT: Shoeless Joe Jackson, described by many as one of the greatest natural hitters who ever lived. Joe came to the bigs with the A's in 1908, but homesickness got him sent back to South Carolina. He came back with Cleveland in 1910 and stuck. In 1915 he was traded to the White Sox. Joe was thirty-three years old when he was banned from organized ball in 1921, leaving behind a .356 lifetime average, third on the all-time list behind Cobb and Hornsby.

Happy Felsch, center fielder on the 1919 White Sox. He was with the club from 1915–20, until he was booted out of baseball. Happy was a .293 lifetime hitter.

Ray Fisher, right-handed pitcher who worked for the Yankees from 1910–17 and the Reds from 1919–20. Lifetime record: 100–94.

Heinie Groh and his specially designed "bottle" bat. A third baseman, Heinie played for the Reds and Giants from 1912–26, finishing up with the Pirates in 1927. With or without his unique bat, Heinie was a good hitter, batting .292 lifetime.

White Sox southpaw Dickie Kerr, known as "Honest Dickie" after winning two games in the 1919 Series. The little left-hander had a short career—1919–21, 1925—and compiled a 53–34 record.

A 24-game winner in his first full year, Claude Hendrix pitched for the Pirates and Cubs from 1911–20, with two years out for the Federal League. His major league record is 98–91.

Claude "Lefty" Williams, talented left-handed ace of the 1919 White Sox. After a brief time with the Tigers in 1913–14, he joined the Sox in 1916 and was an immediate success. Thrown out of baseball in 1921, he left behind a 82–48 record.

Some action from the tainted 1919 World Series. It's the sixth inning of game 2 and Cincinnati's Greasy Neale is being tagged out on an attempted steal of second. Swede Risberg is making the play. Watching from the mound is Lefty Williams.

Swede Risberg, shortstop on the 1919 White Sox. He came to the majors with the Sox in 1917 and batted .243 over his short career.

Eddie Collins. He batted over .340 ten times.

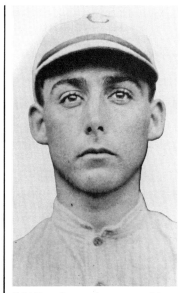

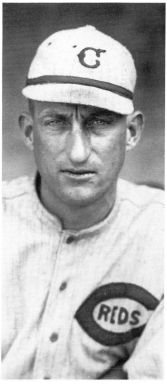

Edd Roush was known as "the Tris Speaker of the National League," which tells you something. Edd was a big-league regular from 1916–29 and in 1931, most of it spent with the Reds. Winner of two batting crowns, he batted over .300 12 times, and .323 lifetime.

Slim Sallee, who pitched for the Cardinals, Giants, and Reds from 1908–21, compiling a 173–143 record.

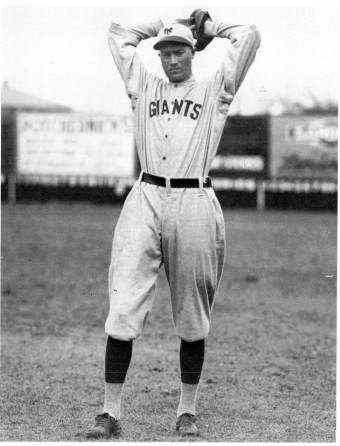

Jesse Barnes toiled on the National League mounds from 1915–27, for the Braves, Giants, and Dodgers. Lifetime record: 153–149.

White Sox third baseman Buck Weaver, who was not in on the plot but who had knowledge of it and chose to remain silent. It cost him his career. Buck played his entire career (1912–20) with the White Sox, batting .272.

Dutch Ruether, a talented left-hander who pitched for five teams in both leagues from 1917–27, leaving behind a 137–95 record.

Babe Ruth

1920

The start of America's most zany decade was also one of the most tumultuous years in major league history. Babe Ruth began the lively ball era by putting on the most thundering display of slugging ever seen. The record book was shattered like so much fine crystal, and in man-sized ways: Ruth hit 54 home runs (25 more than his own previous record, which he broke with his 30th home run on July 16), scored 158 runs, and mounted an .847 slugging average (still the all-time record), while George Sisler of the Browns set an all-time standard with 257 hits. Many team and league hitting records were established that year, only to be broken and reestablished again the next year, and over and over again during that hit-happy decade.

It was a year for the bizarre, the unique, and the tragic. There was an unassisted triple play in the World Series, by Cleveland second baseman Bill Wambsganss; there was the bronzed-in-legend May 1 game between the Dodgers and Braves in which Brooklyn's Leon Cadore and Boston's Joe Oeschger pitched to a 26-inning 1–1 tie, the longest game by innings ever played; there was baseball's only on-the-field fatality, occurring at the Polo Grounds on August 16, when the Yankees' Carl Mays hit the Indians' Ray Chapman in the temple with a pitch, Chapman never regaining consciousness and dying the next day.

Amid all this there were two pennant races: one, in the American League, that should have been won by the White Sox, but that club was beset by rumors and torn by dissension all summer, and finally, like an overheated boiler, it blew apart with two weeks to go. Seven White Sox players were suspended for conspiring to throw the 1919 World Series: pitchers Eddie Cicotte and Lefty Williams, first baseman Chick Gandil (who had retired after 1919), outfielders Joe Jackson and Happy Felsch, shortstop Swede Risberg, and utility infielder Fred McMullin. An eighth, third baseman Buck Weaver, got caught in the vortex not for complicity but for knowing what was going on and choosing what he thought was an honorable silence. All eight were ultimately barred forever from organized baseball by the man the major league club owners hired late in 1920 to be their first commissioner, Kenesaw Mountain Landis, a Federal judge of severe and unforgiving temperament, invested by the owners with virtually limitless authority over their game.

Until losing so many of their star players, the White Sox had been contending in

1920- Mr. Ruth's Game 1929

Mr. Ruth in 1920.

Kenesaw Mountain Landis. He was named for a Civil War battle in which his surgeon father was wounded.

a blistering race with the Indians and the Yankees. The Chicago staff had an unprecedented four 20-game winners: Red Faber (23–13), Williams (22–14), Cicotte (21–10), and Dickie Kerr (21–9). Joe Jackson left with a .382 batting average, while honest man Eddie Collins batted .369.

Cleveland was a first-time winner, edging out the White Sox (who were forced to play a number of second-line players during the crucial final days of the season) by two games and the Yankees by three. The Indians had a 30-game winner in Jim Bagby (31–12), though most of the Cleveland players insisted the ace was Stanley Coveleski (24–14). Ray Caldwell (20–10) gave the club a trio of big winners. Left-hander Walter "Duster" Mails was brought up late in the season and went 7–0 down the stretch. Player-manager Tris Speaker batted .388, leading an attack that had six .300 hitters in the lineup and hit the lively ball for a .303 average.

Along with Ruth's explosive bat, the Yankees had a 26-game winner in Mays and a 20-gamer in Bob Shawkey. St. Louis, with batting champion George Sisler (.407) and 20-game winner Urban Shocker, had a .300-hitting outfield in Johnny Tobin (.341), Ken Williams (.307), and Baby Doll Jacobson (.355), a trio that would each hit over .300 for four straight years. As a team, the Browns batted .308.

Walter Johnson, bothered by the first sore arm in his career, fell to an 8–10 record. Nevertheless, Walter had his first and only no-hitter, against Boston on July 1, winning 1–0, losing a perfect game on an error by rookie second baseman Bucky Harris, who later atoned by knocking in the game's only run. Earlier in the season, on May 14, Walter chalked up his 300th victory.

In the National League, a rather surprising Brooklyn team went all the way, winning their second pennant, coming in seven games ahead of the Giants. Burleigh Grimes

led Wilbert Robinson's staff with a 23–11 record, while Zack Wheat topped the Dodger hitters with a .328 average. Grimes was one of a small number of spitball pitchers permitted to throw a wet ball after the spitter and all other freak deliveries had been banned (the leagues had agreed that any pitcher who relied heavily on the spitter would otherwise be deprived of his livelihood). The sudden outlawing of these "unnatural" pitches was another factor in the abrupt rise of batting averages.

The Giants were second despite having three 20-game winners—Fred Toney (21–11), Art Nehf (21–12), and Jesse Barnes (20–15), and Ross Youngs's .351 batting average.

The Cardinals' Rogers Hornsby, who possessed the league's most flawless swing as well as, according to contemporaries, the coldest pair of eyes in baseball, began committing six years of the highest-average mayhem in baseball history with a league-leading .370.

The lively ball seemed not to intimidate Grover Cleveland Alexander, who turned in a 27–14 season for the fifth-place Cubs, leading the league with a 1.91 ERA. Other 20-game winners were Pittsburgh's Wilbur Cooper (24–15) and St. Louis's Bill Doak (20–12). The Phillies' Cy Williams was the home run leader with 15. The Phillies, with 64 home runs, were the only team in the major leagues Babe Ruth did not out-homer.

Still a best-of-nine affair, the World Series was won by Cleveland over Brooklyn in seven games. Along with Wambsganss's unassisted triple play in game 5, the Series saw the first home run by a pitcher (Bagby) and the first Series grand slam, by Cleveland's Elmer Smith, both in that same fifth game. Stanley Coveleski was the hero of the generally tightly pitched pageant, winning three complete games.

Ken Williams

1921

For the third straight year Babe Ruth set a new major league home run record: 29 in 1919, 54 in 1920, and now 59 in 1921. The Babe's breathtaking hitting and charismatic personality helped rub from the public's mind the ignominy of the "Black Sox" scandal. Led by Ruth's bat, the Yankees won their first pennant, finishing 4½ games ahead of Cleveland.

Miller Huggins's club had a big winner in Carl Mays (27–9), while Waite Hoyt won 19 and Bob Shawkey 18. Outfielder Bob Meusel backed up the Babe with a .318 batting average and 24 home runs, tying him for second place with the Browns' Ken Williams. Ruth set a new RBI record with 171 and another pair of records that still stand —457 total bases and 177 runs scored—in addition to an .846 slugging mark.

With four teams batting over .300 in the new lively ball circus, extravagant averages were commonplace. Detroit's Harry Heilmann, beginning a peculiar odd-numbered-year series of batting titles, led with a booming .394 average, followed by teammate Ty Cobb's .389, Ruth's .378, and George Sisler's .371. Heilmann and Cobb led a Tiger team that rapped out 1,724 hits and batted .316, both American League records still on the books (one of those 1,724 hits was Cobb's 3,000th career safety, which came on August 19). But without quality pitching, all it earned the Tigers was sixth place. For the American League as a whole, it was the highest batting average in its history—.292.

Along with Mays, the league's big winners were Cleveland's Stanley Coveleski (23–13), St. Louis's Urban Shocker (27–12), Boston's Sam Jones (23–16), and Chicago's Red Faber (25–15). Faber's 2.48 ERA was the highest yet seen for a league leader.

John McGraw's Giants made it New York's first "Subway Series" by taking the National League pennant, winning by four games over the Pirates. McGraw had a .298-hitting lineup, led by the dynamic Frank Frisch at .341. George Kelly, who led the league with 23 home runs, was one of three Giants to drive in 100 or more runs, Frisch and Ross Youngs being the others. The small, cagey left-hander Art Nehf led the Giants staff with a 20–10 record.

Second-place Pittsburgh had a 20-game winner in Wilbur Cooper (22–14), while Brooklyn's Burleigh Grimes (22–13) and Boston's Joe Oeschger (20–14) were the league's other top winners.

The Cardinals, finishing third, shell-shocked National League pitchers with a .308 team batting average, led by Rogers Hornsby's league-high .397. Hornsby also led in RBIs (126), hits (235), runs (131), doubles (44), triples (18), slugging (.639), and total bases (378)—and he was

Rogers Hornsby

nowhere near his peak yet. Hornsby was one of seven Cardinals regulars who machine-gunned .300 averages (thirty-five National League regulars batted .300 that year). One of them, twenty-six-year-old Austin McHenry, who batted .350 and seemed on the verge of a high-caliber career, took ill a year later and died.

On August 5, baseball entered the technological age. On that date, station KDKA went on the air with the first ever broadcast of a major league game. The precedent-setting game saw the Pirates defeat the Phillies, 8–5, at Philadelphia, with Harold Arlin doing the play-by-play.

The first of the many all–New York World Series went to the Giants in eight games (this was the last of the best-of-nine Series format). Waite Hoyt was brilliant in defeat for the Yankees, pitching three complete games, winning two, losing one, and allowing no earned runs in 27 innings. Phil Douglas and Jesse Barnes each won twice for the Giants.

1922

New York remained the capital of baseball for a second straight year as both the Yankees and the Giants repeated as pennant winners.

For Miller Huggins's Yankees it was an excruciatingly close-run race, with the team penalized by the loss of their two top hitters, Babe Ruth and Bob Meusel, until May 20. In defiance of baseball law and of a direct warning from Commissioner Landis, Ruth and Meusel had gone barnstorming after the 1921 World Series (a peculiar rule forbade Series participants from doing this). The judge responded by hitting the players with hefty fines and suspensions.

Despite the early-season loss of their two best hitters, the Yankees stayed at the top of the league and then spent the rest of the summer fighting off the St. Louis Browns. The Browns, with an average of .313, were the hardest-hitting team in the league. They were led by George Sisler, at his incomparable best that year with a .420 batting average, followed by solid, .300-plus seasons from second baseman Marty McManus, catcher Hank Severeid, and the Johnny Tobin–Ken Williams–Baby Doll Jacobson outfield. Williams was the home run and RBI leader with 39 and 155, respectively. Ruth, playing in 43 fewer games, hit 35 long ones.

The Yankees beat out the Browns by just one game, although outhit by 26 points and outscored by over 100 runs. The difference was pitching (which the great-hitting Yankees teams of the 1920s always had plenty of). The Browns had Urban Shocker leading their staff with a 24–17 record, followed by Elam Vangilder (19–13); the Yankees had Joe Bush (26–7), Bob Shawkey (20–12), and Waite Hoyt (19–12).

In winning his second batting title and going over .400 for the second time, Sisler had 246 hits. George had to be at the top of his game to win that year, since Cobb dogged him all summer and wound up at .401. Sisler spiced his .420 season with a 41-game hitting streak, breaking Cobb's modern major league record by one.

The league's top winner, ironically, came from the seventh-place Athletics (out of the cellar for the first time in eight years), for whom Eddie Rommel went 27–13. Connie Mack's years in the wilderness were just about over now, and the man whom sportswriters called "the tall tactician" was about to begin moving his team slowly upward in the standings.

Other 20-game winners in the league were Chicago's Red Faber (21–17) and Cleveland's George Uhle (22–16).

On April 30, Chicago White Sox right-hander Charlie Robertson, a 14–15 pitcher that year and 49–80 for his career, stunned the baseball world by pitching a perfect game against the Tigers, winning by a 2–0 score, throttling a lineup that included Cobb, Harry Heilmann, and

Eddie Rommel

Bobby Veach. (Cobb was by this time Detroit's player-manager, which led some writers to call the club the "Tygers.")

On April 22, the Browns' Ken Williams became the first American Leaguer to hit three home runs in a game—another trumpet blast for the arrival of the lively ball. (In 1922, the two major leagues combined for 1,055 home runs; in 1918, the figure was 237.)

In the National League, McGraw's Giants had things comfortably in hand throughout the season. Without benefit of a 20-game winner (Art Nehf led the staff with a 19–13 record), the Giants hammered away with a bruising offensive attack, with six regulars batting over .320, led by catcher Frank Snyder's .343 and outfielder Irish Meusel's .331 (he was the brother of the Yankees' Bob). George Kelly, Frank Frisch, Dave Bancroft, and Ross Youngs were McGraw's other solid hitters, while part-time outfielder Casey Stengel batted .368.

Second-place Cincinnati, buoyed by Eppa Rixey's 25–13 season, paced the Giants and finished seven out. Third-place Pittsburgh, with Wilbur Cooper turning in a 23–14 record, bloodied opposing pitchers with a .308 team average, topped by Carson Bigbee's .350. The Pirates also had a budding star in twenty-two-year-old rookie third baseman Pie Traynor. A .282 hitter that year, Traynor was soon to be acclaimed the finest defensive third baseman since Jimmy Collins.

The league's top buster was Rogers Hornsby. The Cardinal second baseman joined the game's all-time elite with a .401 batting average, 47 points better than runner-up Ray Grimes of the Cubs. Hornsby set a new National League home run record with 42 and a new RBI standard with 152, and still more league records with 250 hits, 46 doubles, 141 runs, .722 slugging average, and 450 total bases (the latter still stands). It all added up to a Triple Crown.

Sixth-place Brooklyn had some of the league's better pitching in Dutch Ruether (21–12) and thirty-one-year-old rookie Dazzy Vance, a journeyman minor leaguer who finally struck big-league paydirt. Vance, who was to become the league's top pitcher throughout the decade, broke in with an 18–12 record and a leading 134 strikeouts, the first of seven straight strikeout titles he would take.

In a game that typified the entire slug-happy decade (during which both leagues averaged .285), the Cubs on August 25 defeated the Phillies, 26–23. With a 25–6 lead in the fourth inning, the Cubs had to struggle to hold on and win.

On September 15, Phillies catcher Butch Henline (later an umpire in the National League) became the first National Leaguer in modern times to hit three home runs in one game.

The Cubs' talented shortstop Charlie Hollocher set a league record by fanning just five times in 152 games, fewest ever by a player in 150 or more games.

The Giants' Jesse Barnes pitched a no-hitter against the Phillies on May 7, winning 6–0. Only a fifth-inning base on balls deprived Barnes of a perfect game.

The Giants made it two in a row over their intracity rivals, beating the Yankees four games to none in the World Series (which was now back to its four-of-seven format), one game ending in a tie. Heinie Groh, the only Giants regular who didn't bat over .300 during the season, led all Series regulars with nine safeties and a .474 average.

1923

New York City remained atop the baseball world for the third year in a row. In the American League, Miller Huggins's Yankees, playing in their brand-new Yankee Stadium (which Babe Ruth christened with a game-winning home run on opening day), ran away with their third straight pennant, finishing 16 games ahead of the Tigers.

Having completed the rape of the Red Sox with the acquisition of left-hander Herb Pennock, the Yankees were able to confront the rest of the league with a starting rotation of Sam Jones (21–8), Pennock (19–6), Joe Bush (19–15), Waite Hoyt (17–9)—all pared from the Red Sox—and Bob Shawkey (16–11). This strong-armed quintet carried the burden of Yankee pitching all season. Only three other pitchers appeared for the Yankees all year—Carl Mays in 23 games, George Pipgras in eight, and Oscar Roettger in five.

Ruth led the league with 41 home runs (the Browns' Ken Williams, with 29, was the only other player in the league to hit more than 18), set a major league record with 170 walks, and batted .393; but Babe's highest career average wasn't good enough for the title, which went to Detroit's Harry Heilmann, who hit .403. Breaking into 13 games at the end of the season for the Yankees (and bat-

Bob Shawkey

ting .423) was twenty-year-old first baseman Lou Gehrig.

Along with Heilmann's mile-high batting average, the Tigers had a 21–13 record from ace right-hander George Dauss, and a .334 rookie season from outfielder Heinie Manush.

Third-place Cleveland had standout performances from skipper Tris Speaker (.380), shortstop Joe Sewell (.353), and outfielder Charlie Jamieson (.345). Also, right-hander George Uhle had a big season at 26–16. Always a good hitter, the burly Uhle batted .361 and set a major league record for pitchers with 52 hits.

The Browns were without the services of George Sisler, who was forced to sit out the entire season because of an eye ailment. He returned the next year, but was never the same hitter again. For the fourth year in a row Urban Shocker was a 20-game winner for the Browns, going 20–12.

Red Sox first baseman George Burns (not to be confused with the National League outfielder of the same name) pulled an unassisted triple play against Cleveland on September 14. Other outstanding individual performances were no-hit games pitched by the Yankees' Sam Jones against the Athletics on September 4, a 2–0 win, and by Boston's Howard Ehmke against the A's on September 7, for a 4–0 win. An oddity of this game was that in the sixth inning A's pitcher Slim Harriss lined a clean shot to left-center and made it safely to second base, but was then called out for not touching first, nullifying the hit. In his next start, Ehmke, who was 20–17 for the last-place Red Sox, pitched a one-hitter.

John McGraw stayed right with Miller Huggins, the Giants taking their third straight pennant, again by hammering the opposition into submission with an array of smoking bats. Frank Frisch batted .348 and Ross Youngs .336, while George Kelly and Dave Bancroft also hit over .300. The club's .295 batting average helped a slightly laggard pitching staff that had Rosy Ryan and Jack Scott the top winners with but 16 apiece.

Second-place Cincinnati, 4½ games out at the end, had the league's strongest rotation in Dolf Luque (27–8, with a 1.93 ERA, by far the league's lowest), Eppa Rixey (20–15), and Pete Donohue (21–15). Edd Roush, called "the National League's Tris Speaker" for his fine all-around play, batted .351. Between 1917 and 1926, Roush never batted below .321.

In Chicago, the thirty-six-year-old Grover Cleveland Alexander was still spinning his curves keenly enough to rack up a 22–12 ledger (and walking just 30 batters in 305 innings). Other 20-game winners were Pittsburgh's "Jughandle" Johnny Morrison (25–13), Brooklyn's Burleigh Grimes (21–18), and St. Louis' Jesse Haines (20–13).

Rogers Hornsby took his fourth straight batting title with a .384 average, illness limiting the slugger to 107 games. Right behind Rogers was teammate Jim Bottomley, a young first baseman playing his first full season and batting .371. On September 16, Bottomley set an all-time major league record when he drove in 12 runs in a game against the Dodgers at Ebbets Field. Philadelphia's Cy Williams was the home run leader with 41, one under Hornsby's league record.

At the end of the season the Braves brought up a young shortstop named Ernie Padgett. Getting into just four games, Ernie shot into the record book in one of them. On October 6, in a game against the Phillies, the rookie had the heady experience of executing an unassisted triple play. It was the highlight of an otherwise brief, undistinguished career.

The Yankees finally upended the Giants and won their first World Series, souring John McGraw's beer in six games. Ruth hit three home runs for the Yankees, while Casey Stengel hit two game-winning home runs for the Giants.

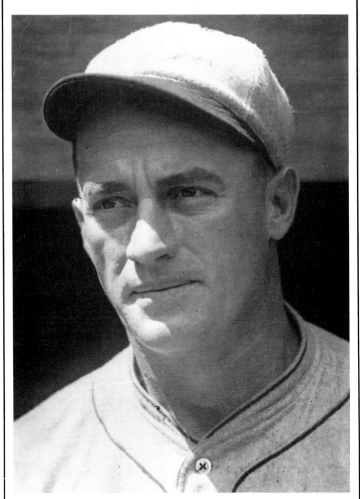

Urban Shocker

1924

The Washington Senators had a new manager in 1924; he was their twenty-seven-year-old second baseman Bucky Harris, a tough, born-to-lead type who steered the team to its first pennant. The Washington pennant appealed to sentimentalists everywhere, for it gave Walter Johnson his first crack at a World Series, after 18 years in the big leagues. Indeed, Walter was one of the prime architects of his club's unexpected success; the now thirty-six-year-old legend still had enough smoke left to put up a 23–7 record and lead the league in strikeouts for the 12th time with 158 and in ERA for the fifth time with 2.72.

For a change, Walter got the batting support that had always been missing—young slugger Goose Goslin batted .344 and led the league in runs batted in with 129, Sam Rice batted .334 and led in hits with 216, and Joe Judge batted .324.

The Washington victory was a truly surprising upset —the Yankees had been expected to roll to a fourth straight pennant, and that they didn't was hardly Babe Ruth's fault. The big man hit 46 home runs and led the league in batting with a .378 mark. On the mound, the Yankees had substantial winners in Herb Pennock (21–9), Waite Hoyt (18–13), and Joe Bush (17–16), and made it a narrow miss—finishing just two games out.

Detroit, still hitting hard and leading the league in most offensive categories (including a .298 team batting average), finished third, undone by shaky pitching. From 1921 through 1926, the Tigers as a team averaged .302, with only one second-place finish to show for it.

The White Sox had five regulars hit over .320 and Hollis (Sloppy) Thurston win 20 games, but still finished last. Cleveland had three regulars hit over .340 and left-hander Joe Shaute win 20, but finished sixth. Connie Mack now had his Athletics up to fifth place, helped along by a lethal young gunner named Al Simmons, who batted .308 in his first go-around.

In winning an unprecedented fourth straight pennant, John McGraw found his competition coming from a most unexpected source—the Brooklyn Dodgers. Thanks largely to the powerful pitching tandem of Dazzy Vance (28–6) and Burleigh Grimes (22–13), the Dodgers hung in all summer and made a race of it till the end, finishing 1½ games out. For the second year in a row McGraw won a pennant (his 10th and last) with a couple of 16-game winners topping his staff (Jack Bentley and Virgil Barnes).

While Brooklyn got some fine hitting from the veteran Zack Wheat (.375) and first baseman Jack Fournier, who batted .334 and hit a league-leading 27 home runs, they were unable to match the Giants' up-and-down-the-lineup firepower. Sporting a .300 team batting average, the Giants had Ross Youngs at .356, Frank Frisch at .328, George Kelly at .324, Irish Meusel at .310, and Travis

Bucky Harris, "Boy Manager" of the Washington Senators.

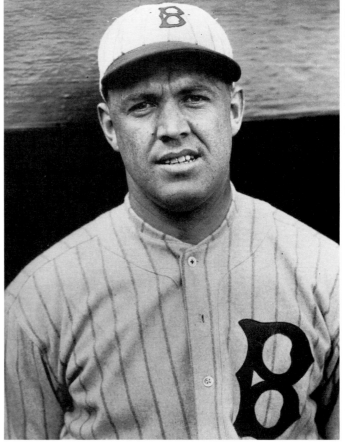

Burleigh Grimes

Jackson and Frank Snyder each at .302.

Pittsburgh, finishing in third place just three games behind, received good pitching from Wilbur Cooper (20–14), Ray Kremer (18–10), and Emil Yde (16–3) and a .354 season from rookie outfielder Kiki Cuyler, soon to become one of the league's brightest stars.

Carl Mays, sold to Cincinnati by the Yankees (a prickly sort, Mays had trouble getting along with Miller Huggins), rang up a 20–9 record. The Cardinals' Jesse Haines, suffering through an 8–19 year, had his moment of glory on July 17, when he delivered the Cardinals' first no-hitter of modern times, snuffing Boston, 5–0.

Rogers Hornsby made another season-long assault on the record books, and when it was over he owned the highest batting average ever recorded in modern baseball—.424, created out of 536 at-bats and 227 hits.

While Hornsby was far and away the hitter of the year, the top pitcher unquestionably was Vance. Brooklyn's big, colorful fastballer had, in fact, the greatest year enjoyed by a National League pitcher in the 1920s. Along with his 28–6 record, he fanned 262 (only one other pitcher in the league, Grimes with 135, struck out more than 86 batters), had a 2.16 ERA, by far the lowest, and at one point ran off 15 consecutive wins.

On September 20, thirty-seven-year-old Grover Cleveland Alexander, 12–5 on the year for the Cubs, beat the Giants for his 300th lifetime win, joining Mathewson, Johnson, and Plank as modern baseball's only 300-game winners.

In a thrilling seven-game World Series, the Senators edged aside the Giants for the championship. The final game, with Walter Johnson pitching in relief for Washington after having lost his two starts, was decided in the bottom of the 12th inning on a bad-hop single by Earl McNeely that bounced over the head of Giant third baseman Fred Lindstrom and allowed the winning run to score. Goose Goslin hit three home runs for Washington.

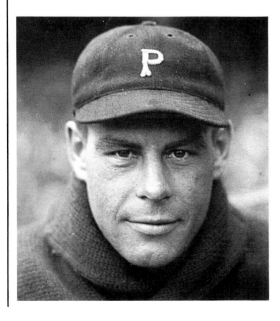

Emil Yde

1925

Connie Mack was suddenly back in contention, his Athletics giving the Washington Senators a lively fight for the pennant until August, when the A's spun into a 12-game losing streak, enabling the Senators to coast in by 8½ games for a second straight pennant.

For Bucky Harris, it was two pennants in two years as a manager (it wasn't always going to be that smooth; Harris would manage in the major leagues for another 27 years and only win once more). Walter Johnson was a 20-game winner for the 12th and final time (20–7), while former Cleveland ace Stanley Coveleski was 20–5. Washington's hitting was again topped by Sam Rice (.350) and Goose Goslin (.334). Harris and shortstop Roger Peckinpaugh gave the club excellent defense in the middle of the infield, while third baseman Ossie Bluege was considered the league's top glove at his position.

The second-place A's had a 20-game winner in Eddie Rommel and got a sizzling .384 season from sophomore outfielder Al Simmons. Simmons, who amassed a gargantuan 253 hits, was third in the batting race to Harry Heilmann's .393 and Tris Speaker's .389, while the fires of autumn burned fiercely in thirty-eight-year-old Ty Cobb, who batted .378. With Al Wingo at .370, Detroit's outfield of Cobb, Heilmann, and Wingo averaged .382.

Connie Mack broke in three new men that year—catcher Mickey Cochrane, who batted .331; pitcher Lefty Grove, who was 10–13 but the strikeout leader with 116; and a rosy-cheeked seventeen-year-old strongboy named Jimmie Foxx, who batted nine times and got six hits.

With Babe Ruth out until June because of abdominal surgery, the Yankees dropped to seventh place, despite Bob Meusel's league-leading 33 home runs and 138 runs batted in. On June 2, the team's veteran first baseman Wally Pipp reported to Yankee Stadium with a nagging headache. Miller Huggins gave him the day off and inserted young Lou Gehrig into the lineup. The next time Pipp started a game at first base it was for Cincinnati in 1926, as Gehrig went on to play 2,130 consecutive games for the Yankees. The streak actually started the day before, when Lou pinch hit. The man Gehrig batted for, shortstop Pee Wee Wanninger, had on May 6 replaced Everett Scott at shortstop, ending Scott's streak of 1,307 consecutive games, which was the record Gehrig was eventually to break. Gehrig batted .295 in 1925.

There were a couple of landmark hits during the season—the 3,000th hits in the careers of Tris Speaker (May 17) and Eddie Collins (June 3), while on May 5 Cobb put on a show when he hit three home runs, a double, and two singles in one game.

Cleveland shortstop Joe Sewell (a .336 hitter) set a major league record for fewest strikeouts in 150 or more games when he fanned just four times (in 608 at-bats).

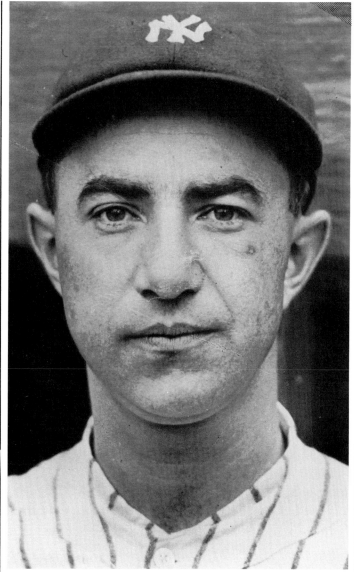

Everett Scott

Cincinnati had two of the league's three 20-game winners in Eppa Rixey (21–11) and Pete Donohue (21–14), while Brooklyn's Dazzy Vance was the other (22–9). On September 13, Vance pitched the major leagues' only no-hitter of the season, beating the Phillies, 10–1.

Rogers Hornsby continued his drumbeat assault on National League pitching with a .403 batting average and sixth batting title in a row. Hornsby, who took over as player-manager of the Cardinals early in the season (replacing Branch Rickey), now had averaged .402 for the last five years. Hornsby also led in home runs with 39 and RBIs with 143, winning his second Triple Crown. In a decade running amok with base hits (in 1925 each league averaged .292), Hornsby was establishing statistical standards that seemed to become less approachable with passing time.

On May 7, Pirate shortstop Glenn Wright pulled an unassisted triple play against the Cardinals.

In the World Series between Washington and Pittsburgh, the Pirates became the first team to come from a three-games-to-one deficit and win the championship, defeating the Senators in seven. For the second year in a row, Goose Goslin homered three times for Washington, as did teammate Joe Harris. Walter Johnson, who was shellacked in the final game, won two games for Washington, while Ray Kremer and Vic Aldridge each won twice for Pittsburgh.

George Sisler, who started the season with a 34-game hitting streak, batted .345 and said dejectedly that "this isn't hitting." The Browns' first baseman was speaking, of course, from the perspective of a one-time .420 hitter.

The White Sox' Ted Lyons, another coming star in the league, was 21–11.

In the National League, Bill McKechnie led the Pirates to their first pennant since 1909, dislodging the Giants from the top after four years. McGraw had to settle for second place, 8½ games behind.

The Pirates batted .307 as a team, with seven regulars over .300. This almost perpetual hitting attack was led by Kiki Cuyler (.357) and the veteran Max Carey (.343), at thirty-five still spry enough to lead in stolen bases for the 10th time. The Pirates established a league record with four men having over 100 RBIs—Glenn Wright, Pie Traynor, Cuyler, and Clyde Barnhart. Lee Meadows, a bespectacled right-hander, topped the Pirate staff with a 19–10 record, followed by 17-game winners Ray Kremer, Johnny Morrison, and Emil Yde.

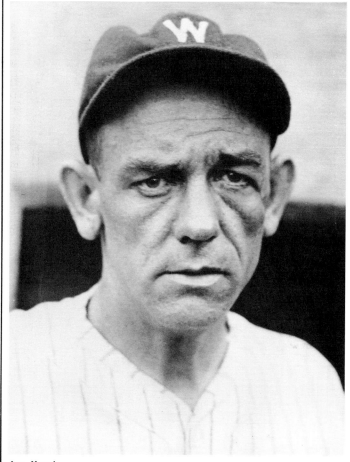

Joe Harris

1926

The Yankees ended Washington's two-year tenure atop the American League, Miller Huggins's team winning by three games over Cleveland, after having led by as many as ten games in mid-August.

Babe Ruth exploded to a typical Babe Ruth season—leading the league by far with 47 home runs (more than five other teams in the league) and 145 runs batted in, and collecting a .372 batting average, which placed him second to Detroit's Heinie Manush, who led with .378. In his second year, the impending crown prince, Lou Gehrig, hit 16 home runs and drove in 107 runs. The ace of the Yankee staff was Herb Pennock at 23–11, followed by ex-Browns spitballer Urban Shocker, who was 19–11.

Cleveland's second-place finish was generated primarily by first baseman George Burns, who batted .358 and set a new major league record with 64 doubles, and George Uhle, who was 27–11.

While Lefty Grove was only 13–13 for the third-place

Lou Gehrig

Athletics, the left-hander with the volcanic temperament and blazing fastball led in ERA with 2.51 and in strikeouts with 194. (Emulating Dazzy Vance in the National League, Grove would lead his league in strikeouts his first seven years.)

The sixth-place Tigers again had an outfield with most regal batting averages: league-leader Manush, .378, and Harry Heilmann and Bob (Fats) Fothergill, .367 each. The trio was good enough and consistent enough to keep player-manager Ty Cobb on the bench much of the season, the thirty-nine-year-old Tyrus getting into 79 games and batting .339. After the season, Cobb was released, ending his 22-year career with the Tigers. He then signed with the Athletics, where he played for the last two years of his career.

On August 21, Chicago's Ted Lyons pitched a no-hitter against the Red Sox, winning 6–0. And on August 28, Cleveland's Emil Levsen in a sense put an era to rest, on that day becoming the last man to pitch two complete-game victories in one day, defeating the Red Sox (losers of 107 games that year), 6–1 and 5–1. The Cleveland right-hander, 16–13 on the year, achieved the iron-man feat for the 24th time in modern baseball history.

Though his own batting average took a precipitous plunge from .403 to .317, player-manager Rogers Hornsby had enough firepower in the lineup to see the Cardinals win their first pennant (this left the St. Louis Browns as the only big-league club not to have won a pennant). With the help of Jim Bottomley's 120 RBIs (the league high) and solid years from third baseman Les Bell and outfielder Taylor Douthit, the Cardinals squeezed past the Reds by two games.

Cardinal pitching was headed by Flint Rhem (20–7) and left-hander Bill Sherdel (16–12). Thirty-nine-year-old Grover Cleveland Alexander proved to be a crucial mid-season pickup, going 9–7, after a 3–3 record with the Cubs, where he had been unable to get along with rookie manager Joe McCarthy.

Along with Rhem, three other league pitchers won 20 on the nose—Cincinnati's Pete Donohue and Pittsburgh's Ray Kremer and Lee Meadows. The Pirates brought up young outfielder Paul Waner, destined to become one of baseball's greatest hitters. Waner broke in with a .336 batting average and a major league rookie record 22 triples. Chicago's Hack Wilson, acquired from the Giants when through a clerical error he was left unprotected in the baseball draft, led the league with 21 home runs. (When John McGraw heard about the snafu, "he didn't hit the ceiling," one writer said, "he went right through it.")

The Reds' Bubbles Hargrave became the first catcher to win a batting title when he hit .353. Hargrave had only 326 official at-bats and 25 walks; under later rules, which

Bubbles Hargrave

1927

The 1927 N.Y. Yankees: Babe Ruth, 60 home runs (more than any other *team* in the league hit), 164 RBIs, .356 batting average; Lou Gehrig, 47 home runs, 175 RBIs, .373 batting average; Earle Combs, 231 hits, .356 batting average; Bob Meusel, 103 RBIs, .337 batting average; Tony Lazzeri, 102 RBIs, .309 batting average. Pitching: Waite Hoyt, 22–7; Herb Pennock, 19–8; Urban Shocker, 18–6. Miller Huggins even had a rarity for the time—an ace relief pitcher, Wilcy Moore, who started 12 games, relieved in 38, and was 19–7 with a league-low 2.28 ERA.

Were they, as many historians claim, the greatest of all teams? Given the balance of devastating hitting and outstanding pitching, the answer is yes. Only seven pitchers in the league had ERAs of 3.00 or less, and four of them were Yankees—Hoyt, Moore, Pennock, and Shocker. The team set many offensive records, including a .489 slugging average that still stands. Overall, the club batted .307, leading in everything except doubles (they were second) and stolen bases. They cut a mighty swath through the league, winning 110 and losing 44, their win total a league record until the 1954 Indians won 111.

The Yankees finished 19 games ahead of an Athletics team Connie Mack had been patiently putting together for years. Connie's top thumper was Al Simmons, who batted .392 but trailed Detroit's Harry Heilmann at the end by six points as Harry continued his peculiar pattern of odd-numbered-year championships, having won previously in 1921, 1923, and 1925. The A's set the American League record for fewest strikeouts by a team, 326 (the major league record was set by Cincinnati in 1921 with 308).

The American League saw the departure that year of two notable Johnsons. Ban Johnson, organizer of the circuit and its president since 1901, resigned. Walter Johnson pitched his 21st and final season for the Washington Senators, leaving with a 5–6 record for the year and a lifetime 416–279 ledger, the league record for victories, and 3,508 strikeouts, for decades the all-time major league standard, as well as the all-time record for shutouts, 110, to which no one has come remotely close.

In addition to Hoyt, there were two other 20-game winners in the league: Philadelphia's Lefty Grove (20–12, and getting better) and Chicago's Ted Lyons (22–14).

On May 31, Detroit first baseman Johnny Neun pulled off an unassisted triple play against Cleveland. It was the seventh in history and the sixth in the 1920s. It would be 41 years before the major leagues saw another one.

On July 19, Ty Cobb, now with the Athletics (for whom he batted .357), laced a double against his former Detroit teammates for his 4,000th career hit.

In the National League, the Pittsburgh Pirates, under Donie Bush, won a pennant race that was a direct contrast

mandated 502 plate appearances to qualify for the crown, Bubbles wouldn't have made it.

The underdog Cardinals upset the Yankees in a seven-game World Series, during which Ruth belted a record four home runs. The Series was highlighted by two complete-game victories by Alexander and then the old master's now legendary bases-loaded strikeout of Tony Lazzeri in the seventh inning of the final game, when Alex came in to relieve Jesse Haines and finish the game.

Despite leading his club to their first pennant and the world championship, Rogers Hornsby found himself traded to the Giants for Frank Frisch on December 20. Hornsby had always been outspoken and brutally candid with everyone, including Cardinals owner Sam Breadon, who finally got fed up. Cardinals fans were vociferous in their denunciations of the deal, but Frisch's fiery play soon made them forgive and forget. (The multitalented Frisch had been made available only because of an increasingly rancorous relationship with McGraw that each found intolerable.)

Three eminent names serving in their twilights for the 1927 Athletics (left to right): Eddie Collins, Ty Cobb, Zack Wheat.

1928

In 1928 the Yankees made it three pennants in a row for the second time in the decade; this time, however, it wasn't so easy, for now the looming shadow of Connie Mack's rebuilt Philadelphia Athletics was upon them. The A's were in fact one-half game in front on September 8, but the next day a mammoth crowd of over 85,000 packed Yankee Stadium and watched Miller Huggins' team sweep the A's in a doubleheader and go on from there to win the pennant by 2½ games.

Ruth and Gehrig were again torrid, the Babe with 54 home runs, 142 RBIs, and .323 batting average; Lou with 27 home runs, 142 RBIs (tying Ruth for the lead), and .374 batting average. George Pipgras led the staff with a 24–13 record ("We averaged almost six runs a game that year," the big right-hander said later. "It was my own fault that I didn't win 30."), followed by Waite Hoyt's 23–7.

Lefty Grove was 24–8 for the A's, while forty-four-year-old right-hander Jack Quinn was 18–7. Another Philadelphia senior citizen, Ty Cobb, playing his final season at the age of forty-one, batted .323, while suffering the embarrassment of not being able to run down some long fly balls in the outfield. ("Ty might have cost us the pennant," one A's player said later. "But Mr. Mack was fascinated by him and kept him in there.")

The Browns' Heinie Manush and the Senators' Goose Goslin put on a bruising race for the batting crown, with Goslin winning, .379 to .378, despite Manush's 241 hits. Browns right-handers Alvin Crowder (21–5) and Sam Gray (20–12) were big winners for their club.

The National League race wasn't decided until the very end, and when it was over, the Cardinals were narrow two-game winners over the Giants. Managed by Bill McKechnie (who had won with the Pirates in 1925), the Cardinals had two of the league's finest all-around players in Frank Frisch and outfielder Chick Hafey, who batted .337 and intimidated baserunners with the league's strongest throwing arm. ("He hit line drives and he threw them,"

to the American League's—the Pirates won it on the last day of the season, edging the Cardinals by 1½ games, with the Giants two behind.

Leading the league with a .305 team batting average, the Pirates had the batting champion in Paul Waner, who tattooed the ball for a .380 average, abetted by his younger brother Lloyd, who broke in with a .355 mark, setting rookie records with 223 hits and 198 singles. Paul had 237 hits, giving the brothers 460 between them. Paul set a major league record when he connected for extra-base hits (12 doubles, 4 triples, 4 home runs) in 14 straight games from June 3–19. Pittsburgh's big winners were Carmen Hill (22–11), Ray Kremer (19–8), and Lee Meadows (19–10).

Second-place St. Louis had a pair of 20-game winners in Jesse Haines (24–10) and the forty-year-old Grover Cleveland Alexander (21–10), a 20-game winner for the ninth and final time. Frank Frisch, replacing Hornsby at second for the Cardinals, batted .337 and stole a league-high 48 bases.

Hornsby batted .361 for the third-place Giants, leading a hard-hitting infield of Bill Terry, Travis Jackson, and Fred Lindstrom, all four of whom would one day reunite in the Hall of Fame. Philadelphia's Cy Williams and Chicago's Hack Wilson tied for the home run lead with 30 apiece. Hack's Chicago teammate Charlie Root was the league's top winner with a 26–15 record.

On May 30, shortstop Jimmy Cooney of the Cubs executed an unassisted triple play against the Pirates, just one day before Detroit's Johnny Neun pulled the same defensive stunner in a game against Cleveland.

The Pirates were a fine team indeed, but it was the year of the '27 Yankees, and in the World Series Miller Huggins' team rolled to the championship in four straight.

Lou Gehrig (right) and Babe Ruth.

one writer said of Hafey.) Bill Sherdel was 21–10 for the Cardinals and Jesse Haines 20–8, with the veteran Alexander squeezing a 16–9 year from his forty-one-year-old right arm.

The Giants, who had traded the always difficult Hornsby to the Braves, no doubt missed the Rajah's magic bat as much as they did not his testy personality. (Hornsby hit .387 for Boston to take his seventh batting crown, outdistancing Paul Waner's .370.) Fred Lindstrom led the Giants with a .358 average and led with 231 hits, while McGraw's nineteen-year-old prodigy Met Ott, in his first full season, batted .322, and first baseman Bill Terry hit .326. McGraw also had the league's top winner in Larry Benton (25–9) and another ace in knuckleballer Fred Fitzsimmons (20–9).

Chicago's Hack Wilson, built like a fire hydrant, again tied for the league's home run title, this time with the Cardinals' Jim Bottomley, each hitting 31. Sunny Jim was the RBI leader with 136. Bottomley also turned in the rare feat of hitting 20 or better in each extra-base category, getting 42 doubles and 20 triples to go along with his 31 long-distance shots.

Fourth-place Pittsburgh led the league with a .309 team average (from 1921 through 1930 the Pirates averaged a remarkable .299), with Burleigh Grimes tying Benton with 25 wins.

Brooklyn's Dazzy Vance was 22–10 for his sixth-place club and led for the seventh straight (and final) time in strikeouts with 200. As an indication of how hard the thirty-seven-year-old Vance was still throwing, his 200 whiffs were more than half the total of the staffs of four other clubs. Between 1918 and 1936 Vance, who did it three times, was the only National League pitcher to attain 200 strikeouts in a season.

The World Series was a Yankee runaway, a sweep of the Cardinals in four. It was also a Ruth-Gehrig circus, the Wham & Smash duo combining for seven home runs and a .592 batting average, with Ruth hitting all three of his home runs in the fourth game.

Hack Wilson making contact.

1929

"With those two monsters in the league," Cleveland manager Roger Peckinpaugh said ruefully, "you started the season fighting for third place."

The "monsters" Peckinpaugh was referring to were the New York Yankees and Philadelphia Athletics, at the time two of major league baseball's all-time bruisers.

In 1929, Connie Mack made it back to the top for the first time since 1914, smashing the three-year Yankee domination with a decisive 18-game first-place margin. This A's team featured four of the greatest players of all time: first baseman Jimmie Foxx, outfielder Al Simmons, catcher Mickey Cochrane, and pitcher Lefty Grove.

In 1929, Grove (20–6) teamed with George Earnshaw (24–8) and left-hander Rube Walberg (18–11) to give the A's the league's best pitching. Grove's 2.81 ERA was the only one in the major leagues under 3.00 that year. Simmons batted .365 and led with 157 runs batted in, Cochrane batted .331, and Foxx .354. In addition, outfielders Bing Miller and Mule Haas batted .335 and .313, respectively, and infielder Jimmy Dykes was at .327.

Philadelphia's .296 team batting average was a point better than the Yankees' .295 (Detroit outhit them both with a .299 mark, but a 4.96 staff ERA sank them into sixth place). Babe Ruth and Earle Combs each batted .345, with Ruth blasting 46 homers (including his 500th career shot on August 11) and driving in 154 runs; Tony Lazzeri batted .354, and rookie catcher Bill Dickey (who for decades vied with Cochrane as "the greatest catcher of all time") broke in with a .324 batting average. The best the Yankees could muster on the mound was George Pipgras's 18–12 record, as nominal aces Waite Hoyt and Herb Pennock suddenly became .500 pitchers, though southpaw Tom Zachary was 12–0, setting a record for most wins in a season by an undefeated pitcher.

Third-place Cleveland had the batting champion in first baseman Lew Fonseca (.369) and a sparkling new pitcher in twenty-one-year-old right-hander Wes Ferrell, who was 21–10. Cleveland third baseman Joe Sewell, for a decade the toughest man in baseball to strike out, went down on strikes just four times in 578 at-bats, at one point going 115 straight games and 437 at-bats without fanning.

The Yankees' season ended in tragedy when manager Miller Huggins suddenly took ill and died on September 25, at the age of fifty.

Joe McCarthy, who was to win eight pennants managing the Yankees, starting in 1932, won his first flag as skipper of the Chicago Cubs in 1929. With the league as a whole averaging .294, the Cubs bashed what seemed like an ever-livelier ball for a .303 team average. McCarthy's crushers, who finished 10½ games ahead of second-place Pittsburgh (which also batted .303), were led by Rogers

Miller Huggins

Hornsby—playing with his fourth team in four years—who smoked the air with a .380 average, the seventh time he had reached this exalted figure. He had 39 home runs and drove in 149 runs. Among his teammates, Kiki Cuyler batted .360, Riggs Stephenson .362, and Hack Wilson .345. Wilson also hit 39 homers and led the league with 159 RBIs.

McCarthy's pennant-winning staff was topped by Pat Malone (22–10), Charlie Root (19–6), and Guy Bush (18–7). Malone was the league's only 20-game winner.

The league's leading hitter was Philadelphia's Lefty O'Doul, a failure as an American League pitcher with the Yankees and Red Sox earlier in the decade. Lefty batted a resonant .398 and set a new league record with 254 hits, one of four Phillies who had 200 or more hits (the only National League team ever to have that many 200-hit collectors). The other shareholders in this feat were Chuck Klein (219), Fresco Thompson (202), and Pinky Whitney (200). The club batted .309, but still finished fifth, thanks to a staff ERA of 6.13. Klein drove in 145 runs and set a new National League home run record with 43.

Other high achievers in this year of the bat were New York's Bill Terry (.372), Brooklyn's colorful Babe Herman (.381), New York's Mel Ott (42 home runs, 151 RBIs), and so on through a hit-booming league that saw 16 men drive in over 100 runs (the Cubs and Phillies tied the league record with four players apiece), and an even dozen rap out 200 or more hits. Brooklyn's rookie outfielder Johnny Frederick led with 52 doubles, highest total ever for a freshman. Not surprisingly, the ERA leader, New York left-hander Bill Walker, had the highest mark ever for a league leader, 3.09.

The league's extravagant hitting was symbolized most thunderously by the Cardinals on July 6. In the second game of a doubleheader that day the Cards scored ten runs in the first inning and again in the fifth, on their way to a 28–7 crushing of the Phillies. The 28 runs and the Cards' 28 hits are both single-game National League records.

With the plethora of hitting in the league these past few years, there hadn't been a no-hitter pitched since 1925. The drought was broken on May 8, when the Giants' screwballing left-hander Carl Hubbell, beginning to develop the form that would soon elevate him to greatness, no-hit the Pirates on May 8, 11–0.

Cincinnati right-hander Red Lucas earned himself an odd distinction. Lucas was 19–12 for the seventh-place Reds, leading the league in complete games with 28 as well as in pinch hits with 13. Always a sharp hitter, Red led again in pinch hits in 1930 and 1931.

The Athletics provided further mayhem in their five-game World Series victory over the Cubs. Included were a ten-run seventh inning rally in game 4 that turned an 8–0 deficit into a 10–8 win, and a three-run rally in the bottom of the ninth of game 5 that gave Mack's team a 3–2 win and the world championship. This was the Series in which Mack bypassed Grove, Earnshaw, and Walberg to start veteran Howard Ehmke in the opener, with Ehmke responding by fanning a Series record 13 Cubs on the way to a 3–1 victory.

Wilbert Robinson, catcher for the Baltimore Orioles in the 1890s and manager of the Brooklyn Dodgers from 1914–31.

Tris Speaker, center fielder and manager of the 1920 world champion Cleveland Indians. Tris set a good example for the boys that year with a .388 batting average.

Jim Bagby, Cleveland's 31-game-winning right-hander in 1920. Pitching for three clubs in 1912 and from 1916–23, Jim was 127–87 for his career.

Joe Sewell, baseball's most difficult strikeout (114 times in 7,132 official at-bats). Joe played from 1920–33, 11 years for Cleveland and 3 for the Yankees, batting .312. Joe's credo for seldom striking out? "You've got to keep your eye on the ball."

Ray Chapman, baseball's only on-the-field fatality. A cracker-jack shortstop from 1912–20, Chapman, who died at the age of twenty-nine, batted .278 lifetime.

The mound stalwarts of Connie Mack's 1929–31 pennant winners (left to right): Rube Walberg, Lefty Grove, and George Earnshaw.

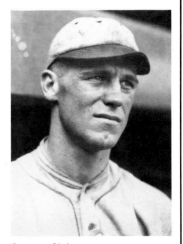

George Sisler

Stanley Coveleski, a high-class pitcher in 1912 and 1916–28, working for four American League clubs, primarily Cleveland. Five times a 20-game winner, he was 215–142 lifetime.

William "Baby Doll" Jacobson, one of the heavy gunners on the hard-hitting St. Louis Browns clubs of the early 1920s. An 11-year veteran, Baby Doll batted over .300 seven straight years, retiring in 1927 with a .311 average.

Grover Cleveland Alexander with the Cubs in the early 1920s.

Jack Tobin, big-league outfielder in 1916 and from 1918–27, most of it spent with the Browns, for whom he batted over .300 six times. Jack, who collected over 200 hits four straight years (1920–23), batted .315 lifetime.

Brooklyn's Leon Cadore, best remembered for his 1–1, 26-inning duel with Joe Oeschger in 1920. He pitched from 1915–24, virtually all of that time with the Dodgers, retiring with a 68–72 record.

It's the bottom of the first inning of the historic fifth game of the 1920 World Series between Cleveland and Brooklyn. The first two Indians batters singled and then Tris Speaker bunted. Dodger pitcher Burleigh Grimes lost his footing as he tried to field the ball, loading the bases. As Burleigh lands on Cleveland's rather patchy infield grass, Charlie Jamieson can be seen arriving safely at third.

A moment after the action portrayed in the previous picture, Cleveland's Elmer Smith hit the first grand slam home run in World Series history, sending home ahead of him (from top to bottom), Charlie Jamieson, Bill Wambsganss, and Tris Speaker. The black arm bands the Cleveland players are wearing are in memory of Ray Chapman.

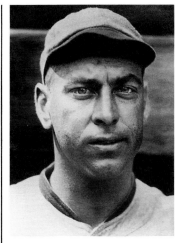

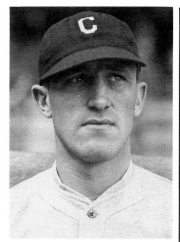

Right-hander Joe Oeschger, whose name will always be linked with that of Leon Cadore. Joe pitched for four National League teams from 1914–25, with a 83–116 record.

Cleveland second baseman Bill Wambsganss: one spectacularly unforgettable moment in a career otherwise noted for its near anonymity. Bill played from 1914–26, most all of it with Cleveland, batting .259.

Babe Ruth

LEFT: Jimmy Dykes, shown here as a young infielder with the Athletics in 1921. Jimmy enjoyed one of the longest careers in major league history, from 1918–39 as a player and also as a manager for six different major league clubs for 21 years, until 1961. Jimmy was a lifetime .280 hitter.

Carl Mays

Bill Wambsganss completing his unassisted triple play in the fifth inning of the fifth game of the 1920 World Series. The Cleveland second baseman has leaped and caught Clarence Mitchell's line drive, stepped on second to put out Pete Kilduff (who has already rounded third base and is looking back), and is about to tag a disbelieving Otto Miller, with umpire Hank O'Day watching it happen. In the foreground are Cleveland third baseman Larry Gardner and umpire Bill Dinneen.

Frankie Frisch, one of the most gifted and dynamic of all ballplayers. He came from the campus of Fordham straight to the New York Giants in 1919, was traded to the Cardinals after the 1926 season, where he played and managed, retiring as an active player in 1937. Thirteen times a .300 hitter, Frisch had a .316 lifetime average.

LEFT: Outfielder Charlie Jamieson. He came up with the Senators in 1915, went to the Athletics in 1917, then to Cleveland two years later, when he began a string of solid seasons that lasted right through the 1920s. He retired in 1932 with a .303 career average.

Yankee Stadium under construction in 1922.

Wally Schang

Wally Schang, who caught for five American League teams from 1913–31, including seven pennant winners. Lifetime average: .284.

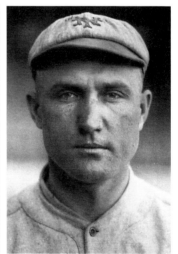

Dave Bancroft

George Kelly, a big leaguer from 1915–17, 1919–30, and 1932. George had his prime years in the early 1920s as part of four McGraw pennant winners. Known as "Highpockets," Kelly was a two-time National League RBI leader and batted .297 overall.

LEFT: Pittsburgh's Wilbur Cooper, one of baseball's top left-handers from 1912–26, all but the last two years spent with the Pirates. He was 216–178 lifetime.

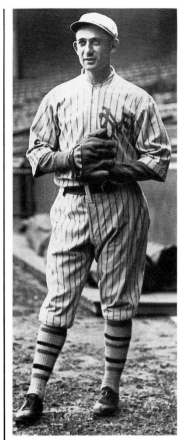

One of the National League's cannier left-handers from 1915–29, Art Nehf pitched for four teams, most notably as one of McGraw's aces on the 1921–24 pennant winners. He was 184–120 for his 15-year career.

Times Square crowds watching the progress of the 1921 World Series as reported on a mechanical diamond on the side of the Times Building.

Emil "Irish" Meusel, older of the two Meusel brothers. Irish, a solid .310 lifetime hitter, did his whacking for the Phillies, Giants, and Dodgers from 1918–27. He was one of the stars of McGraw's 1921–24 pennant winners.

The Cardinals' Austin McHenry, who died in November 1922, at the age of twenty-seven. He batted .302 for a career that ran from 1918–22.

George Uhle, who pitched from 1919–34 and in 1936, winning 200 and losing 166. Working for four clubs, George had his best outing with Cleveland in the 1920s, winning 26 in 1923 and 27 in 1926.

RIGHT: Sam Jones, who pitched for every American League club except the Tigers and Athletics from 1914–33, retiring with a record of 229–217.

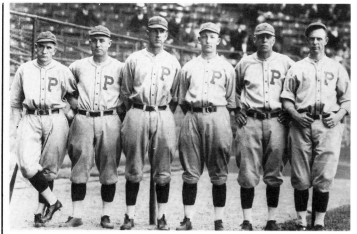

Six members of the 1921 Pittsburgh Pirates (left to right): Rabbit Maranville, Cotton Tierney, Charlie Grimm, Clyde Barnhart, Ray Rohwer, and George Cutshaw.

Howard Ehmke, a productive right-hander for the Tigers, Red Sox, and Athletics from 1916–17 and 1919–30. Lifetime record: 166–164.

Frank "Pancho" Snyder, catcher for the Cardinals and Giants from 1912–27. Career average: .265.

Max Carey loosening up before a game.

Eppa Rixey

A tough day at the office for Frankie Frisch.

BELOW: First baseman Jack Fournier, who played for five clubs in both leagues from 1912–18 and 1920–27, did some fancy hitting for the Dodgers in the 1920s, twice hitting .350 and leading in home runs in 1924. Lifetime average: .313.

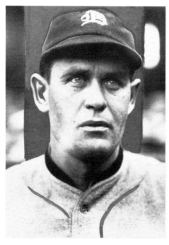

First baseman Lu Blue, who played from 1921–33, batting .287. His best years were with Detroit in the 1920s.

RIGHT: Willie Kamm, American League third baseman with Chicago and Cleveland from 1923–35, during which he batted .281.

Bullet Joe Bush

Philadelphia's Shibe Park in the early 1920s.

An outfielder with the White Sox from 1920–28 and then with the Indians through 1931, Bibb Falk batted over .300 eight times and .314 for his career.

The Babe launching one at the Polo Grounds, the Yankees' home park until 1922.

Considered one of the outstanding defensive center fielders of his day, Johnny Mostil spent his entire ten-year career with the White Sox, retiring in 1929 with a .301 average.

This picture was taken in August 1921 during a break in the trial of the White Sox players accused of throwing the 1919 World Series. Sitting left to right: defense attorney William Fallon, Joe Jackson, Buck Weaver, Eddie Cicotte, Swede Risberg, Lefty Williams, and Chick Gandil. Two other players, Fred McMullin and Happy Felsch, were out of the room when the picture was taken.

Pete Donohue, three-time 20-game winner for the Reds in the 1920s. Pitching for four teams from 1921–32, he was 134–118.

"Jughandle" Johnny Morrison, Pirate right-hander from 1920–27, finishing up with the Dodgers in 1929–30. A 25-game winner in 1923, he was 103–80 lifetime.

Rogers Hornsby. Lifetime average: .358.

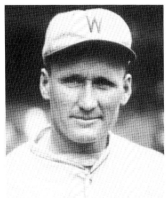

RIGHT: Walter Johnson

Babe Ruth acknowledging the cheering crowd after blasting a home run in the 1923 World Series.

Travis Jackson, Giant shortstop from 1922–36. He was a .291 career hitter.

Cy Williams, long-balling out-fielder for the Cubs and Phillies from 1912–30. Four times the home run leader, he compiled a .292 career average.

It's opening day at the Polo Grounds in 1924 and the Giants' Frank Frisch (left) and the Dodgers' Zack Wheat are starting the new season off with a handshake.

Goose Goslin, who played the outfield for the Senators, Browns, and Tigers from 1921–38, hitting hard and driving in runs wherever he played. The American League batting champion in 1928, Goose batted .300 11 times and drove in 100 or more runs in a season 11 times. Lifetime average: .316.

A big leaguer at the age of eighteen, Fred Lindstrom starred for the Giants through the 1920s, later playing for the Pirates, Cubs, and Dodgers in a career that ran from 1924–36. He twice collected 231 hits in a season and in 1930 batted .379. He was a .311 hitter lifetime.

LEFT: Dazzy Vance, Brooklyn's colorful, hard-throwing ace. Over a 16-year career that ended in 1935, Vance, pitching for five different teams but primarily with the Dodgers, was 197–140, despite not winning his first big-league game until he was thirty-one years old.

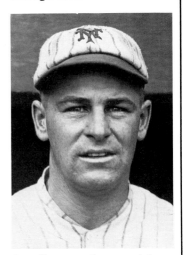

Ross Youngs, who was nick-named "Pep" for the ener-getic hustle he put out on a ball field. A New York Giant from 1917–26, he was a .300 hitter every year except one. He batted .322 for his career, which was shortened by an illness that took his life in 1927, when he was thirty years old.

LEFT: Right-hander Dolf Luque, who had a long National League career, pitching for four clubs from 1914–15 and 1918–35. The bulk of his career was spent with the Reds, for whom he won 27 in 1923. He was 193–179 lifetime.

The slick-fielding Joe Judge, who played first base for the Washington Senators from 1915–32, finishing up with the Dodgers and the Red Sox in 1933–34. Nine times a .300 hitter, Joe batted .298 lifetime.

The president is getting game 3 of the 1925 World Series under way with a ceremonial toss. Left to right: Mrs. Coolidge, Pirates skipper Bill McKechnie, President Calvin Coolidge, Senators manager Bucky Harris, and Commissioner Landis.

Fred "Firpo" Marberry, a relief specialist for the Washington Senators in the 1920s. The right-hander led American League pitchers in appearances six times. In a career that ran from 1923–36, Marberry was 147–89.

Ossie Bluege, who played third base for the Senators from 1922–39 and was regarded as one of the great defensive players of his era. His lifetime average is .272.

RIGHT: Wally Pipp, Yankee first baseman from 1915–25 and then with the Reds through 1928. In 1925, he suffered baseball's most famous headache. He was a .281 career hitter.

LEFT: Detroit's Harry Heilmann, who won batting titles in odd-numbered years—1921, 1923, 1925, 1927. Harry came up with the Tigers in 1914 and finished up with Cincinnati in 1930 and 1932. Primarily a line-drive hitter, the right-handed-hitting Heilmann batted over .300 12 times and a lusty .342 for his career. Among right-handed hitters in this century, only Hornsby's .358 tops him.

Rookie first baseman Lou Gehrig at the Yankees' St. Petersburg spring training site in March 1925.

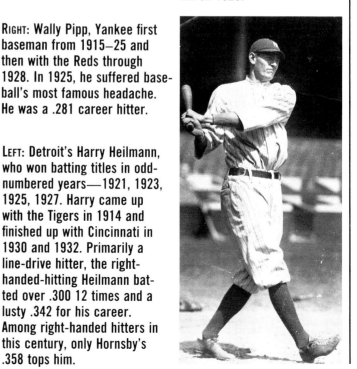

ABOVE: Sam Rice, one of the most consistent of hitters. Over a 20-year career (1915–34), all but the last year of it spent with Washington, he never batted under .293. Thirteen times a .300 hitter, he batted .322 lifetime. He had a career total of 2,987 hits, but never seemed interested in picking up those last 13.

A couple of top-notch shortstops turned managers. Shown in this 1925 photo are the Phillies' Art Fletcher (left) and the Braves' Dave Bancroft, who was still an active player then.

Lee Meadows, a solid right-hander who pitched for the Cardinals, Phillies, and Pirates from 1915–29, winning 188 and losing 180.

Hazen "Kiki" Cuyler, one of the best all-around ballplayers of his time. Playing for the Pirates, Cubs, Reds, and Dodgers from 1921–1938, he batted over .300 ten times and .321 for his career. He led the league in stolen bases four times.

LEFT: "If Ted Lyons had pitched for the Yankees," Joe Mc-Carthy said, "he would have won 400 games." Ted, however, pitched his entire career (1923–42, 1946) for the White Sox, posting a 260–230 ledger.

BELOW: Carson Bigbee, Pittsburgh outfielder from 1916–26. Lifetime average: .287.

The exterior of Fenway Park.

Al Simmons. He played for the Athletics (for whom he had his greatest years), White Sox, Tigers, Senators, Braves, and Reds from 1924–41. He batted over .300 13 times (including four times over .380), drove in over 100 runs 12 times, and had a lifetime average of .334.

Second baseman Hughie Critz, who divided his 12-year career (1924–35) between the Reds and Giants, batting .268.

RIGHT: The Babe—always the center of attention.

A bench full of Phillies in 1925. Left to right: Lew Fonseca (who was the American League batting champion with Cleveland in 1929), pitcher Jimmy Ring, infielder Wally Kimmick, pitcher Clarence Mitchell, outfielder George Burns, and outfielder George Harper; the last player is unidentified.

National League outfielder Taylor Douthit, who spent his prime years with the Cardinals in the 1920s. He batted .291 over his 11-year career (1923–33).

Ray Kremer, top-line Pirates right-hander from 1924–33. He was 143–85 lifetime.

Yankee second baseman Tony Lazzeri, who joined the club in 1926 and played in New York through 1937. His final two years were spent with the Cubs, Dodgers, and Giants. Tony drove in over 100 runs seven times and batted .292 lifetime, but is chiefly remembered today for having been struck out with the bases loaded in the seventh game of the 1926 World Series by Grover Cleveland Alexander.

Not everything was a home run. Here is Ruth legging out an infield hit. The first baseman is Phil Todt; pitcher Howard Ehmke, who stumbled over the bag while covering, is on the ground.

Bob "Fats" Fothergill, good-hitting outfielder for Detroit in the 1920s and later for the White Sox and Red Sox. Playing from 1922–33, Fats averaged an impressive .326.

Bob O'Farrell, who caught in the National League for four teams from 1915–35, batting .273. He was behind the plate when Alexander fanned Lazzeri in the seventh game of the 1926 World Series.

Pie Traynor, the automatic selection at third base on many all-time all-star teams. He was with Pittsburgh from 1920–35 and in 1937, batting .320.

Heinie Manush, for 17 years (1923–39) one of baseball's most adept line-drive bats. Playing for six teams in both leagues, Heinie batted over .300 11 times and .330 for his career.

Grover Cleveland Alexander in 1926.

One of the great first baseman in National League history, Sunny Jim Bottomley starred for the Cardinals from 1922–32, later playing for the Reds and the Browns, retiring in 1937 with a .310 batting average.

Jesse Haines. He got into one game for the Reds in 1918, then from 1920–37 pitched for the Cardinals, winning 210 and losing 158.

Jimmy Ring, a hard-throwing right-hander who pitched for four National League clubs from 1917–28, compiling a 118–149 record.

The Babe looking deep. He's watching the flight of one of the three home runs he hit against the Cardinals in the fourth game of the 1926 World Series. The catcher is Bob O'Farrell.

Right-hander Red Lucas, who pitched in the big leagues for 15 years, mostly with Cincinnati and Pittsburgh, retiring in 1938 with a 157–135 record. He was also one of the great-hitting pitchers of all time, batting .281. Frequently used as a pinch hitter, he led the National League four times in pinch hits.

Luke Sewell, who caught for four American League teams from 1921–39 and 1942, the first 12 of those years with Cleveland. A .259 lifetime batter, Sewell in 1944 managed the St. Louis Browns to their only pennant.

A couple of well-known names getting together during the 1926 World Series. Babe Ruth (left) and Rogers Hornsby.

After 22 years with the Tigers, Ty Cobb joined the Athletics in 1927.

The outfield of the 1927 Yankees. Left to right: Earle Combs, Babe Ruth, and Bob Meusel. Combs played his entire 12-year career (1924–35) with the Yankees, batting .325. Meusel played from 1920–30, all but the last year with the Yankees, batting .309.

Paul Waner, three-time batting champion and one of the greatest hitters in National League history. He was with Pittsburgh from 1926–40, then played for three other teams until 1945. He hit over .300 his first 12 years and 14 times overall, with a lifetime average of .333.

Lloyd Waner, who teamed with his brother Paul in the Pirate outfield from 1927–40 and then played for four other teams (plus a second stint with Pittsburgh) until 1945. A slap hitter with terrific running speed, Lloyd batted over .300 ten times and .316 for his career.

Glenn Wright, hard-hitting shortstop with Pittsburgh and Brooklyn from 1924–33, finishing up with the White Sox in 1935. Lifetime average: .294.

Knuckleballer Fred Fitzsimmons, who had a long career with the Giants and Dodgers from 1925–43, winning 217 and losing 146.

"Jumping" Joe Dugan, third baseman on the '27 Yankees. Joe was with four other clubs in a career that ran from 1917–29 and 1931. He batted .280 lifetime.

A .300 gunner eight straight times, George Grantham played first base and second base for the Pirates and three other clubs from 1922–34, retiring with a .302 average.

LEFT: Sam Gray, right-hander with the Athletics and Browns from 1924–33. A 20-game winner for the Browns in 1928, he was 112–115 lifetime.

Waite "Schoolboy" Hoyt. Hoyt was an ace right-hander on six Yankees pennant winners in the 1920s. He also pitched for six other teams in both leagues during the course of a long career (1918–38), during which he won 237 and lost 182.

Wilcy Moore, who had a spectacular 19–7 year as a reliever for the '27 Yankees, his rookie year. Moore pitched for the Yankees and Red Sox from 1927–33, logging a 51–44 record.

Herb Pennock, southpaw ace for the Yankees in the 1920s. He also pitched for the Athletics and Red Sox during a career that ran from 1912–17 and 1918–34. Lifetime record: 240–162, plus a perfect 5–0 record in World Series competition.

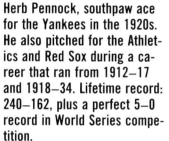

Ethan Allen, who played the outfield for six big-league clubs from 1926–38, batting an even .300.

Al Simmons

Robert Moses "Lefty" Grove. Tough, irascible, likable, and damn near unbeatable. He was a force on American League mounds from 1925–41, dividing his career between Philadelphia and Boston. Eight times a 20-game winner, nine times the ERA leader, he retired with a 300–141 career history.

Charlie Grimm, long-time first baseman and manager. He played in 1916 and from 1918–36, mostly for the Pirates and Cubs, batting .290. He also managed the Cubs for thirteen years (over three separate stints) and the Braves for five.

Larry Benton, who pitched from 1923–35, working the hill for the Braves, Giants, and Reds. A 25-game winner for the Giants in 1928, he was 127–128 lifetime. He is shown here tuning up at the Giants' spring training camp at Hot Springs, Arkansas, in late February 1928.

With some encouragement from Babe Ruth (number 3), Lou Gehrig comes sliding safely home well ahead of the relay.

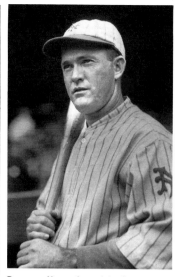

Rogers Hornsby with the Giants in 1927.

Right-hander Irving "Bump" Hadley, who made his way around the big leagues from 1926–41. Pitching for six different teams in both leagues, he was 161–165.

Hack Wilson, one of the slugging stars of the hard-hitting 1929 pennant-winning Chicago Cubs, for whom he drove in a league-leading 159 runs. In 1930 he set a National League record with 56 home runs and a major league record with 190 RBIs. Lifetime average: .307.

Jimmie Foxx. They called him "the right-handed Babe Ruth," which was all you needed to know. Jimmie came up with the Athletics in 1925, was dealt to the Red Sox in 1936 and finished up in the National League in 1942 and 1944–45. Jimmie had 534 lifetime homers, drove in over 100 runs 13 times (consecutively), batted over .300 12 times, and had a career average of .325.

Sparky Adams, infielder with four National League clubs from 1922–34. He batted .286 lifetime.

A .336 lifetime hitter, Riggs Stephenson hit line drives for the Indians and Cubs from 1921–34.

Lou Gehrig taking his rips in the cage at the Yankees' St. Petersburg training camp on February 28, 1929.

Mickey Cochrane, top candidate for greatest catcher of all time. Mickey was behind the plate for the Athletics and Tigers from 1925–37, when a Bump Hadley fastball ended his career and almost his life. Lifetime average: .320.

A couple of Philadelphia Phillies boomers in 1929. Chuck Klein (left) and Lefty O'Doul. Chuck batted .356 that year and Lefty a league-high .398.

Lou Gehrig. Thirteen consecutive years of over 100 runs batted in (7 times over 150), 493 home runs, .340 career batting average.

1930

In contrast to the staggering national economy, baseball's batting averages soared even further in 1930. All of the concentrated slugging of the decade just ended seemed to culminate in this one season, particularly in the National League.

In the American League, the Philadelphia Athletics took to heart Connie Mack's credo, "A team cannot be considered great unless it repeats," and gave their manager a second straight pennant, winning by eight games over the Washington Senators (who were now managed by Walter Johnson).

Lefty Grove was spectacular all season, with a 28–5 record and an earned run average of 2.54, lowest in the league by far (the next lowest was Wes Ferrell's 3.31). George Earnshaw was 22–13. Al Simmons won the batting title with a .381 average, two points ahead of Lou Gehrig, hit 36 home runs and drove in 165 runs. Jimmie Foxx batted .335, hit 37 homers, and drove in 156 runs. Mickey Cochrane batted .357.

Washington had a flood of .300 hitters, including Heinie Manush (.350), Sam Rice (.349), and Joe Cronin (.346). Cronin was beginning to establish himself as one of the hardest-hitting shortstops of all time. The Senators, however, like the third-place Yankees, suffered from a lack of front-line pitching. The Yankees batted a lusty .309 and led the league in every offensive category except doubles (Cleveland set an American League record with 358 that year) and stolen bases and scored 1062 runs to the Athletics' 951, but the A's had Grove and Earnshaw, and that was the difference. New York's top pitcher was Red Ruffing (15–5), who had been acquired in an early-season steal-of-a-deal with the Red Sox. The Yankees' tremendous hitting was highlighted by Lou Gehrig's 41 home runs, 174 runs batted in, and .379 batting average; Babe Ruth's 49 homers, 153 RBIs, and .359 average; a .344 season from Earle Combs; and a .339 turnout from young Bill Dickey.

Cleveland's Wes Ferrell was 25–13, Chicago's Ted Lyons 22–15, and St. Louis's Lefty Stewart 20–12.

When the season was over, the American League's shell-shocked pitchers had thrown the fewest shutouts in history (36) and been shredded for a 4.65 ERA.

The hitting in the National League in 1930 was even more devastating, the ball so lively that the scoring approached levels of near travesty. Slightly embarrassed by it all, and perhaps suffering whiplash from watching runners whirl around the bases,

1930– Surviving the Depression 1939

George Earnshaw

club officials that winter had some of the high-octane stimulus drained from the ball, bringing averages back to normal levels in 1931.

The cannonading of 1930 has a slightly farcical look to it today. Some guardians of the record books even wonder if some of the feats accomplished during that noisy summer have true validity, given the vibrant spirit of the baseball. These are some of the things that happened:

Chicago's Hack Wilson set a National League record with 56 home runs and a major league record with 190 runs batted in.

The top five batters were New York's Bill Terry, .401; Brooklyn's Babe Herman, .393; Philadelphia's Chuck Klein, .386 and Lefty O'Doul, .383; New York's Fred Lindstrom, .379. Overall, 11 players who appeared in 100 or more games batted .350 or better.

Terry tied O'Doul's league record with 254 hits, Klein had 250, Herman 241. Twelve players had over 200 hits.

Boston's Wally Berger set a rookie home run record with 38.

Hack Wilson (56) and Gabby Hartnett (37) set a league mark for teammates with 93 home runs.

Klein's 158 runs scored are a league record.

The St. Louis Cardinals' eight regulars all batted over .300. The Cards set a major league record with 373 doubles and a National League mark with 1,004 runs.

Six teams batted over .300, led by the Giants' major league record high of .319. The Phillies had a major league record 1,783 hits in 156 games (an average of more than 11 hits a game), batted .315, and finished last, thanks to

the highest team ERA in history—6.71.

The National League batted a record .303 for the season, with the beleaguered pitchers leaving behind a 4.97 ERA, a league high.

Brooklyn's Dazzy Vance emerged from the sustained bombardment as something of a miracle man, posting a 2.61 ERA; the next lowest was more than a full run behind —Carl Hubbell's 3.76. Chicago's Pat Malone (20–9) and Pittsburgh's Ray Kremer (20–12) were the league's only 20-game winners.

The St. Louis Cardinals and their .314 team batting average emerged from baseball's version of the Western Front as pennant winners, Gabby Street's club finishing two games ahead of the Cubs. Bill Hallahan at 15–9 was the Cards' top winner.

The Athletics made it two world championships in a row when they defeated the Cardinals in the World Series four games to two. Grove and Earnshaw each won two games for the A's.

The season marked the end of the career of Grover Cleveland Alexander. The forty-three-year-old Alex had been released by the Cardinals and returned to Philadelphia, where it had all started for him in 1911. But now the magic was long gone and the veteran was 0–3, hit hard in the few games he worked. Alexander left with 373 victories, leaving him in a tie with Christy Mathewson at the top of the National League scrolls.

Pat Malone

1931

With the baseball not as frisky as it had been in 1930, a more traditional balance between offense and defense returned to the game in 1931. The American League batting average dropped from .288 to .278, while the National's went from an unrealistic .303 to .277.

Nevertheless, there was still plenty of impressive hitting, particularly in the American League, where Ruth, Gehrig, and a few others made the ball look as lively as ever. The Yankees' home run twins tied for the lead in homers with 46 apiece, with Lou setting an American League RBI record with 184, the Babe right behind with 163.

The Yankees scored an all-time major league record 1,067 runs, 209 more than the Athletics—and finished second, 13½ games behind Connie Mack's bruisers, who made it three in a row. The A's had the league's leading hitter in Al Simmons, who scorched the ball at a .390 clip, and had some more solid hitting from Jimmie Foxx, Mickey Cochrane, and Mule Haas. But the big difference was again on the mound. Whereas the best the Yankees had was young Lefty Gomez (21–9), the A's had Lefty Grove at his peak (31–4), George Earnshaw (21–7), and Rube Walberg (20–12). The A's won 107 games, making them the first American League club to win over 100 for three straight years.

Grove's mountaintop record included a 16-game winning streak, which tied him with Joe Wood and Walter Johnson for the league record. The streak ended on August 23, when the Browns' Dick Coffman shut out the A's, 1–0, the run scoring on a misjudged fly ball. After the game the temperamental Mr. Grove dismantled much of the clubhouse.

Cleveland's Wes Ferrell made it three big seasons in a row with a 22–12 record, including the league's first no-hitter in almost five years, a 9–0 win over the Browns on April 29. Wes, the most complete ballplaying talent since the early days of Babe Ruth, set a major league record for pitchers by hitting nine home runs. His Cleveland teammate Earl Averill had his own fine season, batting .333 and driving in 143 runs.

Red Sox outfielder Earl Webb set an all-time major league record for doubles with 67. Like Owen Wilson, who hit 36 triples in 1912, Webb was an unexceptional player who crashed the record books with one remarkable season in an otherwise unremarkable career. On August 21, Babe Ruth hit his 600th career home run. On August 8, Washington left-hander Bobby Burke fired a no-hitter against the Red Sox, winning 5–0.

For the first time in its history, the National League failed to have a 20-game winner. The St. Louis Cardinals had one of the league's three top winners in left-hander Bill Hallahan, whose 19 victories tied him with Pittsburgh's Heinie Meine and Philadelphia's Jim Elliott. The Cardinals also got strong seasons from rookie Paul Derringer (18–8) and the veteran Burleigh Grimes (17–9). This solid pitching enabled St. Louis to take a second straight, rather easy pennant, coming in 13 games ahead of the Giants. For skipper Gabby Street, it was two pennants in two years on the job.

The Cardinals' Chick Hafey won the closest batting race in history, his .3489 edging out teammate Jim Bottomley's .3481 and Bill Terry's .3486. The driving force behind the Cardinals, however, remained second baseman Frank Frisch, dynamic in the field and on the basepaths, whose .311 batting average was his 11th straight year over .300.

Third-place Chicago had Charlie Grimm, Rogers Hornsby, and Kiki Cuyler all around .330, but Hack Wilson's home runs dropped from 56 to 13 and his RBIs from 190 to 61. Philadelphia's Chuck Klein was the leader in home runs (31) and RBIs (121).

The Baseball Writers Association of America began voting its Most Valuable Player Award in 1931, with the first winners being Frisch in the National League and Grove in the American.

Trying for their third straight world championship, the Athletics were upended in seven games by the Cardinals. The driving force in the Series was the Cardinals' rookie center fielder Pepper Martin, who collected 12 hits, batted .500, and stole five bases.

Wes Ferrell

Chick Hafey

1932

With second-year manager Joe McCarthy in charge, the Yankees ended the Athletics' three-year reign as league champions, winning handily, their 107 wins earning them a 13-game lead at the end.

Babe Ruth, fat and thirty-seven, turned in his last year of heavy production, hitting 41 home runs and batting .341, while Lou Gehrig batted .349, hit 34 homers, and drove in 151 runs. This hard-hitting Yankee team also got solid years from Tony Lazzeri, Earle Combs, Ben Chapman, and Bill Dickey. The '32 Yankees earned the distinction of being the only club in history to go through an entire season without being shut out.

The New Yorkers saw Lefty Gomez blossom to a 24–7 season and also had winning records from Red Ruffing (18–7) and Johnny Allen (17–4), the latter a talented but fiercely hot-tempered right-hander who McCarthy finally had to unload a few years later.

The Yankee pennant was the 12th straight for an Eastern club in the American League, with Cleveland in 1920 being the last Western contingent to win. In fact, up to this point, 24 of the league's 32 pennants had been won in the East, a dominance that would continue, the East winning 48 of the first 64 flags.

With Lefty Grove "slumping" to 25–10 (down from 31–4), the A's finished second (Connie Mack would manage for another 18 years and never finish that high again). Jimmie Foxx, the MVP that year, generated some excitement by challenging Ruth's home run record, ending up with 58. Jimmie led with 169 RBIs and just missed the Triple Crown, batting .364 to .367 for the leader, Dale Alexander, a good-hit, no-field first baseman who started

Dale Alexander

the year with Detroit and was traded early on to Boston. Al Simmons drove in 151 runs for the A's, giving them a lethal swat team.

Washington finished third, thanks largely to a 26–13 season from Alvin Crowder (who had a 15-game winning streak) and a surprise 22–10 effort from rookie Monte Weaver. Cleveland's Wes Ferrell set a record by winning 20 games again (23–13), making it four such outings in his first four major league seasons.

The Indians and the Athletics played the game of the year on July 10. This was an 18-inning orgy that the A's won, 18–17, with Cleveland's Johnny Burnett collecting a record nine hits. Relief pitcher Eddie Rommel picked up a rather checkered victory—going the last 17 innings and allowing 29 hits and 14 runs.

The noisiest one-man detonation of the year came on June 3 at Philadelphia's Shibe Park, when Gehrig became the first American Leaguer to clout four home runs in a game, exploding against the Athletics in a 20–13 Yankees victory.

After 31 tumultuous, controversial, and sometimes triumphant years, John McGraw, weary, ailing, and burned out, resigned as manager of the New York Giants. The date was June 3 (the same day that Gehrig's fireworks lit up the American League). McGraw's hand-picked successor was his first baseman, Bill Terry, with whom the skipper had been conducting an icy, virtually wordless feud for years. Nevertheless, McGraw admired Terry's leadership abilities, even as he had been offended by his star player's strong and independent personality. (McGraw died on February 25, 1934, at the age of sixty.)

With his club in second place on August 2, Cubs manager Rogers Hornsby, as thorny a character as ever, was bounced by owner William Wrigley and replaced by first baseman Charlie Grimm, who took the team to the pennant, winning by four games over the Pirates.

The Cubs had the league's best pitcher in Lon Warneke (22–6) and a 19-game winner in Guy Bush, while rookie second baseman Billy Herman, veteran outfielder Riggs Stephenson, and Grimm led the hitters.

The second-place Pirates got their usual high-grade hitting from Pie Traynor (.329), Paul Waner (.341), Lloyd Waner (.333), and this year added rookie shortstop Arky Vaughan, who batted .318.

Third-place Brooklyn had the league's only other 20-game winner in left-hander Watson Clark (20–12) as well the league's leading hitter, Lefty O'Doul (.368). O'Doul's career was brief—only six full seasons and parts of five others—but highly decorated, with two batting titles and an impressive .349 lifetime average.

New York's Mel Ott and Philadelphia's Chuck Klein tied for the home run lead with 38 apiece, while Klein led in slugging (.646), hits (226), runs (152), and stolen bases

Guy Bush

(20), all of which earned him the MVP Award.

It was a good year for rookies in the National League. In addition to Herman and Vaughan, the St. Louis Cardinals introduced a lanky, garrulous, hard-throwing youngster who was shortly to become baseball's top pitcher, biggest drawing card, and most colorful character—Dizzy Dean. The twenty-one-year-old Dean was 18–15 for the seventh-place Cards, leading in strikeouts with 191. Getting into 26 late-season games for the Cards and batting .349 was another rookie, twenty-year-old Joe Medwick, soon to become the league's big bopper.

In the World Series, the Yankees flattened the Cubs in four straight, with Gehrig hitting three home runs and batting .529. It was Ruth's final Series, and in game 3 the Babe put on a bravura performance when he allegedly "called" his home run. Called or not, it was one of the longest blasts ever hit in Chicago's Wrigley Field. Following their sweeps of the Pirates in 1927 and the Cardinals in 1928, the Yankees now had won 12 straight World Series games.

1933

When the Washington Senators last won a pennant, in 1925, it was under the driving force of second baseman–manager Bucky Harris. Eight years later another player-manager, shortstop Joe Cronin, led the club to the last pennant it would ever win in the nation's capital.

In his first year as manager, the twenty-six-year-old Cronin starred on a hard-hitting team that featured .300 hitters in first baseman Joe Kuhel, second baseman Buddy Myer, outfielder Heinie Manush, and Cronin himself. At the top of the Washington staff were Alvin Crowder (24–15) and left-hander Earl Whitehill (22–8).

The Senators finished seven up on the Yankees, who were hurt by Red Ruffing's 9–14 season and the fading of Babe Ruth, who "dropped" to 34 home runs, 103 RBIs, and a .301 batting average. On August 17, Lou Gehrig played in his 1,308th consecutive game, breaking the previous endurance record set by Everett Scott. A few weeks before, the Yankees were shut out for the first time since August 3, 1931, a record span of 308 games. The man who hung the goose eggs on Joe McCarthy's sluggers was Lefty Grove.

Grove was 24–8 for the third-place Athletics, for whom Jimmie Foxx had another big year. Jimmie had a Triple Crown season that earned him his second straight MVP Award: 48 home runs, 163 RBIs, .356 batting average.

Alvin Crowder

BASEBALL

For the second time in less than 20 years, Connie Mack was in the process of breaking up his ball club. Al Simmons, Mule Haas, and Jimmy Dykes had already been sold to the White Sox for needed cash; over the next few years Foxx and Grove would go to the Red Sox, Mickey Cochrane to the Tigers, and George Earnshaw to the White Sox. Declining attendance and stock market losses were forcing Connie into this divestment.

On May 16, Washington rookie Cecil Travis set a major league record when he collected five hits (all singles) in his first game, which was a 12-inning affair.

The first All-Star Game was played that year, on July 6, at Chicago's Comiskey Park. The American League won it, 4–2, on Ruth's home run. Intended as a one-time-only spectacular, the game was so popular the owners decided to make it an annual event.

Philadelphia was home to a pair of Triple Crown winners that year—Jimmie Foxx in the American League with the Athletics, and Chuck Klein in the National with the Phillies. Klein took his honors on the basis of 28 home runs, 120 runs batted in, and a .368 batting average, built on 223 hits. For Klein it was now five full years in the major leagues and five years of 200 hits or more, a record also set by Al Simmons that same year. After the season, he was sold to the Cubs; injuries and the loss of Baker Bowl's neighborly walls soon cost him his superstar status.

Despite his Triple Crown, Klein was not the league's MVP; the honor went instead to New York's Carl Hubbell. The Giants left-hander, beginning five straight years of greatness, was 23–12, with the best ERA, 1.66, built on a foundation of 10 shutouts. Abetted by Hal Schumacher (19–12), Hubbell helped pitch the Giants to the pennant. On July 2, "King Carl" turned in one of baseball's all-time pitching performances, an 18-inning 1–0 victory over the Cardinals at the Polo Grounds, yielding just six hits and no walks. Shortly after, on July 13, Hubbell began a string of 46 consecutive scoreless innings.

The Giants, who took over first place on June 10 and led the rest of the way, had just one regular who was a .300 hitter—first baseman–manager Bill Terry, who batted .322.

Finishing four games behind, the Pirates, who outhit the Giants .285 to .263, were undone by shaky pitching, their top man being southpaw Larry French at 18–13.

There were three other 20-game winners in the league: Chicago's Guy Bush (20–12), Boston's Ben Cantwell (20–10), and St. Louis's Dizzy Dean (20–18). On July 30, Dean fanned 17 Chicago Cubs, setting a new one-game major league record.

In the World Series it was all New York, the Giants easily beating Washington in five games, with Hubbell winning twice and giving up no earned runs in 20 innings.

1934

Detroit became in 1934 the first Western team since Cleveland in 1920 to win the American League pennant. The Tigers attributed their success (by seven games over the Yankees) to the acquisition of catcher Mickey Cochrane from the Athletics to be player-manager.

Cochrane brought to Detroit not only his insatiable winning spirit, but a .320 batting average, making him one of seven regulars who were .300 hitters on the club, which batted .300 as a unit. Along with Cochrane (the league's MVP) in the elite class were young slugger Hank Greenberg (.339), the great second baseman Charlie Gehringer (.356), third baseman Marv Owen (.317), and outfielders Gerald Walker (.300), Jo-Jo White (.313), and Goose Goslin (.305). Greenberg, one of the team's four 100-RBI men, led the league with 63 doubles.

Detroit's fine pitching staff was topped by Schoolboy Rowe (24–8), called by Gehringer "the most beautifully coordinated athlete I ever saw," and curveballer Tommy Bridges (22–11), backed by 15-game winners Eldon Auker and Fred Marberry. Of Rowe's 24 wins, 16 came in succession from June 15 to August 25, tying the league record held by Joe Wood, Walter Johnson, and Lefty Grove.

Lou Gehrig put together a Triple Crown season for the second-place Yankees, hitting 49 home runs, driving in 165 runs, and batting .363. In his final Yankees season, Babe Ruth hit 22 homers, drove in 84 runs, and batted .288. On July 13, Ruth hit his 700th home run. On February 26, 1935, he was released and signed by the Boston Braves.

The Yankees' Lefty Gomez had his greatest season, going 26–5 and leading in ERA (2.33), strikeouts (158), and shutouts (6, a tie with Cleveland's Mel Harder). Red Ruffing won 19, but after that Joe McCarthy's pitching thinned out considerably.

Cleveland had a 20-game winner in Mel Harder and received some lusty hitting from rookie first baseman Hal Trosky (35 home runs, 142 RBIs, .330 batting average)

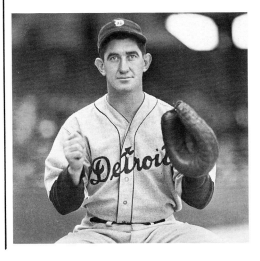

Mickey Cochrane

Paul Dean (left) and brother Dizzy.

and outfielder Joe Vosmik (.341), but still finished third under skipper Walter Johnson, whose most vehement expression, according to one player, was "Dad gum!"

There were a couple of notable hard-luck experiences in the league this year. On June 30, Gehrig hit three triples in 4½ innings against the Senators, only to have the game washed away by rain before the trailing Senators could complete their at-bats in the bottom of the fifth. And on September 16, the Browns' colorful Bobo Newsom pitched nine no-hit innings against the Red Sox, then gave up two walks and a hit in the 10th and lost, 2–1 (the other run he yielded was unearned).

The All-Star Game was played at New York's Polo Grounds on July 10, and the American League won it, 9–7, but not before Carl Hubbell made history by fanning in succession Ruth, Gehrig, Jimmie Foxx, Al Simmons, and Joe Cronin.

It was the year of the Gashouse Gang in the National League, as Frank Frisch's raucous, hard-playing Cardinals clawed, dove, and battled their way to the pennant, finishing two games ahead of the Giants. New York, in first place most of the summer, lost it on the basis of a 14–13 September, while the Cardinals rang up a 21–7 record that month.

St. Louis got 49 victories from the Dean brothers, Dizzy and Daffy. Dizzy posted a scintillating 30–7 season, which earned him the MVP Award. His 50 mound appearances included 17 in relief, during which he scored 4 of his 30 wins. Daffy (whose real name was Paul and who was as quiet and reserved as his older brother was outspoken and flamboyant) was 19–11.

Cardinals first baseman Rip Collins led the league with 35 home runs, drove in 128 runs, and batted .333, while the burgeoning young Joe Medwick batted .319 and had 106 RBIs.

The second-place Giants got a .354 year from skipper Bill Terry, .331 from outfielder Jo-Jo Moore, and .326 with a league-high 135 RBIs from Mel Ott (who tied Collins with 35 homers), and had a pair of aces in Hal Schumacher (23–10) and Hubbell (21–12), but it all fell short by two games.

Chicago's Lou Warneke was 22–10 for the Cubs, the league's only other big winner. Pittsburgh's Paul Waner was the batting champion with a .362 average, while teammate Arky Vaughan hit .333. (Vaughan batted .300 or better his first ten big-league seasons.)

On September 21, the Deans pitched a doubleheader shutout against the Dodgers in Ebbets Field, Dizzy pitching a three-hitter in the opener and Daffy a 3–0 no-hitter in the nightcap.

In a tumultuous seven-game World Series, the Cardinals emerged as world champions, with each Dean brother winning twice (as Dizzy had predicted they would). The Cardinals' 11–0 slaughter of Detroit in the final game was marked by an altercation between Medwick and Tigers' third baseman Marv Owen (Joe had made a vigorous Gashouse slide into the base), after which the irate Tigers fans bombarded Joe in left field with so much debris the game had to be halted. The fans weren't placated until Commissioner Landis had ordered Joe removed from the premises.

BASEBALL

1935

After a slow start, Mickey Cochrane's Tigers slugged their way to a second successive pennant, beating out the Yankees by three games.

Tigers first baseman Hank Greenberg hammered his way to the MVP Award with 36 home runs (tying him with Jimmie Foxx for the league lead), a mammoth 170 RBIs (Gehrig was next with 119), and .328 batting average. Charlie Gehringer batted .330 while playing the smoothest second base in the league, Pete Fox hit .321, and Cochrane .319. Once again the Tigers' good hitting was balanced by excellent pitching, with Tommy Bridges topping the staff with a 21–10 record, followed by Schoolboy Rowe (19–13) and Eldon Auker (18–7).

The Yankees bats were comparatively quiet this year, the club hitting just 104 home runs, their lowest since 1924, and scored their fewest runs (818) since 1925. Only Gehrig and George Selkirk, Ruth's successor in right field, hit with any real authority all season.

Washington second baseman Buddy Myer was the batting champion, edging out Cleveland's Joe Vosmik, .349 to .348, with Jimmie Foxx right behind at .346. Jimmie was part of an eighth-place Athletics team whose lineup featured, in addition to Foxx, outfielders Wally Moses, Bob Johnson, and Doc Cramer, whose respective batting averages were .325, .299, and .332.

The fourth-place Red Sox got big seasons from Wes Ferrell (25–14) and Lefty Grove (20–12). Always a good man with the bat, Wes batted .347 and tied George Uhle's record for pitchers with 52 hits. New Red Sox owner Tom Yawkey had shelled out $250,000 to pry shortstop Joe Cronin loose from Washington and installed him as Boston's player-manager. The season was a negative landmark of sorts for Chicago's Al Simmons; after driving in over 100 runs in every one of his 11 big-league seasons, Al slipped to 79.

Cleveland's Mel Harder was a 20-game winner again (22–11), and Chicago's Vern Kennedy pitched the league's only no-hitter, stopping Cleveland, 5–0, on August 31.

For the third year in a row, the American League won the All-Star Game, by a 4–1 score. The game was played at Cleveland Stadium on July 8.

Baseball history was made in Cincinnati on the night of May 24, when the Reds beat the Phillies, 2–1, in the first major league game played under lights. The lights had been installed at the behest of Reds general manager Larry MacPhail, despite the misgivings of most of the other clubs. In the words of Washington owner Clark Griffith, "Night baseball is a passing fad." The National League limited the Reds to just seven night games that first season. (Within 13 years every big league team, with the exception of the Cubs, had installed lights.)

The year also marked the final passage of Babe Ruth. Playing with the Braves, Ruth was hitting a feeble .181 when he retired in early June. A few days before, on May 25, Ruth had set off one final demonstration of the old Hercules when he hit three majestic home runs in Pittsburgh's Forbes Field, the 712th, 713th, and 714th of his career. Ruth ended his career with a Boston Braves team that lost 115 games, up to that time the greatest number of defeats in history.

While the Giants and Cardinals battled for the top spot most of the summer, the Cubs hung just close enough; then, in September, Charlie Grimm's team put on a sizzling 21-game winning streak and caught and passed both of their competitors, winning the pennant by four games over second-place St. Louis.

Grimm came down the stretch with a strong rotation in Bill Lee (20–6), Lon Warneke (20–13), and Larry French (17–10). The Cubs' top hitters were second baseman Billy Herman (.341 with 57 doubles), catcher Gabby Hartnett, the league's MVP (.344), third baseman Stan Hack (.311), outfielder Frank Demaree (.325), and outfielder Augie Galan (.314), who set an unbreakable record

Augie Galan

by playing in 154 games and grounding into no double plays.

The Dean brothers came close to repeating their 1934 season combined win total of 49, Dizzy going 28–12 and Paul 19–12 (a sore arm all but ended Paul's career the following year. Many National League hitters claimed the twenty-one-year-old younger Dean threw harder than his famous brother). Joe Medwick, rapidly becoming the league's most dangerous hitter, batted .353.

The Giants were third, with .300 seasons from Bill Terry, Travis Jackson, Mel Ott, and Hank Leiber, while Carl Hubbell continued to cruise through the league with a 23–12 record. Pittsburgh also had four .300 hitters in Paul and Lloyd Waner, Woody Jensen, and Arky Vaughan, who won the batting crown with a snow-capped .385 average, highest ever for a National League shortstop, an average which no National Leaguer has since exceeded. Boston's Wally Berger was the home run and RBI leader, with respective figures of 34 and 130. Cincinnati's Paul Derringer, one of the great National League pitchers of his time, was 22–13 for his sixth-place club.

In its fifth try, Detroit finally won its first World Series, defeating the Cubs in six games, winning the finale, 4–3, in the bottom of the ninth on Goose Goslin's pop fly single.

Goose Goslin

1936

It was the year of the "Golden Rookies" in the American League. The Yankees brought up a twenty-one-year-old center fielder who was being proclaimed a star before he played his first game. (He had batted .398 with San Francisco of the Pacific Coast League in 1935.) Nor did Joe DiMaggio disappoint, not in his rookie year, not ever. The new man batted .323, hit 29 home runs, and drove in 125 runs.

DiMaggio was one of five Yankees to drive in over 100 runs this year (a record). Along with Joe were Lou Gehrig (152), Bill Dickey and George Selkirk (107 each), and Tony Lazzeri (109). Dickey's .362 batting average remains the highest ever for a catcher. Gehrig, who led the league with 49 home runs, was voted Most Valuable Player. On May 24, Lazzeri hit two grand slam home runs and drove in an American League record 11 runs in the Yankees' 25–2 win over the Athletics.

Joe McCarthy's club had six .300 hitters in the lineup, with Lazzeri's .287 lowest among the regulars. With Red Ruffing going 20–12, Monte Pearson 19–7, and four others winning in double figures, the Yankees won it easily, by 19½ games over Detroit.

The defending Tigers had their problems in 1936, with slugging first baseman Hank Greenberg out virtually the entire season with a broken wrist and catcher-manager Mickey Cochrane missing over 100 games because of illness. The Tigers did get superb seasons from Charlie Gehringer (.354, 227 hits, 60 doubles), Gerald Walker (.353), Goose Goslin (.315), and a sort of last hurrah from Al Simmons, whom they had purchased from the White Sox. Al batted .327 and drove in 112 runs, one of four Tigers to drive in over 100 (the others were Gehringer, Goslin, and third baseman Marv Owen). Tommy Bridges was 23–11 for Detroit and Schoolboy Rowe 19–10.

The league's other "Golden Rookie" was Cleveland's seventeen-year-old fastballer Bob Feller, signed off the Iowa sandlots for a one-dollar bonus the year before. Deemed too precious to risk in the minor leagues, the youngster came straight to the top, being added to the roster in midseason after fanning eight Cardinals in three innings in a July exhibition game. He got into only a handful of games, winning five and losing three, but capturing the imagination of the baseball world when he fanned 17 Philadelphia Athletics on September 13, tying Dizzy Dean's major league record.

With Dickey setting an all-time high batting average for catchers, Chicago's Luke Appling did the same for shortstops with his league-leading .388 mark. (Appling was the first and thus far only White Sox player to win a batting title.) Luke had to go high to beat out Cleveland's Earl Averill, who batted .378. Earl's Cleveland teammate, first baseman Hal Trosky, pounded out his own spectacu-

Hal Trosky

lar season, hitting 42 home runs, leading with 162 RBIs, and batting .343. It was, in fact, a year of heavy hitting throughout the entire circuit, to the extent that American League pitchers were clobbered for a collective 5.04 ERA, the highest ever. On September 22, the Tigers applied the most crushing double shutout ever when they swarmed over the Browns (managed by Rogers Hornsby) by scores of 12–0 and 14–0.

Vern Kennedy was 21–9 for the White Sox, Johnny Allen 20–10 for Cleveland, and Wes Ferrell was a 20-game winner for the sixth and last time, going 20–15 for the Red Sox.

The National League finally won its first All-Star Game, beating the American League in the game played on July 7 at Braves Field, Boston.

It was a three-team race in the National League, with the Giants finally coming out on top, five games ahead of the Cubs and Cardinals, who tied for second place. Bill Terry's club owed if not all then a considerable share of their pennant to Carl Hubbell, who turned in his greatest year—26–6, including his last 16 wins in a row, from July 17 to the end of the season. It brought the screwballing left-hander his second MVP Award. Mel Ott was New York's top hitter with a league-leading 33 home runs and 135 RBIs, second to Joe Medwick's 138.

The Cubs got 18-win seasons from Larry French and Bill Lee, plus good performances from Billy Herman (.334 and for the second straight year 57 doubles) and Frank Demaree (.350), but Carl Hubbell winning 20 more games than he lost was the difference.

Dizzy Dean won 24 for the Cardinals, but the club's pitching suffered a crippling loss when a sore arm reduced Paul Dean to a 5–5 record. The Cardinals' fertile farm system turned up another gem in first baseman Johnny Mize, who broke in with a .329 batting average. Medwick, in addition to his 138 RBIs, batted .351 and set a league record with 64 doubles.

The batting champion was Pittsburgh's Paul Waner, taking his third title with a .373 average.

Dizzy Dean, who had led in strikeouts in each of his four years, yielded the crown this year to Brooklyn's high-kicking, hard-throwing right-hander Van Lingle Mungo. Pitching for a seventh-place Dodgers club (managed by Casey Stengel), Mungo was 18–19 with 238 strikeouts, highest in the league since Dazzy Vance's 262 in 1924.

Chuck Klein, reacquired by the Phillies from the Cubs, put in his most thunderous day at the office on July 10, hitting four home runs in a 10-inning victory over the Pirates at Forbes Field.

In the first all-New York World Series since 1923, the Yankees beat the Giants in six games. With all the big names in their lineup, the hitting star for the Yankees turned out to be outfielder Jake Powell, who had 10 hits and a .455 batting average. Lefty Gomez was 2–0 for the Yankees.

Jake Powell

1937

The Yankees blasted their way to a second straight pennant in 1937, with DiMaggio exceeding everything he had done in his stellar rookie season. The young Yankees center fielder hit 46 home runs (tops in the league), drove in 167 runs, and batted .346. Lou Gehrig, enjoying his last super season, hit 37 homers, drove in 159 runs, and batted .351, while Bill Dickey drove in 133 runs and batted .332. The bulwarks of Joe McCarthy's pitching staff were Lefty Gomez (21–11) and Red Ruffing (20–7) —the league's only 20-game winners—and relief pitcher Johnny Murphy.

Finishing 13 games down the road in second place was Detroit, despite some thunderous hitting of their own. Big Hank Greenberg came within one of Gehrig's league RBI record with a towering 183, Henry's hits including 40 home runs. Charlie Gehringer earned the MVP Award with the league's best batting average, .371. Along with Greenberg (.337) and Gehringer, the Tigers also received solid hitting from Pete Fox (.331), Gerald Walker (.335), and rookie catcher Rudy York, who hit 35 home runs, drove in 103 runs, and batted .307. This band of compulsive hitters tied a record set by the 1929 Phillies with four men collecting 200 or more hits: Walker (213), Gehringer (209), Fox (208), and Greenberg (200). For Gehringer it was a fifth consecutive season of 200 hits, tying the record coheld by Al Simmons and Chuck Klein.

Although the Tigers received winning pitching from Roxie Lawson (18–7) and Eldon Auker (17–9), the team suffered an irreplaceable loss when Schoolboy Rowe was forced to sit out most of the year with a sore arm. An even more grievous loss was that of the club's catcher, Mickey Cochrane. Manager Cochrane was hit in the head so severely by an errant fastball delivered by the Yankees' Bump Hadley early in the season, it ended Mickey's playing career and nearly his life.

Cleveland's Johnny Allen set a league record for winning percentage with .938, based on a 15–1 record, with all of the wins coming in a row and the lone loss on the last day of the season. Hampered by a sore arm, young Bob Feller was 9–7, but still averaged better than a strikeout an inning (150 whiffs in 149 innings), a remarkable statistic for the time.

With a .285 team batting average, the eighth-place St. Louis Browns outhit every team in the league except Detroit. The Browns had an all-.300 outfield in Beau Bell (.340), Sammy West (.328), and Joe Vosmik (.325), in addition to a hard-hitting third baseman, Harlond Clift, who hit 29 home runs, drove in 118 runs, and batted .306. But eighth place was spelled out by the pitching staff's 6.00 ERA.

Chicago's Bill Dietrich pitched the only no-hitter of the year, stopping the Browns, 8–0, on June 1.

Sammy West

The American League resumed its dominance of the National by winning the All-Star Game, 8–3, played at Washington's Griffith Stadium on July 7. The game was marked by an injury to Dizzy Dean that would soon lead to an end of his meteoric career. In the bottom of the third inning Cleveland's Earl Averill scorched a low line drive that hit Dean on the foot and broke a toe. In trying to come back too soon from the injury, Dean altered his pitching motion to try and compensate for the pain he still felt, and a few weeks later injured his arm, losing the fastball that had made him for several years the game's most celebrated pitcher and biggest drawing card. Dizzy hung on for a few more years, throwing slow curves, a slim shadow of his former self.

The National League pennant went to the Giants again in 1937, but just about every batting honor went to the Cardinals' Joe Medwick, and with them came the Most Valuable Player Award. In sweeping the Triple Crown (the last National League player to do so), the St. Louis slugger hit 31 home runs (tying Mel Ott), drove in 154 runs, and batted a hard .374. Joe also led with 111 runs, 237 hits, 56 doubles, 406 total bases, and .641 slugging average. Joe's Cardinal teammate Johnny Mize backed him up with a .364 batting average. In spite of this two-man hit parade, the Cards still finished fourth.

BASEBALL

Bill Terry's Giants won the pennant, finishing three games ahead of the Cubs, thanks to Carl Hubbell's 22–8 season and a 20–9 record by rookie left-hander Cliff Melton. The Giants didn't have anyone breaking loose with a spectacular offensive season (Ott's 95 RBIs led the club), but rather presented a solid up-and-down attack; outfielders Jimmy Ripple and Jo-Jo Moore batted .317 and .310, respectively, while shortstop Dick Bartell was at .306. Hubbell opened the season with 8 straight wins, giving him 24 in a row, dating back to July 1937, before losing to Brooklyn on May 27.

The fifth-place Boston Braves had the league's feeblest attack with a .247 average, but surprised everyone by turning up a couple of rookie 20-game winners, though they were rookies by designation only. Right-handers Lou Fette (thirty years old) and Jim Turner (thirty-three years old) had respective records of 20–10 and 20–11. Along with the Giants' Melton, it gave the league three rookie 20-game winners. None of the three ever came close to repeating their freshman success.

The Yankees continued their domination of the universe of baseball with an easy five-game victory over the Giants in the World Series, with Gomez again winning two games.

Four of 1937's 20-game winners gathering in spring training in 1938. Left to right: Red Ruffing, Jim Turner, Lefty Gomez, and Lou Fette.

1938 It was a year of memorable individual performances in both leagues. In the American League there were explosive seasons turned in by Detroit's Hank Greenberg and Boston's Jimmie Foxx, the MVP. Big Henry hit 58 home runs and drove in 146 runs, while Jimmie hit 50 long ones and drove in a man-sized 175 runs. On the last day of the season, when Greenberg was taking his final shots at Ruth's 60–home run record, he ran into a nineteen-year-old buzzsaw named Bob Feller, who fireballed his way to a new strikeout record by fanning 18 Tigers. For Feller, who whiffed 240 (highest in the league since Walter Johnson's 243 in 1913), it was the first of his seven strikeout titles (the youngster also set a major league record with 208 walks). In addition to leading in RBIs, Foxx was also on top with a .349 batting average, but his 50 homers weren't enough to give him his second Triple Crown.

The Yankees were still unbeatable, rolling to their third straight pennant, outdistancing second-place Boston by 9½ games. Joe McCarthy's big winners were Red Ruffing (21–7), Lefty Gomez (18–12), and Monte Pearson (16–7), who pitched the league's only no-hitter, a 13–0 garroting of his former Cleveland teammates on August 27.

Beginning to show the erosion of the fatal disease that was to take his life in three years, Lou Gehrig dropped to .295, with 29 home runs and 114 runs batted in. For most men, a season of pride; but for Lou Gehrig those statistics were a melancholy tolling. Joe DiMaggio drove in 140 runs, which was only good enough for third place in this year of the big RBI bruisers.

Second-place Boston batted .299, 25 points better than the Yankees (who nevertheless outscored them, 966–902). The league's meanest lineup was saturated with .300 hitters: Foxx, .349; Ben Chapman, .340; Joe Cronin, .325; Joe Vosmik, .324; Pinky Higgins, .303; Doc Cramer, .301. Higgins set a major league record with 12 consecutive hits over the course of two doubleheaders on June 19 and 21. At the age of thirty-eight, Red Sox veteran Lefty Grove slow-curved his way to a 14–4 record and eighth ERA title (3.08).

With over thirty .300 hitters, the league batted .281, a figure it has not bettered since. Cleveland had three men at .330 or more—Hal Trosky (.334), Jeff Heath (.343), and Earl Averill (.330), while Washington's keystone combination of Buddy Myer and Cecil Travis batted .336 and .335, respectively.

Bobo Newsom joined Ruffing as the league's only 20-game winners, Bobo being 20–16 for the seventh-place Browns. Chicago White Sox right-hander Monty Stratton was 15–9 and showed every indication of getting better, but that fall the twenty-six-year-old pitcher blew off his leg in a hunting accident. (Stratton was later the subject of a motion picture starring Jimmy Stewart.)

The All-Star Game, played that year at Cincinnati's Crosley Field, went to the National League, 4–1.

History was also made in the National League that year, most conspicuously by Cincinnati's talented but sometimes erratic fastballing left-hander Johnny Vander Meer. Johnny turned in one of baseball's all-time achievements by pitching successive no-hitters, on June 11 against Boston and on June 15 against the Dodgers (in the first night game at Ebbets Field). The scores were 3–0 and 6–0. With three hitless innings in his next start, Vander Meer (who was 15–10 for the season) piled up a league record 21 straight innings without giving up a hit, three under Cy Young's major league record, set in 1904.

The pennant winners were the Chicago Cubs, who continued to follow a curious every-third-year pattern, having won in 1929, 1932, 1935, and now again in 1938. It was a four-team race between the Cubs, Pirates, Giants, and Reds. With the Giants and Reds eliminated on September 25, the Cubs and Pirates squared off for a three-game shootout in Chicago on September 27, with the Pirates 1½ games in front.

Sore-armed Dizzy Dean (bought from the Cardinals that spring for $185,000) slow-balled the Cubs to a 2–1 win in the first game (Dean was just 7–1 for the year). The following day Chicago baseball history was made. With the score tied, 5–5, in the botton of the ninth and darkness setting in, catcher-manager Gabby Hartnett (who had replaced Charlie Grimm in midseason) belted a stunning game-winning home run—"The homer in the gloamin' " of National League lore—off of Pirates reliever Mace Brown. The Cubs won their tenth straight the next day, crushing the demoralized Pirates, 10–1, and went on to win the pennant, thanks to a sizzling 21–4 September.

Hartnett's aces were Bill Lee (22–9, with nine shutouts) and Clay Bryant (19–11), with Stan Hack topping the hitters with a .320 batting average. Incredibly, the top RBI man for the pennant winners was Augie Galan with just 69.

Mel Ott's 36 home runs led the league, while Joe Medwick's 122 RBIs gave him a record-tying third straight title (Cobb, Ruth, Wagner, and Hornsby had done it previously—quite a gallery to join). Cincinnati's Ernie Lombardi became only the second catcher to lead in batting, his .342 taking the title. Ernie was also voted the league's MVP. Cincinnati's rookie first baseman Frank McCormick broke in handsomely, with a league-high 209 hits and a .327 average, while teammate Paul Derringer was 21–14.

On July 4, the Phillies' 51-year tenancy at cozy, archaic Baker Bowl came to an end when they moved over to share Shibe Park with the Athletics. The Phillies also made a trade on June 13 that was to influence National League pennant races for the next few years when they dealt right-hander Bucky Walters to the Reds.

The Yankee steamroller continued its flattening pace in the World Series. McCarthy's club won an unprecedented third straight championship by beating the Cubs in four straight.

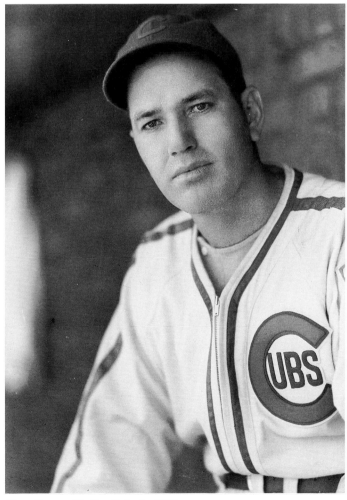

Dizzy Dean with the Cubs in 1939.

Mace Brown

1939

It was a year of triumph and sadness for the New York Yankees. Joe McCarthy's club tied the record of John McGraw's 1921–24 Giants by taking a fourth straight pennant. On May 2, however, Lou Gehrig, suffering from amyotrophic lateral sclerosis, a rare muscle-killing disease, took himself out of the starting lineup for the first time since June 2, 1925, ending his consecutive game streak at 2,130. (Gehrig died two years later, on June 2, 1941, 17 days short of his 38th birthday.)

For the fourth year in a row Red Ruffing was a 20-game winner for the Yankees (21–7). No one else won more than 13, but with the team winning 106 games, McCarthy's deep staff had records like this: Atley Donald, 13–3; Lefty Gomez, 12–8; Bump Hadley, 12–6; Monte Pearson, 12–5; Steve Sundra, 11–1; Oral Hildebrand, 10–4.

Most Valuable Player Joe DiMaggio hit his career peak of .381 (a late-season tail-off cost him a shot at .400), rookie Charlie Keller broke in at .334, while Red Rolfe, Bill Dickey, and George Selkirk all cleared .300. Rolfe set a major league record by scoring runs in 18 straight games, from August 9 through 25, scoring 30 times during that span.

Boston, a distant second (17 games out), again outhit the champs, .291 to .287, but was once again scuttled by their pitching. Lefty Grove led the staff with a 15–4 record, winning his ninth ERA title with a 2.54 mark. Jimmie Foxx's .360 batting average was second in the league to DiMaggio's .381. The Red Sox had four other plus-.300 sticks in the lineup, the most lethal of which belonged to twenty-year-old rookie Ted Williams, a stylish swinger with crushing power. Launching the 22-year career that would see him become the greatest of all hitters, Williams hit 31 home runs, drove in an all-time rookie record (and league-leading) 145 runs, and batted .327. Ted's first big-league hit was a long double in Yankee Stadium on April 20. Foxx, with 35 home runs, led the league for the fourth time.

Cleveland's Bob Feller burst forth with his first big year, the twenty-year-old fireballer going 24–9, with 246 strikeouts. Other 20-game winners were Washington's Dutch Leonard (20–8), and Bobo Newsom (20–11), who split his season between the Browns and the Tigers.

On May 16, the Athletics entertained the Indians under the newly installed Shibe Park lights for the first night game in American League history.

The All-Star Game was played at Yankee Stadium that year, with the American League winning, 3–1.

The Cincinnati Reds, behind the spectacular pitching of ace right-handers Paul Derringer and Bucky Walters, won their first pennant since 1919. Walters (the league's

Ted Williams

MVP), a converted infielder, was 27–11, while Derringer was 25–7 for skipper Bill McKechnie, who won a pennant with his third different team (Bill previously had won with the Pirates and Cardinals). A manager who was known as the epitome of conservatism, McKechnie's team was built primarily on pitching and defense, though the Reds did have some rugged hitting from Ernie Lombardi, Ival Goodman (.323), and sophomore Frank McCormick (.332), who made it two-for-two in leading the league in hits (209) and also led in RBIs (128), ending Joe Medwick's three-year reign as RBI leader. (Joe was second with 117.)

The Cardinals, in second place 4½ games out, had the home run (28) and batting leader (.349) in first baseman Johnny Mize. Right-hander Curt Davis was 22–16 for St. Louis. Third-place Brooklyn, coming to life under freshman manager Leo Durocher after six years of door-mat status, had a surprise 20-game winner in veteran right-hander Luke Hamlin (20–13). The defending champion Cubs finished fourth, the first time since 1927 they had come in that low.

The fifth-place Giants had an inning of explosive glory on June 6. In the fourth inning of a 17–3 mauling of the Reds, the New Yorkers set a record when Harry Danning, Frank Demaree, Burgess Whitehead, pitcher Manny Salvo, and Jo-Jo Moore all hit home runs.

A significant event occurred on August 26 at Brooklyn's Ebbets Field when NBC-TV set up its cameras and for the first time televised a major league game (between Brooklyn and Cincinnati). The broadcast, to the handful of television receivers then in use, covered a radius of about 50 miles.

The Yankees made it two straight October sweeps by burying the Reds in four straight. It was New York's fourth successive world championship, extending the record they had established the year before. This "unbreakable" record would last for 14 years.

Lefty Grove

Mule Haas, center fielder on Connie Mack's pennant-winning Athletics of 1929–31. A 12-year major leaguer who split his time between the A's and White Sox from 1928–38, Mule batted .292 lifetime.

A rather informal contract signing. George Earnshaw is using skipper Connie Mack's shoulder as a desk. Bearing witness is Rube Walberg. The impromptu signing took place in Savannah, Georgia, in the early 1930s as the club was on its way to spring training. Earnshaw pitched from 1928–36 and had a 127–93 record; Walberg pitched from 1923–37, with a 155–141 record.

Al Simmons. A teammate said of him, "He loathed opposing pitchers. He considered them his mortal enemies."

Lou Gehrig at bat in spring training 1930.

Sixteen years in the big leagues (1921–36) added up to a .312 career average for Bing Miller. One of the stars of the 1929–31 Athletics, he also played for the Senators, Browns, and Red Sox.

Rick Ferrell, one of the American League's solid catchers from 1929–45 and 1947, working for the Browns, Red Sox, and Senators, batting .281. He formed a family battery with his brother Wes in both Boston and Washington.

Hack Wilson's super season in 1930 evidently led to some endorsements.

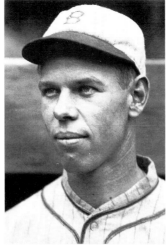

In his heyday in the early 1930s, left-hander Wild Bill Hallahan threw as hard as anybody. Bill pitched from 1925–26 and 1929–38, spending the bulk of his time with the Cardinals. Lifetime record: 102–94.

Babe Herman, a genuine buster. He hit .381 and .393 in back-to-back seasons for the Dodgers in 1929–30. He came up in 1926 and played for five clubs until 1937, then came back briefly as a pinch-hitter for the Dodgers in 1945. He batted .324 lifetime.

A couple of veteran Philadelphia pitchers meeting in the spring of 1930. The Athletics' forty-seven-year-old Jack Quinn (left) is talking with the Phillies' forty-three-year-old Grover Cleveland Alexander. Quinn, whose big league career began in 1909, pitched until 1933, minus a few years in the minors and in the Federal League. His major league record is 212–181. He pitched for seven teams.

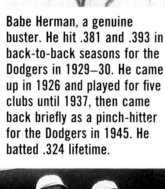

A quartet of Phillies in the Baker Bowl sunshine in 1930. Left to right: Chuck Klein, Don Hurst, Spud Davis, and Pinky Whitney.

A couple of distinguished visitors at Chicago's Wrigley Field. Left to right: Cubs coach Jimmy Burke, Ring Lardner, George M. Cohan, and Cubs manager Joe McCarthy.

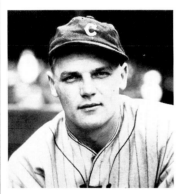

Joe Vosmik. Joe was a premier hitter for the Indians from 1930–36. He later played for the Browns, Red Sox, Dodgers, and Senators, retiring in 1944 with a .307 average. He led the American League in hits in 1935 and 1938.

The ebullient Pepper Martin. He played outfield and third base for the Cardinals throughout the 1930s. Hero of the 1931 World Series, Pepper led the league in stolen bases three times. He batted .298 lifetime.

One of the American League's top sluggers, Earl Averill played from 1929–41, most all of it for Cleveland, for whom he hit over .300 eight times, peaking at .378 in 1936, a year he led with 232 hits. He batted .318 lifetime.

Earl Webb played for five clubs in a seven-year career that was undistinguished except for his 1931 season with the Red Sox—the year he hit an all-time record 67 doubles. He retired in 1933 with a .306 average.

After failing as a pitcher with the Yankees and Red Sox in the early 1920s, Lefty O'Doul came back as an outfielder with the Giants, Phillies, and Dodgers from 1928–34. Twice the National League batting champion, he batted a towering .349 over his relatively short career.

Dick Bartell, top-flight shortstop from 1927–43 and 1946, playing for the Pirates, Phillies, Giants, Cubs, and Tigers. Lifetime average: .284.

Babe Ruth in 1932.

Jimmie Foxx and the trophy he received for being the American League's Most Valuable Player in 1932.

Billy Herman, one of the finest second basemen of all time. He played with the Cubs, Dodgers, Braves, and Pirates from 1931–43 and 1946–47. He had his best years with the Cubs in the 1930s. Seven times a .300 hitter, he batted .304 lifetime.

Bill Jurges, National League shortstop from 1931–47, playing for the Cubs and Giants, batting .258.

Third baseman on Chicago Cub pennant winners in 1932, 1935, 1938, and 1945, Stan Hack was one of the most consistent players of his era. Playing from 1932–47, he compiled a batting average of .301.

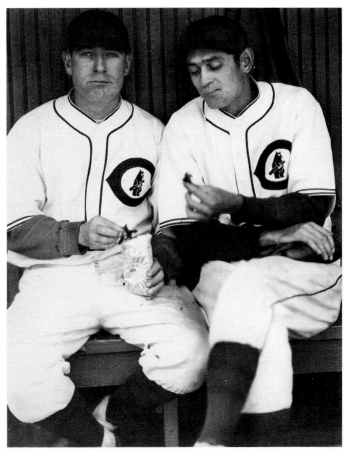

Cubs right-handers Charlie Root (left) and Guy Bush sharing a chaw. Charlie pitched for the Browns in 1923, then for the Cubs from 1926–41, retiring with a 201–160 record. A longtime Cubs pitcher, Bush pitched for five teams overall, from 1923–38 and 1945, winning 176 and losing 136.

It's opening day at the Polo Grounds, April 12, 1932, and the Giants' Travis Jackson and the Phillies' Pinky Whitney are starting it off with a handshake. Pinky was with the Phillies and Braves from 1928–39, batting .295.

A couple of New York sluggers meeting in 1933: Mel Ott of the Giants and Babe Ruth. Ott played for the Giants from 1926–47, managing the club from 1942–48. Six times the league home run champ, he hit 511 career shots, batting .304.

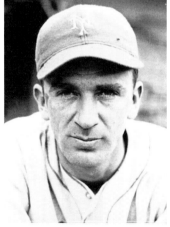

Mel Ott

Paul Waner

One of the National League's ace pitchers in the 1930s, Lon Warneke pitched for the Cubs and Cardinals from 1930–43 and 1945. Three times a 20-game winner for the Cubs, he was 193–121 lifetime.

Carl Hubbell, one of the greatest left-handers in history. "King" Carl spent his entire career with the Giants (1928–43), winning 253 and losing 154.

Longtime National League catcher Gus Mancuso. Gus was behind the plate for five teams, getting into World Series with the Cardinals in 1930–31 and Giants in 1933 and 1936–37. Lifetime average: .265.

Buddy Myer, a gifted second baseman with the Senators and Red Sox from 1925–41. Playing all but two of those years with the Senators, Buddy, the American League batting champion in 1935, batted over .300 nine times and .303 overall.

Earl Whitehill, a classy south-paw with the Tigers, Senators, Indians, and Cubs from 1923–39. Lifetime record: 218–185.

Joe Kuhel played over 2,000 games at first base for the Senators and White Sox from 1930–47, batting .277.

Some infield byplay in the 1933 World Series. Washington short-stop Joe Cronin is firing on to first to complete a double play in the eighth inning of the fifth and final game. The base runner is the Giants' Kiddo Davis. Second baseman Buddy Myer is watch-ing the action and umpire Charlie Pfirman is making the call.

Giants outfielder Jo-Jo Moore. Jo-Jo played for the Giants from 1930–41, batting .298.

Dizzy Dean. His prime years were few but memorable. Life-time record: 150–83.

Bill Terry, generally regarded as the greatest of National League first basemen. He spent his entire career (1923–36) with the Giants, whom he also managed from 1932–41. The last National Leaguer to bat .400 (.401 in 1930), he hit over .300 11 times and a re-sounding .341 lifetime.

RIGHT: Guess who's pitching the final game of the 1933 season for the Yankees? It's that old southpaw Babe Ruth. The Babe won it, 6–5, pitching a 12-hitter and going the full nine. The victory completed his pitch-ing record at 94–46. The bat-ter is Boston's Smead Jolley.

Chuck Klein, a premier National League bopper from 1928–44. His best years were with the Phillies from 1928–33, during which he had 200 or more hits five straight times. He batted .320 lifetime.

Gerald "Gee" Walker, outfielder with five clubs in both leagues from 1931–45. Walker had his best years with Detroit in the 1930s, including a .353 average in 1936. He was a .294 lifetime hitter.

Chuck Klein teeing off in the first inning of the 1933 All-Star Game. The catcher is Rick Ferrell. The umpire is Bill Dinneen.

Detroit manager Mickey Cochrane (left) and pitcher Schoolboy Rowe. A Tiger ace in the 1930s, Rowe later pitched for the Dodgers and Phillies, retiring in 1949 with a career mark of 158–101.

Two all-time catching greats at the 1933 All-Star Game, the Yankees' Bill Dickey (left) and the Cubs' Gabby Hartnett. Dickey played for the Yankees from 1928–43 and 1946, batting .313. Hartnett caught for the Cubs from 1922–40, finishing up with the Giants in 1941. His throwing arm was so strong that fans would come out to watch him in pregame drills. He batted .297 for his career.

Ripper Collins, first baseman on the 1934 Cardinals pennant winners. Rip came up in 1931, played nine years for the Cardinals, Cubs, and Pirates, and batted .296.

"Indian" Bob Johnson, an outfielder who lathered the ball for Connie Mack's A's in the 1930s. He came up in 1933 and was with the A's until 1942, then played for the Senators and Red Sox until 1945. A .296 lifetime batter, he drove in over 100 runs for seven straight seasons (1935–41).

Right-hander Mel Harder spent 20 years (1928–47) with Cleveland, winning 223 and losing 186.

The funeral of John McGraw in late February 1934, outside New York's St. Patrick's Cathedral.

Detroit's Hank Greenberg. One of the great power hitters in baseball annals, Big Henry played one game in 1930 and from 1933–41 and 1945–47, the last year for Pittsburgh. Four times the American League home run leader, Hank batted .313 lifetime.

Dizzy Dean, Damon Runyon, Will Rogers, and Mrs. Dean at dinner during the 1934 World Series.

Right-hander Eldon Auker, who pitched for the Tigers from 1933–38 and then for the Red Sox and Browns, retiring in 1942 with a 130–101 record.

RIGHT: Bill Werber, third baseman with the Yankees, Red Sox, Athletics, Reds, and Giants. An 11-year veteran who retired in 1942, Billy led the American League in stolen bases three times and had a career batting average of .271.

Joe Medwick

LEFT: Frankie Frisch, player-manager of the Gashouse Gang.

Curveballer Tommy Bridges, one of the mainstays of the Tigers pitching staff from 1930–43 and 1945–46. The three-time 20-game winner was 194–138 in the big leagues.

Zeke Bonura's sluggish fielding made him, one contemporary said, "a conversation piece." But there were no jokes about Zeke's hitting. Playing for four clubs in both leagues from 1934–40, he batted .307, with a .345 high for the White Sox in 1937.

Pepper Martin heading for first base the Pepper Martin way.

Charlie Gehringer, Detroit's near-flawless second baseman from 1924–42, whose consistent high-caliber excellence earned him the nickname "The Mechanical Man." Thirteen times a .300 hitter (he was the batting champion in 1937), seven times with over 200 hits, he was a lifetime .320 batter.

RIGHT: Bill Lee, right-handed ace on the 1935 and 1938 Chicago Cubs pennant winners. Lee pitched from 1934–47, working for the Cubs, Phillies, and Braves. Lifetime record: 169–157.

"Just a good ole hitter," was one teammate's description of Rip Radcliff. Rip was in the outfield for the White Sox, Browns, and Tigers from 1934–43, batting .311.

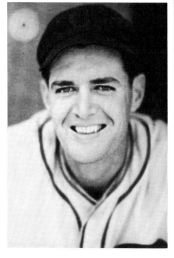

Joe Medwick sliding into Detroit's Marv Owen in the seventh game of the 1934 World Series. Joe's aggressiveness provoked a memorable brawl.

Hank Greenberg tying into one.

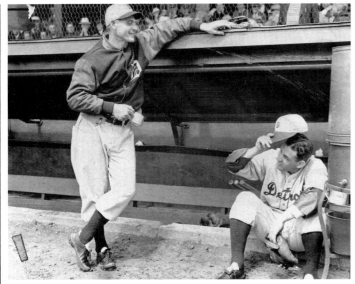

Tigers outfielder Pete Fox (left) demonstrating the fine art of squirting water through one's teeth. The man trying to avoid the shower is Charlie Gehringer. A steady man at bat, Pete played for the Tigers and Red Sox from 1933–45, batting .298.

Joe Medwick making contact. The National League's top hitter in the 1930s, Joe came up with the Cardinals in 1932, was traded to Brooklyn in 1940 and later played for the Giants and Braves. A .300 hitter in all but 3 of his 17 seasons (1932–48), Joe batted .324 lifetime. He had over 220 hits three straight seasons (1935–37).

RIGHT: "You mark him down for .300 on the first day of spring training and forget about it." That was White Sox manager Jimmy Dykes talking about his shortstop Luke Appling. Luke played for the White Sox from 1930–50, with one year out for military service. Twice the league batting champion, with a .388 high in 1936, Luke batted .300 in 14 of his 17 full seasons, averaging .310 for his career.

Cecil Travis, Washington's sharp-hitting shortstop in the 1930s and early '40s, when military service interrupted his career. Seven times a .300 hitter, with a high of .359 in 1941, Travis retired in 1947 with a .314 average.

Arky Vaughan, one of the great shortstops of all time. He joined the Pirates in 1932 and hit over .300 his first ten years, peaking with a .385 batting title in 1935. He was traded to Brooklyn in 1942 and retired in 1947 with a .318 career average. He was out of baseball from 1944–46.

A classy left-hander for the Pirates, Cubs, and Dodgers from 1929–42, Larry French was a steady winner, retiring with a 197–171 record.

Known equally for his withering line drives and slowness afoot, Ernie Lombardi caught for Brooklyn, Cincinnati (ten years), Boston, and New York in the National League. One of the great hitting catchers of all time, he batted over .300 ten times, won two batting championships, and had a lifetime average of .306. He played from 1931–47.

LEFT: Monte Pearson pitched for Cleveland and the Yankees from 1932–40, finishing up with Cincinnati a year later. The right-hander was 100–61 lifetime.

Wally Berger (left) and Babe Ruth of the Boston Braves in 1935, as Ruth's career was winding down. Wally played for four teams from 1930–40, batting an even .300.

Five American League managers sharing a laugh at the 1936 winter meetings. Sitting left to right: New York's Joe McCarthy, Boston's Joe Cronin, and Detroit's Mickey Cochrane. Standing left to right: Chicago's Jimmy Dykes and Washington's Bucky Harris.

Joe DiMaggio's Yankees debut on May 3, 1936. He had been delayed by an injury.

Van Lingle Mungo, Brooklyn's big fastballer of the 1930s. Mungo pitched for the Dodgers from 1931–41, then for the Giants, winding up in 1945. Lifetime record: 120–115.

BELOW: Beau Bell, who had a couple of hot seasons for the Browns in 1936 and 1937, batting .344 and .340. Beau's career was short; he played for the Browns, Tigers, and Indians from 1935–41, averaging .297.

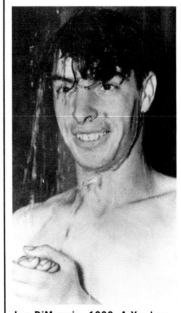

Gus Suhr, Pirates first baseman from 1930–39, finishing up with the Phillies in 1940. At one point he played in 822 consecutive games, which for a time was the National League record. He was a lifetime .279 hitter.

Joe DiMaggio, 1936. A Yankee from 1936–42 and 1946–51, Joe batted over .300 eleven times, drove in over 100 runs nine times, and batted .325.

A hard-hitting third baseman, Harlond Clift starred for the Browns from 1934–43, then finished up with the Senators in 1944–45. Lifetime average: .272.

Baseball's one and only prodigy: Mr. Robert William Andrew Feller, seventeen-year-old fastballer of the Cleveland Indians in 1936. He pitched for Cleveland from 1936–56, with the better part of four seasons out for military service. Six times a 20-game winner and seven times the strikeout champ, his lifetime record is 266–162.

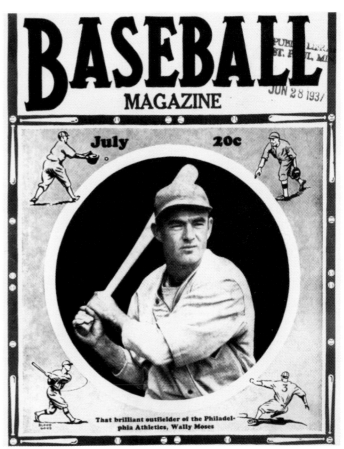

That brilliant outfielder of the Philadelphia Athletics, Wally Moses

Wally Moses's steady hitting earned him a place on the cover of the July 1937 issue of *Baseball Magazine*. Wally came up with the Athletics in 1935 and was a .300 hitter for his first seven years. He later played for the White Sox and Red Sox, retiring in 1951 with a career average of .291.

Harry Danning, New York Giants catcher from 1933–42. Lifetime average: .285.

BELOW: Monty Stratton, White Sox right-hander whose career ended when he lost a leg in a hunting accident. Pitching from 1934–38, he logged a 36–23 record.

A Yankees ace from 1930–42, Lefty Gomez was a four-time 20-game winner and was a perfect 6–0 in World Series competition. Lifetime he stands 189–102.

After the 1936 season, Bob Feller returned home to graduate from high school in Van Meter, Iowa. The population of Van Meter at that time was 450.

Young Joe DiMaggio in 1937, prepared to enjoy the bright lights of New York.

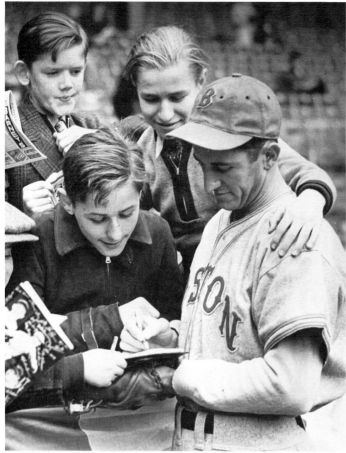

Braves catcher Al Lopez obliging some young fans at the Polo Grounds in 1936. Al came to the big leagues in 1928 and caught for the Dodgers, Braves, Pirates, and Indians, retiring in 1947. His 1,918 games behind the plate was the major league record until broken by Bob Boone in 1987. A lifetime .261 hitter, Al later managed the Indians and White Sox.

A couple of handsomely turned out Chicago Cubs en route to spring training in February 1936. That's Charlie Grimm on the left, and Gabby Hartnett.

Carl Hubbell (left) and Lou Gehrig during the all—New York 1936 World Series.

Johnny Mize, first baseman with the Cardinals, Giants, and Yankees from 1936–42 and 1946–53. Big John hit over .300 his first nine years in the major leagues and .312 lifetime. He was the National League home run leader four times and drove in over 100 runs eight times.

Third baseman Red Rolfe, a key man on six Yankees pennant winners. Red played from 1934–42, batting .289.

The Yankees' George Selkirk, who had the unenviable job of replacing Babe Ruth in right field. George played from 1934–42, hit .300 five times and .290 overall.

One of the top batteries in Yankee history: Bill Dickey (left) and Lefty Gomez.

Cliff Melton, the New York Giants' 20-game-winning rookie southpaw in 1937. He pitched for the Giants until 1944, retiring with a 86–80 record.

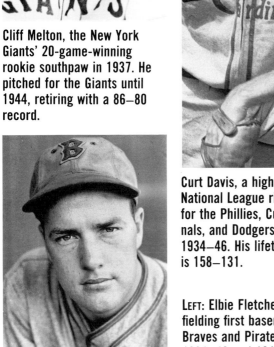

Curt Davis, a highly efficient National League right-hander for the Phillies, Cubs, Cardinals, and Dodgers from 1934–46. His lifetime record is 158–131.

LEFT: Elbie Fletcher, slick-fielding first baseman with the Braves and Pirates from 1934–43 and 1946–48. Lifetime average: .271.

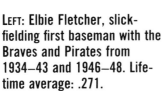

Lou Gehrig

A quintet of New York Giants passing the time during some old-fashioned travel. Riding in a Pullman compartment in this 1937 picture are (left to right) shortstop Blondy Ryan, pitcher Hal Schumacher, infielder Mickey Haslin, pitcher Harry Gumbert, and pitcher Cliff Melton.

Three rather studious-looking St. Louis Cardinals. Left to right: Pepper Martin, catcher Mickey Owen, and Lon Warneke.

Jimmie Foxx (left) and Joe Cronin. Cronin, one of the heaviest-hitting shortstops in baseball history, came to the majors with the Pirates in 1926, joined the Senators in 1928, and was sold to the Boston Red Sox in 1935, playing until 1945. He drove in over 100 runs eight times and batted .301 for his 20-year career. He was a player-manager from 1933–45 and was later president of the American League.

Pinky Higgins getting his record-making twelfth straight hit on June 21, 1938. A third baseman, Pinky came up with the Athletics and played for the Red Sox and Tigers, retiring in 1946 with a .292 lifetime average.

RIGHT: Taft Wright played nine years in the bigs and hit over .300 in six of them, compiling a .311 career average. He came up with the Senators in 1938, playing later for the White Sox and A's.

LEFT: A couple of 1938's golden boys meeting at the All-Star Game: Bob Feller (left) and Johnny Vander Meer.

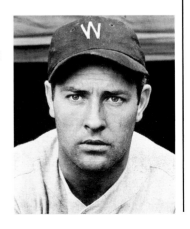

Right-hander Bobo Newsom, who came up to the majors with the Dodgers in 1929 and then followed the most tangled course in baseball history: Cubs, Browns, Senators, Red Sox, Browns, Tigers, Senators, Dodgers, Browns, Senators, Athletics, Senators, Yankees, Giants, Senators, Athletics. The Senators kept reacquiring him, it was said, because owner Clark Griffith enjoyed Bobo's pinochle game. Rubber-armed ("Rubber-headed, too," said one teammate), Bobo finally retired in 1953 with a 211–222 record.

LEFT: Joe Cronin, Jimmie Foxx, Lefty Grove, and Doc Cramer (left to right) of the Boston Red Sox in 1938. Cramer played in the American League for 20 years (1929–48), appearing for the Athletics, Red Sox, Senators, and Tigers, batting .296.

Jeff Heath, a 14-year major-league outfielder for the Indians, Senators, Browns, and Braves from 1936–49. He was a .293 lifetime hitter.

Joe DiMaggio in 1939.

Jimmie Foxx (left) and young Detroit slugger Rudy York. Rudy came up in 1937 and slugged them out of American League ball yards until 1948, playing for the Tigers, Red Sox, White Sox, and Athletics, leaving behind a .275 career average.

A trio of relaxed Cleveland Indians in 1938. Left to right: infielder Odell Hale, catcher Rollie Hemsley, and pitcher Johnny Allen. Hale batted .289 over a 10-year career, Hemsley caught in the big leagues for seven clubs in a 19-year career, and Allen was a hot-tempered right-hander who pitched for five teams in a 13-year career, compiling a fine 142–75 record.

Johnny Vander Meer, who made baseball history in June 1938. The fastballing lefty came up with the Reds in 1937 and pitched in the big leagues until 1951 (with two years out during World War II), finishing up with the Cubs and Indians. Three times the strikeout leader, he had a lifetime record of 119–121.

A converted infielder, Bucky Walters went on to become the National League's top pitcher. He led the league in ERA in Cincinnati's pennant-winning years of 1939–40 and was a three-time 20-game winner. He broke in as an infielder with the Braves in 1931 and played some infield for the Red Sox and Phillies, who began converting him to the mound in 1934. He joined Cincinnati in 1938 and finished his career in 1950. Lifetime record: 198–160.

Dodgers manager Burleigh Grimes, coach Babe Ruth, and shortstop Leo Durocher in 1938. Babe was primarily a batting practice attraction. Leo, a 17-year major leaguer with a .247 batting average, took over as Dodgers manager in 1939. He later managed the Giants, Cubs, and Astros.

RIGHT: Frank McCormick, crack first baseman for Cincinnati's 1939–40 pennant winners. Frank played in 1934 and from 1937–48, putting in his prime years with the Reds. He also played for the Phillies and Braves, finishing with a .299 average.

One of the National League's ace pitchers from 1931–45, Paul Derringer pitched for the Cardinals, Reds, and Cubs. A four-time 20-game winner, he was 223–212 lifetime.

Johnny Vander Meer at work at Ebbets Field on the night of June 15, 1938. It was the occasion of Vander Meer's second consecutive no-hitter and the first night game ever played in Ebbets Field.

Lou Gehrig Appreciation Day at Yankee Stadium on July 4, 1939.

Ted Williams

1940

The New York Yankees didn't make it five in a row in 1940, but they came close, as the American League put on a fascinating three-way pennant race. The Yankees, sunk in the basement in May, made a strong recovery and finished third, two games out. Cleveland was second, one game behind the pennant-winning Tigers.

Del Baker's Tigers featured strong hitting and just enough pitching—Bobo Newsom was 21–5 and Schoolboy Rowe 16–3. The hitting came from a tough lineup headed by MVP Hank Greenberg, who led the league with 41 home runs and 150 RBIs, while batting .340; young outfielder Barney McCosky, who matched Big Henry's .340; powerful first baseman Rudy York, who hit 33 home runs, drove in 134 runs, and batted .316; and the great veteran Charlie Gehringer (.313).

Second-place Cleveland had Bob Feller, who turned in a herculean 27–11 season, leading in strikeouts with 261 (almost 100 more than runner-up Newsom), and starting the season with baseball's only opening day no-hitter, a 1–0 smothering of the White Sox. The Indians introduced a sparkling new player to the league in shortstop Lou Boudreau, who batted .295 and drove in 101 runs.

The Indians broke out in midseason rebellion against their manager Oscar Vitt. The players demanded that ownership fire the unpopular Vitt and hire another manager, but the front office refused. The episode led to the team being labeled "The Crybabies" and, in the opinion of some, the smoldering dissension ended up costing the Indians the pennant.

The third-place Yankees dropped 28 points in team batting average (to .259, lowest since the 1918 club) and scored 150 fewer runs. The Bronx Bombers were dropping lower-yield shells this year —even though they did lead in home runs with 155—with DiMaggio the only regular player clearing the .300 mark with a league-leading .352. Chicago's steady-as-the-rain Luke Appling was second with .348 and Ted Williams third with .344. Ted was one of four Boston hitters to drive in over 100 runs (the others were Jimmie Foxx, Joe Cronin, and Bobby Doerr). Jimmie also hit his 500th home run, on September 22.

The National League won the All-Star Game, 4–0, played at St. Louis's Sportsman's Park on July 9.

The Brooklyn Dodgers opened the season with nine straight wins, climaxed by a no-hitter from Tex Carleton over the Reds on April 30, 3–0. Soon after, how-

1940-
War
and Revolution
1949

Hank Greenberg (left) and Barney McCosky.

1941

In 1941, the last of the pre-war seasons, history, baseball style, was made, as two of the game's imperishable figures cast their shadows deep into the future.

It was the year of Joe DiMaggio's 56-game hitting streak and Ted Williams's .406 batting average. For DiMaggio it was a midseason festival as he put together his wondrous cable of continuity, hitting safely in every Yankee game from May 15 until the night of July 17, in Cleveland, when he was finally brought down by a combination of pitchers Al Smith and Jim Bagby Jr. and some flashy glovework by third baseman Ken Keltner, who intercepted a pair of DiMaggio scorchers.

For Williams it was a season-long odyssey across the mutinous seas and over the high tors to the magical realm of .400. Batting .405 at the All-Star break, the Red Sox' strong, slender hitting genius finished at .406, with wholly fitting last-day dramatics. Batting .3995 on the final day, with a doubleheader scheduled against the Athletics, Wil-

ever, the Reds began a drive that eventually carried them to the pennant, coasting in 12 games ahead of Brooklyn.

Bill McKechnie's repeaters again featured the pitching of Bucky Walters (22–10) and Paul Derringer (20–12). First baseman Frank McCormick led the league in hits (191) for the third year in a row, batting .309, driving in 127 runs, and winning the MVP Award.

Second-place Brooklyn coaxed a 16–2 year out of veteran knuckleballer Freddy Fitzsimmons and received some solid hitting from first baseman Dolph Camilli and outfielder Dixie Walker, the latter salvaged from the American League scrap heap, as was pitcher Whitlow Wyatt (15–14). With general manager Larry MacPhail spending furiously to try and build a winner, the Dodgers acquired Joe Medwick from the Cardinals in a deal involving players and $100,000 in Brooklyn money. The deal was consummated on June 12; a week later Cardinal pitcher Bob Bowman beaned Medwick at the plate in Ebbets Field so severely that Joe was never the same player again. It was believed—on the Brooklyn side anyway—that the beaning had been less than accidental; indeed, the volatile MacPhail tried to have Bowman thrown out of baseball, a demand that league president Ford Frick ignored.

The Cardinals' Johnny Mize led in home runs with 43 and runs batted in with 137, while Pittsburgh's Debs Garms won the batting crown with a .355 average. Cubs right-hander Claude Passeau was 20–13, the only other pitcher besides Walters and Derringer to win 20.

The Cincinnati victory was tempered by an episode of deep sadness and tragedy. On August 3, reserve catcher Willard Hershberger committed suicide, slashing his throat in a Boston hotel room. No one ever knew why the thirty-year-old Hershberger took his life.

In a hard-fought World Series, the Reds defeated the Tigers in seven games, with Walters and Derringer running true to form and winning two games apiece.

Ken Keltner

liams refused to sit it out, went on and played both games, got a stinging six-for-eight, and inscribed his enthralling .406, a beacon for all subsequent batters to aspire to.

When *56* was weighed against *.406* in the MVP voting, the streak tipped the scales in DiMaggio's favor, and the Yankee won the award.

There was also a pennant race in the American League, though not a very suspenseful one. The Yankees clinched on September 4—the earliest date in history—and finished 17 games ahead of the Red Sox, who led the league in batting for the fourth straight year and still had no cigars to show for it. DiMaggio batted .357, third in the league to ".406" and Washington's Cecil Travis's .359. Joe D. was the RBI leader with 125 and struck out just 13 times in 541 at bats, a remarkable statistic for a power hitter. Joe McCarthy won his pennant with Lefty Gomez and Red Ruffing his top winners at 15 apiece.

In addition to his regal batting average, Williams led with 37 home runs and .735 slugging average, which no one in either league has topped since. Ted's teammate Jimmie Foxx had his last productive season, driving in 105 runs, giving him 13 straight years of over 100 RBIs, tying him with Gehrig for the major league record. There was also a landmark moment for another Red Sox glory name: on July 25 Lefty Grove won his 300th and final big league game, struggling to a 10–6 win over Cleveland.

The first wave of the concussive turmoil of the European war reached baseball when Detroit's Hank Greenberg left for military service after just 19 games. (The first big leaguer to go into service was Philadelphia Phillies right-hander Hugh Mulcahy.)

It was a big year for Cleveland's Jeff Heath, with 32 doubles, 20 triples, 24 home runs, 123 RBIs, and a .340 batting average. Teammate Bob Feller remained the league's top pitcher with a 25–13 record, including 260 strikeouts. The only other 20-game winner was White Sox left-hander Thornton Lee at 22–11.

The All-Star Game, played at Detroit's Briggs Stadium on July 8, remains one of the most memorable in history. The American League won it, 7–5, on Williams's three-run homer in the bottom of the ninth.

Spending lavishly and trading shrewdly, Larry MacPhail had put together in Brooklyn a blend of youth and experience good enough to win the Dodgers' first pennant since 1920. Brooklyn's big gun was MVP first baseman Dolph Camilli, who led the league with 34 home runs and 120 runs batted in. In twenty-two-year-old center fielder Pete Reiser, playing his first full major league season, the Dodgers had the batting champion (.343). Leo Durocher's team also had the league's only 20-game winners in right-handers Whitlow Wyatt (22–10) and Kirby Higbe (22–9).

The Dodgers were on top of their game all summer,

Ted Williams (left) and Joe DiMaggio moments after Ted's game-winning home run in the 1941 All-Star Game.

and they had to be to beat out a spirited Cardinal team that won 97 games and finished 2½ behind. The Cards had four .300 hitters in Johnny Mize, Jimmy Brown, Enos Slaughter, and Johnny Hopp, while at the end of the season they brought up young outfielder Stan Musial, threw him into the end of a grueling pennant race, and saw the twenty-year-old rookie hit .426 in 12 games. The Cardinals' veteran right-hander Lon Warneke pitched the major leagues' only no-hitter that year, stopping the Cincinnati Reds, 2–0, on August 30.

The Reds, noted for their good pitching during these years, came up with another winner in right-hander Elmer Riddle, who was 19–4 and led the league in ERA (2.24).

In the World Series, the Yankees, who had won seven times in seven outings since 1927, made it eight straight with a four-games-to-one win over the Dodgers. The heart went out of the Dodgers in game 4. Trailing in games, 2–1, Durocher's team took a 4–3 lead into the top of the ninth inning, only to lose it and the game when catcher Mickey Owen missed a third strike with two out and nobody on base, after which the Yankees scored four runs and won the game, 7–4.

1942

Joe McCarthy's Yankees took another smoothly paved highway to the pennant, winning 103 games and finishing nine ahead of the Red Sox, who were pulling their fourth second-place finish in five years.

The Yankees had the MVP in second baseman Joe Gordon, who hit 18 home runs, drove in 103 runs, and batted .322. The Yanks also had the league's top pitcher in forkballer Ernie Bonham (21–5) and other high-percentage winners in Spud Chandler (16–5) and Hank Borowy (15–4).

The Red Sox had a Triple Crown winner in Ted Williams, who hit 36 home runs, drove in 137 runs, and batted .356. (Ted's failure to win the MVP Award is probably the most conspicuous example of wrong-headed voting in the history of the award.) Shortstop Johnny Pesky broke in with the Red Sox and led the league with 205 hits, batting .331. Boston also had the league's other 20-game winner in right-hander Tex Hughson, 22–6. Hughson and Washington's Bobo Newsom tied for the league strikeout lead with 113 apiece, the lowest for a leader in major league history. (Bob Feller, who would have had that amount by the Fourth of July, had enlisted in the Navy.)

The White Sox' forty-one-year-old Ted Lyons turned in a season of remarkable efficiency: 20 starts, 20 complete games, a 14–6 record, and a league-low 2.10 ERA. Then when the season was over, he joined the Marines.

The All-Star Game, played at New York's Polo Grounds on July 6, was won by the American League, 3–1.

In the National League, Leo Durocher's Dodgers were breezing along with a 10½-game lead in mid-August when general manager Larry MacPhail accused them of complacency and overconfidence. MacPhail had been watching Billy Southworth's Cardinals scratching and hustling for every base, every run, every game. "They haven't quit," MacPhail warned his team, "and they won't quit."

Putting on one of the most relentless charges in baseball history, the Cardinals won 43 of their last 51 games, including 21 of 26 in September, finally catching and passing the Dodgers, who won 104 games but finished second to the Cards, who won 106.

Southworth had a pair of 20-game winners in MVP Mort Cooper (22–7) and rookie Johnny Beazley (21–6). For Cooper it was a scintillating season, as he pitched 10 shutouts and posted the lowest ERA, 1.78. The 1942 Cardinals were a classic case of baseball homogeneity—every man on the club with the exception of veteran pitcher Harry Gumbert was a graduate of the St. Louis farm system, which had been built and nurtured by Branch Rickey, who would soon move on to Brooklyn, where he would build another farm system and also make a bit of history.

The Cardinals, who played as an interlocking unit as

Johnny Pesky

Johnny Beazley

few teams ever have, had their top hitter in Enos Slaughter, who batted .318, followed by young Stan Musial at .315. Shortstop Marty Marion and center fielder Terry Moore provided some of the best defense ever seen in the National League.

Johnny Mize, whom the Cardinals had dealt to the Giants, led in RBIs with 110, lowest for a league leader since 1920. Johnny's Giants teammate Mel Ott led for the sixth time in home runs, hitting 30. Ernie Lombardi, catching for the Boston Braves now, won the batting crown for the second time (.330). On May 13, the Braves' Jim Tobin became the only pitcher in major-league history to hit three home runs in a game when he connected three times against the Cubs. On June 19, another Boston player got into the history books when Paul Waner, the long-time Pirate star, singled against his old team for his 3,000th career hit, the sixth player in modern times to attain that total.

After losing the first game of the World Series to the Yankees, the underdog Cardinals took the next four in a row, recording one of the great upsets in Series history. Beazley capped his superb rookie year with a pair of victories. He then entered the military, injured his arm pitching for his service team in Hawaii, and was never the same again.

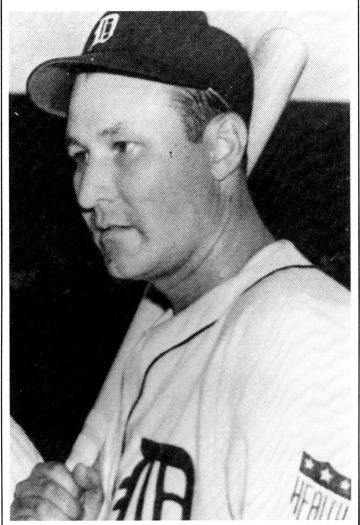

Rudy York

1943

Baseball was beginning to scramble now to find competent players with which to fill out their rosters. The great names had all gone off to war—Greenberg, Feller, DiMaggio, Williams, Reiser, and others like Pee Wee Reese, Phil Rizzuto, Enos Slaughter, Johnny Pesky, and Cecil Travis were gone or soon would be.

With some of his fine veterans squeezing out one more year's play before going off to war, Joe McCarthy's Yankees made it seven of the last eight pennants, finishing 13½ games ahead of Washington. Bill Dickey, Charlie Keller, and Joe Gordon gave the team a solid core before departing for military service, while Spud Chandler had a pitcher's dream season—20–4 record, league-leading 1.64 ERA, and the MVP Award. Spud and Detroit's Dizzy Trout (20–12) were the league's only 20-game winners.

The leading hitter, for the second time in his career, was Chicago's Luke Appling, the thirty-six-year-old shortstop batting .328. In the second spot was Detroit's Dick Wakefield at .316. Wakefield had received a $52,000 bonus from the Tigers in 1941; despite his excellent rookie year, he never delivered the career that most baseball men felt he was capable of.

Detroit's Rudy York, one of the last bona fide power hitters still in the league, led in home runs (34) and RBIs (118).

The palm for futility went to Connie Mack's Athletics, finishing last for the fourth year in a row. During the course of the season (in which they lost 105 games) they endured a 20-game losing streak, tying the league record set by the 1906 Red Sox and 1916 Athletics.

On July 13, the All-Star Game was played under lights for the first time, at Philadelphia's Shibe Park, the American League winning by a score of 5–3.

Billy Southworth's Cardinals easily made it two in a row in 1943, winning 105 games and finishing 18 ahead of the second-place Reds. For Stan Musial it was the first of his many dominating seasons. On his way to the Most Valuable Player Award, Musial won his first batting crown (.357) and also led in hits (220), doubles (48), and triples (20). Catcher Walker Cooper batted .318, while the St. Louis infield displayed uncanny consistency with these batting averages: first baseman Ray Sanders .280, second baseman Lou Klein .287, shortstop Marty Marion .280, and third baseman Whitey Kurowski .287.

Mort Cooper, Walker's brother, turned in another 20-game season for the Cards, going 21–8, tying Cincinnati's Elmer Riddle and Pittsburgh's Rip Sewell for most wins. Sewell was now regaling fans and frustrating hitters with his amusing "blooper" ball, a pitch that Rip rolled off his fingertips, arced some 20 feet into the air, and parachuted through the strike zone.

The Cooper brothers, Mort (left) and Walker.

Chicago's Bill Nicholson led the league in the two prime power categories—home runs (29) and runs batted in (128).

Despite four regulars and two part-timers with .300 batting averages, the Brooklyn Dodgers finished third. Billy Herman was their top hitter—and second in the league to Musial—at .330. The Dodger roster, like most others, reflected the patchwork jobs being done by big-league managers. The Brooklyn lineup that summer went from forty-two-year-old Johnny Cooney and forty-year-old Paul Waner (still with a live .311 bat) down to nineteen-year-old Gil Hodges, who played one game—at third base.

The rematch of the 1942 World Series went to the Yankees, who avenged the 1942 upset by taking the Cardinals in five. Spud Chandler won two games for New York, with a sparkling 0.50 ERA for 18 innings of work. In game 5, Chandler pitched a 2–0, 10-hit shutout.

1944

It took a World War to do it, but the St. Louis Browns in 1944 finally won the first (and only) pennant in their history. And they did it dramatically, too, on the last day of the season. Going into the final day they were tied with the Detroit Tigers, who were playing the Washington Senators. The Browns won their game, 5–2, over the Yankees on a pair of two-run homers by Chet Laabs, while the Tigers were losing, 4–1, to the Senators.

Luke Sewell's unexpected pennant winners, who had opened the season with nine straight wins, had a staff of veteran pitchers in Nelson Potter—the ace at 19–7—Jack Kramer, Bob Muncrief, Denny Galehouse, and a career minor leaguer with the bouncy name of Sigmund Jakucki (who won that final game). With a .252 team batting average, the Browns were next to last in hitting, though only Boston outscored them (739 to 684). Veteran outfielder Mike Kreevich led the club with a .301 average, but the big belter was shortstop Vern Stephens, who batted .293, hit 20 home runs (second in the league to New York's Nick Etten, who had 22), and had a league-leading 109 RBIs.

Detroit's strength lay in a formidable pitching duo, left-hander Hal Newhouser and righty Dizzy Trout. Newhouser, a mediocre prewar pitcher, mowed down the ragged opposition lineups and built a 29–9 record (earning him the MVP Award) while Trout was 27–14. Detroit's big hitter was Dick Wakefield, who spent half the season in the service, hitting .355 for his 78 games.

Joe McCarthy's third-place Yankees had the league's best all-around player in second baseman George Stirnweiss. Stirnweiss turned in a flashy season with a .319 batting average and league-leading figures in runs (125), hits (205), triples (16), and stolen bases (55).

Cleveland's twenty-six-year-old shortstop-manager Lou Boudreau led the league with a .327 average, edging out Boston's Bobby Doerr, who was hitting .325 before departing for the service in late August. Right-hander Tex Hughson also left for the military in August, leaving behind an 18–5 record. Their departures killed any hopes the Red Sox had for a pennant run.

The National League won for only the fourth time in 12 All-Star Games, defeating the Americans, 7–1, on July 11 at Forbes Field, Pittsburgh.

There were no surprises in the National League. The St. Louis Cardinals were expected to win and they did. In taking their third straight pennant, the Cards became the first National League team to win 100 games three years in a row. Billy Southworth's club left no doubts, winning 73 of their first 100 games and finishing 14½ games ahead of the runner-up Pirates.

The St. Louis lineup included Stan Musial (.347), Johnny Hopp (.336), and Walker Cooper (.317). Mort

George Stirnweiss

Joe Nuxhall in 1944.

Cooper at 22–7 was a 20-game winner for the third year in a row and rookie Ted Wilks, up from the Cardinals' ever-productive farm system, entered the majors with a 17–4 record. The Cardinals also had the MVP for the third straight year, shortstop Marty Marion edging the Cubs' Bill Nicholson by one vote, 190–189.

Other 20-game winners in the league were Cincinnati's Bucky Walters (23–8), Pittsburgh's Rip Sewell (21–12), and New York's rookie Bill Voiselle (21–16). Seventh-place Brooklyn had its only glory in batting champion Dixie Walker, who led with a .357 average. Joe Medwick, banging away for the Giants now, batted .337. For the second year in a row Nicholson was the home run and RBI leader, with respective totals of 33 and 122.

Boston's Jim Tobin, 18–19 on the year, coughed up the league's first no-hitter in almost three years when he dropped the noose around the Dodgers on April 27, 2–0, embellishing his effort with a home run. Just four days before, the knuckleballing Tobin had one-hit the Phillies. On June 22, Tobin pitched a five-inning, 7–0 no-hitter against the Phillies, the game being called because of darkness. On May 15, however, Tobin swallowed some of his own medicine when Cincinnati left-hander Clyde Shoun pitched a 1–0 no-hitter against Tobin and the Braves.

With ballplayers becoming ever more scarce, Cincinnati on June 10 sent left-hander Joe Nuxhall to the mound for a nightmarish two-thirds of an inning against the Car-

dinals, during which he surrendered two singles and issued five walks. Nuxhall was at the time six weeks short of his sixteenth birthday and remains the youngest player ever to appear in a major league game. He returned to the bigs with the Reds in 1952 and pitched for 15 years thereafter, winning 135 games.

Cincinnati catcher Ray Mueller earned an "iron-man" distinction by catching in every one of his team's 155 games.

On November 25, Kenesaw Mountain Landis, baseball's first and most notable commissioner, died at the age of seventy-eight. The following April his successor, former Kentucky Governor and United States Senator Albert B. (Happy) Chandler, was signed to a seven-year contract.

The underdog Browns took a two-games-to-one advantage in baseball's only all–St. Louis World Series, but then the strong Cardinal pitching kicked in as Harry Brecheen, Mort Cooper, and Ted Wilks limited the Browns to two runs over the last three games to give the Cards the title in six.

1945

The man who was to become the symbol of wartime baseball was employed as an outfielder by the St. Louis Browns in 1945. He was Pete Gray, a twenty-eight-year-old outfielder, who had lost his right arm in a childhood accident. Gray, who began moving up through the minor leagues as the war lengthened and players became scarcer, had developed a skill in catching a ball with his gloved left hand, flipping the ball into the air, catching it with his now bare left hand, and firing it in. After batting .333 with Memphis of the Southern Association in 1944, Gray was brought up to the majors by the Browns. In 77 games he batted .218.

For the second year in a row the Tigers were involved in a pennant race that narrowed down to the last day of the season. This time their opponents were the Washington Senators, and this time Steve O'Neill's Detroit club won it, in as close to storybook fashion as it was possible to get. Released from the service in midseason, Hank Greenberg had immediately rejoined the club and began hitting as though he had never been away. On the last day of the season, with the Tigers losing to the Browns, 3–2, in the top of the ninth inning, Greenberg came up with the bases loaded and hit a home run, giving the Tigers the ball game and the pennant.

Pete Gray

Excelling against the wartime opposition for the second year in a row, Detroit lefty Hal Newhouser (25–9) was again voted the MVP, although there was strong support for second baseman Eddie Mayo, who gave the Tigers fine all-around play throughout the season. Greenberg got into 78 games, hit 13 homers, drove in 60 runs, and batted .311.

Washington's second-place club had a staff that included four knuckleballers—ace Roger Wolff (20–10), Dutch Leonard (17–7), left-hander Mickey Haefner (16–14), and Johnny Niggeling (7–12). They were caught, bravely and uncomplainingly, by the veteran Rick Ferrell. The Red Sox brought up rookie right-hander Dave Ferriss, who pitched shutouts in his first two starts and put together a 21–10 record.

The league had only three .300 hitters, with George Stirnweiss's .309 average edging out Chicago's Tony Cuccinello by one point. Stirnweiss was again the league's best ballplayer; in addition to his batting title, the Yankees second baseman led in runs (107), hits (195), triples (22), and stolen bases (33). Another Yankee, first baseman Nick Etten, led in RBIs with 111, while the Browns' Vern Stephens became the first, and thus far only, shortstop to win the American League home run crown, with 24.

The Athletics' Dick Fowler pitched the league's first no-hitter in more than five years, stopping the Browns on September 9, 1–0, the run coming in the last of the ninth.

The season's overtime award went to the Athletics and Tigers, who on July 21, played to a 24-inning, 1–1 tie.

Because of government-imposed travel restrictions, the 1945 All-Star Game was not played.

On July 27, the Yankees and Cubs engineered an interleague deal that ultimately won the 1945 pennant for the Cubs. Hank Borowy, New York's best pitcher (10–5), was sold to the Cubs for around $100,000. Borowy pitched to an 11–2 record with the Cubs, bolstering a strong wartime pitching staff that already included Hank Wyse (22–10), Claude Passeau (17–9), and Paul Derringer (16–11).

Charlie Grimm's Cubs also had the batting titlist and MVP in first baseman Phil Cavarretta, who batted .355, and received productive seasons from veteran third baseman Stan Hack and outfielders Andy Pafko and Peanuts Lowrey.

Failing in their quest for a fourth straight pennant, the Cardinals finished second, three games behind. St. Louis had the league's top winner in Red Barrett (23–12) and pulled another big-winning rookie from the farm system, Ken Burkhart, who was 19–8, as well as a gifted young player in Red Schoendienst, who batted .278 (Breaking in primarily as an outfielder, Red switched to second base a year later).

The most exciting hitting of the season came from Boston's Tommy Holmes. From June 6 through July 8,

Tommy Holmes

Holmes batted safely in 37 consecutive games, setting a new modern record for the National League (the previous record had belonged to Rogers Hornsby—33 straight in 1922). The streak was the highlight of a terrific season for Holmes: .352 batting average, 117 RBIs, and league-leading totals in home runs (28), hits (224), and doubles (47), in addition to striking out just nine times in 154 games (636 at-bats), an astonishing statistic for a home run leader.

Topping the league in RBIs was the previous year's batting titlist, Brooklyn's Dixie Walker, with 124. Dixie's Dodgers teammate Eddie Stanky set a new league record with 148 walks.

The World Series was a seven-game affair, with the Tigers finally winning it, despite some heroic pitching by Borowy, who started three times for the Cubs and relieved once, ending with a 2–2 mark.

The biggest baseball news of that year, and as far as many are concerned, for any year, broke on October 23. On that day, Brooklyn general manager Branch Rickey announced the signing of a pair of Negro ballplayers— infielder Jackie Robinson and pitcher Johnny Wright—to contracts with Brooklyn's International League farm club at Montreal. Baseball's long-standing color barrier had finally been breached. Condemned, vilified, ridiculed ("He thinks he's Abraham Lincoln," one American League executive said), Rickey was suddenly all alone, receiving no support or encouragement whatsoever from any big-league club executive. He did, however, have the quiet support of Commissioner Chandler.

1946

The war was over and they were all back now—Di-Maggio, Williams, and all the rest, as baseball enjoyed its most prosperous and exhilarating season in years. There was, however, one troublesome bump in the road. A millionaire Mexican named Jorge Pasquel, intent upon establishing a Mexican League, was luring American players south of the border with extravagant (for the time) contracts. Succumbing to the sound of falling pesos were such front-line players as pitcher Max Lanier and second baseman Lou Klein of the Cardinals and catcher Mickey Owen and outfielder Luis Olmo of the Dodgers. The New York Giants were the hardest hit, losing top relief pitcher Ace Adams, outfielder Danny Gardella, young pitcher Sal Maglie, and five others. Stan Musial was offered a tempting five-year contract calling for the then-princely total of $130,000, but turned it down.

Commissioner Chandler immediately decreed that the jumpers would be barred from organized ball for five years. When the disillusioned began returning home— Mickey Owen was first, coming back late that summer— they found Chandler adamant. By 1949, however, Chandler relented and some of the jumpers began filtering back.

But the big show went on, regardless of the threat from Mexico. In the American League, a hard-hitting Red Sox club got off to a torrid start and ran away to an easy pennant, finishing 12 games ahead of second-place Detroit.

Ted Williams came back to an MVP season, hitting 38 home runs, driving in 123 runs, and batting .342. Williams was joined by shortstop Johnny Pesky, who took up where he left off in 1942 by batting .335 and leading in hits with 208. Center fielder Dominic DiMaggio batted .316 and second baseman Bobby Doerr and first baseman Rudy York each drove in over 100 runs.

For a change, the Red Sox had a strong mound staff, presided over by Dave Ferriss (25–6), Tex Hughson (20–11), and left-hander Mickey Harris (17–9). In winning 104 games, the club gave skipper Joe Cronin his only pennant in 13 years as Red Sox manager.

Detroit got a 26–9 season from lefty Hal Newhouser and some powerhouse hitting from Hank Greenberg, who led the league with 44 home runs and 127 RBIs. (To everyone's surprise, Big Henry was waived to the Pirates after the season.)

The most exciting pitching of the year was turned in by Cleveland's Bob Feller. Feller, who had returned in the middle of 1945 and pitched to a 5–3 record, turned in a sizzling 26–15 season, replete with ten shutouts and 348 strikeouts, one under Rube Waddell's American League record. Bob also fired his second no-hitter, throttling the Yankees, 1–0 (on catcher Frank Hayes's ninth-inning home run) on April 30. Feller no-hit a lineup that included

Bob Feller

Joe DiMaggio, Phil Rizzuto, Tommy Henrich, Charlie Keller, Joe Gordon, and Bill Dickey.

The Yankees' Spud Chandler, at 20–8, was the league's other 20-game winner. Thirty-one-year-old Joe DiMaggio, fighting three years of rust, batted .290 as the Yankees went without a .300 hitter in their everyday lineup for the first time since 1917.

The surprise batting leader was Washington first baseman Mickey Vernon with a .353 average, the first time in his six-year career he had surpassed .300.

In the All-Star Game, played on July 9 at Boston's Fenway Park, the American League shot down the National with a lopsided 12–0 victory. The game was highlighted by Ted Williams' eighth-inning home run off one of Rip Sewell's blooper pitches. It was the only time anyone ever hit one of Rip's high floaters out of the park.

In direct contrast to the American League runaway, the National League put on the tightest pennant race in its history; it ended, in fact, in a dead heat between the Dodgers and Cardinals, calling for a best-of-three playoff, the first ever in baseball. The Cardinals won the opener in St. Louis, 4–2, behind left-hander Howie Pollett, then went to Brooklyn and won there, 8–4, to clinch the pennant. The game ended with southpaw Harry Brecheen fanning Brooklyn's Howie Schultz with two out and the bases loaded in the bottom of the ninth.

Pollett was 21–10 for Eddie Dyer's Cardinals, followed by Murry Dickson (15–6) and Brecheen (15–15). Back from the service after a one-year hiatus, Stan Musial ripped league pitching for his second batting crown (.365), including top marks in hits (228), doubles (50), and triples (20), earning his second MVP Award. Stanley was abetted by Enos Slaughter, who batted .300 and led with 130 RBIs.

The second-place Dodgers had one .300 hitter in Dixie Walker (.319), while their top winner was Kirby Higbe (17–8). Right-hander Ed Head pitched a no-hitter against the Braves on April 23, winning 5–0. Head came down with a sore arm shortly after and won only two games the rest of the season. Brooklyn's dynamic center fielder Pete Reiser set a major league record with seven steals of home.

Boston's curveballing Johnny Sain joined Pollett as the league's only 20-game winners with a 20–14 season. Joining the Boston staff early in the season and gradually working his way back into shape after three years of military service was twenty-five-year-old left-hander Warren Spahn. Ultimately to become the most prodigious southpaw winner in history, Spahn started slowly in 1946, with an 8–5 record.

Another notable rookie in the league was Pittsburgh outfielder Ralph Kiner, the home run leader with 23, the first of a record seven straight home run crowns he would either win or tie for.

A thrilling seven-game World Series between the Red Sox and the Cardinals went to St. Louis. The seventh game was tied 3–3 in the bottom of the eighth when, with Enos Slaughter on first base, Harry Walker dropped a soft hit into short left-center, unleashing Slaughter, who made a now legendary dash around the bases, running through a stop sign at third base and scoring when Red Sox shortstop Johnny Pesky hesitated for an instant before throwing the relay home. Slaughter's "mad dash" was the winning run in the Cardinals' 4–3 victory. Harry Brecheen won three games for the Cardinals.

Harry Brecheen

1947

The Red Sox failed to repeat—they finished third—despite Ted Williams's Triple Crown season. In becoming the first American Leaguer to win two Triple Crowns (Rogers Hornsby had done it in the National League), Williams hit 32 home runs, drove in 114 runs (the only man in the league with over 100), and batted .343. Johnny Pesky led in hits with 207 while batting .324, giving him three hit titles in his three seasons. A combination of off seasons and sore arms for Tex Hughson, Dave Ferris, and Mickey Harris sank the Red Sox.

The pennant winners, back on top after four years, were Bucky Harris's Yankees, led by Joe DiMaggio's .315 batting average and Allie Reynold's 19–8 record, plus excellent work from left-handed reliever Joe Page, who was 14–8 with 17 saves. (Not then a recognized statistic, saves have been computed retroactively.) The Yankees, winning by 12 games over second-place Detroit, used a 19-game winning streak as a springboard away from the pack. The streak, which ran from June 29–July 17, tied the American League record set by the 1906 White Sox.

The Tigers got a .320 season from up-and-coming third base star George Kell, acquired the previous season from the Athletics. Connie Mack had traded him because he didn't think Kell would hit. Bob Feller continued rolling, though a bit less spectacularly, with a 20–11 record and 196 league-leading strikeouts.

On July 5, Cleveland introduced the American League's first black player, twenty-three-year-old Larry Doby, then a second baseman. Used sparingly, Doby got into 29 games and batted .156. The man who signed Doby, thereby breaking ranks with his fellow American League club owners, was Cleveland's spiritedly independent and innovative boss, Bill Veeck. Another bit of Cleveland baseball history was made on July 10, when right-hander Don Black pitched a no-hitter against the Athletics, winning 3–0. The A's got a no-hit performance of their own later in the season, turned in by right-hander Bill McCahan over the Senators on September 3. In winning 3–0, McCahan missed a perfect game only because first baseman Ferris Fain made a throwing error in the second inning.

Despite Williams's Triple Crown season, some unaccountably benighted voting by the sportswriters gave the Most Valuable Player Award to DiMaggio.

The All-Star Game was played that year at Chicago's Wrigley Field on July 8 and resulted in a 2–1 American League win.

The Brooklyn Dodgers formally integrated major league baseball in 1947 with the promotion of Jackie Robinson to their big league roster, following Robinson's sensational season at Montreal in 1946.

Robinson, who played first base in his historic first

George Kell

year, helped the Dodgers to the pennant with his sharp hitting (.297) and exciting baserunning (he led with 29 stolen bases). Robinson's fine performance on the field came despite beanballs, attempted spikings, and torrents of unconscionable abuse hurled at him from the stands as well as from opposing dugouts. Jackie's stoic, turn-the-other-cheek attitude—imposed on this fiery, militant man by Branch Rickey for the sake of "the cause"—under the season-long pressure was a sculpture of resolution and nobility, helping to direct the way for all of the black players who followed him.

There was other turmoil in Dodgerland that year. Just before the opening of the season, Commissioner Chandler suspended manager Leo Durocher for one year, for what Chandler described as "conduct detrimental to baseball." Among the vaguely defined charges was Leo's alleged association with gamblers; but more to the point, perhaps, was Chandler's distaste for Durocher's flashy life-style, which earlier that year included marriage to actress Laraine Day.

With Durocher sidelined for the entire season, Rickey replaced him with Burt Shotton, a soft-spoken, white-haired former ballplayer who managed from the dugout wearing civilian clothes.

In May there were rumors that the St. Louis Cardinals would strike rather than appear on the same field with Robinson. Into this cauldron stepped National League President Ford Frick. A mild-mannered person of no known strong feelings, Frick surpassed himself with a ringing statement that threatened suspension to any player who dared strike. "This is the United States of America," Frick had to remind the grumblers, "and one citizen has as much right to play as another." It was Ford Frick's finest moment, and the purported strike threat passed.

Branch Rickey

Ewell Blackwell

There was also a baseball season in the National League that year, with Brooklyn winning over the Cardinals by five games. Pete Reiser's .309 led the club, and young Ralph Branca's 21–12 record topped the pitching staff, followed by lefty Joe Hatten's 17–8, along with the outstanding relief pitching of Hugh Casey.

The third-place Braves had a pair of big winners in Johnny Sain (21–12) and Warren Spahn (21–10), plus the MVP in third baseman Bob Elliott, who earned the honor with a .317 batting average and 113 RBIs. There was also some very loud thunder in the league, coming from New York and Pittsburgh. The Giants' Johnny Mize and the Pirates' Ralph Kiner tied for the home run lead with 51 apiece, with Mize the RBI king with 138. Kiner's year of excitement was capped by an early September outburst during which he set a record by hitting eight home runs in four games. Led by Mize, the Giants established a new major league home run record with 221. Behind Big John were Willard Marshall with 36, Walker Cooper with 35, and Bobby Thomson with 29.

Harry Walker (brother of Dixie), traded by the Cardinals to the Phillies early in the season, was the batting champion with a .363 average.

All of the Giants' home run power could lift them no higher than fourth, despite a superb 21–5 season from rookie right-hander Larry Jansen. The league's fifth 20-game winner, and most dominant pitcher of 1947, was Cincinnati's tall, sidewheeling right-hander Ewell Blackwell, who was 22–8. Blackwell's accomplishments that year included a 16-game winning streak and a 6–0 no-hitter against the Braves on June 18. In his next start, against the Dodgers four days later, Blackwell came within an eyelash of duplicating Johnny Vander Meer's 1938 feat of two consecutive no-hitters. Holding the Dodgers hitless for 8⅓ innings, Blackwell was nicked for a hit in the top of

the ninth when Eddie Stanky hit a sharp ground ball through the mound that Blackwell failed to get down to in time. (Adding to the drama of the moment was Blackwell's teammate, Vander Meer, sitting on the bench watching it all happen. "I would have been the first one out there to congratulate him, if he had done it," Johnny said later.)

This was the year that saw the installation of a Rookie of the Year Award, with one selection covering both leagues (individual league selections began in 1949). The first winner was Jackie Robinson.

The 1947 World Series went resoundingly into the history books, primarily for the events of game 4. Yankees right-hander Bill Bevens (a 7–13 pitcher that year) took a 2–1 lead and no-hitter against the Dodgers into the bottom of the ninth. Wild throughout the game, Bevens walked two men, and with two out pinch-hitter Cookie Lavagetto doubled off the wall in right field, scoring both runs to give the Dodgers a clamorous 3–2 win and deprive Bevens of the first no-hitter in World Series history. In game 6, Dodger left fielder Al Gionfriddo etched his name on World Series scrolls with a breathtaking catch of a DiMaggio drive that looked like a game-tying three-run homer, helping Brooklyn to an 8–6 win. In spite of these individual heroics, the Yankees went on to win in seven.

1948

The Boston Red Sox and Cleveland Indians ran the American League's first dead-heat finish in 1948, elbow-locked at 96–58 apiece. It was, in fact, a three-way race until the season's penultimate day, when the Yankees were eliminated.

So it came down to a one-game playoff (American League rules called for a single game of decision in the event of a tie) between Lou Boudreau's Indians and Joe McCarthy's Red Sox at Fenway Park. (McCarthy had resigned as Yankee manager in 1946 and returned to baseball in 1948 as skipper of the Red Sox.) The Indians sent their left-handed knuckleballer Gene Bearden to the mound, while the Red Sox started Denny Galehouse. With the help of some heavy hitting by skipper Boudreau (two singles and two home runs), Bearden won it for Cleveland (their first pennant in 28 years), by a score of 8–3.

It was perhaps the most spirited year ever in Cleveland baseball. With a winning team and owner Bill Veeck's promotions and giveaways, the club drew a then-record 2,620,627 customers. The heart and soul of the club was Boudreau, shortstop and manager, who put together an MVP season with his .355 batting average and 106 RBIs. Along with the lead-by-example skipper were third baseman Ken Keltner (31 homers, 119 RBIs), second baseman Joe Gordon (32 homers, 124 RBIs), and outfielders Dale Mitchell (.336) and Larry Doby (.301).

In addition to Bearden, who was 20–7, the Indians also had on the mound converted outfielder Bob Lemon (20–14) and Bob Feller (19–15).

Second-place Boston had Ted Williams take his fourth batting title with a .369 mark and also received strong seasons from Bobby Doerr, Vern Stephens (137 RBIs), and Billy Goodman. Jack Kramer (18–5) was Boston's top pitcher.

The Yankees got winning pitching from Vic Raschi (19–8), Eddie Lopat (17–11), and Allie Reynolds (16–7), plus an old-fashioned Joe DiMaggio season from their reigning king—39 home runs and 155 RBIs (both tops in the league) and a .320 batting average, in addition to .300 seasons from Tommy Henrich, Johnny Lindell, Bobby Brown, and Yogi Berra. It was, however, Cleveland's year.

Cleveland's Lemon pitched the league's only no-hitter, stopping the Tigers on June 30, 2–0. The biggest one-man detonation of the year came on July 18, when Chicago's Pat Seerey belted four home runs in an 11-inning game against the Athletics.

In the All-Star Game, played on July 13 in St. Louis's Sportsman's Park, the American League won, 5–2.

The most thunderous National League headline of the 1948 season went to a not unfamiliar subject—Leo Durocher. Leo had completed his year's suspension and returned as Brooklyn's manager. By midseason the team was floundering and Branch Rickey was losing patience with his controversial manager. Also spinning in a vortex to nowhere were the New York Giants, under skipper Mel Ott. Deciding to do something radical to shake up his club, Giants owner Horace Stoneham sought to obtain Rickey's permission to talk to Burt Shotton, Brooklyn's 1947 manager, with the view of hiring Burt to take over the Giants. Rickey instead told Stoneham he could have Durocher. Stoneham agreed.

The moves were announced on July 16—Ott was given a front-office job, Durocher replaced Ott, and Shotton returned as the Dodgers manager. Brooklyn fans were stunned, while Giant fans were outraged—the long-despised Durocher was suddenly managing their team.

Although the Dodgers surged after Shotton took over, the best they could do was a third-place finish. Fireballer Rex Barney's 2–0 no-hitting of the Giants on September 9 proved to be the season's highlight for Dodger fans.

The surprise pennant winners were Billy Southworth's Boston Braves, coming in 6½ games ahead of the

Rex Barney. One of the fastest pitchers of all time. Wildness cost him a chance at greatness.

Cardinals. It was the year of "Spahn and Sain and pray for rain," with Warren 15–12 and Johnny the year's big winner at 24–15.

The Braves presented a surprisingly productive lineup that included second baseman Eddie Stanky at .320, Rookie of the Year shortstop Alvin Dark at .322, and outfielders Tommy Holmes (.325), Mike McCormick (.303), and former American Leaguer Jeff Heath (.319). (Stanky was sidelined in July with a broken ankle and played in just 67 games.)

For the Braves, it was their first pennant since the "Miracle" club of 1914.

For second-place St. Louis it was all Stan Musial and Harry Brecheen. In winning his third MVP Award, Musial led in batting (.376), runs (135), hits (230), doubles (46), triples (18), slugging (.702, which remains the league's highest since 1930), total bases (429, also the highest since 1930), and runs batted in (131). With New York's Johnny Mize and Pittsburgh's Ralph Kiner again tying for the home run lead, this time with 40 apiece, Musial, with 39 homers, just missed the Triple Crown. Brecheen was 20–7 and was the ERA leader with 2.24, based largely on his seven shutouts.

Along with Dark, the National League took the wrappings off two other outstanding rookies—Phillies outfielder Richie Ashburn, who batted .333, and his teammate Robin Roberts, who broke in with a 7–9 record, the stamp of greatness vividly apparent.

The World Series, won by Cleveland in six games, is largely remembered for a play in the opening game. The game was scoreless in the bottom of the eighth, Feller dueling Sain. The Braves had Phil Masi on second base when Feller whirled and fired to Boudreau covering. Masi looked to be out, but umpire Bill Stewart thought otherwise. When play resumed, Tommy Holmes singled to left, scoring Masi with the game's only run. Later in the Series, however, the tight pitching of Lemon, Bearden, and Steve Gromek prevailed for Cleveland.

Gene Bearden

1949

The Yankees had a new manager in 1949, though he was hardly an unfamiliar name. Casey Stengel had been around, and around, and around, as player, coach, minor league executive, minor league manager, and major league manager with the Dodgers and Braves. Part sage, part buffoon, a wit, a tactician, adored by some, belittled by others, he began in 1949 the greatest run of managerial success in baseball history.

Stengel's first pennant was his toughest. Coming down to the season's end he was one game behind the Red Sox with two games to play, at Yankee Stadium—with Boston. The Yankees won the Saturday game, 5–4, tying the Sox for first place and setting a full table for the Sunday finale. With the gritty Vic Raschi on the mound, the New Yorkers won it, 5–3.

Making the Yankees victory the more impressive was the fact that they were injury-riddled for much of the season. The biggest void was created by the absence of Joe DiMaggio until the end of June because of a bone spur on his heel. When he finally broke into the lineup it was against the Red Sox in a three-game series at Fenway, in which Joe hit four home runs and drove in nine runs in leading the Yankees to a sweep. The performance remains one of the shining jewels in the DiMaggio diadem. In his 76 games that year, Joe batted .346 and drove in 67 runs. No full-time Yankee batted .300 or attained 100 RBIs.

The injuries did not touch the Yankee pitching, and here lay the team's strength. Raschi was 21–10, Allie Reynolds 17–6, lefties Tommy Byrne 15–7 and Eddie Lopat 15–10, while Joe Page had another sterling year in relief, going 13–8 with 27 saves.

The Red Sox had four .300 hitters in Bobby Doerr, Johnny Pesky, Dom DiMaggio, and Ted Williams. Williams had another colossal season, leading with 43 home runs, tying teammate Vern Stephens for the RBI lead at 159 apiece, and batting .343. Winning his second MVP Award, Ted missed his third Triple Crown by an eyelash—losing the batting title to Detroit's George Kell, .3429 to .3427.

Boston's starting pitching was essentially two men—left-hander Mel Parnell (25–7) and Ellis Kinder (23–6). No one else won more than 14.

Third-place Cleveland had a 22-game winner in Bob Lemon, while .317-hitting Dale Mitchell collected 23 triples, which remains the most in the league since 1917.

Athletics rookie left-hander Alex Kellner was 20–12, Detroit's young slugger Vic Wertz drove in 133 runs, and Chicago's forty-two-year-old shortstop (playing 141 games at the position) Luke Appling batted .301, clearing the .300 barrier for the 14th time. The Browns' Roy Sievers, a .306 hitter, was the league's Rookie of the Year.

The American League won the All-Star Game, played July 12 at Brooklyn's Ebbets Field, by a score of 11–7.

Warren Spahn (left) and Mel Parnell at the 1949 All-Star Game.

The National League matched the American in pennant-race excitement, the older league also waiting until the final day to decide its winner. Burt Shotton's Dodgers cut their victory even finer, winning the pennant in extra innings in the last game of the season, beating the Phillies in ten, 9–7. It gave them a one-game margin over second-place St. Louis.

About to become the league's dominant team for the better part of the coming decade, the Dodgers used power, speed, and defense to shore up a sometimes shaky pitching staff. Gil Hodges at first base, Jackie Robinson at second, Pee Wee Reese at short, Billy Cox at third, Roy Campanella catching, and Duke Snider and Carl Furillo in the outfield were a set lineup for the next several years.

In 1949 Robinson was the league's MVP, on the strength of his 124 RBIs (second to Ralph Kiner's 127), daring baserunning, and league-leading .342 batting average. Hodges and Furillo, who batted .322, also drove in over 100 runs. Brooklyn pitching was topped by Rookie of the Year Don Newcombe, who was 17–8, and left-hander Preacher Roe, 15–6.

Second-place St. Louis got .338 and .336 years, respectively, from Stan Musial and Enos Slaughter, and a 20–9 record from Howie Pollett, but it wasn't enough.

Defending champion Boston fell to fourth, despite Warren Spahn's 21–14 season, while Leo Durocher was busy tearing apart and rebuilding his fifth-place Giants.

Catcher Walker Cooper was dealt to the Reds and in August Johnny Mize was waived to the Yankees. After the season, Leo pulled a critical trade when he dispatched shortstop Buddy Kerr and slow-footed sluggers Willard Marshall and Sid Gordon to the Braves for a brand new keystone combination of Alvin Dark and Eddie Stanky, who immediately began to breathe new life into the Giants.

Pittsburgh's Ralph Kiner won his fourth straight home run title with his greatest season—54 home runs, 127 RBIs, .310 batting average. The biggest home run outburst of the year occurred on June 2, when the Phillies tied a major league record by homering five times in one inning—two by Andy Seminick, and one each by Del Ennis, Willie Jones, and pitcher Schoolboy Rowe.

Another Phillies player, first baseman Eddie Waitkus, broke into the news on June 15. While staying at the club's Edgewater Beach Hotel in Chicago, Waitkus received a late-night message from a young woman inviting him to her room. When he entered the room of nineteen-year-old Ruth Ann Steinhagen, Waitkus received a .22-caliber rifle bullet in the chest. Waitkus, batting .306 at the time, recovered but did not play again that season. Miss Steinhagen, who professed a romantic interest in the ballplayer, was committed to psychiatric therapy.

In a somewhat dull World Series, which began with the teams exchanging 1–0 victories, the Yankees beat the Dodgers in five games. The opener featured a textbook pitching duel between the Yankees' Reynolds and the Dodgers' Newcombe, which Tommy Henrich settled with a bottom-of-the-ninth home run.

Eddie Waitkus

Rudy York

Ted Williams answering some fan mail.

Willard Hershberger. His suicide on August 3, 1940, was never explained. Thirty years old at the time, Hershberger was in his third big-league season. He had a .316 lifetime average.

Bucky Walters

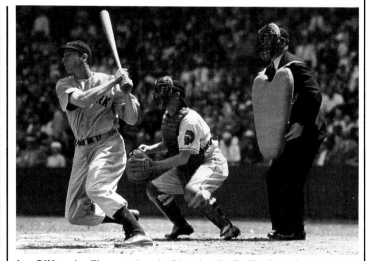

Joe DiMaggio. The catcher is Cleveland's Rollie Hemsley.

Tommy Henrich, one of the most popular of all New York Yankees. He played from 1937–50, with three years out for military service, batting .282.

LEFT: Dolf Camilli. The long-balling first baseman of the '41 Dodgers came to the majors with the Cubs, and then played for the Phillies and Dodgers, with whom he had his peak years. He had over 20 home runs for eight consecutive years and five times drove in over 100 runs. He played for the Red Sox in 1945, his final year. Lifetime average: .277.

RIGHT: Ted Williams. Lifetime average: .344.

BELOW: Second baseman Joe Gordon was with the Yankees from 1938–43 and 1946, and then with Cleveland until 1950. A flashy fielder with a long-ball bat, he batted .268.

A Dodger fan who had taken exception to some of umpire George Magerkurth's decisions has come down to the field after the game to have a discussion about them. Umpire Bill Stewart is running up to lend a hand. The fan was given some time in the cooler to reflect on it all. This post-game action took place at Ebbets Field in September 1940.

Gathered together at the family's Fisherman's Wharf restaurant in San Francisco are the three baseball-playing DiMaggio brothers. Left to right: Vince, Joe, and Dom. Vince played for five National League clubs from 1937–46, batting .249. Dom spent his entire 11-year career with the Red Sox, retiring in 1953 with a .298 average.

Claude Passeau, one of the National League's solid right-handed pitchers from 1935–47. Pitching for the Pirates, Phillies, and Cubs, he compiled a 162–150 record.

Charlie Keller, hard-hitting Yankees outfielder. He came up in 1939 and played until 1952, batting .286.

Sam Chapman, good-hitting outfielder who came up with the A's in 1938 and played in the major leagues until 1951. He batted .266.

Left-hander Thornton Lee, most of whose 16-year major league career was spent with the White Sox. In 1941 he won 22 games and led the American League in ERA. He retired in 1948 with a 117–124 record.

Fastballer Kirby Higbe. He came up in 1937 and pitched for the Cubs and Phillies before joining the Dodgers in 1941 and helping them to a pennant with 22 victories. He later pitched for the Pirates and Giants, retiring in 1950 with a 118–101 record.

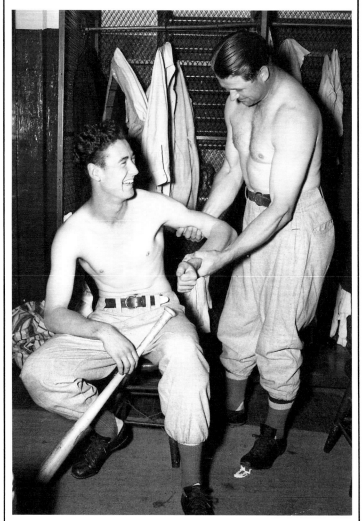

Jimmie Foxx (right) searching for the source of Ted Williams's power.

RIGHT: Pee Wee Reese, one of the finest shortstops in National League history, played his entire career with the Dodgers—1940–58, with three years out for military service. His career average is .269. He was at shortstop for seven Dodger pennant winners.

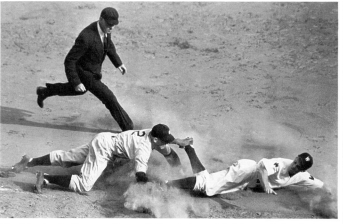

Philadelphia Athletics manager Connie Mack (center) and his 1941 infield. Left to right: second baseman Benny McCoy, shortstop Al Brancato, Mack, first baseman Dick Siebert, and third baseman Pete Suder.

Washington's George Case sliding into a third base defended by the Yankees' Red Rolfe. One of the speediest men of his time, Case came up with the Senators in 1937 and played for 11 years. He led in stolen bases six times and batted .282.

Stan Spence, who came up with the Red Sox in 1940 and later played with the Senators and Browns, retiring in 1949. He was a lifetime .282 batter.

Brooklyn's 1941 pennant-winning infield. Left to right: third baseman Cookie Lavagetto, shortstop Pee Wee Reese, second baseman Billy Herman, and first baseman Dolf Camilli.

Whitlow Wyatt bounced around the American League for a decade, with arm trouble always limiting his efficiency. Acquired by the Dodgers in 1939 he soon became their ace, leading the league in shutouts in 1940 and 1941. He retired in 1945 with a record of 106–95.

Aerial view of Ebbets Field in September 1941.

RIGHT: Hugh Casey, who started and relieved for the 1941 Dodgers. Hugh pitched in the majors for nine years, most of the time with Brooklyn, retiring in 1949 with a 75–42 record.

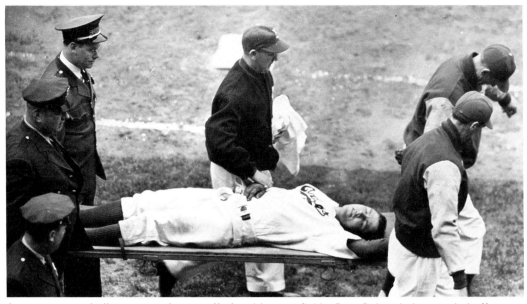

A scene enacted all too many times on National League fields: Pete Reiser being carried off on a stretcher. This time it was after an April 1941 beaning.

Elmer Riddle. He came up with the Reds in 1939 and pitched in the National League for ten years, finishing with Pittsburgh in 1949. He gave the Reds two big years—1941 when he was 19–4 and 1943 when he was 21–11. Lifetime record: 65–52.

Sergeant Henry Greenberg

Stan Musial, one of the National League's all-time superstars. With the exception of one year in military service, he was with the Cardinals from 1941–63, winning seven batting crowns and batting .331.

RIGHT: Pirates Frank Gustine (left) and Arky Vaughan at Pittsburgh's San Bernadino, California, training base in March 1941. Gustine, a popular, hustling infielder, played from 1939–50, batting .265.

Brooklyn's "Pistol" Pete Reiser, whose blazing talents were crippled by injuries. The National League batting champion in 1941 (his first full season), he played from 1940–42 and 1946–52, with Brooklyn and three other clubs. Called by Branch Rickey "the greatest young ballplayer I ever saw," Pete batted .295 lifetime.

One of the darkest moments in the history of Brooklyn baseball. It's the top of the ninth inning of game 4 of the 1941 World Series between the Dodgers and the Yankees. Tommy Henrich has swung and missed for strike three—ostensibly the final out in a 4–3 Dodgers victory. But catcher Mickey Owen does not have control of the ball. The next picture shows Henrich on his way to first base —even as the umpire is calling him out—as a frantic Owen goes after the rolling baseball. The gates were opened for a devastating four-run game-winning Yankees rally.

Yankees' ace Ernie Bonham demonstrating his forkball grip. Today the pitch is called the split-fingered fastball. Ernie pitched for the Yanks and the Pirates from 1940–49, winning 103 and losing 72.

Paul Derringer

Knuckleballer Emil "Dutch" Leonard, who pitched in the big leagues from 1933–53, most of it with the Washington Senators. Working also for the Dodgers, Phillies, and Cubs, he had a lifetime record of 191–181.

Known primarily for his spectacular center-field play, Terry Moore did his share of hitting —a .280 lifetime average. He spent his entire career (1935– 42 and 1946–48) with the Cardinals.

Yankees' shortstop Phil Rizzuto fouling off a bunt attempt in April 1942. The catcher is the Browns' Bob Swift, the umpire Harry Geisel. Shortstop on nine Yankees pennant winners, Phil played from 1941–56, with three years out for military service. Lifetime average: .273.

One of baseball's legendary hustlers, Enos Slaughter played in the major leagues from 1938–59, with three years out for military service. He played with the Cardinals until 1954, when he was dealt to the Yankees. His career average is .300.

Four of the National League's solid timbermen at the 1942 All-Star Game. Left to right: Brooklyn's Joe Medwick, Boston's Ernie Lombardi, and New York's Mel Ott and Johnny Mize.

Washington manager Bucky Harris (left), a former "boy manager," talking in 1942 to a latter-day version, Cleveland's twenty-five-year-old shortstop-manager Lou Boudreau. Lou played from 1938–52, all but the last year with Cleveland, whom he managed for nine years. He batted .295 lifetime.

"Stylish" is the word they always used to describe Howie Pollett. He joined the Cardinals in 1941 and pitched in the big leagues until 1956, working also for the Pirates, Cubs, and White Sox. His career totals are 131–116.

Hank Borowy, who pitched for five teams in both leagues from 1942–51. He had a career record of 108–82.

Outfielder Dick Wakefield, who received a then-enormous $52,000 bonus to sign with Detroit in 1941. He played until 1952, appearing briefly with the Yankees and Giants at the end of his career. Despite a few good years, the free-spirited Wakefield never lived up to his early promise, finishing with a .293 mark.

Whitey Kurowski, Cardinals third baseman, whose home run in the ninth inning of game 5 of the 1942 World Series gave the Cards their upset victory over the Yankees. Whitey played for St. Louis from 1941–49, batting .286.

Marine pilot trainee Ted Williams in the winter of 1942.

Rip Sewell demonstrating his blooper ball delivery. Rip pitched for the Pirates from 1938–49. Lifetime record: 143–97.

The relay has bounced out of Cardinal catcher Walker Cooper's glove as Philadelphia's Danny Litwhiler prepares to slide safely in. The umpire is Jocko Conlan. The action occurred in Philadelphia on September 13, 1942.

Four members of the Pittsburgh Pirates in 1942. Left to right: Vince DiMaggio, Babe Phelps, Elbie Fletcher, and Bob Elliott.

In all of baseball history, no pitcher was harder to beat than the Yankees' Spud Chandler. With the Yankees from 1937–47, Spud put up a 109–43 record, good for a .717 winning percentage.

Relaxing at the tarpaulin cylinder is the Red Sox' Tex Hughson. The talented right-hander pitched from 1941–49, with one year lost to military service. He finished with a 96–54 record.

RIGHT: It is May 8, 1942, and a packed house at Ebbets Field is watching the flag-raising ceremony prior to a twilight game between the Dodgers and Giants. The Dodgers players are lined up along the right-field foul line. Proceeds from the game were donated to the Navy Relief Fund.

Max Lanier. Max pitched for the Cardinals from 1938–46, then jumped to the Mexican League in the spring of 1946. He returned in 1949, later pitching for the Giants and Browns, retiring in 1953 with a 108–82 record.

Marty Marion, who ranged far and wide at shortstop for the Cardinals from 1940–50, finishing up with the Browns in 1953. Considered by many the top fielding shortstop of his era, Marion posted a .263 lifetime average.

Nelson Potter, ace of the St. Louis Browns' 1944 pennant winners. Potter pitched for five teams in both leagues over 12 years, retiring in 1949 with a 92–97 record.

Stan Musial

Members of the 1944 St. Louis Browns, the only Browns team to win a pennant. Front row (left to right): third baseman Mark Christman, infielder Ellis Clary, second baseman Don Gutteride, first baseman George McQuinn. Back row (left to right): infielder Floyd Baker, outfielder Mickey Chartak, shortstop Vern Stephens.

Left to right: Pitchers Ted Wilks, Mort Cooper, and Harry Brecheen of the 1944 pennant-winning St. Louis Cardinals.

Hal Newhouser (left) and Dizzy Trout, aces of Detroit's 1945 pennant winners. Newhouser came up in 1939, pitched 17 years in the American League, and had a 207–150 record. Trout pitched from 1939–52, almost all of it for Detroit, compiling a 170–161 record.

LEFT: Bobby Doerr, greatest second baseman in Boston Red Sox history. He came up in 1937 and played until 1951, retiring prematurely because of a bad back. He drove in over 100 runs six times and had a career average of .288.

RIGHT: Red Sox right-hander Dave Ferriss. He broke in with two 20-game-winning seasons (1945–46), but a sore arm soon dented his career and he retired in 1950 with a 65–30 record.

Dixie Walker, one of the most popular players in Brooklyn Dodgers history. In his 18-year career, he played for the Yankees, White Sox, Tigers, Dodgers, and Pirates. The National League batting champion in 1944, ten times a .300 hitter, Dixie left with a .306 lifetime average.

Outfielder–first baseman Phil Cavaretta, a 22-year major league veteran. He was with the Cubs from 1934–53, then played his final two years for the White Sox. The National League batting champion in 1945, he batted .293 lifetime.

Bill "Swish" Nicholson, a heavy gunner for the Cubs in the 1940s. After a brief trial with the Athletics in 1936, he joined the Cubs in 1939, was dealt to the Phillies in 1949 and retired in 1953. Bill was a .268 lifetime hitter.

BELOW: A popular performer wherever he played, Andy Pafko came up with the Cubs in 1943, was traded to the Dodgers in 1951, and then to the Braves in 1953. He played for 17 years, batting .285.

It's July 6, 1945, and the Braves' Tommy Holmes has just whacked the base hit that established a new National League record for consecutive game hitting streaks. Holmes later had players of both teams autograph the picture. Tommy played for the Braves from 1942–51 and finished up with the Dodgers a year later. Lifetime average: .302.

Hank Greenberg in 1946.

Rookie Jackie Robinson is the object of autograph seekers. Coach Ray Blades is on the left, pitcher Ralph Branca on the right.

Fenway Park

Bob Feller. They wondered if his years in the Navy had tarnished his skills. He answered the speculation by winning 26 games and striking out 348 in 1946.

Joe Dobson, who came up with Cleveland in 1939 and pitched in the American League until 1954, most of the time with the Red Sox. He was 137–103 lifetime.

Red Sox third baseman Pinky Higgins (number 36) is trying to run down Stan Musial in this 1946 World Series action shot.

A trio of Cardinals pitchers in 1946. Left to right: Murry Dickson, Howard Pollett, and Harry Brecheen. Dickson was 172–181 for 18 years work with five teams; Brecheen was 132–92 for his 12-year career, all but one year of it in the employ of the Cardinals.

Summit meeting, baseball style: Feller versus DiMaggio in 1946.

LEFT: Pete Reiser coming home safely against the Cardinals at Ebbets Field on September 13, 1946. The catcher is Del Rice. Watching the action is Pee Wee Reese.

RIGHT: Jackie Robinson with Montreal in 1946. He played for Brooklyn from 1947–56, helping the team to six pennants. The batting champion in 1949, he batted .311 lifetime.

Larry Doby, the American League's first black player. Spending the bulk of his career with Cleveland, he played from 1947–59, twice leading the league in home runs. He batted .283 lifetime.

The 1946 Red Sox outfield is here drawing a crowd of adoring young fans. Left to right: Ted Williams, Leon Culberson, Dom DiMaggio, George Metkovich, Johnny Lazor, and Wally Moses.

Below: The Cardinals are putting on the "Williams shift" against Ted during the 1946 World Series.

Enos Slaughter completing his memorable dash around the bases in the eighth inning of the seventh game of the 1946 World Series. Enos scored from first on Harry Walker's hit to short left-center. The run gave the Cardinals the game and the championship. The umpire is Al Barlick, the on-deck hitter Marty Marion, and the Red Sox catcher is Roy Partee.

The Red Sox infield quartet in 1948. Left to right: first baseman Jake Jones, second baseman Bobby Doerr, shortstop Vern Stephens, and third baseman Johnny Pesky.

Harry Walker, who, like his older brother Dixie, was a National League batting champion (1947). Harry came up to the bigs with the Cardinals in 1940, was traded to the Phillies early in 1947, and later played for the Cubs and Reds, ending his 11-year career with a .296 batting average.

Red Schoendienst, who played second base for the Cardinals from 1945–56 and then for the Giants and Braves before returning to the Cardinals and retiring in 1963. He later managed the Cards for 12 years. His career average is .289.

Cincinnati's Ewell Blackwell. His whiplash sidearm motion gave right-handed batters nightmares. He pitched for the Reds in 1942 and from 1946–52, finishing up with the Yankees and Athletics. During his ten-year career he won 82 and lost 78, having been slowed down by a sore arm after his brilliant 1947 season.

RIGHT: Sid Gordon, National League infielder-outfielder for the Giants, Braves, and Pirates from 1941–55, with two years out for military service. Sid hit 25 or more home runs for five consecutive years and had a .283 lifetime average.

Eddie Stanky, hustling, sharp-witted second baseman with the Cubs, Dodgers, Braves, Giants, and Cardinals from 1943–53. Lifetime average: .268.

Walker Cooper, hard-hitting National League catcher for six clubs from 1940–57, with a career average of .285.

Johnny Mize and infielder Bill Rigney in the Giants dugout in 1947. Rigney, a lifetime .259 hitter, played for the Giants from 1946–53 and later managed the club.

Right-hander Larry Jansen, a superb pitcher for the Giants from 1947–54. He was 122–89 lifetime.

Philadelphia's fleet-footed center fielder Richie Ashburn. He was with the Phillies from 1948–59, later playing with the Cubs and Mets. A two-time National League batting champion, he batted over .300 nine times, retiring in 1962 with a .308 career mark.

Pittsburgh's Hank Greenberg (left) and Ralph Kiner in 1947. Kiner, one of baseball's great home run hitters, played from 1946–55, having his greatest years with Pittsburgh, leading in home runs seven consecutive times. He batted .279 lifetime.

LEFT: Del Ennis, the Phillies' premier long-ball hitter from 1946–56, later played for the Cardinals, Reds, and White Sox, retiring in 1959 with a .284 average. He drove in over 100 runs in a season seven times.

LEFT: Bob Elliott, a steady belter with the Pirates and Braves from 1939–51, finishing up in the American League in 1953. The MVP for the Braves in 1947, he drove in over 100 runs six times, batting .289 lifetime.

Cookie Lavagetto is mobbed by jubilant fans and teammates after his breathtaking game-winning pinch-hit double in the bottom of the ninth inning of game 4 of the 1947 World Series. The hit deprived Yankees pitcher Bill Bevens of the first World Series no-hitter.

Dodger left fielder Al Gionfriddo making his memorable catch of a DiMaggio blast at Yankee Stadium in the sixth game of the 1947 World Series.

A pair of pitching legends: Satchel Paige (left) and Bob Feller. Paige, for two decades a star in the Negro Leagues, finally reached the majors with Cleveland in 1948, after the crumbling of the color barrier. He was forty-two years old at the time. He pitched for the Indians and Browns until 1953, winning 28 and losing 31.

Stunned and dejected, Yankees Bill Bevens (left) and Joe DiMaggio head for the Yankees clubhouse through the Ebbets Field runway moments after Lavagetto's hit.

The dramatics of the 1947 World Series belonged to the Dodgers, but the ultimate victory went to the Yankees. Four of the architects of that victory, left to right: infielder (and future president of the American League) Bobby Brown, third baseman Billy Johnson, and pitchers Joe Page and Allie Reynolds.

Six members of Detroit's 1948 pitching staff line up to have their picture taken. Left to right: Ted Gray, Hal Newhouser, Virgil Trucks, Art Houtteman, Fred Hutchinson, and Dizzy Trout.

Gene Bearden (center) has just beaten the Red Sox in the American League's first pennant playoff, at Fenway Park on October 4, 1948, giving Cleveland its first pennant in 28 years. Owner Bill Veeck is at the left and pitcher Steve Gromek is in the middle.

The Braves' Rookie-of-the-Year shortstop Alvin Dark in 1948. He starred for the Braves and Giants and also played for three other National League teams in a 14-year career that ended in 1960. Lifetime batting average: .289.

The ivy-covered walls of Chicago's Wrigley Field.

Right-hander Johnny Sain, who would throw you a curve on three-and-oh. Four times a 20-game winner for the Braves in the 1940s and 1950, he later helped the Yankees to three pennants, retiring in 1955 with a 139–116 record.

Ralph Kiner

Right-hander Virgil Trucks. They called him "Fire," and that's what he could do. He pitched for five American League clubs from 1941–58, with two years out for military service. Lifetime record: 177–135.

Vic Wertz, outfielder–first baseman and power hitter for five American League clubs from 1947–63. Five times a 100-RBI man, he was a career .277 hitter.

Fred Hutchinson, who pitched for Detroit from 1939–41 and 1946–53. Known as a gritty competitor, his career record is 95–71.

Detroit's Tiger Stadium from on high.

Roy Sievers, one of the top power hitters of his time (1949–65). He played for the Browns, Senators, White Sox, and Phillies. He had nine straight years of 20 or more home runs and a career batting average of .267.

Ted Williams (left) and right-hander Ellis Kinder celebrating a Red Sox victory in September 1949. Kinder was 23–6 that year. Pitching for four clubs in both leagues from 1946–57, Ellis had a career 102–71 record.

Jackie Robinson stealing home against the Phillies. The catcher is Andy Seminick, the batter Gil Hodges.

The National League's Most Valuable Player in 1949, Jackie Robinson, receiving the emblematic plaque from league president Ford Frick.

Mickey Mantle

1950

In 1949, the Yankees survived key injuries and went on to win the pennant; in 1950, their two closest rivals suffered key injuries but failed to demonstrate similar resilience. Detroit lost its 19-game-winning right-hander of 1949 Virgil Trucks to arm miseries early in the season, and the Red Sox lost Ted Williams for most of the season's second half after Ted suffered a fractured elbow in the All-Star Game. Detroit finished three games behind New York, Boston four.

In winning a second straight pennant, Casey Stengel was blessed again with great pitching. Vic Raschi was 21–8, Eddie Lopat 18–8, Allie Reynolds 16–12, Tommy Byrne 15–9, and just for good measure the club brought up young southpaw Whitey Ford in June. Ford, destined to become the greatest of all Yankees pitchers, set an American League record by winning his first nine starts (he was 9–1 overall).

With Joe DiMaggio batting just .301 but hitting 32 home runs and driving in 122 runs, the Yankee's two top players were MVP shortstop Phil Rizzuto, who batted .324, and catcher Yogi Berra, who batted .322, hit 28 home runs, and drove in 124 runs.

The last major league team to have a .300 batting average (.302), the Red Sox mounted a fierce batting attack all season, even with Williams missing most of the second half. The lineup was so potent that the league's leading hitter, Billy Goodman (.354), had to be content with utility status, playing infield and outfield. Rookie of the Year first baseman Walt Dropo broke in thunderously, hitting 34 home runs, driving in 144 runs, and batting .322 (a year he never came close to repeating). Bobby Doerr batted .294 and drove in 120 runs, shortstop Vern Stephens batted .295 and tied Dropo at the top of the league with 144 RBIs, third baseman Johnny Pesky batted .312, catcher Birdie Tebbetts .310, outfielder Al Zarilla .325, and outfielder Dom DiMaggio .328. Williams, in his 89 games, hit 28 homers, drove in 97 runs, and batted .317. But with Mel Parnell at 18–10 the team's big winner, pitching once again was Boston's bugaboo.

On June 7 and 8 at Fenway Park, the Red Sox flexed their muscles against the St. Louis Browns. On the seventh, the Sox flattened the Browns by a score of 20–4. But that proved to be just a warm-up. The next day Boston delivered a 29–4 drubbing, setting records for most runs in a major league game, most runs in two straight games, and numerous other scoring, long ball, and total base records.

Second-place Detroit was sparked by

1950–
a
Yankees Decade
1959

Walt Dropo

third baseman George Kell, a .340 hitter with a league-leading 56 doubles, and a .300-hitting outfield of Vic Wertz, Johnny Groth, and Hoot Evers. Stylish young right-hander Art Houtteman led the staff with a 19–12 record.

Fourth-place Cleveland had the home run leader in third baseman Al Rosen (37) and the league's top winner in Bob Lemon (23–11), as well as the ERA champ in Early Wynn, whose 3.20 mark was the highest of any ERA leader in history.

An era—it seemed more like a millenium—came to an end with the retirement of eighty-seven-year-old Connie Mack as manager of the Philadelphia Athletics, after a reign of 50 years. Connie was succeeded in 1951 by Jimmy Dykes.

The National League won the All-Star Game, played at Chicago's Comiskey Park on July 11, 4–3, in 14 innings, on Red Schoendienst's home run.

They called the 1950 National League pennant-winning Philadelphia Phillies "The Whiz Kids" for the number of young players in the lineup. The squad included shortstop Granny Hamner (twenty-three years old), third baseman Willie Jones (twenty-four), outfielders Del Ennis (twenty-five) and Richie Ashburn (twenty-three), and pitchers Robin Roberts (twenty-three) and Curt Simmons (twenty-one). But before the pulsating pennant climax was

achieved, the "whiz" came perilously close to "fizz."

Through the agencies of bad luck and bad timing, the Phillies came close to blowing an "insurmountable" lead in the season's waning days. The bad luck occurred in injuries to starting pitchers Bob Miller and Bubba Church (who was almost decapitated by a Ted Kluszewski line drive), and the bad timing involved southpaw ace Simmons, called to military duty in September after a 17–8 season. Thus beset, the Phillies saw a 7½-game lead melt away as they lost eight of ten games while the Brooklyn Dodgers put on a charge.

The season's final game saw the Phillies and Dodgers meeting at Ebbets Field, with Eddie Sawyer's Whiz Kids one game up. Starting for the Phillies—for the third time in five games—was Robin Roberts. Opposing him was Don Newcombe.

The game was a gripping 1–1 tie going into the bottom of the ninth. With Dodgers on first and second and none out, Duke Snider singled hard to center. With Cal Abrams carrying the ostensible winning run, center fielder Ashburn rushed in, picked up the ball, and made the throw of his life, getting Abrams at the plate. Roberts then worked out of further hot water. In the top of the tenth, Dick Sisler cracked an opposite-field three-run homer into the lower stands in left and the Phillies went on to win their first pennant since 1915.

Roberts was 20–11 for the Phillies, while reliever Jim Konstanty was 16–7 with 22 saves, appearing in 74 games. Konstanty was voted Most Valuable Player, the first time the award was ever given to a relief pitcher. Philadelphia's hitting was led by Ennis, who had 31 homers, a league-high 126 RBIs, and a .311 batting average.

Second-place Brooklyn got 19–11 years from both Newcombe and Preacher Roe, while Gil Hodges, Carl Furillo, and Snider each had over 100 RBIs, with Hodges, Snider, and Roy Campanella each hitting over 30 home runs. On August 31, Hodges joined an elite group by connecting for four home runs in a 19–3 Dodgers slaughter of the Braves. A few weeks earlier, on August 11, the Braves' Vern Bickford pitched the year's only no-hitter, stopping the Dodgers by a 7–0 score.

The third-place Giants, who finished just five games out, received superb pitching from Larry Jansen (19–13) and Mexican League returnee Sal Maglie (18–4). Maglie, who claimed to have sharpened his curve ball in the thin Mexican air, had a string of 45 consecutive scoreless innings (1⅓ short of Carl Hubbell's league record) which was broken by a 257-foot Polo Grounds home run hit by Pittsburgh's Gus Bell on September 13.

Boston had a pair of 20-game winners in Warren Spahn (21–17) and Johnny Sain (20–13), as well as a 19–14 year from Bickford, but no other Boston pitcher won more than seven. The Braves also had the Rookie of the Year in outfielder Sam Jethroe, who batted .273 and led in

Vern Bickford

1951

It was a year that saw the biggest and the smallest—the biggest hit in baseball history and the smallest batter. The latter stepped up to home plate in an American League game between the St. Louis Browns and Detroit Tigers on August 19. In order to hype the Browns' sagging attendance, their owner, the ever-mischievous Bill Veeck, signed to a contract a three-foot-seven-inch midget named Eddie Gaedel and ordered manager Zack Taylor to use him. Sent up as a pinch-hitter against Tiger left-hander Bob Cain, Gaedel walked on four pitches (all high), went to first base, and was removed for a runner. The crowd loved it, but league president Will Harridge was not amused. He sent Veeck a sternly worded telegram condemning the "stunt," and Eddie Gaedel passed from the roster to the trivia lists.

While Veeck was trying to inject a bit of levity into things, Casey Stengel's Yankees were going methodically about the business of winning a third straight pennant. With Eddie Lopat (21–9), Vic Raschi (21–10), and Allie Reynolds (17–8) heading the pitching, the New Yorkers rolled to a five-game finish over Cleveland, where Al Lopez had three 20-game winners in Bob Feller (22–8), Mike Garcia (20–13), and Bob Lemon (20–13).

In his farewell season, Joe DiMaggio batted a mere .263, enough to singe his pride and send him into retirement. The club broke in nineteen-year-old rookie Mickey Mantle, who batted .267, while the club's star was its MVP catcher, Yogi Berra. The player-rich Yankees also had the Rookie of the Year in infielder Gil McDougald, who batted .306.

The league's sixth 20-game winner that year came from a most unlikely source—the last-place Browns, for whom Ned Garver was 20–12. On September 14, Browns rookie Bob Nieman set a record by homering in his first two big-league at bats. The batting champion was a surprise to everyone. After four big league seasons during which he had never hit .300, Athletics first baseman Ferris

stolen bases with 35, more than double anyone else's total.

In other notable areas it was business as usual—Stan Musial winning his fourth batting title with a .346 average and Ralph Kiner his fifth straight home run crown with 47.

In four tightly played games—the scores were 1–0, 2–1, 3–2, and 5–2—the Yankees swept the Phillies for their second straight World Series victory.

Eddie Gaedel in his one and only major league at-bat. The catcher is Bob Swift.

Fain singled and doubled his way to a .344 batting title. Outfielder Gus Zernial, traded from the White Sox to the Athletics early in the season, brought further glory to the sixth-place A's by leading in home runs with 33 and RBIs with 129.

On July 1, Bob Feller joined Cy Young as the only men in modern history to pitch three no-hitters when he stopped Detroit, 2–1. Allie Reynolds also tied a record by pitching a pair of no-hitters—1–0 over Cleveland on July 12 (beating Feller; the run was Gene Woodling's home run) and 8–0 over Boston on September 28. The Boston game, which also happened to be the Yankees' pennant clincher, ended most dramatically. Facing Reynolds as the game's final batter was Ted Williams. Ted popped up a foul to Yogi Berra, who dropped it. Unfazed, Reynolds fired away again and got the game's greatest hitter to pop up another foul to Yogi, who this time caught it.

The National League won the All-Star Game, 8–3. The game was played on July 10, at Detroit's Briggs Stadium.

Baseball's biggest hit came on the afternoon of October 3 at New York's Polo Grounds. It was struck by the Giants' Bobby Thomson and brought a sudden, crashing, crushing end to one of the most incredible pennant drives ever seen.

On August 12, the Brooklyn Dodgers held a 13½-game lead over Leo Durocher's Giants, who had been expected to contend but who stumbled coming out of the gate, losing 12 of their first 14, including 11 straight. But in May the Giants added to the club twenty-year-old center fielder Willie Mays (the eventual Rookie of the Year) and began playing better ball.

On August 12 the Giants launched a 16-game winning streak, went on to take 37 of their last 44, and finished in a 96–58 tie with the Dodgers, necessitating a three-game playoff.

The Giants won the first game, at Ebbets Field, the Dodgers the second, at the Polo Grounds. Game 3 saw a matchup of aces—the Giants' Sal Maglie and the Dodgers' Don Newcombe. The Dodgers took a 4–1 lead into the bottom of the ninth, only to see the Giants mount a rally. Singles by Alvin Dark and Don Mueller, followed by an out and then a double by Whitey Lockman brought the winning run to the plate. Dodger manager Chuck Dressen relieved the tiring Newcombe with Ralph Branca. The batter was Thomson. The first pitch was a strike, the second became baseball history and American folklore as it disappeared on a ringing line into the lower stands in left. The 5–4 victory, which drove baseball credibility to its extremes, gave the Giants their first pennant since 1937.

Durocher received superb pitching all year long from his two aces, Maglie (23–6) and Larry Jansen (23–11), as well as from Jim Hearn (17–9). Leo also had the league's

Roy Campanella

top RBI man in Monte Irvin (121) and got fine all-around play from Dark, Lockman, Thomson (32 homers), Eddie Stanky, and the wondrous Mays, who batted .274 in his first season, hitting 20 home runs, and playing center field with an élan not seen in years.

The Dodgers got a 22–3 season from Preacher Roe, while Newcombe was 20–9. Roe's .880 winning percentage was the league's highest ever for a 20-game winner.

The Dodgers had earned a tie on the last day of the regular season with an exciting 14-inning win over the Phillies, 9–8, on a Jackie Robinson home run. Robinson led the Dodgers with a .338 batting average, while MVP Roy Campanella batted .325. Gil Hodges hit 40 homers and drove in over 100 runs, as did Campanella and Duke Snider. The strong Brooklyn hitting led the league in every offensive department but triples; but the Giants pitching made the difference.

Stan Musial won his fifth batting title with a .355 average, while Ralph Kiner took home run honors for the sixth straight year with 42.

There were seven 20-game winners in the league this year. Joining the Giants and Dodgers aces were Boston's Warren Spahn (22–14), Philadelphia's Robin Roberts (21–15), and Murry Dickson, who was 20–16 for the seventh-place Pirates. On May 6, left-hander Cliff Chambers became the first Pirates pitcher since Nick Maddox in 1907 to pitch a no-hitter when he stopped Boston, 3–0.

On September 20, the 16 major-league club owners elected National League President Ford Frick to succeed Happy Chandler as commissioner of baseball.

After Thomson's resounding home run, the World Series was something of an anticlimax. The businesslike Yankees took their third straight title in six games, despite 11 hits by the Giants' red-hot Monte Irvin.

1952

Although the inroads were not nearly as serious as those made in World War II, the Korean War subtracted some key players from the major league rosters in 1952, most prominent among them Ted Williams. The Yankees were probably the hardest hit, having lost Whitey Ford a year earlier, and now infielders Bobby Brown and Jerry Coleman and pitcher Tom Morgan.

Nevertheless, the ever-resourceful Stengel fielded a winning combination for the fourth successive year, edging out Cleveland and its strong pitching by two games. Allie Reynolds (20–8) and Vic Raschi (16–6) led the Yankee staff. Young Mickey Mantle, replacing DiMaggio in center field, batted .311 and hit 23 home runs, while Yogi Berra was the team leader in homers with 30 and RBIs with 98, the second year in a row the New York pennant winners failed to have someone drive in 100.

For the second year running, the Indians had three 20-game winners: Early Wynn (23–12), Mike Garcia, and Bob Lemon (both 22–11). A disappointing 9–13 from the aging Bob Feller, however, was costly. Cleveland also had the home run leader in Larry Doby (32) and the RBI leader in Al Rosen (105, lowest league-leading total since 1918).

Fourth-place Philadelphia garnered a large share of individual honors: left-hander Bobby Shantz was the league MVP on the strength of a sparkling 24–7 season, while right-hander Harry Byrd (15–15) was Rookie of the Year, and Ferris Fain won the batting title for the second year in a row, hitting .327.

The Detroit Tigers, pennant contenders just two years before, finished last for the first time in their 52-year history, and it was a resounding last, with 104 losses. Detroit did have a few shining moments, provided by Walt Dropo, who on July 14 and in a July 15 doubleheader tied Pinky Higgins' major league record of 12 consecutive hits, and by Virgil Trucks, who tied yet another major league record (held by Johnny Vander Meer and Allie Reynolds) by pitching two no-hitters. The achievement was curious in light of Trucks's 5–19 season, but on May 15 he stopped the Senators 1–0 (winning on Vic Wertz's homer in the bottom of the ninth) and on August 25 he no-hit the Yankees, again by a 1–0 score.

Rain shortened the All-Star Game, played on July 8 at Philadelphia's Shibe Park, to five innings, the National League winning, 3–2.

Regrouping after their heartbreaking 1951 loss, Chuck Dressen's Dodgers came back to win the 1952 pennant, finishing 4½ games ahead of the Giants. The Giants suffered two crippling losses when big-gun Monte Irvin broke an ankle in spring training and was sidelined for most of the season and Willie Mays entered the Army late in May. Adding to the Giants' woes were back injuries to Sal

Joe Black (left) and Jackie Robinson.

Maglie (18–8) and co-ace Larry Jansen (11–11).

Two twenty-eight-year-old rookie relief pitchers shone through the season—fastballer Joe Black for the Dodgers (a nonroster player in the spring) and knuckleballing Hoyt Wilhelm for the Giants. Appearing in 56 games, Black was 15–4 (the club's top winner) with 15 saves, while Wilhelm was 15–3 with 11 saves in 71 appearances, pitching enough innings (159) to qualify for the ERA title (2.43). Wilhelm provided a curious note to his first big-league victory, which came on April 23. In his first big-league at-bat he won his own game with a home run, and although he pitched in the major leagues for another 20 years, in a record 1,070 games, never hit another home run.

With Black (the Rookie of the Year) shoring up a shaky staff depleted by Don Newcombe's departure for military service, the Dodgers hitting muscled the club to the pennant. Gil Hodges, Jackie Robinson, Duke Snider, Roy Campanella, and Andy Pafko led a solid attack. Carl Erskine, at 14–6 the club's most reliable starter, pitched the league's only no-hitter, stopping the Cubs on June 19, 5–0. Only a third-inning walk to opposing pitcher Willard Ramsdell deprived the Dodgers right-hander of a perfect game.

The Dodgers also put on the season's most extravagant scoring outburst. It came in the first inning of a May 21 shelling of the Reds when the Brooks scored a major league–record 15 runs on the way to a 19–1 hosing.

Twenty-one men went to the plate, including 19 in a row who reached base safely.

The year's most glittering pitching came from Philadelphia's Robin Roberts, who was 28–7, logging the league's highest win total since Dizzy Dean's 30 in 1934. Stan Musial won his third straight batting crown and sixth overall with a .336 average, and Ralph Kiner won his seventh (and final) straight home run title, tying with Chicago's Hank Sauer for the lead with 37 apiece. Sauer, who was voted the MVP Award, was the RBI leader with 121. With most observers expecting the award to go to either Black, Wilhelm, or Roberts, Sauer proved a surprise choice.

The Yankees and Dodgers played it all the way out in the World Series, with the Yankees winning their fourth straight championship, Raschi and Reynolds each winning two games. Duke Snider tied a Ruth-Gehrig record by hitting four home runs in the seven-game Series, while Johnny Mize hit three for the Yankees. Gil Hodges, however, did not fare as well; the Dodger first baseman went 0-for-21.

Duke Snider

1953

Casey Stengel, who had never been able to win in the National League, was finding it impossible to lose in the American. A fast start, buoyed by an 18-game winning streak begun in late May, carried the Yankees through to an 8½-game finish over Cleveland, the third straight second-place windup for Al Lopez and his Indians.

Whitey Ford, back from military service, was the Yankee ace with an 18–6 record, followed by Eddie Lopat's 16–4. Yogi Berra with 27 home runs and 108 RBIs topped the club in these power categories, with Gene Woodling's .306 the best average.

Cleveland had only one 20-game winner this year, Bob Lemon at 21–15, though Mike Garcia (18–9) and Early Wynn were not far behind. The Indians had the MVP in third baseman Al Rosen, who had a sensational year, hitting 43 home runs, driving in 145 runs, and batting .336, missing the Triple Crown on the last day of the season when Washington's Mickey Vernon edged him with a .337 average.

Yankee Mickey Mantle delivered the year's most thunderous hit, a 565-foot home run belted in Griffith Stadium on April 17 off Washington left-hander Chuck Stobbs. Detroit had the Rookie of the Year in shortstop Harvey Kuenn, a line-drive hitter who batted .308 and led with 209 hits. Also breaking into the Tiger lineup, albeit for just 30 games, was eighteen-year-old outfielder Al Kaline, fresh out of a Baltimore high school.

Another rookie made baseball's most memorable starting debut. In his first big-league start, on May 6, the Browns' Bobo Holloman fired a no-hitter against the Athletics, winning 6–0. But it was strictly a freak occurrance,

Whitey Ford

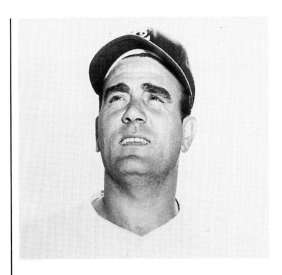

Bobo Holloman

for Holloman never completed another game, and at the end of July was optioned to the minors, never to return to the big leagues, leaving behind a 3–7 record, a 5.23 ERA, and one moment of unaccountable glory.

Other 20-game winners this year were Washington's Bob Porterfield (22–10, with nine shutouts), Boston's Mel Parnell (21–8), and Virgil Trucks, who was a combined 20–10 pitching for St. Louis and Chicago. Ted Williams returned from military service in August, got into 37 games for the Red Sox and batted .407, with 13 home runs among his 37 hits.

On June 18 the Red Sox lit up the Tigers at Fenway park by a 23–3 score, which included a 17-run, 14-hit seventh inning, during which Gene Stephens became the first player in modern baseball history to collect three hits in an inning (two singles and a double).

The All-Star game, played at Cincinnati's Crosley Field on July 14, was won by the National League, 5–1.

Charlie Dressen's Dodgers were the first Brooklyn team to repeat, finishing a strong 13 games ahead of the Milwaukee Braves. The Braves were now located in the Wisconsin city after the league approved their transfer in the spring. After years of declining attendance in what was, and always had been, a Red Sox town, owner Lou Perini felt he had no choice but to make a move. The wisdom of the move was quickly affirmed: in 1952 the club had drawn just 281,278—a figure they passed in their 13th Milwaukee home game (their season's total was 1,826,397). The Braves' success had other owners reaching for their geography books; the era of peripatetic franchises had begun.

The 1953 Dodgers were one of the most powerful combines in baseball history. MVP Roy Campanella hit 41 home runs, drove in 142 runs, and batted .312; Carl Furillo won the batting title with a .344 average; Duke Snider hit 42 home runs, drove in 126 runs, and batted .336; Gil Hodges hit 31 homers, had 122 RBIs, and batted .302; Jackie Robinson batted .329 and drove in 95 runs. In addition, the team had the Rookie of the Year in second

baseman Jim Gilliam, who batted .278. The Dodgers were the first National League team to have two 40-home run men in the same season. In winning a club-record 105 games, the Brooks were shut out just once, a record they share with the 1970 Reds.

Furillo may have owed his batting title to Leo Durocher. After being nicked with a pitch by Giants pitcher Ruben Gomez in a game at the Polo Grounds in early September, Furillo, believing that the offending pitch had been ordered by Leo, charged the Giants dugout. In the ensuing brawl, Furillo suffered a broken hand and missed the rest of the season (he returned for the World Series), freezing his batting average. The Cardinals' Red Schoendienst took a September shot at the stationary target, but fell short at .342.

Carl Erskine was the Dodger ace with a 20–6 record.

Milwaukee fans cheered the lusty hitting of sophomore third baseman Eddie Mathews, whose 47 home runs led the league and dethroned seven-time champ Ralph Kiner, who was traded to Chicago in a ten-man June 4 blockbuster deal. Kiner hit 35 long ones, while Cincinnati's Ted Kluszewski had 40, giving the league four men with 40 or more.

Milwaukee's Warren Spahn (23–7) and Philadelphia's Robin Roberts (23–16) were the league's top winners. St. Louis's rookie left-hander Harvey Haddix broke in with a 20–9 mark.

Stengel's Yankees broke all records for sustained dominance by taking their fifth straight world championship, beating the Dodgers in six. In game 3, Erskine set a new single-game Series record with 14 strikeouts. Yankees second baseman Billy Martin had 12 hits, the record for a six-game Series.

After the season, Dodgers manager Chuck Dressen resigned after being refused a three-year contract. Owner Walter O'Malley's best offer was a one-year pact. Dressen was replaced by Brooklyn farm system skipper Walter Alston.

Harvey Haddix

1954

The Cleveland Indians finally found a way to stop the Yankees' pennant march, which had by now assumed an aura of inevitability. The sure way to win more games than any other American League team had ever done, and this was exactly what Al Lopez's boys did in 1954, racking up 111 victories, exceeding by one the old league record set by the 1927 Yankees. Nor were the Indians being extravagant with 111 wins—the Yankees won 103, more than any of Stengel's ten pennant winners ever did.

The Indians traded on what had become their perennial strength—good pitching. Bob Lemon was 23–7, Early Wynn 23–11, Mike Garcia 19–8, Art Houtteman 15–7, and Bob Feller, in his last winning season, 13–3. Also on the staff, considered by many the greatest of modern times, were a couple of first-rate relief pitchers, Ray Narleski and left-hander Don Mossi. The staff ERA of 2.78 was the league's lowest since the dead-ball 1919 season.

Cleveland also had the batting champion in second baseman Bobby Avila (.341), the home run (32) and RBI (126) leader in Larry Doby, and a 100-RBI man in Al Rosen.

The Indians didn't settle definitively with the tenacious Yankees until September 12. Trailing by 6½ games, the Yankees came into Cleveland for a doubleheader, only to have Lopez's club drop them twice (before a rip-roaring crowd of 84,587), which pretty much ended Stengel's dream of a sixth straight pennant.

The Yankees got .300 seasons from Mickey Mantle, Andy Carey, rookie first baseman Bill Skowron (.340 in 87 games), Irv Noren, and Yogi Berra, who won his second MVP Award. The Yankees also had a rookie 20-game winner in Bob Grim (20–6), the last freshman to win 20 until Cincinnati's Tom Browning in 1985. Grim was voted the league's Rookie of the Year.

Detroit's sophomore shortstop Harvey Kuenn again led in hits with 201, tied with White Sox second baseman Nelson Fox. In 631 at-bats Fox struck out just 12 times—one of 11 years he led in fewest strikeouts, a major league record.

Major league baseball's second franchise shift in two years occurred this year, the St. Louis Browns melting away and reappearing as the Baltimore Orioles. The seventh-place Orioles had one shining asset in fastballing right-hander Bob Turley (14–15, with a league-high 185 strikeouts), upon whom the Yankees began casting coveting eyes. In December the Yankees got Turley along with pitcher Don Larsen, who were part of a massive, two-step, 18-player deal. The Yankees wanted Larsen in spite of the big right-hander's wretched (and misleading) 3–21 record.

The All-Star Game went to the American League,

Bob Grim

11–9. The game was played in Cleveland's Municipal Stadium on July 13.

Willie Mays was back with the Giants in 1954, and that was the crucial fact in deciding the pennant race. With Willie putting together a sensational MVP year—41 home runs, 110 RBIs, a league-leading .345 batting average—Leo Durocher's Giants upset the favored Dodgers and won by five games. Willie won his batting title on the season's final day, edging out teammate Don Mueller (.342) and Brooklyn's Duke Snider (.341).

In February the Giants had traded their 1951 pennant hero Bobby Thomson to the Braves in a six-man deal that brought them young left-hander Johnny Antonelli. Johnny promptly became the ace with a 21–7 record, followed by Ruben Gomez's 17–9. The Giants also received marvelous relief pitching from Hoyt Wilhelm and Marv Grissom.

Second-place Brooklyn got 40-homer seasons from Snider and Gil Hodges, each of whom drove in 130 runs. The league's biggest gun was Cincinnati's muscular first baseman Ted Kluszewski, who led everybody with 49 homers and 141 runs batted in. Chicago's Hank Sauer, with 41 homers, and Milwaukee's Eddie Mathews, with 40, gave the league six men with 40 or more big belts, a major league record for an eight-club league (tied the next year).

On April 23, Milwaukee rookie Henry Aaron belted the first of his record 755 major league home runs, the shot coming against the Cardinals, served up by ex-

Yankee Vic Raschi. On May 2, Stan Musial, who launched 35 one-way shots that year, set a new major league record by hitting five home runs in a doubleheader against the Giants. Another man-sized outburst was delivered by Milwaukee's Joe Adcock against the Dodgers on July 31. Adcock hit four home runs and a double, accumulating a one-game record 18 total bases. The next day he was beaned and carried off the field on a stretcher. Coincidence, the Dodgers said, was part of baseball.

Philadelphia's Robin Roberts was the league's big winner with a 23–15 record, while Milwaukee's Warren Spahn maintained a good habit by winning 21 games. Another Milwaukee pitcher, right-hander Jim Wilson, pitched the majors' only no-hitter of the year, chilling the Phillies on June 12, 2–0. The Cardinals had the Rookie of the Year in outfielder Wally Moon, who batted .304. Brooklyn rookie southpaw Karl Spooner made his first major league start one for the record books when he fanned 15 Giants (most ever by a pitcher in his first game) on his way to a 3–0 shutout. After he shut out the Pirates in his next start, Dodgers fans were heard to mutter, "We shoulda had Spooner sooner."

After winning 111 regular-season games, the Indians never won another as the Giants swept them in four straight in the World Series. The Series was highlighted by Mays's breathtaking running catch of a Vic Wertz drive to the deepest reaches of the Polo Grounds, a defensive play that saved game 1 for the Giants, and by the lethal pinch-hitting of Dusty Rhodes, who delivered three times, including a three-run game-winning home run in the tenth inning of the opener.

1955

Getting closer and closer to the superstardom that had been predicted for him since 1951, the Yankees' Mickey Mantle hit 37 home runs to lead the American League and help return Casey Stengel's Yankees to the top. New York's sixth pennant in seven years was won by three games over a dogged Cleveland team.

Yogi Berra won his third MVP Award, hitting 27 homers and driving in 108 runs while catching 145 games. With the American League going without a 20-game winner for the first time in its history, Whitey Ford topped the league as one of three 18-game winners, along with Cleveland's Bob Lemon and Boston's Frank Sullivan. Bob Turley, in his first year with the Yankees, was a 17-game winner.

Although without a 20-game winner for the first time in nine years, the Indians did break in one of the most spectacularly talented pitchers in years in twenty-two-year-old left-hander Herb Score. The Rookie of the Year speedballer was 16–10, setting a new rookie record with 245 strikeouts.

Playing his second full season, Detroit's Al Kaline

Jim Wilson

Al Kaline

became a twenty-year-old batting champion with a .340 average, tying him with Tiger predecessor Ty Cobb as the youngest-ever batting titlist. Kaline would play another nineteen years and bat over .300 eight more times, but never again as high as he did this year. The early batting crown gave a special luster to Kaline's long and splendid career that never faded.

On June 24, Washington's nineteen-year-old Harmon Killebrew hit the first of his 573 big-league home runs, and on September 17 the Orioles for the first time played eighteen-year-old Brooks Robinson at third base.

The RBI leaders were Detroit's Ray Boone and Boston's Jackie Jensen, with 116 apiece. The massacre of the year took place on April 23, when the White Sox battered the Athletics by a 29–6 score, tying the major league record for runs scored in a single game. The Athletics were now receiving their mail in Kansas City, having received permission to migrate from Philadelphia, making it three big-league franchise movements in three years.

Thirty-six-year-old Bob Feller was near the end of his long career now, showing a 4–4 record for the Indians (he retired the next year after an 0–4 season); but on May 1 there was one final flash of the old "Rapid Robert" when he pitched his major league–record 12th one-hitter in beating the Red Sox.

The National League won the All-Star Game, played at Milwaukee's County Stadium on July 12, when Stan Musial's home run in the bottom of the 12th gave them a 6–5 victory.

After stumbling in his first year as Dodgers manager, Walter Alston won the pennant in 1955. "Actually," Alston said later, "I don't think that team even needed a manager."

The Dodgers came charging out of the gate with blazing speed, winning their first 10 games and 22 of their first 24, coasting to an ultimate 13½-game margin over second-place Milwaukee. Once more the team was dominated by its hitters. Duke Snider hit 42 home runs, Roy Campanella (who won his third MVP Award) 32, Gil Hodges 27, and Carl Furillo 26, with Hodges, Snider, and Campanella each driving in over 100 runs, Snider's 136 leading the league.

Sharing in the club's lusty hitting was ace right-hander Don Newcombe. In addition to his 20–5 record, Big Newk swung a hot bat all year, batting .359 and setting a new standard for pitchers with seven home runs and tying Burleigh Grimes's league record for pitchers with 42 hits.

Breaking in with a 2–2 record for the Dodgers was Sandy Koufax, a nineteen-year-old left-hander who was extremely fast and extremely wild.

Once again the league had six men with 40 or more home runs, led by Willie Mays's 51. Following Willie were Cincinnati's Ted Kluszewski with 47, Chicago's Ernie Banks (44), Snider (42), Milwaukee's Eddie Mathews (41), and Cincinnati's Wally Post (40). Among Banks's total were five grand slams, a new one-season major league record.

Philadelphia's Richie Ashburn, who hit just three home runs, was the batting champion with a .338 average. Teammate Robin Roberts was a 20-game winner for the sixth straight year with a 23–14 mark.

For the second year in a row a Cardinal outfielder was voted Rookie of the Year, Bill Virdon (.281) following Wally Moon as the sportswriters' choice. Another rookie, albeit a seasoned one, the Cubs' Sam Jones, pitched the majors' only no-hitter, bottling up the Pirates on May 12, 4–0. The twenty-nine-year-old hard-throwing right-hander did it with dramatic flair, too. After walking the first three Pirates in the top of the ninth, Sam fanned the next three—Dick Groat, twenty-year-old rookie Roberto Clemente, and Frank Thomas.

The World Series started off like another Yankee festival, Stengel's team winning the first two games. The Series then moved to Ebbets Field where the Dodgers won three straight. The Yankees won game 6. Then, behind the shutout pitching of Johnny Podres and helped by a memorable running catch by left-fielder Sandy Amoros in the sixth inning that turned a Yankee rally into a double play, the Dodgers won the only world championship in their long Brooklyn history. Duke Snider hit four home runs for the Dodgers, tying the record he already shared with Ruth and Gehrig.

Bill Virdon

1956

The Yankees had been waiting for it to happen, the other clubs in the league had been dreading it, and finally, like a colossus in eruption, Mickey Mantle in 1956 did it all. With stunning power from either side of the plate, with terrific running speed, with a charisma conferred upon him by millions of fans, the Yankees center fielder slugged his way to a Triple Crown via 52 home runs, 130 runs batted in, and .353 batting average. Inevitably, he was the MVP.

Sparked by the hitting of Mantle, Gil McDougald, Bill Skowron, and Yogi Berra, and the pitching of Whitey Ford (19–6), Johnny Kucks (18–9), and Tom Sturdivant (16–8), Stengel's club finished nine games ahead of second-place Cleveland. It was the sixth straight year that New York and Cleveland had finished first or second.

The Indians once again had pitching to boast of—three 20-game winners in Early Wynn (20–9), Herb Score (20–9), and Bob Lemon (20–14), but Cleveland's .244 team batting average was no match for New York's power-laden .270. Score led in strikeouts with 263, and in only his second year seemed on course for a Hall of Fame career.

Detroit had four .300 hitters in their regular lineup in Harvey Kuenn (.332), Charlie Maxwell (.326), Al Kaline (.314, 128 RBIs), and Ray Boone (.308), as well as big winners in Frank Lary (21–13) and left-hander Billy Hoeft (20–14), but still finished fifth. Chicago's talented southpaw Billy Pierce, with a 20–9 record, gave the league six 20-game winners for the year. Another White Sox player, shortstop Luis Aparicio, was Rookie of the Year.

On July 14, Boston left-hander Mel Parnell no-hit the White Sox, winning 4–0.

Washington's Griffith Stadium was the scene of the All-Star Game, on July 10, with the National League winning, 7–3.

Mel Parnell (right) after his no-hitter. With him is catcher Sammy White.

The National League race was a back-alley brawl between the Dodgers, Braves, and Reds, three heavy hitters who smashed 577 home runs between them. Cincinnati had the most thunderous attack, hitting 221 homers to tie the record set by the 1947 New York Giants. To an already potent offense, the Reds this year added twenty-year-old outfielder Frank Robinson, who tied Wally Berger's rookie home run record of 38. Robinson, one day to become baseball's first black manager, was voted Rookie of the Year. Other Cincinnati fence busters included Wally Post (36 home runs), Ted Kluszewski (35), Gus Bell (29), and Ed Bailey (28). The Reds, however, had only one dependable starter, Brooks Lawrence, who was 19–10.

Walter Alston's Dodgers took a one-game lead into the season's final day and held it, finishing one up on Milwaukee and two over the Reds. Alston had a yearlong pitching bulwark in Don Newcombe, who was a spectacular 27–7. Newk's memorable season brought him the MVP Award as well as the newly instituted Cy Young Award, which until 1967 was given to just one pitcher. (Cy Young had died the year before, at the age of eighty-eight, and the memorial award to be given annually for pitching excellence and named for him was the idea of National League president Ford Frick.)

On May 15 the Dodgers picked up Sal Maglie on waivers from the Cleveland Indians, who had obtained him from the Giants the previous July. Maglie pitched superbly for the Dodgers; Brooklyn's one-time most despised opponent was 13–5, including a 5–0 no-hitter against the Phillies on September 25. Maglie's was one of two Dodger no-hitters in 1956; on May 12, Carl Erskine pitched the second of his career, allowing the Giants no hits in a 3–0 victory.

Brooklyn's top gunners were Duke Snider with a league-high 43 home runs and Gil Hodges with 32.

Second-place Milwaukee had a strong starting rotation in Warren Spahn (20–11), Lew Burdette (19–10), and Bob Buhl (18–8). They also had the batting champion in Henry Aaron, whose .328 average was the lowest for a National League leader since Edd Roush's .321 in 1919. Henry hit 26 homers, while teammates Joe Adcock and Eddie Mathews had 38 and 37, respectively.

Pittsburgh's Dale Long generated some excitement when he set a record by hitting home runs in eight consecutive games (one per game) from May 19–28, before being stopped by Newcombe.

The Giants' Johnny Antonelli was the league's third 20-game winner, posting a 20–13 record for the sixth-place Giants, while Robin Roberts was a hefty 19–18, making it the first time since 1950 that the great Phillies right-hander had not won 20.

Yankees right-hander Don Larsen emerged from the 1956 World Series wearing a halo, for it was in this Series

Johnny Antonelli

that he pitched his perfect game, sealing off the Dodgers 2–0 in game 5. The last three games of this seven-game Series, in fact, were shutouts: Brooklyn's Clem Labine (normally a relief pitcher, and a superb one) pitched a ten-inning 1–0 shutout in game 6, defeating an equally brilliant Bob Turley; and then right-hander Johnny Kucks won it all for the Yankees by stopping the Dodgers in game 7, 9–0. Yogi Berra and Mickey Mantle each had three homers for the Yankees in the seven-game Series, Yogi driving in 10 runs.

Mickey Mantle

1957

There was Ol' Man River and there was the New York Yankees, and both just kept rolling along. Stengel's group of noblemen (baseball style) won their third straight pennant and eighth in nine years, muscling ahead of runner-up Chicago's popgun offense by eight games. (For White Sox manager Al Lopez, hired away from Cleveland over the winter, it was six second-place finishes in the last seven years.)

Led by MVP Mickey Mantle, who hit 34 homers and batted .365 (146 walks kept his RBIs down to 94), the Yankees took first place away from the surprising White Sox in midseason and never looked back. Mantle, Bill Skowron, Yogi Berra, and their mates were joined by Rookie of the Year Tony Kubek, a versatile youngster who played infield and outfield with equal skill and batted .297.

With a sore shoulder limiting Whitey Ford to an 11–5 season, Stengel's top pitcher was Tom Sturdivant, who was 16–6.

Lopez, who had been blessed with good pitching in Cleveland, inherited some more in Chicago, particularly in Billy Pierce (20–12) and Dick Donovan (16–6). The White Sox also got the year's only no-hitter, when Bob Keegan shut down the Senators, 6–0, on August 20. One of the men silenced by Keegan that day was Roy Sievers, who was the first Washington player to lead in home runs (42); his 114 RBIs also led the league (the only other Senator to do that was Goose Goslin in 1924). Detroit's Jim Bunning, with a 20–8 record, was the league's other 20-game winner.

In the spring, Boston owner Tom Yawkey had offered the Indians $1,000,000 cash for Herb Score. The Indians refused it. On May 7, while pitching to the Yankees' Gil McDougald, the young left-hander was struck in the eye by a sizzling line drive hit right back at him. Score did not pitch again in 1957, and when he returned, his once incomparable skills were gone.

Boston's thirty-eight-year-old Ted Williams turned in a season of pure splendor with a .388 batting average (including 38 home runs), that left Mantle's .365 in second place and earned the game's greatest hitter his fifth batting title and the distinction of being baseball's oldest titlist. Ted's slugging average was .731, a figure no one has come even remotely close to since.

The American League won the All-Star Game, played at Busch Stadium in St. Louis on July 9, by a 6–5 score.

After missing by a single game in 1956, Fred Haney's Milwaukee Braves went all the way in 1957, beating second-place St. Louis by eight games, while an aging Dodgers team finished third.

The Braves combined solid hitting with good starting pitching, the latter being the province of Cy Young Award

Bob Buhl

winner Warren Spahn (21–11), Bob Buhl (18–7), and Lew Burdette (17–9), with strong relief work from Don Mc-Mahon, who joined the club in midseason. The hitting came from MVP Henry Aaron, who led with 44 home runs and 132 RBIs; Eddie Mathews, with 32 home runs, and Red Schoendienst, who batted .310 after coming to the Braves in a June deal with the Giants.

Stan Musial vied with Ted Williams for senior citizen honors by leading the league with a .351 average. For the thirty-six-year-old Cardinal icon, it was his seventh batting crown. Another signal personal achievement was Duke Snider's 40 home runs, giving the Dodger center fielder a league record by having hit 40 or more long ones five years in a row. Chicago's Ernie Banks hit 43 homers.

The Rookie of the Year was no callow youngster— he was Philadelphia's twenty-eight-year-old right-hander Jack Sanford, who was 19–8 with 188 league-leading strikeouts. Willie Mays continued to display his dazzling all-around abilities by hitting 35 home runs, batting .333, and leading in triples (20) and stolen bases (38), in addition to playing the most complete center field in baseball.

The World Series went to Milwaukee, the Braves beating the Yankees in seven. Milwaukee's twin stars were Aaron with 11 hits (including three home runs) and Burdette, who hurled three complete-game victories, becoming the first pitcher since Stanley Coveleski in 1920 to accomplish this.

The biggest baseball news of the year, however, took place in the executive suites of the New York Giants and Brooklyn Dodgers. On August 19, Giants owner Horace Stoneham announced that his club, a National League fixture in New York since 1883, was moving to San Francisco. And shortly after the close of the season, Brooklyn's chief executive Walter O'Malley confirmed the rumors that had been swirling all summer when he announced that starting in 1958 his club would be known as the Los Angeles Dodgers.

1958

It was becoming routine now, one of life's more dependable expectations— the Yankees winning the pennant. Stengel's marauders made it four straight and nine of ten, rolling home ten games ahead of the second-place White Sox and Al Lopez, who seemed to have taken a lease on the slot.

Though his batting average fell from .365 to .304, Mickey Mantle still blasted 42 home runs, leading the league by one over Cleveland's Rocky Colavito. Mickey was joined in the Yankees .300 circle by Norm Siebern and Elston Howard, though for the second year in a row the pennant winners were without a 100-RBI man. The Yanks did have the Cy Young Award winner in Bob Turley, who had his greatest year with a 21–7 record, the league's only 20-game winner that year.

The Red Sox had the MVP in outfielder Jackie Jensen, who hit 35 homers and drove in 122 runs. They also had the batting leader again, and for the second year in a row it was Ted Williams setting a new record as the oldest titlist, this time with a .328 average, as Ted beat out teammate Pete Runnels (.322) in the season's waning days.

Both of 1958's no-hitters were pitched in the American League: the first, on July 20, by Detroit's Jim Bunning over the Red Sox, 3–0; the second, by Baltimore's Hoyt

Jim Bunning

Wilhelm (in a rare start), 1–0, over the Yankees on September 20.

Eighth-place Washington supplied the Rookie of the Year in outfielder Albie Pearson, who batted .275.

The All-Star Game was played at Baltimore's Memorial Stadium on July 8, the American League winning, 4–3.

While the Dodgers and Giants moved themselves and their venerable (and profitable) rivalry from one coast to the other, the Milwaukee Braves struck another blow for the heartland, winning their second straight pennant for Fred Haney, repeating their eight-game margin, this time over Pittsburgh. Warren Spahn was 22–11 and Lew Burdette 20–10, leading the Braves staff. Henry Aaron, solidifying his superstar status year after year, hit 30 home runs and batted .326, while Eddie Mathews banged out 31 homers and part-timer Wes Covington hit 24 homers and batted .330.

The second-place Pirates, in their best windup since 1944, had a 20-game winner in Bob Friend (22–14) and a big clouter in third baseman Frank Thomas (35 home runs, 109 RBIs), as well as .300 hitters in shortstop Dick Groat and outfielder Bob Skinner.

The transplanted Giants fared better in their new time zone than the Dodgers, finishing third to L.A.'s seventh. The San Franciscans introduced a lusty young slugger in Rookie of the Year first baseman Orlando Cepeda, who hit 25 home runs, drove in 96 runs, and batted .312. Teammate Willie Mays was no less magical in California than he was in New York, hitting 29 home runs and batting

.347. Willie lost out on the batting crown to Philadelphia's Richie Ashburn, who won for the second time with a .350 average.

The league's MVP was the Cubs' Ernie Banks, a shortstop who hit like an outfielder. Banks led in home runs (47) and RBIs (129), while batting .313. The fifth-place Cubs were a hard-hitting outfit this year, with five men hitting 20 or more homers—Banks, first baseman Dale Long (20), and outfielders Walt Moryn (26), Lee Walls (24), and Bobby Thomson (21). But the team had only one pitcher win as many as ten games.

Though posting just a 14–13 record, the Cardinals' Sam Jones fanned 225, most in the league since Van Mungo's 238 in 1936.

Playing in the lopsided Los Angeles Coliseum (designed, as one writer said, for every possible human activity except a baseball game) while awaiting construction of their new park, the Dodgers were an artistic failure but a commercial success, from the opening-day record 78,672 fans they drew to their total attendance of 1,845,556, highest in franchise history. Among the several reasons for their abrupt decline in the standings was the club's loss of catcher Roy Campanella, who had been paralyzed from the neck down in an automobile accident in January.

The Yankees got off to a 1–3 predicament in games in the World Series, but then, thanks to the strong pitching of Turley (two wins and a save), turned it around and became the first team since the 1925 Pirates to emerge from that deficit and win it all. New York's Hank Bauer tied a Series record with four home runs.

Hank Bauer

Orlando Cepeda

1959

Two strange and unaccountable occurrences took place in 1954 and again in 1959, giving certain people a disoriented feeling; for these were the years—the only years—between 1949 and 1964 that the New York Yankees did not win the American League pennant.

In 1959, that perennial second-place occupant Al Lopez proved that persistence was its own reward, that if you hung around outside of a door long enough eventually someone would open it and let you in. Lopez's Chicago White Sox won their first pennant in 40 years—since the notorious 1919 team.

The Yankees stumbled badly in the early going and never really regained their footing, finishing third, 15 games out. The second-place club was Cleveland, five games behind. The White Sox showed the Indians who was boss that year by sweeping Cleveland in a four-game late-August series that was significant in deciding the race.

This White Sox team was known as "The Go-Go Sox" for their hustle. And hustle they did, making up for the lowest number of home runs in the league (97) and the sixth-highest number of runs (669). The hustle came most conspicuously from shortstop Luis Aparicio, the top base stealer with 56 (he led in steals in his first nine years in the big leagues); second baseman Nelson Fox, at .306 the club's top hitter; and outfielder Jim Landis. What little power the club had was supplied by catcher Sherman Lollar, who hit 22 home runs and drove in 84 runs, most on the club.

Good pitching, always the hallmark of an Al Lopez team, was at the heart of Chicago's success. The staff featured Early Wynn (22–10), Bob Shaw (18–6), Billy Pierce (14–15), and an effective pair of relievers, Gerry Staley and Turk Lown.

The Indians had a big buster in Rocky Colavito, who tied Washington's Harmon Killebrew for the home run lead at 42. Rocky went into the record books when he hit four home runs in one game against the Orioles on June 10. Cal McLish was 19–8 for the Indians. The long decline that was to distress the Cleveland franchise for decades was about to set in.

Detroit had the leading hitter in Harvey Kuenn. The former shortstop, who had been switched to the outfield, batted .353, his 198 hits giving him the league lead for the fourth time. The RBI leader was Boston's Jackie Jensen with 112, one more than Colavito. (A fear of flying drove the thirty-two-year-old Jensen from baseball the next year.)

The oddball game of the year was played between the White Sox and the Kansas City Athletics on April 22. In an unbelievable seventh inning, the Sox scored 11 runs on ten walks, three errors, one hit batter, and just one hit— a single. The final score was 20–6.

Early Wynn won the Cy Young Award and Nelson Fox was the MVP, while Rookie of the Year distinction went to Washington's Bob Allison, who hit 30 home runs.

Beginning this year, two All-Star Games were scheduled. The first, played on July 7 at Pittsburgh's Forbes Field, went to the National League, 5–4. The second game, on August 3 at the Los Angeles Memorial Coliseum, went to the American League by the score of 5–3.

With eight games left to play, the San Francisco Giants led the Braves and the Dodgers by two games. As they went about making the necessary preparations for the anticipated World Series, the Giants received a three-day visit from the Dodgers. The Dodgers swept their hosts, the Giants went on to lose seven of those last eight games, and the Dodgers and Braves ended the season tied for first place.

In the best-of-three playoff, the Dodgers won the first game in Milwaukee, 3–2. Coming back to L.A., Walter Alston's club beat the Braves and clinched the pennant in a hair-raising 12-inning thriller, 7–6, after having scored three times in the bottom of the ninth to tie.

The Dodgers' 88 wins (counting the two playoff victories) were the lowest total ever for a National League pennant winner. Alston's ace was Don Drysdale, 17–13 with 242 league-leading strikeouts, while Duke Snider at .308 and Wally Moon at .302 were the top hitters.

Milwaukee had the batting champion in Henry Aaron, who reached a career-high .355, hit 39 home runs, drove in 123 runs, and led with 223 hits. Eddie Mathews was the home run champ with 46. The Braves' aces were

Henry Aaron

Warren Spahn and Lew Burdette, with identical 21–15 records. The Giants' Sam Jones, the league's other 20-game winner, had the same 21–15 mark.

Despite Aaron's superb season, the MVP Award went to the Cubs' Ernie Banks for the second year in a row. Banks hit 45 home runs, led with 143 RBIs, and batted .304. Rookie of the Year honors went to the Giants' Willie McCovey, who played in just 52 games and batted .354. Called up in early August, McCovey launched his Hall of Fame career by smashing two singles and two triples in his first game, the hits coming off no less than Robin Roberts.

The greatest-pitched game in major league history occurred on May 26. Working against the hard-hitting Milwaukee lineup, Pirates left-hander Harvey Haddix spun out 12 perfect innings in a 0–0 duel with Lew Burdette. In the bottom of the 13th, Haddix's streak of 36 consecutive outs was broken by a throwing error by third baseman Don Hoak. A sacrifice, an intentional walk, and a hit by Joe Adcock followed, sending Haddix down to a 1–0 defeat.

Haddix's Pirate teammate, reliever Elroy Face, had a near-impeccable season, going 18–1, the first 17 coming consecutively. Face's .947 winning percentage is the highest in big-league history for a pitcher with 16 or more decisions. With a runover of five straight wins from the previous season, Face had racked up 22 consecutive wins, falling two shy of Carl Hubbell's all-time record.

On August 31, the Dodgers' Sandy Koufax, gradually reaching toward greatness, set a new National League record when he struck out 18 Giants (tying Bob Feller's major league record). Koufax was 8–6 for the year, with 173 strikeouts in 153 innings.

Behind the overpowering relief pitching of Larry Sherry, the Dodgers defeated the White Sox in six games to win the world championship. Sherry appeared in all four Dodger victories, winning two and saving two. The hitting star of the Series was White Sox first baseman Ted Kluszewski, the former Cincinnati slugger hitting three home runs, driving in 10 runs, and batting .391. Kluszewski's 10 RBIs are the record for a six-game Series.

Casey Stengel eyeing the troops. Joe Page is on the right.

BELOW: First baseman Luke Easter, who hit the long ball for Cleveland in the early 1950s. He played from 1949–54, batting .274.

LEFT: Gus Zernial, home run–hitting outfielder with the White Sox, Athletics, and Tigers from 1949–59. Lifetime average: .265.

The Yankees did a lot of celebrating in the 1950s. Here are (left to right) Gene Woodling, Vic Raschi, and Johnny Mize with the smiles of winners. They were part of the Yankees' five consecutive world championship clubs (1949–53).

Phillies third baseman Willie Jones (left) and Robin Roberts smiling up a victory. Willie, known as "Puddin' Head," played most of his career (1947–61) with the Phillies, batting .258.

After joining the Phillies as an exceptionally gifted young bonus player in 1947, Curt Simmons pitched in the big leagues until 1967, having his best years with the Phillies and Cardinals. He was 193–183 lifetime.

Granny Hamner, shortstop on the 1950 pennant-winning Phillies. Coming to the big leagues in 1944, Hamner had a long career, retiring in 1959. He spent virtually his entire big-league tenure with the Phillies, batting .262.

RIGHT: First baseman Ferris Fain, two-time American League batting champion. He played for four clubs from 1947–55, batting .290.

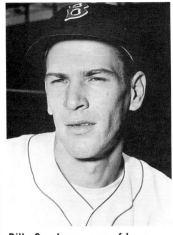

Billy Goodman, one of baseball's paragons of versatility. He played from 1947–62, most notably with the Red Sox and White Sox, giving a good game at first, second, third, or the outfield, as well as at home plate. The batting champion in 1950, he batted over .290 11 years in a row, an even .300 lifetime.

Brooklyn's Cal Abrams being tagged out at home by Phillies catcher Stan Lopata in the bottom of the ninth inning of the crucial Dodgers-Phillies game on the last day of the 1950 season.

Jim Konstanty, who pitched in the majors for 11 years, retiring in 1956 with a 66–48 record. Working for five clubs, he had one season of pure brilliance—1950, for the Phillies.

Sam Jethroe, the Braves' 1950 Rookie-of-the-Year outfielder. Sam played just three full seasons, batting .261.

LEFT: Whitey Lockman came up with the Giants in 1945, played for them until 1956 and then for three other clubs, retiring in 1960 with a .279 career average.

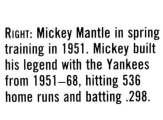

RIGHT: Mickey Mantle in spring training in 1951. Mickey built his legend with the Yankees from 1951–68, hitting 536 home runs and batting .298.

Enos Slaughter (left) and Stan Musial in 1950.

BELOW: Allie Reynolds firing the last pitch of his second no-hitter of 1951, on September 28 against the Red Sox. The batter is Ted Williams, who fouled to Yogi Berra (after Yogi had dropped one, above right).

Yogi Berra about to snare a foul pop. Yogi was with the Yankees from 1946–63, then played a handful of games with the Mets in 1965. A lifetime .285 hitter, he was later a pennant-winning manager with both the Yankees and Mets.

Ted Williams

National League President (and future Commissioner) Ford Frick (left) and Commissioner Happy Chandler.

Ned Garver, who pitched for four American League clubs from 1948–61, winning 129 and losing 157.

Not a bad all-time outfield. Left to right: Joe DiMaggio, Mickey Mantle, and Ted Williams.

Willie Mays. He joined the Giants in 1951, spent most of 1952 and all of 1953 in the army, then played for the Giants from 1954–72, when he was traded to the Mets, with whom he finished his career in 1973. Willie hit 660 home runs (third on the all-time list) and batted .302.

Left: Stan Musial cranking it up in spring training.

Giants manager Leo Durocher (center) with two of his 1951 aces, Sal Maglie (left) and Jim Hearn. Maglie joined the Giants in 1945, jumped to the Mexican League a year later and rejoined the club in 1950. He later pitched for four other clubs, retiring in 1958 with a 119–62 record. Hearn pitched for three National League teams from 1947–59, winning 109 and losing 89.

The Polo Grounds

Right-hander Gerry Staley, a steady winner for the Cardinals in the early 1950s. He later pitched for five other clubs in both leagues, retiring in 1961 with a 134–111 record.

The Giants' Henry Thompson (left, in the mirror) and Monte Irvin. A nine-year big leaguer, Thompson batted .267. Irvin played for eight years, batting .293.

Bobby Thomson. He joined the Giants in 1946 and played for them until 1954, then for four other clubs in both leagues, retiring in 1960. He hit 263 home runs besides *that* one, batting .270.

Bobby Thomson connecting for the most resounding home run in baseball history. The catcher is Brooklyn's Rube Walker.

Bobby Thomson coming home.

Willie Mays at bat in the 1951 World Series. Yogi Berra is the catcher.

Ralph Branca. He pitched in the big leagues for 12 years, most of them for the Dodgers, for whom he was a 21-game winner at the age of twenty-one in 1947. He won 88, lost 68; but as far as history is concerned, he threw just one pitch.

Vic Raschi working against the Giants in the 1951 World Series. The first baseman is Joe Collins.

Yankees (left to right) Phil Rizzuto, Eddie Lopat, and Gil McDougald celebrating Lopat's 13–1 victory over the Giants in the fifth game of the 1951 World Series. McDougald hit a grand slammer in the game.

Celebrating a Cleveland win over the Yankees in 1952 are (left to right) catcher Birdie Tebbetts, outfielder Dale Mitchell, and pitcher Steve Gromek. Tebbetts caught in the American League for 14 years, batting .270; Mitchell was a .312 lifetime hitter for his 11 years; and Gromek, who pitched for 17 years, was 123–108.

LEFT: Bobby Shantz, 24–7 for the Athletics in 1952 and the American League's Most Valuable Player. He pitched for seven teams in both leagues from 1949–64, winning 119 and losing 99.

BELOW: Hoyt Wilhelm pitched in 1,070 games, more than anyone in major league history. Joining the Giants in 1952, he continued pitching until 1972, working for nine different teams. Lifetime record: 143–122.

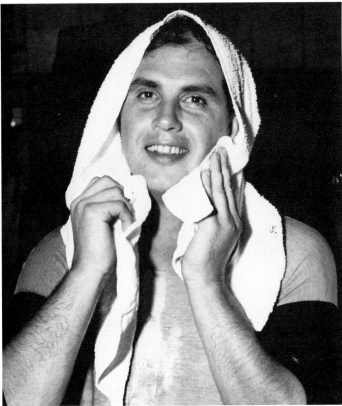

Robin Roberts, Philadelphia's greatest pitcher since Grover Cleveland Alexander. He was with the Phillies from 1948–61, and then with the Orioles, Astros, and Cubs, retiring in 1966 with a 286–245 record. When asked for a capsule summary of his ace, Phillies manager Eddie Sawyer replied, "Speed, control, stamina—and guts."

Dee Fondy, first baseman with the Cubs, Pirates, and Reds from 1951–58. He was a .286 career hitter.

RIGHT: Right-hander Bob Rush was a solid starting pitcher for the Cubs from 1948–57. He also pitched for the Braves and White Sox, retiring in 1960 with a 127–152 record.

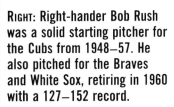

Pitching for the Dodgers from 1948–59, Carl Erskine was 122–78.

Crack double-play combination of the White Sox in the early 1950s: Chico Carrasquel (left) and Nelson Fox. Chico played shortstop for four American League clubs from 1950–59, batting .258. Fox, a 19-year veteran, 14 of those years with the White Sox, batted .288 lifetime, four times leading in hits. He struck out just 216 times in 9,232 official at bats.

Ask the man who was one !

Ted Williams
BASEBALL STAR

UNITED STATES MARINES

Back in the service for the second time during the Korean War, Ted Williams was a Marine Corps poster boy.

Brooklyn's Gil Hodges. A power hitter and brilliant fielder, he played in 1943 and from 1947–63, when he finished up with the Mets, whom he later managed to their "miracle" 1969 world championship. He drove in more than 100 runs seven times and had a career average of .273. Note those muscles.

Royalty, Brooklyn style: Duke Snider. The Dodgers' great center fielder played from 1947–64, most of it for the Dodgers, finishing up with the Mets in 1963 and the Giants a year later. He drove in over 100 runs six times, hit 407 home runs, and batted .295.

The American League's MVP in 1953, third baseman Al Rosen played for Cleveland from 1948–56, batting .285.

The colorful, controversial Jimmy Piersall, described by Casey Stengel as "the greatest defensive outfielder I ever saw." He came up with the Red Sox in 1950 and was traded to Cleveland in 1959. He later played for three other clubs, retiring in 1967 with a .272 career average.

LEFT: Brooklyn's ace relief pitcher in the 1950s, Clem Labine. The sinkerballing right-hander pitched for 13 years, retiring in 1962 with a 77–56 record.

BELOW: Jackie Robinson and Dodgers owner Walter O'Malley.

A tense Billy Cox (right) watching Roy Campanella gather in a pop foul in the 1952 World Series. One of the greatest glove men of all time, Cox came up in 1941 as a shortstop with the Pirates. After four years in the military, he rejoined the Pirates in 1946 and was traded to Brooklyn in 1948. He retired in 1955 after one year with the Orioles. Lifetime average: .262.

President Eisenhower admiring the silver bat awarded Mickey Vernon for being the American League's 1953 batting champion. Mickey, who also won the title in 1946, played in the big leagues from 1939–43 and 1946–60, primarily for Washington. He played more games at first base than anyone in big-league history—2,237. Lifetime average: .286.

RIGHT: Right-hander Bob Turley spent most of his 12-year career with the Yankees, retiring in 1963 with a 101–85 record.

A pair of Dodgers southpaws: the veteran Preacher Roe (left) and Johnny Podres. Roe was 127–84 over his 12-year career, while Podres pitched for 15 years and was 148–116.

A pair of 1953's fine rookies: Milwaukee's Bill Bruton (left) and Brooklyn's Jim Gilliam. Bruton, who led in stolen bases his first 3 years, played for 12 years and batted .273. Gilliam played 14 years with the Dodgers, compiling a .265 average.

The Chicago Cubs outfield in 1953. Left to right: Ralph Kiner, Frank Baumholtz, and Hank Sauer. A 10-year major leaguer, Baumholtz batted .290; Sauer played for 15 years, had over 30 homers in a season six times, and batted .266 lifetime.

RIGHT: Vic Wertz's bald head is being used to deliver the message that Cleveland has just clinched the 1954 American League pennant.

Jim Hegan, one of the most admired defensive catchers of his time. He caught in the majors for 17 years, most of it with Cleveland, batting .228. He retired in 1960.

RIGHT: One of the most popular players in Chicago White Sox history, Minnie Minoso had his best years with the Chisox during the 1950s. He also played for the Indians, Cardinals, and Senators during his 15-year career. Lifetime average: .298.

Jackie Jensen came to the majors with the Yankees in 1950, was traded to Washington and then to the Red Sox, for whom he had his best years. A three-time leader in runs batted in, he was a .263 career hitter. He retired in 1961.

Second baseman Bobby Avila, the 1954 American League batting champion. He spent 10 of his 11 major league seasons with the Indians, batting .281.

Bob Porterfield's major league career extended from 1948–59, embracing five teams in both leagues. A 20-game winner for the Senators in 1953, he was 87–97 lifetime.

Carl Furillo, who brought to the ball park with him a line-drive bat and a line-drive throwing arm. The Dodgers' classy right fielder played from 1946–60, won the batting title in 1953, and hit .299 lifetime.

Cleveland's 1954 pitching staff, regarded as one of the best in baseball history. Front row (left to right): Mike Garcia, Hal Newhouser, manager Al Lopez, Don Mossi, and Bob Feller. Back row (left to right): Early Wynn, Bob Lemon, Bob Hooper, Art Houtteman, Dave Hoskins, and Ray Narleski.

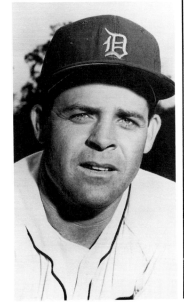

Infielder Ray Boone. He played from 1948–60, mostly for the Indians and Tigers. The RBI leader in 1955, he batted .275.

It's the spring of 1954 and Enos Slaughter has just learned that, after nearly two decades in the Cardinals organization, he has been traded to the Yankees. "You get a few handshakes," he said, "and walk away from twenty years of your life. I cried like a baby."

Ruben Gomez (right) is giving catcher Ray Katt a hand loosening up at the Polo Grounds in 1954. Gomez, who had his best years with the Giants, pitched for four clubs for ten seasons, compiling a 76–86 record.

Joe Adcock played from 1950–66, having his best years with the Braves from 1953–62. He hit 336 career home runs and batted .277.

Bill Skowron, Yankees first baseman from 1954–62, later playing for four other clubs until 1967. His career average is .282.

On July 31, 1954, Joe Adcock hit four home runs and a double against the Dodgers at Ebbets Field. This sequence of pictures shows what happened in the fourth inning the next day. Clem Labine was on the mound for the Dodgers. The catcher is Rube Walker, the umpire Bill Engle. Adcock was not seriously hurt.

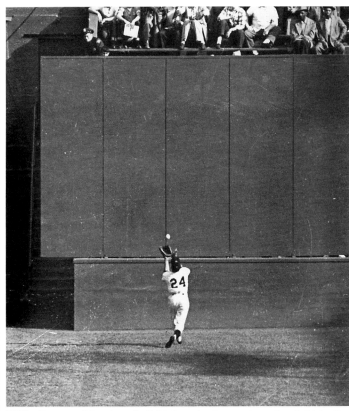

Willie Mays making baseball history in deepest center field in the Polo Grounds in the opening game of the 1954 World Series. The ball was hit by Vic Wertz. Willie's catch helped preserve a tie and allow the Giants to win in extra innings.

Johnny Podres, who won the big one for the Dodgers in the 1955 Series.

Don Newcombe, Brooklyn's big, hard-throwing right-handed ace from 1949–51 and 1954–57. He later pitched for the Reds and Indians, ringing up a 149–90 lifetime record.

RIGHT: Early Wynn came to the major leagues in 1939 and didn't leave until 1963, pitching for Washington, Cleveland, and the Chicago White Sox. Five times a 20-game winner, he was 300–244 lifetime.

The turning point in the seventh game of the 1955 World Series: Sandy Amoros's catch of Yogi Berra's bid for an extra-base hit. What looked like a game-tying hit was turned into a double play.

211

The victory smiles are being flashed by (left to right) left-handers Don Mossi and Herb Score and outfielder Jim Busby. Mossi was 101–80 for a 12-year career that ended in 1965; Score, whose scintillating career was ruined when he was hit in the eye by a line drive, pitched from 1955–62 and was 55–46; Busby was with six teams in a 13-year career that wound up in 1962, batting .262.

Frank Lary, Detroit's outstanding right-hander. Spending most of his 12-year career with the Tigers, Lary retired in 1965 with a 128–116 record.

Catcher Ed Bailey, who had some fine years with Cincinnati in the middle 1950s. He later caught for four other teams, retiring in 1966 with a lifetime average of .256.

Ted Williams waiting his turn at Yankee Stadium. "He could affect a game just by being in the on-deck circle," Joe McCarthy said. "The pitcher would keep looking over at him and worrying about him. There never was another hitter like Ted."

RIGHT: Gus Bell, part of Cincinnati's home run attack in the 1950s. Gus came up with the Pirates in 1950, joined the Reds in 1953, and later played for two other clubs, retiring in 1964. Lifetime average: .281.

Roger Craig came to the majors with Brooklyn in 1955 and later pitched for four other National League teams, retiring in 1966. Two crushing seasons with inept Mets teams, during which he lost 46 games, helped capsize his lifetime record to 74–98.

LEFT: Wally Post, long-ball-hitting outfielder with the Reds in the 1950s. He played for four other clubs in a career that ran from 1949–64, checking out with a .266 career average.

One of the National League's genuine busters with the Reds from 1947–57, Ted Kluszewski had 40 or more homers three years in a row. Seven times a .300 hitter, Ted later played for the Pirates, White Sox, and Angels, retiring in 1961 with a .298 lifetime average.

Stan Musial

Frank Thomas. This hard-hitting outfielder came up with the Pirates in 1951 and later played for six other National League clubs. He played for 16 years, batting .266.

His Pirates teammates are gathered to greet Dale Long after the first baseman homered in his seventh consecutive game, on May 27, 1956, setting a new record. Long extended the record the next day before being stopped. Long played for six teams over the course of a ten-year career, batting .267.

RIGHT: Rocky Colavito had 20 or more home runs for 11 straight seasons. He came up to the majors with Cleveland in 1955 and played for five other clubs, retiring in 1968 with 374 home runs and a .266 batting average.

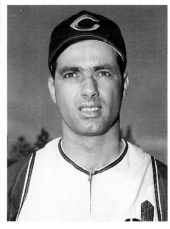

Warren Spahn, the most successful left-handed pitcher in baseball history. He pitched for the Braves in 1942 and from 1946–64, finishing up with the Mets and Giants in 1965. He was a 20-game winner 13 times and overall was 363–245.

The Yankees' versatile Tony Kubek, who played with them from 1957–65, compiling an average of .266.

Jack Sanford, the Phillies' Rookie of the Year in 1957 and in 1962 a 24-game winner for the Giants. Jack pitched until 1967, putting together a 137–101 record.

Don Larsen delivering the final pitch of his perfect game against the Dodgers in the 1956 World Series. Second baseman Billy Martin is in the background.

Sherman Lollar, American League catcher with four clubs from 1946–63, the last 12 with the White Sox. Career average: .264.

LEFT: Frank Robinson, one of baseball's all-time great hitters and its first black manager. Robinson played for 21 years (1956–76), with the Reds, Orioles, Dodgers, Angels, and Indians. His 586 career home runs are fourth on the all-time list. Lifetime average: .294.

There was a brawl between the Yankees and White Sox in the summer of 1957 and New York's Enos Slaughter was in the middle of it.

Del Crandall joined the Braves in 1949 as a 19-year-old catching prodigy and remained with them until 1963. He also played for three other clubs, retiring in 1966 with a .254 career average.

They said Ted Williams could hit with his eyes closed. Well . . .

BELOW: The Yankees' Gil McDougald (left) and Elston Howard meeting the press after New York's 7–0 victory in game 5 of the 1958 World Series. McDougald played his entire 10-year career for the Yankees, batting .276, while Howard played for 14 years, finishing up with the Red Sox in 1968, compiling an average of .274.

Lew Burdette, Milwaukee's hero of the 1957 World Series. A Milwaukee ace throughout the 1950s, Lew also pitched for five other teams. For his 18-year major league career he was 203–144.

Eddie Mathews. A third baseman with a booming bat, Eddie played from 1952–68, most of it with the Braves. He hit 512 home runs and batted .271.

Luis Aparicio, whose magic glove at shortstop earned him a place in the Hall of Fame. He played for the White Sox, Orioles, and Red Sox from 1956–73, batting .262. He led the league in stolen bases his first nine years. His 2,581 games at shortstop are a major league record.

The Tigers traded young Billy Pierce to the White Sox in 1949 and it was a mistake; Billy went on to become one of the league's top southpaws. He finished up with the Giants in 1964. Lifetime record: 211–169.

Vic Power, one of the flashiest first basemen of his time. He played with five clubs from 1954–65, batting .284.

Dick Donovan pitched for five major league clubs from 1950–65, winning 122 and losing 99.

Orlando Cepeda, who played from 1958–74. Nine times a .300 hitter, Cepeda played for six teams and batted .297.

One of baseball's fine relief pitchers, Elroy Face. He pitched from 1953–69, virtually all of it with the Pirates, logging a 104–95 record.

It's April 18, 1958, and the Los Angeles Dodgers and San Francisco Giants are introducing major league baseball to the west coast. The opening-day crowd at the Dodgers' Los Angeles Coliseum was 78,672, an all-time record for opening day. Note the proximity of the left-field screen as opposed to the endless acreage in right and center fields.

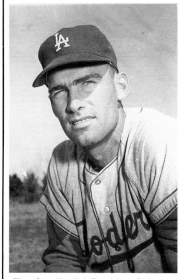

The Cardinals' Rookie of the Year in 1954, Wally Moon later helped the Dodgers to a pennant in 1959. Splitting his 12-year career between St. Louis and Los Angeles, Wally was a .289 career hitter.

Left to right: Vic Wertz, Frank Malzone, and Pete Runnels of the Red Sox. Malzone spent most of his 11-year career with Boston, batting .274. Runnels played the bulk of his 14-year career with the Senators and Red Sox. A two-time batting champion, he hit .291 lifetime.

The Dodgers' Carl Furillo (number 6) is shown reaching first base safely as the throw from the Braves' Felix Mantilla sails past first baseman Frank Torre. ABOVE RIGHT: The errant throw allowed a jubilant Gil Hodges (on the right) to score the winning run in the bottom of the 12th inning in the second and final game of the playoff for the 1959 National League pennant. Maury Wills is rushing to congratulate Hodges while a dejected Del Crandall walks off.

Ernie Banks played his entire 19-year career (1953–71) for the Cubs, dividing his time between shortstop and first base. A two-time MVP, he hit over 40 homers in a season five times, drove in over 100 runs eight times, hit 512 career home runs, and batted .274.

Pirates manager Danny Murtaugh (left) consoling Harvey Haddix after Harvey had pitched 12 perfect innings against the Braves on May 26, 1959, only to lose in the 13th. Haddix pitched in the majors for 14 years to a 136–113 record.

Harvey Kuenn's educated line-drive bat earned him a lifetime .303 batting average for his 15-year career, spent with five clubs in both leagues from 1952–66. He led the American League in hits four times and was the batting champ with Detroit in 1959.

Willie Mays

Sam Jones is holding the trophy he won for leading the National League in strikeouts in 1958. Sam pitched for six clubs in both leagues. His 12-year career added up to a 102–101 record.

RIGHT: Larry Jackson pitched for the Cards, Cubs, and Phillies from 1955–68, winning 194 and losing 183.

Sandy Koufax

1960 Everything was returned to proper orbit in the American League in 1960 as the Yankees once again won the pennant, their 10th in the last 12 years, all under Casey Stengel. One reason for this resumption of success was the arrival in New York (via a trade with Kansas City) of right-fielder Roger Maris, a twenty-five-year-old power hitter with a left-handed stroke made to order for the Yankee Stadium right-field fence. Roger broke in with an MVP year—39 home runs and a league-leading 112 RBIs. Right there with him was Mickey Mantle, whose 40 home runs led the league.

Yankees pitching was slim pickings this year, with Art Ditmar on top with a 15–9 record; but all around the league it wasn't a year for big performances. Boston's Pete Runnels was the batting champ with a .320 average, while for the second time in its history the league was without a 20-game winner, or even a 19-gamer—the top men were Baltimore's Chuck Estrada and Cleveland's Jim Perry with 18 apiece.

Baltimore, finishing second, eight games out, and Chicago in third place, ten games out, had any last lingering hopes scrubbed away by the Yankee's season-ending 15-game winning streak. Along with second place, Paul Richards's Orioles also netted Rookie of the Year honors with shortstop Ron Hansen. The year also marked the retirement of Ted Williams, and the great Boston slugger bowed out as no other superstar ever has—hitting his 521st home run in his final at-bat, against Baltimore's Jack Fisher.

In what was now the annual All-Star doubleheader, the National League won the first game, 5–3, played July 11 at Kansas City's Municipal Stadium, and then made it a sweep by scoring a 6–0 victory in the second game, played two days later at Yankee Stadium.

The Pirates put an end to a pennant drought that had existed for them since 1927 by winning it all in the National League, finishing seven games ahead of Milwaukee. Danny Murtaugh's team had the league's leading hitter (.325) and MVP in shortstop Dick Groat (three shortstops had led the league in hitting and each had been a Pirate —Wagner, Vaughan, and now Groat), and at second they had Bill Mazeroski, a .273 hitter and acclaimed as one of the great defensive second basemen of all time. Also on the club was right-fielder Roberto Clemente, a .314 hitter that year and in the anteroom of superstardom.

In addition to the MVP, the Pirates also had the Cy Young Award winner in Vernon Law (20–9) and an 18-game win-

(Central diamond graphic: 1960– Our Changing Game 1969)

Dick Groat

no-hitting of the Cardinals on May 15. It was the first time the Cardinals had been no-hit since 1919, the longest any team had ever gone without suffering such embarrassment.

Statistically, the Yankees crushed the Pirates in the World Series, hitting ten home runs to the Pirates' four, scoring 55 runs to the Pirates' 27, and batting a whopping .338 to the Pirates' .256. Four Yankees had ten or more hits, Mantle drove in 11 runs, and Bobby Richardson a record 12. But still Pittsburgh won it in seven games, the crowning blow coming in the bottom of the ninth inning of the seventh game when Mazeroski hit a home run off Ralph Terry to break a 9–9 tie and give the Pirates a 10–9 win and the world championship. The key play of the game, and one of the most memorable in Series history, came in the bottom of the eighth inning when a Bill Virdon grounder that looked like a double-play in the making took a bad hop and struck Yankee shortstop Tony Kubek in the throat, prolonging the inning and helping the Pirates to a five-run rally.

After the Series the Yankees fired their seventy-year-old manager Casey Stengel, citing Casey's age as the reason. Perhaps, but other reasons were rumored. The skipper had become crotchety, alienating his employers as well as some of his players. It was deemed time for a change, and the club appointed coach Ralph Houk to replace the man who had won 10 pennants in 12 years.

ner in Bob Friend, and more fine work from reliever Elroy Face, who won 10 and saved 24.

Milwaukee's Henry Aaron hit 40 homes runs—the leader was Ernie Banks with 41—and drove in 126 runs, best in the league and two more than teammate Eddie Mathews, who had 39 bangers. Warren Spahn (21–10) was a 20-game winner for the 11th time, and Ernie Broglio went 21–9 for the Cardinals. On July 19, twenty-two-year-old Juan Marichal broke in with the San Francisco Giants, pitching a one-hitter against the Phillies, going on to a 6–2 record. Marichal was the first picher in modern National League history to break in with a one-hitter. The Rookie of the Year was Los Angeles' outfielder Frank Howard, a six-foot-seven-inch masher who hit 23 home runs (some of which didn't come down for days) and batted .268.

For the thirty-nine-year-old Spahn, who seemed immune to the erosions of time, the season also saw his first no-hitter. It came on September 16 against the Phillies with Spahn, normally not a strikeout pitcher, emphasizing the effort with 15 strikeouts. It was the league's third no-hitter of the season, following Spahn's Milwaukee teammate Lew Burdette's 1–0 job against the Phillies on August 18 (a hit batsman in the fifth inning kept Burdette from a perfect game), and the Cubs' Don Cardwell's 4–0

Ernie Broglio

1961

It was one of the most tumultuous years in baseball history, particularly in the American League. For the first time in its 61-year existence, the league expanded, adding two new clubs: the Los Angeles Angels (they became the California Angels in 1965) and a new Washington Senators team to replace the one that shifted to Minneapolis-St. Paul and became the Minnesota Twins. The new clubs were stocked with players made available by the other eight American League teams in an expansion draft, dooming the new clubs to the more airless regions of the standings—Washington finished tenth, Los Angeles eighth.

The additional clubs called for an entirely new playing schedule to be drawn, adding eight games to the length of the season, leading to a brand-new kind of baseball controversy. It centered around Yankee Roger Maris's exciting challenge of Babe Ruth's record of 60 home runs in a season. As Maris slugged his way ever closer to the record the question of what constituted a season was hotly debated in baseball forums all around the country. When Roger finished game 154 with 59 homers, the traditionalists and the sentimentalists breathed easier; when Roger clubbed number 60 in game 159 and then number 61 in game 162, the controversy flared anew. Who holds the record, Ruth or Maris? The record books show two entries—for the 154-game season (Ruth) and for the 162-game season (Maris). In essence, Ruth and Maris coexist. The eight extra games do not, however, diminish Roger's

achievement, for no one has since come close to challenging his "61 in '61" record.

Adding drama to Maris's quest was the home run production of teammate Mickey Mantle, who paced Roger most of the season and ended with his own monumental total of 54. Mantle drove in 128 runs, while Maris, the MVP for the second year in a row, led with 142. The entire Yankee team was explosive that year, setting a major league record with 240 four-baggers. Following the M&M combine and their two-man record total of 115 homers were Bill Skowron with 28, Yogi Berra (22), Elston Howard (21), and part-timer Johnny Blanchard (21). Six players with 20 or more home runs each was a new record (later tied by the Minnestoa Twins in 1964 and the Milwaukee Braves in 1965).

Whitey Ford put together his greatest season with a 25–4 record (winning the Cy Young Award), followed by Ralph Terry's 16–3 and a 15–5 season from one-year-wonder reliever Luis Arroyo, who also saved 29 games. All told, Ralph Houk's busters won 109 games, finishing eight ahead of a spirited Detroit team. The Yankees' 65–16 home record remains the best in major league history.

The Tigers had the league's other 20-game winner in right-hander Frank Lary (23–9). Lary had a knack of beating the great Yankees teams of his era, mounting a lifetime 28–13 record against them. The Tigers also had the batting champion in first baseman Norm Cash, who whaled away at .361—the only time in his 17-year career he batted over .300.

Generally, it was a year for power hitting in the American League, with six men hitting over 40 home runs (a league record): in addition to Maris and Mantle, Cash hit 41 and his Tiger teammate Rocky Colavito 45; Baltimore's Jim Gentile and Minnesota's Harmon Killebrew each had 46. Where in the past two seasons no American Leaguer had posted a slugging average over .581, this year five men went over .600, with Mantle's .687 the best. Gentile tied Ernie Banks's major league record by hitting five grand slams, including two in successive innings against Minnesota on May 9.

Boston Red Sox right-hander Don Schwall, with a 15–7 record, was named Rookie of the Year.

The All-Star Game, still a two-games-a-year affair, saw one win and one no decision. The National League won the first game, played July 11 in San Francisco's Candlestick Park, 5–4 in 10 innings. The game achieved a special place in All-Star history when a gale force wind nudged pitcher Stu Miller from the mound in the ninth inning, forcing an act-of-God balk to be called. The second game, played at Boston's Fenway Park on July 31, ended in a 1–1 nine-inning tie called by rain.

The surprise team in the National League in 1961— the final year of the eight-team league—was Fred Hutch-

Roger Maris (left) and Mickey Mantle.

Joey Jay

inson's Cincinnati Reds. The tough, hard-driving Hutchinson led a good-hitting team with just enough pitching to Cincinnati's first pennant in 21 years.

The heart of the club was MVP Frank Robinson, who hit 37 homes runs, drove in 124 runs, and batted .323. Robinson's outfield mate Vada Pinson also turned in a superb year, batting .343 and leading with 208 hits. Right-hander Joey Jay was the ace of the staff with a 21–10 record, while left-hander Jim O'Toole was 19–9.

Second-place Los Angeles (four games behind) got Johnny Podres's best season (18–5) and had Sandy Koufax at the brink of greatness now with an 18–13 record and 269 strikeouts (in 256 innings), which broke Christy Mathewson's National League standard of 267, set in 1903.

The third-place Giants had the league's best one-two punch in Orlando Cepeda, who led in home runs (46) and RBIs (142), and Willie Mays (40 homers, 123 RBIs), but the club's pitching fell back, with reliever Stu Miller's 14 wins topping the staff. On April 30, Mays had his biggest day at bat when he hit four home runs in one game against Milwaukee. The Braves themselves were no strangers to dramatic outbursts this year: on June 8 they set a new record when Eddie Mathews, Henry Aaron, Joe Adcock, and Frank Thomas homered successively in one inning. Though not successively, five Giants tied a record when they homered in one inning on August 23. They were Cepeda, Felipe Alou, Jim Davenport, Mays, and John Orsino.

Warren Spahn was a 20-game winner for the 12th time, going 21–13 (winning 13 of his last 15 decisions). The forty-year-old Spahn embellished his season with his second career no-hitter, stopping the hard-hitting Giants on April 28 (two days before Mays's four–home run performance), winning 1–0. On August 11 he won his 300th game, the first pitcher since Lefty Grove in 1941 to reach this plateau of success.

The Cubs had the Rookie of the Year in sweet-swinging young outfielder Billy Williams, who batted .278 and hit 25 home runs. The batting champion was Pittsburgh's Roberto Clemente, whose .351 average couldn't prevent the world champs from dropping to sixth place.

The World Series was an all-Yankee show as Ralph Houk's window-breakers took a rather docile Cincinnati club in five. Whitey Ford, who the year before had pitched two shutouts against the Pirates, added another shutout against the Reds and then five more scoreless innings to end the Series with 32 straight runless innings in World Series competition, erasing Babe Ruth's old mark of 29⅔. Between Maris and Ford, it had been, as someone pointed out, a bad year for the Babe.

Whitey Ford

1962

To no one's surprise, the Yankees made it three straight in 1962, winning by five games over second-place Minnesota. Ralph Houk's club did it despite come-down seasons from Whitey Ford (17–8, as compared to last year's 25–4) and Roger Maris (33 home runs to 61) and injuries that kept Mantle out of 39 games. While he was in there, however, Mickey did enough damage with his 30 home runs and .321 batting average to earn his third MVP Award. Second baseman Bobby Richardson had a starring year with a league-high 209 hits and .302 batting average. The club's big winner this year was Ralph Terry with a 23–12 record.

The Twins had the home run and RBI leader in Harmon Killebrew, with respective figures of 48 and 126. Killebrew, a physically imposing man who hit with terrific force, had come up as a third baseman, been moved to first, and was now in the outfield for the Twins who, in the parlance of baseball, were trying to "hide" his slowness of foot and rather sluggish glove.

Minnesota also had right-hander Camilo Pascual, whom many hitters claimed was the toughest man in the league to hit. Pascual was 20–11, with 206 strikeouts, tops in the league. Other 20-game winners this year were Chicago's Ray Herbert (20–9) and Cleveland's Dick Donovan (20–10). Boston first baseman Pete Runnels won his second batting title with a .326 average.

There were four no-hitters in the American League this year, one under the 1917 record. The first was pitched May 5 by the Angels' colorful young left-hander Bo Belinsky, who silenced the Orioles by a 2–0 score. On June 2 Earl Wilson of the Red Sox pitched a no-hitter against Belinsky and the Angels, hit a solo homer, and won, 2–0. On August 1, another Red Sox right-hander, Bill Monbouquette, no-hit the White Sox, 1–0. Minnesota left-hander Jack Kralick pitched the league's fourth beauty on August 26 against the Athletics, winning 1–0. Kralick missed a perfect game when he walked George Alusik on a 3–2 pitch with one out in the ninth. Kralick's opponent in that game, right-hander Bill Fischer, was at the time in the midst of a record-making streak of 84⅓ innings during which he did not walk a batter (from August 3 to September 30). Fischer walked only 8 men in 128 innings, but still wound up with a 4–12 record.

The Yankees had the Rookie of the Year for the fourth time, in shortstop-outfielder Tom Tresh, who batted .286, hit 20 home runs, and had 93 RBIs.

This was the last year that two All-Star Games were played. The National League won the first, played at Washington's D.C. Stadium on July 10, 3–1, and the American League took the second, played at Chicago's Wrigley Field on July 30, by a 9–4 score.

Camilo Pascual

Several Los Angeles Dodgers put together truly spectacular seasons in 1962, one of them of stunning, record-making proportions. The Dodgers' winged-footed shortstop Maury Wills broke Ty Cobb's 1915 record of 96 stolen bases by stealing 104 times (he was caught just 13 times). What Wills also did was usher in a new era of prolific base-stealers, beating a path that would be taken by such future record-setters as Lou Brock and Rickey Henderson.

Wills (the MVP) was joined in his yearlong pyrotechnics by teammate Tommy Davis, a line-drive-hitting outfielder who led the league with a .346 batting average and the prodigious RBI total of 153, highest in the league since Joe Medwick's 154 in 1937.

On the mound, the Dodgers had the league's biggest winner in Don Drysdale (25–9), the strikeout leader (Drysdale, 232), and the ERA leader (Sandy Koufax, 2.54), with Drysdale the Cy Young Award winner.

Despite all this glitter, the Dodgers did not win the pennant, primarily because of a circulatory ailment suffered by Koufax in his pitching hand that caused him to miss most of the season's second half, limiting him to 26 starts and a 14–5 record. Along the way in this first of his five brilliant seasons in a row, Koufax tied his own major league record by fanning 18 Cubs on April 24, and pitched a no-hitter against the brand-new New York Mets on June 30.

The pennant winners—with a touch of déjà vu about

Maury Wills stealing third.

it—were Alvin Dark's San Francisco Giants. Banging out 204 home runs, the Giants were sparked by Willie Mays, who hit 49 and drove in 141 runs, and Orlando Cepeda with 35 homers and 114 RBIs. Giants pitching was led by Jack Sanford, the onetime Phillies Rookie of the Year, who was 24–7 (including a 16-game winning streak), former Orioles left-hander Billy O'Dell at 19–14, Juan Marichal at 18–11, and former White Sox ace Billy Pierce, who was 16–6. Stu Miller headed a strong Giants bullpen, which included one-time Yankee "perfect man" Don Larsen.

Stumbling during the season's final two weeks, the Dodgers lost 10 of their last 13 and ended in a first-place tie with the Giants, setting up a second playoff between these rivals that bore an eerie resemblance to the 1951 Bobby Thomson show. The Giants won the first game (as they had in 1951), the Dodgers won the second (as they had in 1951), and then the Giants took the deciding game with a four-run ninth-inning rally (as they had in 1951). This time there was no Bobby Thomson–like bombshell, but rather a slow and steady boring away with hits and walks that turned a 4–2 Dodgers lead into a 6–4 Giants victory.

The other significant news in the league in 1962 was expansion, the National League adding clubs in New York and Houston. The New York Mets, managed by Casey Stengel, turned in a season-long performance of horrendous ineptitude, losing 120 of their 160 games, saddling talented right-hander Roger Craig with a 10–24 record.

Cincinnati's Frank Robinson turned in a great season of slugging, hitting 39 home runs and 51 doubles, driving in 136 runs, and batting .342, as the defending champs finished third, just 3½ games short of paydirt. The Reds received fine seasons from Bob Purkey (23–5) and Joey Jay (21–14). Henry Aaron hit 45 homers for the Braves,

while forty-one-year-old Stan Musial, after three sub-.300 seasons, revived old memories with a .330 batting average. Musial's 3,431st career hit on May 19 broke Honus Wagner's National League record.

The Cubs had the Rookie of the Year in second baseman Ken Hubbs, who batted .260. A year and a half later, the twenty-two-year-old Hubbs lost his life when the private plane he was piloting crashed in Utah.

The World Series between the Yankees and Giants was an exciting seven-game affair that was won by the Yankees, concluding with the most resounding final out in Series history. With Ralph Terry and the Yankees holding a 1–0 lead in the bottom of the ninth of game 7, the Giants had men on second and third and two out when Willie McCovey lashed a sizzling line drive right at second baseman Bobby Richardson. In the second inning of the opening game, Whitey Ford's record of 33 consecutive scoreless World Series innings was broken.

Willie McCovey

1963

The season saw a landmark victory in the American League. On July 13, forty-three-year-old Early Wynn, back with Cleveland now, pitched the first five innings of a 7–4 win over Kansas City for his 300th and last major league win.

Despite injuries to Mickey Mantle (who played in just 65 games) and Roger Maris (90 games), the Yankees still found the resources to win their fourth straight pennant, coming in 10½ games ahead of the second-place White Sox. Whitey Ford (24–7), Jim Bouton (21–7), and Ralph Terry (17–15) headlined a strong pitching staff for manager Ralph Houk. Catcher Elston Howard was the club's leading hitter at .287 and the league's Most Valuable Player, the eighth Yankee in the past ten years to be so designated.

In a generally passive batting year, Boston's Carl Yastrzemski was the leading hitter at .321. The league as a whole recorded its lowest batting average since the dead-ball days of 1910—.247. There were, however, two big home run hitters—Harmon Killebrew hitting 45 for the Twins and Dick Stuart 42 for the Red Sox.

Along with Ford and Bouton, there were three other 20-game winners in the league: Minnesota's Camilo Pascual (21–9), Boston's Bill Monbouquette (20–10), and Baltimore left-hander Steve Barber (20–13).

One notable explosion occurred on July 31, when four Cleveland players tied a major league record by homering in succession: Woodie Held, pitcher Pedro Ramos, Tito Francona, and Larry Brown.

Rookie of the Year honors went to White Sox left-hander Gary Peters who was 19–8 and the ERA leader with 2.33.

The All-Star Game, played at Cleveland's Municipal Stadium on July 9, was won by the National League, 5–3.

National League hitting in 1963 was as sluggish as American, with a composite .245 batting average. Among the league's tamest bats were those of the Los Angeles Dodgers, outhomered by six teams in the ten-team league and outscored by five, but nevertheless the pennant winners by six games over the Cardinals.

Walter Alston's club, recovering to win after their 1962 heartbreak as the 1952 Dodgers had after theirs, were buoyed by the soaring Sandy Koufax, who was 25–5, the strikeout leader with 306 (breaking his own National League record), the shutout leader with 11 (a major league record for left-handers), and had the lowest ERA, 1.88. These heroics won him both the MVP and Cy Young awards. Behind Koufax were Don Drysdale (19–17) and relief ace Ron Perranoski, who was 16–3 with 21 saves.

The limited Dodger offense was repeat batting champion Tommy Davis (.326), Frank Howard with 28 homers (though just 64 RBIs), and Maury Wills, who batted .302 and dropped from 104 stolen bases to 40, still good enough to lead the league.

A spirited drive by the Cardinals—winning 19 of 20—pulled them to within one game of the Dodgers on September 16 as the teams measured paces for a three-game series. The Dodgers, however, avoided the stigma of another collapse by sweeping the Cardinals and going on to win the pennant. The Cards got strong pitching from budding superstar Bob Gibson (18–9) and Ernie Broglio (18–8). Broglio's record turned out to have hidden benefits for St. Louis, for it made the big right-hander so attractive to the Cubs that the following June they traded Lou Brock to the Cardinals to get him.

For Stan Musial it was a 23rd and final season, Stanley bowing out with a .255 finale, leaving behind a plethora of league records that would in time be broken by Henry Aaron and Pete Rose.

The third-place Giants had an awesome threesome in Willie Mays (38 home runs), Willie McCovey (a league-leading 44), and Orlando Cepeda (34), and a top-shelf pitcher in Juan Marichal, who was 25–8, but overshadowed by the more spectacular Koufax. Milwaukee's Aaron tied McCovey with 44 homers and led in RBIs with 130. Warren Spahn, at the age of forty-two, tied Christy

Pete Rose

227

Mathewson's modern major league record by winning 20 for the 13th (and last) time, posting a 23–7 ledger.

Cincinnati's Jim Maloney, a right-hander with a blazing fastball, was 23–7 with 265 strikeouts, while another big winner was the Cubs' young southpaw Dick Ellsworth, 22–10.

Three no-hitters were pitched in the league this year, Koufax, in what was to be an annual ritual, delivered his second, stopping the tough Giants on May 11, 8–0. On May 17, Houston's Don Nottebart no-hit the Phillies, 4–1, and on June 15 Marichal silenced Houston, 1–0. Seventeen days later, Marichal topped Spahn, 1–0, in a 16-inning classic, the lone run coming on a Mays homer.

The tenth-place New York Mets improved, but it was barely noticeable, cutting their defeats from 120 to 111. For Roger Craig the season was a nightmare: his 5–22 record included an 18-game losing streak, one under the record. "Losing builds character," Craig was later to say. If true, his combined 1962–63 15–46 record made him one of nature's noblemen.

The Rookie of the Year was Cincinnati's second baseman Pete Rose, who broke in with a .273 batting average. Pete's first big-league hit, which later events were to make noteworthy, was a triple off Pittsburgh's Bob Friend on April 13.

In a rather bland four-game sweep, the Dodgers pitching of Koufax, Drysdale, and Johnny Podres held the Yankees to just four runs, 22 hits, and a .171 batting average. In the opener, Koufax fanned 15 for a new Series record.

After it was all over, Yankees manager Ralph Houk, with three pennants in three years, moved up to become the club's general manager and coach Yogi Berra took over as skipper.

Walter Alston

Ralph Houk

Juan Marichal

1964

Despite a third manager in five years, the Yankees under Yogi Berra made it five pennants in a row, tying the record set by the 1949–53 club. It was a close-run race, however, the clinching coming on the next-to-last day of the season, as the Yankees nosed out the White Sox, whose manager, Al Lopez, had his ninth second-place finish since 1951.

Before winning their 14th pennant in 16 years, the Yankees had to make a 22–6 September stretch run that got them past both Baltimore (who finished two games out) and Chicago. The New York pitching, led by Jim Bouton (18–13), Whitey Ford (17–6), and Al Downing (13–8), received a big boost from sinkerballer Mel Stottlemyre, who joined the team in August and won 9 of 12 decisions.

Elston Howard was the team leader with a .313 average, while Mickey Mantle had his last truly productive season, hitting 35 home runs and driving in 111 runs.

The White Sox had the league's best pitching but were unable to match the Yankees' hitting. Gary Peters (20–8) was Lopez's ace, followed by another left-hander, Juan Pizarro (19–9), and Joel Horlen, who had a 1.88 ERA to go with his 13–9 record. Forty-year-old knuckleballer Hoyt Wilhelm appeared in 73 games, winning 12 and saving 27.

Baltimore got a 19–5 season from rookie Wally Bunker (just nineteen years old), and also had the MVP in third baseman Brooks Robinson, who batted .317, led with 118 RBIs, and inhaled everything hit near third base. Boog Powell, an outfielder then, launched 39 home runs for the O's, second in the league to the Twins' Harmon Killebrew, who had 49.

The Twins introduced one of the sweetest-swinging hitters seen in years in outfielder Tony Oliva. Easily the Rookie of the Year, Oliva was the first freshman in modern times to break in as a batting champion, leading with a .323 average, and was also first in hits (217) and doubles (43). With Twins players Rich Rollins and Zoilo Versalles tied for the lead in triples (10), it gave Minnesota the individual leaders in batting, doubles, triples, home runs, and hits. On May 2, the Twins tied a major league record when Oliva, Bob Allison, Jimmie Hall, and Killebrew homered in succession. The club led in home runs (221) and also scored the most runs (737), but still finished seventh.

The best pitcher in the league was Los Angeles's Dean Chance, the Cy Young Award winner, who was 20–9 with 11 shutouts and an immaculate 1.65 ERA, lowest in the league.

The 1964 All-Star Game, played on July 7 at New York's Shea Stadium, was won by the National League, 7–4, on a three-run homer in the bottom of the ninth by Philadelphia's Johnny Callison.

Dean Chance

The 1964 National League pennant race was marked by one of the most memorable end-of-the-season collapses in history. With two weeks to go, the Phillies were leading the league by 6½ games. But then it suddenly became as if the planets had fallen out of conjunction: the Phillies lost ten in a row, the Cardinals ran off an eight-game win streak, the Reds a nine-game win streak, and when those two tumultuous weeks were over, the Cardinals were the winners, by one game over the Reds and Phillies, who tied for second.

As late as mid-August, the Cardinals were in fifth place, nine games out, with rumors running about the imminent firing of manager Johnny Keane. The Cardinals' drive and the Phillies' two-week-long flat tire saved Keane's job, though the skipper would have something to say about that after the World Series.

The Cardinals had the MVP in third baseman Ken Boyer, who led in RBIs with 119, and another hard-hitter at the opposite corner in first baseman Bill White, who batted .303 and drove in 102 runs. Lou Brock, obtained that June from the Cubs, batted .348 in 102 games with St. Louis.

The Cards' top winner was left-hander Ray Sadecki, who was 20–11, but the ace was Bob Gibson, 19–12 with 245 strikeouts. The other big man on the staff was ex-Phillies left-hander Curt Simmons, 18–9.

Third-place Philadelphia had the Rookie of the Year in their enormously gifted third baseman Richie Allen, who batted .318 and hit 29 home runs, some of them, according to Casey Stengel, "over buildings."

The home run leader was Willie Mays with 47. Willie's teammate Juan Marichal was 21–8, while the league's

Sandy Koufax

most prolific winner was Cubs right-hander Larry Jackson, who outdid himself with a 24–11 record. The batting champion, for the second time, was Pittsburgh's Roberto Clemente at .339.

Sandy Koufax, who missed a dozen starts at the end of the season because of a hand injury, was 19–5, leading for the third straight year in ERA with 1.74.

There were three no-hitters in the league this year, each of them bearing a special stamp. The first came on April 23, when Houston right-hander Ken Johnson no-hit the Reds, yet became the first pitcher ever to lose a no-hitter. The Reds scored an unearned run against Johnson in the top of the ninth on two errors (one by Johnson) and won the game, 1–0, without benefit of a hit. On June 4, Koufax pitched his annual no-hitter, stifling the Phillies, 3–0. This third spotless effort tied the Dodger southpaw with Bob Feller for modern baseball's career record for no-hitters. On June 21, the Phillies' Jim Bunning delivered the first perfect game in modern National League history, beating the Mets, 6–0. Having pitched a no-hitter for the Tigers in 1958, Bunning became the first to achieve this success in both leagues.

Casey Stengel's Mets, who had gone from 120 losses in 1962 to 111 in 1963, lost 109 in 1964. "Progress," the old man said ruefully.

The World Series went the full seven, with the Cardinals winning over the Yankees, despite three home runs by Mantle and a record 13 hits by Bobby Richardson. Tim McCarver had 11 hits and a .478 batting average for the Cardinals, while Bob Gibson won twice.

After the Series, Johnny Keane announced he was leaving the world champs to replace Yogi Berra as Yankees manager. By general consensus, Berra, a beloved teammate, had never been taken seriously by those ex-teammates as a skipper, causing some dissension throughout the season. Yogi quickly resurfaced as a coach for Stengel's Mets.

1965

Age, injuries, and a depleted farm system finally brought an end to Yankees dominance. The year 1965 began a decade of decline for the New Yorkers, signaled by a sixth-place finish.

The American League pennant winners were the Minnesota Twins, managed by Sam Mele. The Twins did not hit as thunderously as they had in previous years, though they did have the league's leading hitter again, as Tony Oliva repeated with a .321 average. Mele's ace was Jim "Mudcat" Grant, 21–7, followed by left-hander Jim Kaat at 18–11. The Twins also had the Most Valuable Player in shortstop Zoilo Versalles, a .273 hitter who tied for the leads in doubles (45) and triples (12).

The runner-up Chicago White Sox were seven games behind, making it the tenth second-place finish for skipper Al Lopez. Logging a 14–7 record for the White Sox was twenty-two-year-old left-hander Tommy John, who would still be winning more than two decades later.

After Oliva, there were only two other full-time .300 hitters in the league—Boston's Carl Yastrzemski (.312) and Cleveland's Vic Davalillo (.301). Boston's twenty-two-year-old outfielder Tony Conigliaro was the home run leader with 32. Only two men in the league, Cleveland's Rocky Colavito with 108 and Detroit's Willie Horton with 104, drove in over 100 runs.

The Yankees' Mel Stottlemyre joined Grant as a 20-game winner (20–9), while the league's most overpowering pitcher was Cleveland's big, hard-throwing left-hander Sam McDowell, who fanned 325 in 273 innings while posting a 17–11 record and league-leading 2.18 ERA. Boston's Dave Morehead, 10–18 for the year, came up with a near-perfect game when he no-hit the Indians on September 16, 2–0. A second-inning walk to Colavito cost the Red Sox right-hander a perfect game.

Baltimore outfielder Curt Blefary, who hit 22 home runs and batted .260, was voted American League Rookie of the Year.

The All-Star Game was played on July 13 at Minnesota's Metropolitan Stadium. The National League won by a score of 6–5, giving them seven of the last eight and putting them ahead of their rivals in the annual competition for the first time, 18–17. (At one time the American League had enjoyed a 12–4 advantage.)

Only two teams in the league scored fewer runs than the Los Angeles Dodgers did in 1965, but no team won more games. Once again Walter Alston's club used strong pitching, timely hitting, and Maury Wills's base-stealing prowess to style themselves a pennant.

Sandy Koufax (26–8) and Don Drysdale (23–12) gave the Dodgers one of the most potent 1–2 pitching combines in baseball history. Koufax, again the Cy Young Award

The Houston Astrodome

Don Drysdale

winner (it was still a single designation covering both leagues), set a new all-time one-season strikeout record with 382 (in 336 innings) and for the fourth straight year led in ERA (2.04).

The Dodgers hit 78 home runs, fewest in the league. Instead of the long ball, the club employed the swift foot. Wills stole 94 bases, more than any other team in the league except the Cardinals, where Lou Brock's 63 steals indicated he was catching on to the new game. The Dodgers had a most unique infield—four switch-hitters.

They were first baseman Wes Parker, second baseman Jim Lefebvre (the Rookie of the Year), shortstop Wills (at .286 the team's leading hitter), and third baseman Jim Gilliam.

The Giants finished just two games behind, despite a bombshell year by MVP Willie Mays, who hit 52 home runs, including his 500th career shot on September 13. Willie McCovey had 39 homers for the Giants. The club's ace was Juan Marichal, 22–13 with ten shutouts. The high-kicking right-hander was the central figure in one of baseball's ugliest brawls, which occurred in a Dodgers-Giants game on August 22. Marichal had thrown close to a few Dodger hitters, and when he came to bat in the third inning, Dodger catcher John Roseboro made a return throw to the pitcher that almost hit Marichal (Juan claimed it nicked his ear). This led to words and then to Marichal raising his bat up in the air and bringing it down on Roseboro's head. The results of the fracas were these: Roseboro had severe cuts and bruises, Marichal was suspended for nine days, Roseboro sued the pitcher and won an out-of-court settlement of about $7,500, and the two main eventers later became good friends.

It had been a four-team race going into September, with the Reds and Pirates in it along with the two west coast teams. The Dodgers then put on a 13-game winning streak and the Giants a streak of 14 in a row, effectively losing the Reds and Pirates.

Pittsburgh's Roberto Clemente won his third batting title with a .329 mark, while Cincinnati's Deron Johnson had the year of his life, leading with 130 RBIs. Fifth-place Milwaukee (which announced it was moving to Atlanta in 1966) tied a record by having six men with over 20 home runs apiece: Eddie Mathews and Henry Aaron (32 each), Mack Jones (31), Joe Torre (27), Felipe Alou (23), and

Gene Oliver (21). All of this sound-barrier blasting helped right-hander Tony Cloninger to a 24–11 record. Cincinnati had Sammy Ellis at 22–10 and Jim Maloney at 20–9, and St. Louis's Bob Gibson made it seven 20-game winners with a 20–12 year. Nine National League pitchers had over 200 strikeouts, including Pittsburgh's talented lefty Bob Veale with 276, Gibson (270), and Philadelphia's Jim Bunning (268).

Jim Maloney won the Harvey Haddix Hard Luck Award by no-hitting the Mets for 10 innings and then losing in 11, 1–0, on a home run by Johnny Lewis. Maloney was superb in defeat, fanning 18 in the game, played on June 14. The big fireballer delivered another ten-inning no-hitter on August 19 against the Cubs, this time winning, 1–0, on Leo Cardenas's 10th-inning home run. On September 9, Koufax and the Cubs' left-hander Bob Hendley combined to pitch the stingiest game in major league history. Koufax was perfect—literally. The Dodger nonpareil retired all 27 men he faced to achieve the second perfect game in modern National League history. Hendley walked one and allowed just one hit, losing 1–0 on an unearned run (the game's lone hit, a seventh-inning double by Lou Johnson, didn't figure in the scoring). Koufax made it easy on his teammates by fanning the last six batters, for a total of 14. For Sandy, it was a record-breaking fourth no-hitter.

The Houston Astrodome, the proclaimed "Eighth Wonder of the World," opened this year, giving baseball its first enclosed stadium. Enchanted by the spectacle, Astros fans came out in sumptuous numbers all season—despite their dismal ninth-place club—and tripled 1964's attendance to over 2,100,000.

The Twins won the first two games of the World Series, but then the Dodgers began catching up and won it in seven. Koufax pitched a four-hit shutout in game 5, and then, on two days' rest, a three-hit shutout to win it all in game 7.

Sammy Ellis

1966

On December 9, 1965, the Cincinnati Reds made one of the biggest blunders in the history of their organization when they traded Frank Robinson to Baltimore for right-hander Milt Pappas (a fine pitcher, but not of superstar status, which Robinson was), thereby deciding the 1966 American League pennant race.

With Robinson smashing away to a Triple Crown, MVP year, the Orioles won the pennant, finishing nine ahead of the Twins. Robinson earned his Triple Crown with 49 home runs, 122 RBIs, and .316 batting average (the league's only other .300 hitter was Minnesota's Tony Oliva at .307), not to mention his driving leadership. The MVP was joined in hacking out Baltimore's victory by Brooks Robinson, who hit 23 homers and drove in 100 runs, and first baseman Boog Powell, who had 34 home runs and 109 RBIs. With former White Sox shortstop Luis Aparicio and Brooks Robinson, things on the left side of the Oriole infield were, as manager Hank Bauer put it, "pretty well sealed up."

Twenty-year-old Jim Palmer led the Baltimore staff with a 15–10 record.

Minnesota's Jim Kaat was the league's top winner at 25–13, with Detroit's Denny McLain the only other prime winner (20–14). Minnesota, still with some flashy home run power, tied a major league record on June 9 by hitting five home runs in one inning, struck by Rich Rollins, Zoilo Versalles, Tony Oliva, Don Mincher, and Harmon Killebrew.

The year's only no-hitter was pitched by Cleveland's Sonny Siebert, who shut down the Senators, 2–0, on June 10. The Rookie of the Year was Chicago outfielder Tommy Agee, who hit .273, cracked 22 home runs, and stole 44 bases.

The All-Star Game, played at St. Louis's newly opened Busch Stadium in broiling 105-degree heat on July 12, saw the National League win in ten innings, 2–1.

The Dodgers put on another of their pulsating pennant races, so familiar to Brooklyn fans and now also to those in Los Angeles. With a two-game margin over the Giants on the season's last day, the Dodgers had a doubleheader scheduled against the Phillies, the Giants a single game against the Pirates. The Giants won their game, the Dodgers lost their opener, making it a one-game lead. Another Dodger defeat would force the Giants to play a makeup game against the Reds the next day to try for a tie.

Walter Alston played his last card, and it was an ace —Sandy Koufax. Pitching on two days' rest, the incomparable left-hander beat the Phillies in the nightcap, 6–3, clinching the Dodgers' second straight pennant. For Koufax it was the crown on another Cy Young Award year.

This time he was 27–9 with 317 strikeouts and his fifth straight ERA title (1.73).

Alston also got winning pitching from left-hander Claude Osteen (17–14) and reliever Phil Regan, who was 14–1 with 21 saves. Again it was strong pitching that brought the flag to Los Angeles—with 606 runs, the Dodgers were outscored by seven other National League teams. The club's top RBI man was second baseman Jim Lefebvre with 74, a figure bettered by 19 other players in the league.

The second-place Giants had superb seasons from Juan Marichal (25–6) and Gaylord Perry (21–8), as well as 30-homer seasons from Willie Mays, Willie McCovey, and Jim Ray Hart, but fell short.

The surprising Pirates, just three out at the finish, had the batting champion in Matty Alou (.342), as well as .300 seasons from Roberto Clemente (the MVP), Manny Mota, and Willie Stargell, but foundered on a shallow pitching staff. Philadelphia's Dick Allen exploded with 40 home runs, second to Henry Aaron's 44. There was a brother act at the top of the league batting averages, Atlanta's Felipe Alou finishing second with a .327 mark to Pittsburgh's Matty. The stolen base crown was now all Lou Brock's, the Cardinals flash stealing 74, ending Maury Wills's six-year reign.

The Cardinals' Bob Gibson was 21–12 and the Phillies' Chris Short 20–10.

Cincinnati third baseman Tommy Helms, a .284 batter, was Rookie of the Year. Atlanta right-hander Tony Cloninger had a decent 14–11 season, but on July 3 he made real news with his bat when he achieved something no National Leaguer ever had—two grand slams in one game.

Little noted at the time, but destined to be long remembered, was an event that took place on April 4. The Atlanta Braves had signed young pitcher Tom Seaver of the University of Southern California to a $50,000 bonus contract. A technical violation soon voided the contract and Seaver was declared a free agent. Three teams bid for his services—Cleveland, Philadelpia, and the New York Mets. On April 4, in the office of Commissioner William Eckert, the Mets won an out-of-the-hat drawing and promptly signed Seaver.

Finding that natural grass would not grow in their Astrodome, Houston that year was forced to introduce one of baseball's abominations—Astroturf.

Baltimore pitching stifled the Dodgers in four straight in one of the tamest World Series ever. The Dodgers scored just two runs, none after the third inning of the opening game, thanks to airtight relief pitching by Moe Drabowsky in the opener and then shutouts by Palmer, Wally Bunker, and Dave McNally. The Dodger club batting average of .142 remains the lowest in Series history.

The news went from bad to worse for the Dodgers, for soon after the Series Sandy Koufax was forced into premature retirement because of a degenerative arthritic condition in his left elbow. The ace of aces was thirty-one years old.

Gaylord Perry

Tommy Helms

1967

For New England, it was a summer of excitement, tension, and victory—all of it unexpected. It was the year of "The Impossible Dream," the year the Boston Red Sox went in a single leap and bound from ninth place in 1966 to improbable pennant winners in 1967.

Going into the season's final week it was a four-team race, with the Red Sox, Tigers, Twins, and White Sox a single tight package. The White Sox dropped out first (Eddie Stanky's club had seemed like a reincarnation of the 1906 Hitless Wonders, for no regular batted over .241 or drove in more than 62 runs).

The season's closing weekend saw the Twins one game up on both Boston and Detroit. Postponements caused Detroit to play back-to-back doubleheaders with the Angels, while the Red Sox were entertaining the Twins at Fenway Park. On Saturday, Detroit split and the Red Sox defeated the Twins. On Sunday, the Red Sox won and Detroit again split, and this gave the Red Sox their first pennant since 1946.

Freshman Boston manager Dick Williams said that in 1967, "Carl Yastrzemski was the greatest ballplayer I ever saw." Indeed, in a league that batted a wretched .236, Yastrzemski looked like a superman as he ripped away to a Triple Crown season, leading with a .326 batting average, 44 home runs (tied with Harmon Killebrew), and 121 RBIs, easily winning the MVP Award.

The Red Sox also had the Cy Young Award winner (this was the first year of individual awards for each league) in right-hander Jim Lonborg, who was 22–9 and led with 246 strikeouts.

The Red Sox won despite the personal calamity that befell their young home run–hitting outfielder Tony Conigliaro. Hit in the face with a fastball in August, Conigliaro was lost for the season, his career in jeopardy. Though he recovered, Conigliaro was never the same player again.

Second-place Detroit got a 22–11 season from Earl

Wilson and a 17–16 record from Denny McLain, one year away from stardom now. Third-place Minnesota had the year's other 20-game winner in Dean Chance, who was 20–14. The Twins also had the Rookie of the Year in twenty-one-year-old second baseman Rod Carew, who batted .292 and impressed everyone with his deft bat manipulation.

The ninth-place Yankees, enduring a wretched .225 team batting average, celebrated one moment of old glory on May 15 when Mickey Mantle cracked his 500th career home run.

There were three no-hitters in the American League this year, one of them a combined losing effort. On April 30, Baltimore's Steve Barber pitched 8⅔ hitless innings against the Tigers but blew a one-run lead in the top of the ninth on walks, a wild pitch, and an error, allowing two runs. Stu Miller relieved and pitched a hitless one-third of an inning, but the O's lost it, 2–1. On August 25, Dean Chance no-hit the Indians in a 2–1 victory, and on September 10 the White Sox' Joel Horlen no-hit the Tigers, 6–0.

In a long, dull All-Star Game, played on July 11 at California's Anaheim Stadium, the National League beat the American, 2–1, on Tony Perez's home run in the top of the 15th inning.

After the season, Kansas City Athletics owner Charles Finley received approval from the league to move his club to Oakland, thus completing the transcontinental journey for Connie Mack's old Philadelphia Athletics.

In contrast to the American League's exciting four-team race, the National League generated very little suspense as the St. Louis Cardinals ran away with honors, finishing a sizable 10½ games ahead of second-place San Francisco.

Cardinals skipper Red Schoendienst got a big year out of MVP first baseman Orlando Cepeda, who hit 25 home runs, drove in a league-leading 111 runs, and batted .325. Other big contributors to the Cardinals' success were center fielder Curt Flood (.335) and Lou Brock, with 206 hits and 52 stolen bases. Despite losing ace Bob Gibson for five weeks in the middle of the season with a broken leg (he was shot down on the mound by a Roberto Clemente line drive), the Cardinals pitching held fast, with rookie right-hander Dick Hughes going 16–6, Nelson Briles 14–5, and twenty-two-year-old southpaw Steve Carlton 14–9.

The Giants had the Cy Young Award winner in southpaw Mike McCormick (22–10), but off years by Juan Marichal (14–10) and Gaylord Perry (15–17) could not be overcome. In addition, the thunder was leaving the bat of thirty-six-year-old Willie Mays, who batted .263 with just 22 home runs.

Chicago's Ferguson Jenkins was 20–13—the first of six straight 20-game seasons for the big, hard-throwing

Carl Yastrzemski

Curt Flood

Pitching dominance reached its apex in 1968, "The Year of the Pitcher," turning Louisville Sluggers into palm fronds, with an array of scintillating mound work in both leagues, highlighted by the landmark achievements of Detroit's Denny McLain and St. Louis's Bob Gibson.

The nation became acquainted with the brash, cocky Dennis McLain during the summer of 1968 as the Tiger right-hander rolled up victory after victory, efficiently and methodically, hurling Mayo Smith's club to its first pennant since 1945. McLain was 31–6, the first 30-game winner since Dizzy Dean in 1934. "He not only had great stuff," one of his catchers said, "but he seemed to have a sixth sense out there; he always seemed to know what to throw and when to throw it. In 1968 he was so good he was scary." The Cy Young Award winner as well as Most Valuable Player, McLain pitched 336 innings in completing 28 of his 41 starts, logging a 1.96 ERA (which was fourth best in this year of soggy hitting).

Detroit's second starter was left-hander Mickey Lolich, always a quality pitcher and a 17–9 man this year. Willie Horton was the big gun in the Tigers lineup with 36 home runs and a .285 batting average which, in the Year of the Pitcher, was fourth highest in the league.

right-hander. The Cubs (managed now by Leo Durocher) had one of the league's toughest threesomes in Ernie Banks, Billy Williams, and Ron Santo, and they helped young left-hander Ken Holtzman to a 9–0 record as he went to and from military obligations throughout the season.

Pittsburgh's Roberto Clemente won his fourth batting title with a .357 average; only Hornsby with eight and Wagner and Musial with seven each had won more in the National League. Atlanta's Henry Aaron was the home run king with 39. On July 14, Aaron's Atlanta teammate Eddie Mathews entered an elite circle with his 500th career home run.

Houston's Don Wilson pitched the league's only no-hitter, stopping Atlanta, 2–0, on June 18 in an overpowering performance in which he fanned 15. Another pitcher, the Mets' Tom Seaver, after just one year in the minors, posted a 16–13 record and was voted Rookie of the Year.

The World Series went the full distance, with the Cardinals winning out over Boston. Jim Lonborg won twice for the Red Sox, including a one-hitter in game 2, but the hero of the Series was Bob Gibson, who pitched three complete-game victories, allowing just three runs and 14 hits. The Cards' Lou Brock was the dominant hitter with 12 hits, a .414 batting average, and a Series record seven stolen bases. Carl Yastrzemski had three home runs for Boston.

Dennis McLain

The league's leading hitter was Carl Yastrzemski, winning his third batting crown with a ludicrously low .301 average (the league average of .230 was its all-time low, with the Yankees batting just .214). Washington's Frank Howard provided some offensive respectability with 44 home runs, while the RBI leader was Boston's Ken Harrelson with 109. The highest team batting average was Oakland's .240.

Aside from McLain, the other ace winners were Baltimore's Dave McNally (22–10), New York's Mel Stottlemyre (21–12), and Cleveland's Luis Tiant (21–9). Tiant's leading ERA of 1.60 was the lowest in the American League since Walter Johnson's 1.49 in 1919, the last year of the dead ball. Cleveland's Sam McDowell led in strikeouts with 283, beating out McLain by three. Both leagues set records for shutouts, the American with 154, the National with 185.

Despite the paucity of hitting this year, Detroit's Jim Northrup tied a record by hitting two grand slams in one game against the White Sox on June 24, and five days later hit another. And from Sunday May 12 through Saturday May 18, Howard set a one-week major league record with ten home runs. The year also saw the first unassisted triple play in 41 years, executed by Washington shortstop Ron Hansen against Cleveland on July 29.

There were two no-hitters this year, the first pitched by Baltimore's Tom Phoebus against Boston on April 27, a 6–0 game, and the second a masterpiece by Oakland's twenty-two-year-old Jim (Catfish) Hunter. On May 8 Hunter worked a 4–0 perfect game against Minnesota, the game's final pitch a 3–2 fastball burned past pinch-hitter Rich Reese.

The White Sox staff boasted the league's three most willing arms, having the three top leaders in appearances: Wilbur Wood with 88, forty-four-year-old Hoyt Wilhelm (72), and Bob Locker (70).

The Yankees had the Rookie of the Year in righthander Stan Bahnsen, who was 17–12.

Midway through the season the Orioles ownership became dissatisfied with manager Hank Bauer and replaced him with the man who would become one of the few managerial legends of modern times, Earl Weaver.

The All-Star Game was right in the spirit of the year, the National League winning, 1–0. The game, played on July 9 at Houston's Astrodome, was the Nationals' sixth straight win.

The National League was a bit louder at home plate than the American, hitting .243, with a more traditional batting average at the top of the heap, Pete Rose's .335, which was three points better than Matty Alou, who was bidding for a second title. Nevertheless, the year's headliner was the Cardinals' Bob Gibson. In pitching the Cards to an easy second straight pennant (nine games over the

Bob Gibson

Giants, who finished second for the fourth year in a row), Gibson was awesome. The Cy Young-MVP winner was 22–9 with a record-breaking 1.12 ERA, his year including highs in strikeouts with 268 and shutouts with 13, second in National League history to Grover Cleveland Alexander's 16 in 1916. Along the way, Gibson had a 15-game winning streak.

The Cardinals also received productive years from Nelson Briles (19–11), Ray Washburn, and Steve Carlton. This strong pitching helped pick up a spotty offense that had Curt Flood's .301 average and Mike Shannon's 79 RBIs lead the team.

Only one man in the league drove in over 100 runs—the Giant's Willie McCovey with 105. Willie also led in home runs with 36.

Another record-shattering pitching performance was turned in by the Dodgers' Don Drysdale. Just 14–12 for the year, Drysdale set a new mark by hurling 58⅔ consecutive scoreless innings from May 14 through June 8, breaking by three Walter Johnson's 1913 record. By pitching six straight shutouts over this span, Drysdale set another record. His string of goose eggs was broken by a sacrifice fly by the Phillies' Howie Bedell—who played in 67 major league games in his career and had just three runs batted in.

Atlanta's Henry Aaron hit his 500th career home run on July 14. The year's top winner was the Giants' Juan Marichal at 26–9, but as he had always been by Koufax, was this year overshadowed by Gibson (Marichal never won a Cy Young Award). The league's other 20-game winner was the Cubs' Ferguson Jenkins, who was 20–15.

The year produced three no-hitters in the National League: on July 29 Cincinnati's George Culver stopped the

Phillies, 6–1, and then on September 17 and 18 two clubs swapped no-hitters—the Giants' Gaylord Perry 1–0 over the Cardinals on the 17th and the Cardinal's Ray Washburn over the Giants the next day, 2–0. Another job of pitching splendor took place on July 14 when Houston's Don Wilson tied the single-game strikeout record by fanning 18 Reds in a 6–1 win.

On April 15 the Mets and Astros played baseball's longest shutout game, the Astros winning in 24 innings, 1–0. (The Mets lost another 1–0 game in 17 innings to the Giants on August 19.)

The league's Rookie of the Year was Cincinnati catcher Johnny Bench. The twenty-year-old youngster broke in with a .275 batting average while displaying remarkable maturity behind the plate.

On May 27, the National League voted to expand, accepting into the lodge new franchises in Montreal and San Diego. In July, rules were drawn up for divisional play in both 12-team leagues, to be followed by divisional play-offs to determine pennant winners, the changes to be implemented in 1969.

In early December, the owners nudged Commissioner Eckert from his job and replaced him with Wall Street lawyer Bowie Kuhn.

The World Series again went the distance, with the Tigers winning it, thanks to three route-going victories by the Tigers' Mickey Lolich. Bob Gibson won two games, including a record 17-strikeout performance in the opener, and extended his World Series winning streak to seven before losing the finale. Lou Brock again starred at the plate, batting .464 and tying Series records with 13 hits and seven stolen bases (his own record)—all in a losing cause.

1969

Concerned about the soporific effects of 339 shutouts in 1968 (82 of them by 1–0 scores), baseball sought to animate things the following year by lowering the mound and contracting the strike zone. The leagues responded accordingly, the American raising its average 16 points to .246, the National seven points to .250.

Each league was now broken into East-West divisions, with a pair of best-of-five playoffs deciding the respective pennant winners and World Series opponents.

Divisional play in the American League began with a Baltimore win marathon, Earl Weaver's squad winning 109 games. The heavy hitting was done by first baseman Boog Powell (37 homers, 121 RBIs) and Frank Robinson (32 homers, 100 RBIs), with considerable support from second baseman Dave Johnson and outfielders Paul Blair and Don Buford. The Orioles pitching—the club's hallmark for the next decade—featured Dave McNally, whose 20–7 record included 15 straight wins from the opening of the season; Mike Cuellar at 23–11, and Jim Palmer, 16–4, plus a strong bullpen in right-handers Eddie Watt and Dick Hall, and lefty Pete Richert.

Second in the East were the Tigers (a hefty 19 games behind), with Denny McLain following his 31-win season with a 24–9 record, sharing the Cy Young Award with Cuellar.

The Minnesota Twins, under Billy Martin (fired after the season) won the West by nine games over Oakland. The Twins had the MVP in Harmon Killebrew, who led in

Mickey Lolich

Dave McNally

home runs (49) and RBIs (140), plus a pair of aces in Jim Perry (20–6) and Dave Boswell (20–12), as well as the batting champion in Rod Carew, who won the first of his seven titles with a .332 average and tied Pete Reiser's record by stealing home seven times.

Reggie Jackson, Oakland's sophomore outfielder, made a jump to stardom by belting 47 home runs, while Washington's Frank Howard hit 48. Mel Stottlemyre, the Yankees' sinkerballer, was 20–14, giving the league six 20-game winners. Kansas City had the Rookie of the Year in outfielder Lou Piniella, a .282 hitter.

Jim Palmer pitched the league's only no-hitter, stopping Oakland on August 13, 8–0.

The National League kept winning the All-Star Game, taking its seventh straight, a 9–3 runaway played at Robert F. Kennedy Memorial Stadium on July 23.

The first American League pennant playoff was a clean three-game sweep by Baltimore over Minnesota, including a 4–3 12-inning win and another in 11 innings, 1–0 (pitched by McNally).

Two years before, the Boston Red Sox had high-jumped from ninth place to the pennant, and now in 1969 this same feat was emulated by the New York Mets, in an achievement even more improbable and fantastic. Where the Red Sox had at least won pennants in the past, with names like Ruth, Speaker, and Williams as part of their history, the Mets were virtually without any history or persona, except losing and losers. Nevertheless, under the firm and patient hand of Gil Hodges, the Mets made their bounding leap, primarily upon the skills of a young and immensely talented pitching staff. The ace was Tom Seaver, the Cy Young Award winner, with a 25–7 record, followed by left-hander Jerry Koosman at 17–9, and a bullpen that included Tug McGraw, Ron Taylor, and the twenty-two-year-old, extraordinarily fast Nolan Ryan.

In winning the East by eight games over the Cubs, the Mets came from 9½ games back in early August, propelled by Cleon Jones's .340 batting average (no other regular batted over .279. The team's .242 batting average was the lowest ever for a pennant winner. Tommie Agee's 76 RBIs led the club).

Leo Durocher's Cubs had a pair of 20-game winners in Ferguson Jenkins (21–15) and Bill Hands (20–14) and hard hitters in Ernie Banks, Ron Santo, and Billy Williams, but some late-season weariness in the pitching arms, plus a few dollops of dissension (not unknown on a Durocher-run club), and the irresistible velocity of the Mets' "miracle" doomed the Cubs to second place, their best finish since 1945.

The western division winners were Lum Harris's Atlanta Braves, with knuckleballer Phil Niekro heading the staff with a 23–13 record and Henry Aaron, that paragon of explosive consistency, hitting 44 home runs. San Fran-

cisco, in second place (by three games) for the fifth straight year, had the MVP in Willie McCovey, who for the second year in a row led in home runs (45) and RBIs (120).

Cincinnati's nonstop dynamo Pete Rose was also a repeating winner, taking his second successive batting title with a career-high .348, delivering 218 hits, second to Matty Alou's impressive 231. Rose was three points better than Roberto Clemente's .345. In addition to Clemente, four other Pirates were in the .300 class this year: Alou (.331), Willie Stargell (.307), Manny Sanguillen (.303), and Richie Hebner (.301). The Dodgers had their seventh Rookie of the Year in second baseman Ted Sizemore, a .271 hitter.

The National League had nine 20-game winners in 1969, tying a league record set in 1903 and again in 1914. In addition to Seaver, Jenkins, Hands, and Niekro were the Cardinals' Bob Gibson (20–13), the Giant's Juan Marichal (21–11), the Dodgers' Bill Singer (20–12) and Claude Osteen (20–15), and the Astros' Larry Dierker (20–13).

In what was probably the game of the year, the Cardinals' Steve Carlton set a new major league record by fanning 19 Mets on September 15, only to lose, 4–3, on a pair of two-run homers by Ron Swoboda.

No-hitters abounded in the league this year, with five of them being thrown: on April 17, Montreal's Bill Stoneman stopped the Phillies, 7–0; on April 30, Cincinnati's Jim Maloney pitched his second career no-hitter, beating Houston, 10–0; the following day Houston's Don Wilson reversed the act, pitching his second career no-hitter in beating the Reds, 4–0; on August 19, the Cubs' Ken Holtzman no-hit the Braves, 3–0 (without benefit of a strikeout); and on September 20 the Pirates' Bob Moose no-hit the merry miracle-making Mets, 4–0.

As befitting an expansion team, the last-place Montreal Expos lost 110 games, their season including a 20-game losing streak, three under the 1961 Phillies' major league record (both clubs were managed by Gene Mauch).

The Mets continued rolling in postseason play, sweeping the Braves in the playoffs and then upsetting a vastly superior Orioles team in the World Series. After losing the first game, the New Yorkers took the next four, thanks to some spectacular outfield catches by Tommie Agee and Ron Swoboda, three home runs by first baseman Donn Clendenon, and the handsome pitching of Seaver, Koosman, and Gary Gentry.

Ferguson Jenkins

A 12-year veteran, Ralph Terry retired in 1967 with a record of 107–99. A Yankees ace in the early 1960s, he also pitched for three other teams.

Roberto Clemente: 3,000 hits, 13 times over .300, four batting titles, a career average of .317. He played from 1955–72.

Whitey Ford, the top pitcher in Yankees history. He pitched in 1950 and from 1953–67, winning 236 and losing 106.

Ted Williams's finale at the end of the 1960 season. The press did not let it pass unrecorded.

LEFT: Bob Friend pitched for the Pirates from 1951–65 and closed out with the Yankees and Mets a year later. Lifetime record: 197–230.

Right-hander Vern Law, Pittsburgh's Cy Young Award winner in 1960. He joined the Pirates in 1950 and retired in 1967 with 162–147 record.

One memorable swing of the bat in the 1960 World Series made Bill Mazeroski a Pittsburgh hero forever. He was also one of the greatest-fielding second basemen in baseball history. Playing his entire career (1956–72) for the Pirates, he batted .260.

Ebbets Field undergoing demolition in the spring of 1960. It was replaced by a housing project.

Lindy McDaniel pitched for five clubs in both leagues from 1955–75, compiling a 141–119 record. A top reliever for many years, he appeared in 987 games, second-highest total in history.

A turning point in the seventh game of the 1960 World Series. It's the bottom of the eighth inning and Yankees shortstop Tony Kubek has just been hit in the throat by a bad-hop grounder. Bobby Richardson is asking the umpire to call time.

Mickey Mantle

Bill Mazeroski heading home to a jubilant reception after hitting the home run that ended the 1960 World Series.

Norm Cash came to the majors with the White Sox in 1958, was traded to Detroit two years later, and played there until 1974. He was the American League batting champion in 1961—the only time he hit over .300. For his career the power-hitting first baseman had 377 home runs and a .271 batting average.

Yankee Stadium, as seen from a Mickey Mantle home run.

Roger Maris making baseball history on October 1, 1961. He is just completing the swing that rocketed his record-making 61st home run of the season into the seats at Yankee Stadium. The pitch was delivered by Boston's Tracy Stallard. The blow came in the fourth inning of the season's last game.

RIGHT: A couple of Baltimore Orioles busters: first baseman Jim Gentile (left) and catcher Gus Triandos. Jim had 46 homers for the Orioles in 1961. He batted .260 over his 9-year career. Gus caught in the bigs for 13 years, batting .244.

A fine left-hander with the Orioles in the early 1960s, Steve Barber later pitched for six other clubs in both leagues, retiring in 1974 with a 121–106 record.

Earl Wilson, a top pitcher for the Red Sox and Tigers from 1959–70. Lifetime record: 121–109.

RIGHT: Colorful first baseman Dick Stuart, whose chancy fielding earned him the nickname "Dr. Strangeglove." But they paid Dick to hit, and that he did, with the Pirates, Red Sox, and four other teams, from 1958–66 and 1969. The RBI leader with Boston in 1963, when he hit 42 home runs, he batted .264 lifetime.

Vada Pinson (left) and Frank Robinson in 1961. Pinson spent 18 years in the major leagues, the first 11 with the Reds, rapping 2,757 hits and racking up a .286 batting average.

Willie Mays is illustrating the occasion of having scored his 1,000th major league run, on September 10, 1961.

Leon Wagner played the outfield for five teams from 1958–69, batting .272. He popped 37 homers for the Angels in 1962.

Gary Peters, a classy southpaw for the White Sox and Red Sox from 1959–72. Twice the ERA leader, he was 124–103.

San Francisco's Candlestick Park

The Yankees infield in the early 1960s (left to right): third baseman Clete Boyer, shortstop Tony Kubek, second baseman Bobby Richardson, first baseman Joe Pepitone.

Jim O'Toole. He was with the Reds for nine of his ten big-league seasons, retiring in 1967 with a 98–84 record.

Dick Radatz. They called this big right-handed reliever "The Monster." He had some spectacular seasons with the Red Sox in the early 1960s and later worked for four other clubs, retiring in 1969 with a 52–43 record.

Milt Pappas, known to baseball trivia experts as a 200-game winner who never won more than 17 in a season. Milt pitched for the Orioles, Reds, Braves, and Cubs from 1957–73. Lifetime record: 209–164.

Jim Bouton, 20-game-winning pitcher for the Yankees in 1963. His career shortened by a sore arm, he was 62–63, pitching for four teams. He later coauthored the baseball classic *Ball Four*.

LEFT: One of baseball's most-traveled players, Tommy Davis played for ten clubs during his 18-year career, which began with the Dodgers (with whom he won two batting titles) in 1959. Lifetime average: .294.

RIGHT: The ever-agile Willie Mays escaping an inside delivery. The catcher is the Dodgers' John Roseboro.

Henry Aaron, baseball's all-time home run champion. Aaron built his record through a 23-year career, the first 21 of which were spent with the Braves in Milwaukee and Atlanta. He finished up with the Milwaukee Brewers in 1976. He hit 40 or more home runs in a season 8 times, drove in over 100 runs in a season 11 times, and was a .300 hitter 14 times, twice winning the batting title. Lifetime, he collected 3,771 hits, hit 755 home runs, and batted .305.

Maury Wills (right) taking the measure of Frank Howard, who stood six feet seven inches. Maury played with the Dodgers, Pirates, and Expos from 1959–72, stealing 586 bases and batting .281. Howard played with the Dodgers, Senators, Rangers, and Tigers from 1958–73, hitting 382 home runs and batting .273. He hit over 40 home runs three years in a row for the Senators.

Dodger Stadium

Spending 11 years of his 12-year career with the White Sox, Joel Horlen carved out a 116–117 record. He led in ERA in 1967.

One of the top relief pitchers of his era, Ron Perranoski. He was with the Dodgers for seven years, then with three other clubs, retiring in 1973 with a 79–74 record. He appeared in 737 games, all but one in relief.

Juan Marichal. "When he rocked back in his delivery," one writer said, "it looked like he had one long leg with a spiked shoe at either end."

Marichal pitched for the Giants from 1960–73, then for the Red Sox and Dodgers, retiring in 1975 with a 243–142 record. He was a six-time 20-game winner.

The Alou brothers (left to right): Jesus, Matty, and Felipe. They were all briefly together on the Giants in the early 1960s before going their separate ways. Each had a long and productive career. Lifetime averages: Jesus, .280; Matty, .307; Felipe, .286.

Pete Rose in 1963, his rookie season.

Ken Hubbs (left) and Dick Ellsworth of the Chicago Cubs. The twenty-two-year-old Hubbs was killed in the crash of a private plane in 1964, after three years as a Cubs second baseman. He batted .247. Ellsworth, a 22-game winner for the Cubs in 1963, pitched in the big leagues for five clubs from 1958–71, winning 115 and losing 137.

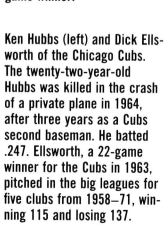

Bill Monbouquette, Red Sox ace during the early 1960s. Pitching for four clubs from 1958–68, he was 114–112.

Two former Brooklyn Dodgers greats winding down their careers with the New York Mets in 1963. Gil Hodges (left) and Duke Snider.

Outfielder—third baseman Mike Shannon (left) and catcher Tim McCarver, who played on three Cardinals pennant winners in the 1960s. Shannon was a .255 lifetime hitter, McCarver (a 21-year major leaguer), .271.

Jim Ray Hart, home run–hitting third baseman of the San Francisco Giants from 1963–73, retiring with the Yankees in 1974. He batted .278 lifetime.

BELOW: Cardinal manager Johnny Keane (left) and Ken Boyer.

The infield of the 1964 pennant-winning St. Louis Cardinals. Left to right: third baseman Ken Boyer, shortstop Dick Groat, second baseman Julian Javier, first baseman Bill White. Lifetime averages: Boyer, .287; Groat, .286; Javier, .257; White, .286.

Pitching for the Yankees from 1964–74, Mel Stottlemyre was a three-time 20-game winner. Lifetime record: 164–139.

Lou Brock came up with the Cubs in 1961 and was traded to the Cardinals in 1964, for whom he played until 1979. The all-time base-stealing leader with 938, he had 3,023 career hits and a .293 batting average.

The Phillies' Jim Bunning firing the final pitch of his June 21, 1964, perfect game against the Mets at Shea Stadium, a third strike past Johnny Stephenson. Bunning had a career record of 224–184.

Outfielder Johnny Callison spent 10 of his 16 years in the big leagues with the Phillies. He retired in 1973 with a .264 average.

Frank Robinson

One of baseball's rare 25-year veterans, southpaw Jim Kaat. He pitched from 1959–83, working for five clubs in both leagues. Three times a 20-game winner, he was 283–237 lifetime.

Harmon Killebrew, one of baseball's all-time busters. He played from 1954–75, the last year with Kansas City after spending his entire career with the Washington Senators-Minnesota Twins. The home run champ six times, he hit over 40 in a season eight times, and 573 over his career, while compiling a .256 batting average.

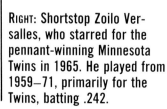

RIGHT: Shortstop Zoilo Versalles, who starred for the pennant-winning Minnesota Twins in 1965. He played from 1959–71, primarily for the Twins, batting .242.

Tony Oliva, Minnesota's sweet-swinging three-time batting champion, whose career was hampered by a knee injury. He led the league in hits five times. He played from 1962–76, batting .304.

Zoilo Versalles is about to steal second base in the first game of the 1965 World Series. Taking the high throw is Dodgers' second baseman Jim Lefebvre.

Part of Minnesota's hard-hitting attack in 1965 (left to right): Harmon Killebrew, Jimmie Hall, Earl Battey, and Bob Allison.

The Marichal-Roseboro brawl on August 22, 1965. Sandy Koufax has run up to try and act as peacemaker.

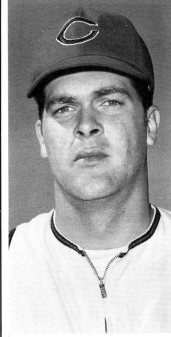

Left-hander Sam McDowell, one of the hardest throwers of all time. He was with Cleveland from 1961–71 and later pitched for the Giants, Yankees, and Pirates, retiring in 1975 with a 141–134 record. He was the American League strikeout leader five times.

Claude Osteen pitched for six clubs in the course of an 18-year career, but had his best outings with the Dodgers from 1965–73. He retired in 1975 after posting a 196–195 record.

Left to right: Maury Wills, Sandy Koufax, and Willie Davis are all smiles after Koufax and the Dodgers trimmed the Twins in the fifth game of the 1965 World Series.

Dodgers first baseman Wes Parker. He played his entire nine-year career with Los Angeles, retiring in 1972 with a .267 average.

RIGHT: Jim Lonborg, ace of the surprise 1967 Red Sox pennant winners. He pitched for three clubs in his 15-year career, retiring in 1979 with a 157–137 record.

ABOVE: Willie Stargell in 1966. He spent his entire career (1962–82) with the Pirates, hitting 475 home runs and batting .282.

RIGHT: Brooks Robinson, who set the standard at third base for the Orioles from 1955–77. He led American League third basemen in fielding a record 11 times, while his 2,870 games at the bag are the most ever. Lifetime batting average: .267.

Bob Veale, Pittsburgh's star left-hander through most of the 1960s. He finished up with the Red Sox in 1974. Lifetime record: 120–95.

Baltimore second baseman Dave Johnson. He played on four Orioles pennant winners. A 13-year career spent with four clubs added up to a .261 batting average. His 43 home runs hit for Atlanta in 1973 are the major league record for second basemen.

Baltimore's Boog Powell. He was with the Orioles from 1961–74, later playing for Cleveland and the Dodgers. He hit 339 home runs and batted .266.

Sandy Koufax. He pitched for the Dodgers from 1955–66. Lifetime record: 165–87. Over his last four years he was 97–27.

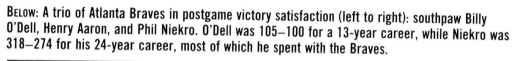

BELOW: A trio of Atlanta Braves in postgame victory satisfaction (left to right): southpaw Billy O'Dell, Henry Aaron, and Phil Niekro. O'Dell was 105–100 for a 13-year career, while Niekro was 318–274 for his 24-year career, most of which he spent with the Braves.

Third baseman–shortstop Rico Petrocelli, who spent his entire 13-year career with the Red Sox, batting .251.

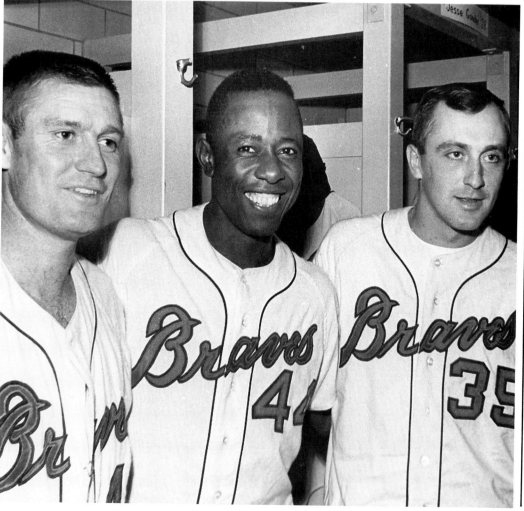

They say the double play is the pitcher's best friend. But Roberto Clemente in right field didn't hurt either.

Orlando Cepeda, the National League MVP in 1967.

Three Red Sox outfielders (left to right): Carl Yastrzemski, Reggie Smith, Tony Conigliaro. Yaz played 23 years for Boston, collecting 3,419 hits, 452 home runs, and batting .285. Smith hit .287 across 17 years, and Conigliaro .264 for an injury-aborted 8-year career.

Second-year man Reggie Jackson in 1968. He played until 1987, hitting 563 home runs and batting .262. His explosive hitting in postseason games earned him the nickname "Mr. October."

Gary Nolan, who spent most of his 10-year career with the Reds, winning 110 and losing 70.

Cincinnati's rookie catcher Johnny Bench in 1967. When he retired in 1983 he was a candidate for greatest catcher of all time. A three-time RBI leader, he hit 389 home runs and batted .267.

Bill Freehan, Detroit catcher from 1961–75. Lifetime average: .262.

Ernie Banks acknowledging the cheers of the crowd after rapping out his 2,500th major league hit. First baseman Joe Torre is less impressed.

Willie Horton, who spent the first 15 years of his 18-year career with Detroit, then made the rounds with five other clubs. A bona fide slugger, Willie had 325 home runs and batted .273.

Outfielder Jimmy Wynn, known as "The Toy Cannon." He spent the bulk of his 15-year career with Houston, batting .250.

Mickey Lolich, star of Detroit's 1968 World Series victory. One of the most durable pitchers of his time, the southpaw pitched 13 of his 16 big-league seasons for the Tigers. He retired in 1979 with a 217–191 record.

Jim "Catfish" Hunter at work during his May 8, 1968, perfect game against the Twins. Hunter pitched for the Athletics and Yankees from 1965–79. Five times a 20-game winner, he was 224–166 lifetime.

Third baseman Ron Santo, who spent his entire 15-year career in Chicago—14 years with the Cubs and 1 with the White Sox. He hit 342 home runs and batted .277.

Don Kessinger, big-league shortstop from 1964–79, most of it spent in the employ of the Cubs. Lifetime average: .252.

It's spring training 1969 and Mickey Mantle is hanging up his number 7 for the last time.

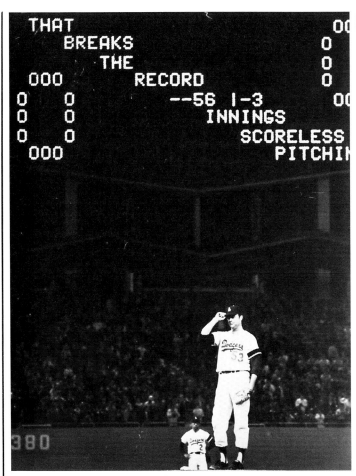

The scoreboard tells the story of Don Drysdale's historic achievement. Drysdale spent his entire 14-year career with the Dodgers, winning 209 and losing 166.

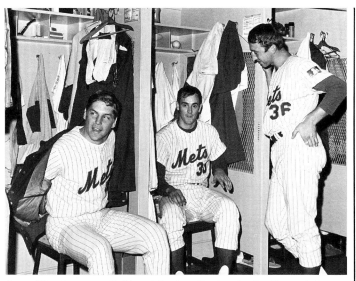

A wealth of young pitching talent gathering in the Mets clubhouse in 1969 (left to right): Tom Seaver, Nolan Ryan, and Jerry Koosman. Seaver went on to a 311–205 record, Koosman 222–209, and Ryan to become the all-time strikeout leader.

Ron Swoboda making a diving grab of a Brooks Robinson drive in the ninth inning of game 4 of the 1969 World Series.

Infielder Dick McAuliffe, who played 14 of his 16 big-league seasons with Detroit, batting .247.

Managers Walter Alston of the Dodgers (left) and Gil Hodges of the Mets.

Mets outfielder Tommie Agee (left) and Jerry Koosman. Agee played for five clubs in his 12-year career, batting .255.

Cincinnati fastballer Jim Maloney (left) and Tom Seaver. Maloney pitched for the Reds for ten years, logging a 134–84 record.

Cleon Jones of the Mets and the Cubs' Billy Williams. Jones played most of his 13-year career for the Mets, batting .281. Williams had a superb 18-year career, the first 16 with the Cubs. The National League batting leader in 1972, he hit 426 home runs and batted .290.

Tommie Agee making one of the two spectacular catches he made to help the Mets win game 3 of the 1969 World Series.

Goose Gossage, one of the most intimidating relief pitchers ever.

1970

The Baltimore Orioles and Minnesota Twins repeated as division winners in the American League, with Earl Weaver's O's winning 108 games. Weaver ran three masterful pitchers through the league all summer—Mike Cuellar (24–8), Dave McNally (24–9), and Jim Palmer (20–10). First baseman Boog Powell turned in an MVP season with 35 home runs and 114 RBIs.

Though 15 games out, the Yankees had the satisfaction of rising from a five-year doldrum and finishing second. The club had a 20-game winner in left-hander Fritz Peterson and the Rookie of the Year in catcher Thurman Munson, a .302 hitter. The California Angels had the batting champion in moody outfielder Alex Johnson, a narrow winner over Carl Yastrzemski, .3289 to .3286. Washington's Frank Howard belted 44 home runs and drove in 126 runs, leading in both departments. Cleveland's Sam McDowell broke the 20-win mark for the first time with a 20–12 record, while leading with 304 strikeouts. Other 20-game winners were Minnesota's Cy Young Award designee Jim Perry (24–12) and California left-hander Clyde Wright (22–12), who was 1–8 the year before.

The most abrupt descent from glory belonged to Detroit's Denny McLain. Winner of 55 games the past two seasons, McLain was suspended in February for alleged past association with gamblers. The fun-loving Denny returned in July, only to suffer two more suspensions for dumping ice water on a couple of reporters and for carrying a gun. With a 3–5 record for the season, McLain was later dealt to Washington. He later drifted on to Oakland and Atlanta, his skills permanently diminished.

On July 3, Wright no-hit Oakland, 4–0, and on September 21 the recently recalled young Oakland southpaw Vida Blue fired a 6–0 no-hitter against the Twins.

Bill Rigney's Twins repeated easily in the American League West, winning by nine over Oakland, led by Perry's 24 wins. The Twins won despite an injury to second baseman Rod Carew that shelved him for two-thirds of the season. Carew was batting .366 when he was forced from the lineup. Tony Oliva's .325 left him four points short of a third batting title, while Harmon Killebrew delivered 41 home runs, the eighth and final time he cleared the 40 barrier.

The National League won its eighth straight All-Star Game, beating the Americans, 5–4, in 12 innings, with Pete Rose scoring the winning run when he crashed into catcher Ray Fosse, who was stunned into dropping the relay. The game was

1970– And Then There Was Free Agency 1979

Jim Perry

Tony Perez

played at Cincinnati's Riverfront Stadium on July 14.

The 1970 pennant playoffs were a repeat of the previous year's, with Baltimore again sweeping Minnesota in three straight.

Miracles are wondrous things, but lack staying power, and so the Mets tumbled to third place in 1970, despite Tom Seaver's 283 strikeouts—a record for a National League right-hander. It was Danny Murtaugh's Pirates winning in the East, by five games over the Cubs, despite a pitching staff that had 15-game winner Luke Walker topping it. Murtaugh's shaky starters were picked up all year long by reliever Dave Giusti, who won 9 and saved 26. Roberto Clemente led the club with a .352 batting average, but lost the title to Atlanta's Rico Carty (.366). Willie Stargell's 31 homers and 85 RBIs were Pittsburgh's main power supply, while catcher Manny Sanguillen batted .325.

The second-place Cubs enjoyed the benefit of Ferguson Jenkins' fourth straight 20-win season (22–16) and a superb year from Billy Williams—42 home runs, 129 RBIs, and a .322 batting average. A weary Williams removed himself from the lineup on September 3, ending a league record iron-man streak of 1,117 consecutive games. "I'm tired, that's all it is," Billy explained.

Under freshman manager Sparky Anderson, the Cincinnati Reds easily won in the West, 14½ games ahead of the Dodgers. Catcher Johnny Bench headlined a team of stars, the MVP designee leading the league with 45 home runs and 148 RBIs. Tony Perez—a third baseman then— hit 40 homers and drove in 129 runs while batting .317.

Three other Reds—Pete Rose, Bobby Tolan, and Bernie Carbo—also hit over .300. This solid hitting supported a staff led by lefty Jim Merritt (20–12) and Gary Nolan (18–7), with reliever Wayne Granger notching 35 saves.

Other 20-game winners in the league were the Giants' Gaylord Perry (23–13) and the Cardinals' Cy Young Award winner Bob Gibson (23–7). Gibson's 274 strikeouts marked the eighth time he had cleared 200 whiffs in a season, breaking a record he had coheld with Walter Johnson and Rube Waddell.

On April 22, Tom Seaver tied Steve Carlton's year-old record by fanning 19 San Diego Padres, including the last ten in a row, the latter a glittering new major league record.

Two National League pitchers joined the ranks of no-hit specialists this year: on June 12 Pittsburgh's Dock Ellis stopped San Diego, winning, 2–0, on the strength of a pair of Willie Stargell homers; and on July 20 the Dodgers' Bill Singer (dubbed "The Singer Throwing Machine") pitched a 5–0 no-hitter over the Phillies.

The year was replete with history-book occasions: On May 10, Hoyt Wilhelm (with Atlanta now) became the first pitcher to work in 1,000 games. On May 12, Ernie Banks hit his 500th career home run. On May 17, Henry Aaron collected his 3,000th career hit, and on July 18 Willie Mays did the same. On August 11, the Phillies' Jim Bunning became the first pitcher in modern history to win 100 games in both leagues. On August 22–23, Roberto Clemente did some scorching hitting and lined ten hits in two games, bettering Stan Musial's old record by one.

Montreal right-hander Carl Morton, with an 18–11 record, was selected the National League's Rookie of the Year.

The National League playoffs went to Cincinnati, as they beat Pittsburgh in three straight by scores of 3–0, 3–1, and 3–2. "We kept getting closer," a rueful Danny Murtaugh said later.

In the World Series, it was Baltimore over Cincinnati in five, thanks in part to some spectacular third base play by Brooks Robinson, who also batted .429.

1971

With 101 wins, the Orioles went over the century mark for the third straight year, giving Earl Weaver a third straight pennant, by 12 games over Billy Martin's Tigers. This time the stellar Orioles pitching outdid itself, becoming the first club since the 1920 Chicago White Sox to have four 20-game winners: Dave McNally (21–5), Pat Dobson (20–8), Mike Cuellar (20–9), and Jim Palmer (20–9). Frank Robinson led the club with 28 homers and 99 RBIs, with outfielder Merv Rettenmund topping the regulars with a .318 average. Among Robinson's home runs was the 500th of his career, on September 13. (Minnesota's Harmon Killebrew observed a similar occasion on August 10.)

Led by the Orioles staff, the league tied a record (set in 1910 and tied in 1920) with ten 20-game winners. In addition to the Orioles aces, there were Detroit's Mickey Lolich (25–14) and Joe Coleman (20–9), Oakland's Vida Blue (24–8) and Catfish Hunter (21–11), Chicago's Wilbur Wood (22–13), and California's Andy Messersmith (20–13). Lolich's 376 innings pitched were the most in the major leagues since Grover Cleveland Alexander's 388 in 1917, and the Detroit lefty also led with 308 strikeouts, with Blue right behind at 301.

Minnesota's Tony Oliva won his third batting title with a .337 average, third baseman Bill Melton's 33 homers made him the first White Sox player ever to lead the league, and Killebrew's 119 RBIs was tops. (Harmon was the only man in the league with over 100 RBIs.)

In the West, Oakland, under skipper Dick Williams, won the first of its five straight division titles, outdistancing Kansas City by 16 games. With MVP and Cy Young Award winner Blue delivering on the expectations aroused by his 1970 no-hitter (he was also the ERA leader with

1.82) and Rollie Fingers emerging as a relief artist, the A's received strong hitting from Reggie Jackson and Sal Bando. On July 9, the A's won the longest shutout in American League history, a 20-inning 1–0 win over California.

The Rookie of the Year was Cleveland first baseman Chris Chambliss, who batted .275.

In the All-Star Game, the American League stopped the Nationals' winning streak at eight with a 6–4 win in the game played at Detroit's Tiger Stadium on July 13.

For the third year running, the Orioles swept the playoffs in three games, with McNally, Cuellar, and Palmer smothering the A's.

After the season, the Washington Senators announced they would be relocating to the Dallas-Fort Worth suburb of Arlington in 1972.

In the National League East, Danny Murtaugh's Pirates made it two in a row, finishing seven ahead of St. Louis, who had the MVP, batting (.363), RBI (137), and hits (230) leader in third baseman Joe Torre.

The Pirates had Dock Ellis (19–9) and Steve Blass (15–8) as their top winners, with fireman Dave Giusti saving 30 games. Pittsburgh's prime ingredient was muscle, with heavy stickers in first baseman Bob Robertson (26) homers, Roberto Clemente (.341), catcher Manny Sanguillen (.319), and Willie Stargell, who led the league with 48 home runs, one more than Atlanta's Henry Aaron, who on April 27 had his 600th career blast. By season's end Aaron had 639 homers, bringing to reality the threat to Babe Ruth's all-time record of 714.

Ferguson Jenkins' 24–13 made him a 20-game winner for the fifth year in a row and earned him the Cy Young Award. The Cardinals' Steve Carlton (20–9), the Mets' Tom Seaver (20–10, with league-leading numbers in strikeouts, 289, and ERA, 1.76), and the Dodgers' Al Downing (20–9), also broke into the pitchers' "magic circle."

Atlanta's Ralph Garr supplemented Aaron's long-ball blasting with a .343 average, and Atlanta catcher Earl Williams, who hit 33 home runs, was Rookie of the Year.

On June 3, the Cubs' Ken Holtzman pitched his second career no-hitter, downing Cincinnati, 1–0. Other no-hitters were delivered by the Phillies' Rick Wise on June 23, Wise hitting two home runs and driving in three runs in the 4–0 victory; and by the Cardinals' Bob Gibson, who no-hit the Pirates on August 14, 11–0.

On September 5, Charlie Fox's Giants held an 8½-game lead over the Dodgers, but then began tumbling, losing 16 of their last 24, barely hanging on and winning the division by one game over the Dodgers. With age slowing Mays and injuries hobbling McCovey, Bobby Bonds picked up the slack with 33 home runs and 102 RBIs. Juan Marichal (18–11) was the club's top winner.

Pat Dobson

Ralph Garr

Houston introduced tall young right-hander J. R. Richard to the league in September, and in his major league debut on the fifth of the month Richard equaled Karl Spooner's debut record by fanning 15 Giants.

Beginning to set league records with regularity, Aaron put a notable one in the books this year by driving in 100 runs for the 11th time, breaking the record he had coheld with Mays and Musial.

The Giants won the opening game of the pennant playoffs against the Pirates, but Murtaugh's team came back to take the next three, riding the crest of four home runs by Robertson.

The Pirates won the World Series, defeating the Orioles in seven games. Pittsburgh, losers of the first two games, had several heroes, including Nelson Briles, who pitched a two-hit shutout in game 5; Roberto Clemente, who batted .414; and Steve Blass, who won two games, including a four-hitter in the finale. In his two wins, Blass allowed just seven hits and two earned runs in 18 innings.

Nelson Briles

1972

Shut down by a players strike that began in spring training, the major league season opened 13 days late, with 86 games scratched from the schedule and never made up. The primary area of contention was the players' pension plan. After some hard bargaining between Marvin Miller and John Gaherin, representing the players and the owners, respectively, the athletes won most of their points.

Billy Martin's Tigers won the American League East, outlasting the Red Sox and winning by just a half game. Mickey Lolich strong-armed another big season (22–14); he and Joe Coleman (19–14) accounted for nearly half of the club's 86 victories. The Tigers won despite a feeble batting attack that saw them outhit by seven other teams and have no regular bat over .262 nor drive in over 61 runs.

The Red Sox were buoyed by the 15–6 record of Luis Tiant, whom they had signed the previous year after most people thought the colorful right-hander was washed up. Tiant was the ERA leader with a 1.91 mark. Another new face in Boston belonged to catcher Carlton Fisk, a .293 hitter who was voted Rookie of the Year.

In the West, it was Oakland again, Dick Williams's club finishing 5½ ahead of the White Sox. The A's did it despite Vida Blue's long holdout, which extended well into the season; the 1971 Cy Young Award winner was just 6–10 for the year. The A's, however, had acquired Ken Holtzman from the Cubs and the left-hander was 19–11, teaming with Catfish Hunter (21–7), Blue Moon Odom (15–6), and reliever Rollie Fingers (11 wins, 21 saves) to give the club the league's best pitching. Outfielder Joe Rudi led the A's with a .305 batting average (the only .300 average the A's had in their three successive world championship seasons) and Bert Campaneris led in stolen bases for the sixth time with 52.

Nolan Ryan, obtained from the Mets for infielder Jim Fregosi in one of baseball's all-time trading blunders, fanned a league-high 329 batters in 284 innings. The twenty-five-year-old Ryan was 19–16, with nine shutouts.

The White Sox had the MVP in ex–National Leaguer Dick Allen, who led in home runs (37) and RBIs (113). They also had a pair of 20-game winners in Wilbur Wood, the left-handed knuckleballer, who was 24–17 and pitched 377 innings, most of any pitcher in the lively ball era, and Stan Bahnsen, the former Yankee, who was 21–16.

Minnesota had the league's leading batter in Rod Carew at .318, who added a footnote to his achievement by being the first American League batting champion not to hit a home run during the season.

Other 20-game winners this year were Baltimore's Jim Palmer (21–10) and Cleveland's Cy Young Award winner Gaylord Perry (24–16). The Indians had acquired

Dick Allen

Perry in a trade with the Giants, giving up Sam McDowell. The deal was a major coup for the Indians.

The National League won the All-Star Game, played at Atlanta Stadium on July 25, by a score of 4–3 in ten innings.

In an exciting five-game series, the A's beat the Tigers in the pennant playoffs.

Disgruntled by Steve Carlton's salary demands, the Cardinals impulsively swapped their big left-hander to the Phillies for pitcher Rick Wise. The trade proved to be exceedingly one-sided. While Wise pitched acceptably for the Cardinals, Carlton went to Philadelphia and had a truly spectacular season. Despite pitching for a sixth-place team that lost 97 games, Carlton was 27–10, winning 46 percent of his team's victories. The Cy Young Award winner led in strikeouts with 310 and ERA with 1.98, in addition to putting together a 15-game winning streak. His 27 wins matched Sandy Koufax's record for a National League left-hander.

For the third straight year the Pirates, managed now by Bill Virdon, won the National League East. World Series hero Steve Blass was the ace with a 19–8 record, helping the Pirates to a breezy 11–game advantage over the second-place Cubs. Willie Stargell was Pittsburgh's main explosive force, hitting 33 home runs and driving in 112 runs. Willie was supported by the .300 bats of Richie Hebner, Roberto Clemente, Al Oliver, and Vic Davalillo. Clemente's final hit of the season was his 3,000th, and the last of his career. On December 31, the Pirates superstar

was on a mercy mission to bring supplies to earthquake-ravaged Managua, Nicaragua, when his plane plunged into the sea off San Juan, Puerto Rico.

Second-place Chicago had the batting champion for only the third time since 1901 when Billy Williams led with .333. Williams also hit 37 home runs and drove in 122 runs. Teammate Ferguson Jenkins was 20–12, a 20-game winner for the sixth straight time. Other elite winners this year were the Mets' Tom Seaver (21–12) and the Dodgers' Claude Osteen (20–11).

Cincinnati won easily in the West, by 10½ games over Houston. Sparky Anderson's club, bolstered by the off-season acquisition of second baseman Joe Morgan from Houston, was beginning to put in place the fear-inspiring team that would soon be known as "The Big Red Machine." Pete Rose, the dynamo's most vivid generator, batted .307, while Johnny Bench, taking his second MVP award, led with 40 home runs and 125 runs batted in. Anderson's sparse band of quality starters had only one with as many as 15 wins, Gary Nolan; however, a solid bullpen that included Clay Carroll, Pedro Borbon, and left-hander Tom Hall shored up the starters.

A transaction drenched with sentimentality occurred early in the season when the fading forty-one-year-old one-time superstar Willie Mays returned to New York, traded by the Giants to the Mets.

On August 1, San Diego's Nate Colbert made the record books shudder as he fired one shell after another in a doubleheader against the Braves. When it was over,

Nate Colbert

Colbert had set a record with 13 RBIs and tied Musial's mark with five home runs. For the year, the San Diego first baseman had 38 homers and 111 RBIs.

The Mets became the first major league team to go through an entire season without a hitter accumulating at least 100 hits. Tommie Agee's 96 hits were high on the team, which batted a feeble .225. The Mets did have the Rookie of the Year in left-hander Jon Matlack, who survived his team's inoffensive offense to post a 15–10 record.

There were three no-hitters in the league this year, two by Cubs pitchers. On April 16 right-hander Burt Hooton stopped the Phillies, 4–0, and on September 2 Milt Pappas pitched a no-hit, near-perfect game against San Diego, 8–0. Pappas had retired the first 26 batters to face him and was one-and-two on pinch-hitter Larry Stahl. The next three pitches missed the strike zone, however, and Stahl walked. Pappas retired the next batter to complete his no-hitter. The other no-hitter was the second of Montreal right-hander Bill Stoneman's career, as he stifled the Mets on October 2, 7–0.

The Pirates were heading for their second straight pennant when they got tripped up by the Reds in the fifth and deciding game of the playoffs. Leading 3–2 in the last of the ninth, the Pirates saw a Johnny Bench home run tie the score, and then a few batters later a Bob Moose wild pitch send home the winning run.

The World Series between Oakland and Cincinnati went the full seven, with six of the games being decided by one run, including the finale, which Oakland won, 3–2. The hitting star was Oakland's Gene Tenace (who was 1-for-17 in the playoffs against Detroit), who hit four home runs (tying a Series record) and drove in 9 of his club's 16 runs. During the season Tenace hit five home runs in 82 games.

1973

Traditionalists winced and sighed as the American League introduced the designated hitter, which took the bat away from the pitchers and put a ninth, nonfielding batter into the lineup. The anomaly had immediate effect —the league batting average jumped 20 points to .259. The National League disdained the innovation, saying it preferred to play "real baseball."

Baltimore was back on top in the American League East, winning its fourth division title in five years, by eight games over the Red Sox. Earl Weaver's ace was Jim Palmer (22–9), a 20-game winner for the fourth straight year. The O's brought up a couple of sharp-hitting young outfielders in Rookie of the Year Al Bumbry (.337) and Rich Coggins (.319) and employed the line-drive bat of Tommy Davis (.306) in the newly established DH role.

Minnesota's Rod Carew won his third batting title and second in a row with a .350 average. Oakland's MVP Award winner Reggie Jackson led with 32 home runs and 117 runs batted in.

With the designated hitter allowing pitchers to stay in longer (complete games jumped from 502 to 614), the American League had a record twelve 20-game winners: in addition to Palmer, there were Boston's Luis Tiant (20–13), Detroit's Joe Coleman (23–15), Milwaukee's Jim Colborn (20–12), Oakland's Catfish Hunter (21–5), Ken Holtzman (21–13), and Vida Blue (20–9), Kansas City's Paul Splittorff (20–11), Minnesota's Bert Blyleven (20–17), California's Nolan Ryan (21–16) and Bill Singer (20–14), and Chicago's Wilbur Wood (24–20). Ryan set a new major league record by striking out 383 (in 326 innings), topping Sandy Koufax's record by one. Wood's rather hefty number of decisions was due to a remarkable 48 starts. Pitching coach Johnny Sain theorized that the ease

Johnny Bench

Rod Carew

with which Wood delivered his knuckler put so little strain on his arm that the heavy workload could be handled. Wood even lifted a page from the old days by starting both ends of a doubleheader against the Yankees on July 20, only to be kayoed twice and lose twice. The Cy Young Award winner was Jim Palmer.

Oakland won its third division title in a row, beating Kansas City by six games. Along with the 20-game arms of Hunter, Holtzman, and Blue, skipper Dick Williams had the relief pitching of Rollie Fingers, perhaps the greatest of all relievers, who this year won 7 and saved 22.

Four no-hitters were tossed in the American League this year: Kansas City's Steve Busby stopped Detroit on April 27, 3-0; on May 15 Ryan no-hit Kansas City, 3-0, and on July 15 did the same to Detroit, 6-0, fanning 17; and on July 30, Texas' Jim Bibby embarrassed Oakland, 6-0.

The National League continued winning the All-Star Game, making it 10 of 11 in beating the American League, 7-1, in the game played on July 24 at Royals Stadium in Kansas City.

The pennant playoff between Oakland and Baltimore went the full five, with the A's winning it for their second straight pennant. Catfish Hunter brought it home for Oakland with a 3-0 shutout in the finale.

The caprices of divisional play were never more evident than in the National League in 1973, when the New York Mets with a season's record of 82-79 ended up as the pennant winner (it was the fourth-best winning percentage in the league, but the best in the East).

Propped up by the strong starting pitching of Tom Seaver, Jerry Koosman, and Jon Matlack, and the spirited relief work of Tug McGraw (who popularized the club's "You gotta believe!" rallying call), Yogi Berra's club won an exceedingly tight eastern division race. When it was over, St. Louis was 1½ games behind, Pittsburgh 2½, and Montreal 3½. Their pursuers each outhit and outscored the Mets (in fact, every team in the league except San Diego outhit and outscored them), but none could match New York's three fine starters.

As late as August 17 the Mets were in last place in the division, but only 7½ games behind. The 1973 "miracle" did not have the proportions of the 1969 working, but it surely was redolent of the improbable and unexpected. Seaver, at 19-10 with league-leading figures in strikeouts (251) and ERA (2.08), won his second Cy Young Award.

Pete Rose's .338 average brought him his third batting title, and his 230 hits also led the league, as did Willie Stargell's 44 home runs and 119 RBIs. Three others attained the 40 mark in home runs and they were all on the same club, the Atlanta Braves, marking the first time one club had three 40-homer men in one season. They were Dave Johnson (43, a new record for second basemen),

Darrell Evans (41), and Henry Aaron (40). Aaron finished the season with 713 lifetime homers, one short of Babe Ruth's career record.

Steve Carlton, still pitching for a last-place Philadelphia club, suffered a stunning reversal of fortunes, going from 27-10 to 13-20. In contrast to the American League's twelve 20-game winners, the National had just one in 1973—San Francisco southpaw Ron Bryant, who was 24-12.

Sparky Anderson's Cincinnati Reds won in the West, outracing the Dodgers by 3½ games. Sparky's best pitching came from Jack Billingham (19-10) and lefty Don Gullett (18-8) and a strong bullpen headed by Pedro Borbon, Clay Carroll, and Tom Hall. The league's most impressive relief work was turned in by Montreal's Mike Marshall, who got into a record 92 games, winning 14 and saving 31.

The year saw the formation of what was to become the most enduring infield in baseball history. Coming together all at once for the first time on June 13 were the Dodgers' Steve Garvey at first base, Davey Lopes at second, Bill Russell at short, and Ron Cey at third. They would not be broken up until 1982.

On August 5, Atlanta's Phil Niekro no-hit San Diego, dancing his knucklers to the tune of a 9-0 victory.

Pete Rose was the MVP, the third Cincinnati player in four years to win the award, and Giants outfielder Gary Matthews, batting .300 on the nose, was Rookie of the Year.

The Mets' strong pitching stopped Cincinnati's good hitting in the playoffs, the Mets winning in five.

In a seven-game World Series, Oakland came from a three-games-to-two deficit to win it, with left-handed reliever Darold Knowles getting into all seven games for the A's and Fingers in six. The Mets' losing effort also marked the final playing appearance of Willie Mays, who had announced his impending retirement earlier in the season. Mays closed out his career with 660 home runs, third on the all-time scroll behind Aaron and Ruth.

Steve Carlton

1974

Earl Weaver's Orioles made it five division titles in six years by beating out the Yankees by two games in the American league East. The O's did it on the strength of an inspired stretch drive that saw them win 28 of their last 34. Making Baltimore's success even more impressive was the fact that they were without the effective services of their best pitcher for much of the year—a sore shoulder limited Jim Palmer to a 7–12 record. Weaver's big three this year were Mike Cuellar (22–10), Ross Grimsley (18–13), and Dave McNally (16–10), all left-handers.

In the West, Oakland (under new manager Alvin Dark) won their fourth straight division title, finishing five games ahead of Billy Martin's Texas Rangers. Oakland's strength was again its power pitching. Catfish Hunter was 25–12, Ken Holtzman 19–17, and Vida Blue 17–15, backed up once more by the classy relief pitching of Rollie Fingers. Neither division winner had a .300 hitter in their lineup.

The bestowing of the American League batting title was becoming more and more like a coronation, Rod Carew's .364 winning it for him for the third straight year and fourth time overall. Carew's average was the best in the league since Ted Williams' .388 in 1957. Chicago's Dick Allen (reportedly baseball's highest-paid player at $250,000 a year) led in home runs with 32, while Texas' Jeff Burroughs carried off the MVP Award on the strength of his league-leading 118 RBIs. Former Cubs ace Ferguson Jenkins was 25–12 for Texas.

Other 20-game winners in the league were Boston's Luis Tiant (22–13), Cleveland's Gaylord Perry (21–13, including 15 in a row), Chicago's Jim Kaat (21–13) and Wilbur Wood (20–19), Kansas City's Steve Busby (22–14), and California's Nolan Ryan (22–16). Ryan was again the strikeout leader with 367 (in 333 innings), third-high-est total in baseball history. On August 12, Ryan tied the major league record by fanning 19 Red Sox batters in one game. The California fireballer, who kept the opposition loose by walking 202 batters, also pitched his third career no-hitter on September 28, stopping the Twins, 4–0, fanning 15. Other no-hitters were pitched by Busby (his second) on June 19 against Milwaukee, the 2–0 masterpiece marred only by a second-inning walk, and by Cleveland's Dick Bosman, 4–0, over Oakland on July 19. Bosman's own throwing error in the fourth inning cost him a perfect game.

On September 24, Detroit's Al Kaline entered an elite inner sanctum when he became the 11th player in modern history to collect 3,000 hits.

Catfish Hunter was the Cy Young Award winner, while Rookie of the Year honors went to Texas' Mike Hargrove, who batted .323.

In the pennant playoffs, Oakland won their third straight by beating Baltimore three games to one, with Blue and Holtzman pitching shutouts.

The National League breezed to another All-Star game victory, 7–2.

With Henry Aaron at 713 lifetime home runs, one short of tying Ruth's at one time almost mystically unapproachable record, Atlanta owner Bill Bartholomay, his mind dancing with the prospect of huge attendance figures, suggested Aaron sit out the team's first three games —in Cincinnati—in order for Henry to make his dramatic record-seeking swings at home. But Commissioner Kuhn, correctly, kayoed the idea.

So it was in Cincinnati, in his first at-bat of the season, that Aaron tagged number 714. Four days later, in Atlanta, Aaron set a new record when he hit number 715 off Dodgers left-hander Al Downing. Later in the season Aaron passed Ty Cobb's career records for most games and most at-bats.

Another record disappeared from the books when the Cardinals' Lou Brock stole 118 bases, easily breaking Maury Wills' 1962 mark of 104. For the thirty-five-year-old Brock, it was his eighth base-stealing title in nine years.

Still another impressive record was established, this one by Dodger reliever Mike Marshall, who surpassed his own standard for appearances of 92 by pitching in 106 of his club's 162 games, posting a 15–12 ledger and saving 21, at one point appearing in 13 consecutive games (from June 18 through July 3, working 26⅔ innings). His 208 innings pitched were the most ever by a relief pitcher. Marshall was the first reliever to win the Cy Young Award. Of his tireless relief pitcher, manager Walter Alston said, "He told me he could do it and I let him. He had his own theories of strength and motion and they bore him out. He was one of a kind."

Ken Holtzman

Henry Aaron hitting his 715th home run.

On July 17, Bob Gibson struck out his 3,000th batter, becoming only the second pitcher in history to attain that level (Walter Johnson was the all-time leader with 3,508).

Despite Brock's nonstop running and .300 batting averages by Lou, Rookie of the Year Bake McBride, and Reggie Smith, and 100-RBI seasons by Smith and young catcher Ted Simmons, the Cardinals finished second, 1½ games behind Pittsburgh. The decline of Gibson, now 38 years old, to an 11–13 record, was a prime factor.

Danny Murtaugh's Pirates had left-handers Jerry Reuss (16–11) and Jim Rooker (15–11) as their top winners. Pittsburgh's superior muscle made the difference in the National League East. Willie Stargell, Richie Zisk, and Al Oliver each were over .300, while Rennie Stennett, Richie Hebner, and Manny Sanguillen also hit well, helping the Pirates to their fourth division title in five years.

Philadelphia's young third baseman Mike Schmidt, playing his second full year, was the home run leader with 36, driving in 116 runs, second to Johnny Bench's league-best 129. Atlanta's Ralph Garr was the batting champion with a .353 average.

Alston's Dodgers won in the West, four games ahead of Cincinnati. The Dodgers had the MVP in first baseman Steve Garvey, who hit 21 homers, drove in 111 runs, and batted .312, while Jim Wynn blasted 32 homers and drove in 108 runs, and Bill Buckner batted .314. Alston's top pitchers were Andy Messersmith (20–6) and Don Sutton (19–9), along with the ever-present Marshall.

Atlanta's Phil Niekro (20–13) was the league's only other 20-game winner.

The Dodgers beat the Pirates in the playoffs, three games to one, thanks to some powerful pitching by Sutton, who won twice, allowing just one run in 17 innings.

In the World Series, Oakland beat Los Angeles in five games, thus becoming the only team other than the New York Yankees to win three world championships in a row. Rollie Fingers, Oakland's answer to Mike Marshall, appeared in four games, winning one and saving two. Marshall was in every game, with a loss and a save. Four of the five games were resolved by scores of 3–2.

After the season, Catfish Hunter and Oakland owner Charles Finley got into a squabble over certain payments stipulated in the pitcher's contract. An arbiter ruled in favor of Hunter, declaring that the contract had been breached and that Hunter was now a free agent. With every big-league club in the bidding for the services of the 25-game winner, the Yankees' George Steinbrenner won out with a five-year contract estimated at around $3 million. It was the first indication the players had as to just how much money the owners were willing to spend for needed talent.

Lou Brock

1975

Every team dreams of finding that rookie player who will bring the dash and strength of youth to the club. In 1975, the dreams of the Boston Red Sox were twice fulfilled, in the form of "The Gold Dust Twins," a pair of young outfielders named Fred Lynn and Jim Rice. Mating these two hard hitters to the already established Dwight Evans, Carl Yastrzemski, Carlton Fisk, and Cecil Cooper, the Bosox slugged their way to the eastern division title.

Lynn, who set a precedent by being named both Most Valuable Player and Rookie of the Year, hit 21 home runs, drove in 105 runs, and batted .331, as well as playing a superlative center field. Rice hit 22 homers, drove in 102 runs, and batted .309. Fisk (hurt part of the year) at .331, Cooper at .311, and second baseman Denny Doyle at .310 gave the club five .300 stickers.

Chronically pitching-poor, the Red Sox had enough this time to give them a 4½-game margin over Baltimore at the end. On his staff, manager Darrell Johnson had Rick Wise (19–12), Luis Tiant (18–14), and left-handers Bill Lee (17–9) and Roger Moret (14–3).

Earl Weaver had a pair of 20-game winners at Baltimore in Cy Young Award winner Jim Palmer (23–11 with ten shutouts) and Mike Torrez (20–9), but the Orioles' hitting couldn't match Boston's.

Other 20-game winners in the league were the Yankees' big acquisition Catfish Hunter (23–14), Oakland's Vida Blue (22–11), and Chicago's Jim Kaat (20–14).

The batting champion, for the fifth time and fourth in a row, was Minnesota's Rod Carew with a .359 average. Oakland's Reggie Jackson and Milwaukee's George Scott tied for the home run lead with 36 apiece.

The Cleveland Indians, seldom in the news in recent years, made a historic move when they hired baseball's first black manager, Frank Robinson. At the age of thirty-nine, Robinson's illustrious playing career was coming to a close; as playing manager (a once common but now all but vanished breed) he got into just 49 games and batted .237. Under Robinson's leadership, the Indians finished fourth.

There was one no-hitter in the league this year, and it was of special significance. On June 1, California's Nolan Ryan tied Sandy Koufax by pitching his fourth no-hitter, stopping Baltimore, 1–0.

Detroit, last in the East, suffered the ignominy of a 19-game losing streak, one under the league record.

Despite the loss of Hunter, Oakland won its fifth straight western division title, buoyed by Blue's fine year and the 18–14 record registered by Holtzman, along with the strong relief work of Rollie Fingers, Jim Todd, and Paul Lindblad.

Second in the West by seven games, Kansas City had a sophomore third baseman whose bat was beginning to attract attention. Twenty-two-year-old George Brett batted .308 and led in hits with 195.

Almost routinely now, the National League won the All-Star Game, played at Milwaukee's County Stadium on July 15, 6–3.

In the pennant playoff, an inspired Red Sox team dethroned the three-time pennant-winning A's in three straight games.

In the National League, Danny Murtaugh's Pirates won in the East for the fifth time in six years, again following the lead of their hard hitting. Led by catcher Manny Sanguillen's .328, the Pittsburgh gunners included Willie Stargell, Rennie Stennett, Dave Parker, Al Oliver, and Richie Zisk. Stennett crashed the record books on September 16 with a record seven hits in a nine-inning game (four singles, two doubles, one triple). Stennett's three hits the next day gave him a two-game total of ten, tying Roberto Clemente's record.

The Pirates, who finished 6½ ahead of the Phillies,

Fred Lynn (left) and Jim Rice.

Al Oliver

had but one big-winning starter, lefty Jerry Reuss, who was 18–11.

The Mets' Tom Seaver was the Cy Young Award winner for the third time. By now nicknamed "Tom Terrific" and "The Franchise," Seaver was 22–9, with a league-leading 243 strikeouts, making him the first pitcher to record 200 or more whiffs in eight straight seasons. San Diego's sinkerballing lefty Randy Jones, at 20–12, was the league's only other double-sawbuck winner.

The Mets' freshman outfielder Mike Vail put together a 23-game hitting streak, setting a record for a rookie.

The western division was ground to a pulp by Sparky Anderson's "Big Red Machine," who won by 20 games over the Dodgers, racking up 108 wins. Joe Morgan's .327 average led a powerful club that included Pete Rose, Tony Perez, Dave Concepcion, George Foster, Johnny Bench, and Ken Griffey—one of the greatest in baseball history. Despite winning 108 games, Anderson's top pitcher won only 15 games, though he had three of them—Don Gullett, Gary Nolan, and Jack Billingham. But the bullpen was deep and talented: Pedro Borbon, Clay Carroll, Rawley Eastwick, and left-hander Will McEnaney.

Morgan was the MVP, giving the Reds four of the last six awards, with more to come. Giants right-hander John Montefusco (15–9) was Rookie of the Year. The batting title went to the Cubs' Bill Madlock. Madlock, who had been acquired from the Texas Rangers for Ferguson Jenkins a few years before, batted .354. The Phillies' Mike Schmidt was again the home run leader with 38.

San Francisco right-hander Ed Halicki pitched the league's only no-hitter, smothering the Mets on August 24, 6–0. It was the fifth time in their 14-year history the Mets had been no-hit.

Cincinnati ran through Pittsburgh in three games to win the pennant, the third time in three meetings they had upended the Pirates in the playoffs.

The Reds also won the World Series, but not before an epic seven-game struggle with the Red Sox. It has been described as the greatest of modern World Series, with the focus on game 6. Down three games to two, and losing, 6–3, in the bottom of the eighth, the Sox tied it on an electrifying three-run homer by pinch-hitter Bernie Carbo (a former Red). After a game-saving catch by Dwight Evans in the 11th inning, Boston won it on Carlton Fisk's just-fair home run in the bottom of the 12th. Cincinnati, however, won the finale the next day, 4–3, on Joe Morgan's bloop single in the top of the ninth.

The months after the 1975 season proved momentous for baseball. It began with a unique challenge to the game's reserve clause, the ball-and-chain clause in every contract that bound a player forever to the club's whims. This clause had been upheld by the courts, so two players, Dodger pitcher Andy Messersmith and Montreal pitcher Dave McNally, took a different approach. (McNally, about

Andy Messersmith

to retire, was lending his name to the suit.) The players agreed that the club could renew a contract for one year after it expired, but that after playing that year without having signed, a player could declare himself a free agent. The contract language did not go beyond that one year, and thus the challenge was made, with both Messersmith and McNally playing the 1975 season under unilaterally renewed contracts.

In December, arbiter Peter Seitz ruled that one year meant one year, and that Messersmith and McNally were free agents, entitled to sign with whomever they wished. (Messersmith soon signed a three-year, million-dollar pact with the Braves.) The owners fired Seitz and appealed his decision in the courts, but Seitz was upheld. The reserve clause was now as good as dead.

In the spring of 1976 the Players Association and the owners began debating a new agreement. The crucial point of what was finally settled was: any player who wished could become a free agent after six years of major league service. Players were also accorded the right to demand to be traded after five years of service with the same team. As a transition measure, anyone playing without a signed contract through the 1976 and 1977 seasons could become a free agent after those seasons. Thus began the era of multimillion-dollar contracts, lawyers, agents, renewal options—and a healthier, more competitively balanced brand of major league baseball.

1976

The rumbling from the new agreement between players and owners began to be felt midway through the 1976 season. Fearing uncompensated loss of his star players to free agency at the end of the season, Oakland owner Charles Finley in June attempted some fancy dealing. For a total of $3.5 million, Finley sold Vida Blue to the Yankees and Joe Rudi and Rollie Fingers to the Red Sox. Commissioner Kuhn, however, stepped in and stopped the deals, calling them "detrimental" to baseball's best interests. The three players remained with the Athletics while Finley challenged Kuhn in the courts (which a year later ruled in favor of the commissioner). Finley did trade Reggie Jackson and Ken Holtzman to Baltimore for Don Baylor and Mike Torrez. (Baltimore was just a pit stop for Reggie; he had his eye on the Big Apple.)

Diverting the fans from court battles and contracts decorated with zeroes was a young Detroit right-hander named Mark Fidrych. Refreshing, uninhibited, and immensely talented, the twenty-one-year-old Fidrych talked to the baseball, waved his arms, joked, laughed—and won 19 games after being called up in May. He was the ERA leader with a 2.34 mark and the league's Rookie of the Year. (Sadly, injuries, for all intents and purposes, aborted Fidrych's career in 1977.)

For the first time in 11 years the Yankees were back on top, winning the eastern division by 10½ games over Baltimore. Manager Billy Martin's pitching staff was topped by right-hander Ed Figueroa (19–10), Catfish Hunter (17–15), and Dock Ellis (17–8), backed up by reliever Sparky Lyle, who saved 23 games. With rookie Willie Randolph at second, MVP Thurman Munson behind the plate, Graig Nettles at third, Chris Chambliss at first, and Mickey Rivers, Roy White, and Lou Piniella in the outfield, the Yankees had a strong, well-balanced attack. Nettles was the league leader in home runs with 32.

Second-place Baltimore had its usual 20-game winners, Jim Palmer gaining his third Cy Young Award with a 22–13 record, and Wayne Garland a surprise 20–7. Baltimore hitting, however, was the division's weakest—.243 —despite Lee May's league-leading 109 RBIs and 27 homers from Jackson.

Despite the turmoil surrounding them, the A's put on a strong show in the West but finished 2½ behind Kansas City. New manager Chuck Tanner had the A's running all year, stealing an American League record 341 bases, topped by Billy North's 75. Whitey Herzog's Kansas City Royals, however, had a lethal weapon in George Brett, who had 215 hits and a league-leading .333 average, edging out teammate Hal McRae by a point and five-time winner Rod Carew by two. Brett went on a tear from May 8–13, collecting three or more hits in six straight games. Dennis Leonard (17–10) was Herzog's ace.

Sparky Lyle

A rare two-man no-hitter was pitched in the league this year. On July 28, the White Sox' Blue Moon Odom and Francisco Barrios combined to no-hit the A's, 2–1. Odom was pulled in the sixth after allowing no hits but walking nine. Barrios came in to complete the no-hitter.

Luis Tiant, with a 21–12 record for the Red Sox, was the league's other 20-game winner. California's Nolan Ryan struck out 327 (in 284 innings) to lead the league, though 183 walks helped saddle him with a 17–18 record.

The All-Star Game ended with the National League's 13th win in 14 games, 7–1. It was played at Philadelphia's Veteran's Stadium on July 13.

The American League pennant playoffs went the full five and ended suddenly and dramatically with Chris Chambliss's home run in the bottom of the ninth of the fifth game, breaking a 6–6 tie and giving the Yankees a 7–6 pennant-winning victory. The blow was followed by the mindless vandalizing of the field by exuberant fans which cost a reported $100,000 to repair.

The Philadelphia Phillies, managed by Danny Ozark, moved their Pennsylvania cousins aside at the top of the National League East, winning by nine games over the Pirates. Ozark got a 20–7 season from Steve Carlton and an 18–10 showing from ex–Red Sox ace Jim Lonborg. The Phillies also had a couple of bruisers in the lineup in Mike

Randy Jones

Schmidt, the home run champ for the third straight time (38) and Greg Luzinski, who hit 21 homers and batted .304. Center fielder Garry Maddox led the team with a .330 average. Schmidt accounted for the year's most eye-catching outburst when he hit four home runs in a noisy ten-inning 18–16 slugfest with the Cubs on April 17.

The Cubs' Bill Madlock won his second straight batting title with a .339 average, edging out the Reds' Ken Griffey (.336) on the last day. Cincinnati's George Foster was the RBI leader with 121. In addition to Carlton, there were four other 20-game winners in the league: San Diego's Cy Young Award–winning Randy Jones (22–14), Los Angeles's Don Sutton (21–10), New York's Jerry Koosman (21–10), and Houston's J. R. Richard (20–15). New York's Tom Seaver extended his own record to nine straight seasons of 200 or more strikeouts, winning his fifth strikeout title with 235.

In the West, Sparky Anderson's Big Red Machine continued to eat up the league, winning 102 games and finishing ten ahead of the Dodgers. Once again the Reds had only a 15-game winner on their staff—Gary Nolan—but had seven pitchers winning in double figures, including ace reliever Rawley Eastwick, who won 11 and saved 26.

Joe Morgan won his second MVP Award in a row, putting together a sensational season. The Reds second baseman batted .320, hit 27 home runs, drove in 111 runs, stole 60 bases, and had the highest slugging average, .576, the first National League second baseman to lead in slugging since Hornsby in 1929. Pete Rose, Ken Griffey, Cesar Geronimo, and George Foster joined Morgan as .300 hitters. Sparky's boys, who led the league in every offensive category, were also blessed with good health all summer—every regular played in at least 135 games. The Reds also had in right-hander Pat Zachry (14–7) a cowinner of the Rookie of the Year Award (with San Diego reliever Butch Metzger, 11–4).

The league saw three no-hitters this year: on July 9 Houston's Larry Dierker no-hit the Expos, 6–0; on August 9 John Candelaria became the first Pirate in 69 years to deliver a no-hitter in Pittsburgh when he stopped the Dodgers, 2–0; and on September 29 the Giants' John Montefusco left the Braves hitless in a 9–0 victory.

The Reds were simply unstoppable this year: in postseason play they stormed past the Phillies in three straight to wrap up their second successive pennant and then took the Yankees in four to make it two world championships in two years. The Series featured a slugging exchange between the catchers—Bench batted .533 for the Reds and Munson .529 for the Yankees. Cincinnati was the first National League team since the 1921–22 New York Giants to win back-to-back World Series.

This was the retirement year for Henry Aaron, who concluded his 23-year career playing for the Milwaukee Brewers. Aaron left as baseball's all-time home run hitter, with 755.

After the season, the American League announced it was expanding to 14 clubs. The additions were Toronto in the East and Seattle in the West. The National League remained at 12 teams.

Butch Metzger

1977

No one plunged into the free-agent market more lavishly or more astutely—in the beginning, anyway—than Yankees owner George Steinbrenner. From the first pool of available talent, the Yankees signed Reggie Jackson and left-hander Don Gullett.

Despite injuries that impaired his season (and soon ended his career), Gullett was 14–4 for Billy Martin's team. Along with Ron Guidry, Ed Figueroa, Mike Torrez, and relievers Sparky Lyle (the Cy Young Award winner) and Dick Tidrow, the Yankees presented a most formidable staff, one that enabled them to repeat as eastern division winners, 2½ games over Boston and Baltimore, who tied for second.

It was a turmoil-filled season for the Yankees. Jackson's amplified self-image clashed with Martin's edgy temperament, to the extent that the two almost came to blows in the dugout one Saturday afternoon in full view of a national television audience.

But Reggie swung a heavy bat, hitting 32 home runs and driving in 110 runs, complementing Graig Nettles' 37 homers and 107 RBIs, and Thurman Munson's 100 RBIs.

Baltimore got some good hitting from Lee May (27 homers), Ken Singleton (.328), and Rookie of the Year Eddie Murray (27 homers), and a 20–11 season from Jim Palmer. The Red Sox were the league's most prolific home run hitters—213. Jim Rice with 39 led the league, followed by the slugging bats of George Scott (33), Butch Hobson (30), Carl Yastrzemski (28), and Carlton Fisk (26). Rice, Hobson, Yastrzemski, and Fisk each drove in over 100 runs. On June 17, 18, and 19 the Sox exploded against the Yankees with a record barrage of 16 home runs in three games. Ragged pitching, however, torpedoed Boston—reliever Bill Campbell's 13 wins were the most on the staff.

The most impressive hitting seen in decades came from the high-caliber bat of Minnesota's Rod Carew, who won his sixth batting title with a lofty .388 average, baseball's best since Ted Williams raised the same average in 1957. Carew had 239 hits, most in the league since 1928.

Repeating in the West were Whitey Herzog's Kansas City Royals, led by the hitting of George Brett, Al Cowens, and Hal McRae, who had 54 doubles. Herzog's top winners were Dennis Leonard (20–12), Jim Colborn (18–14) and Paul Splittorff (16–6). Minnesota's Dave Goltz (20–11) was the league's other premier winner.

Second-place Texas (by eight games) made some managerial headlines before and during the season. In spring training, skipper Frank Lucchesi was belted by one of his players, Lenny Randle, then was fired in midseason. His replacement, Eddie Stanky, managed for one game, decided that this wasn't for him, and resigned; he was followed by interim manager Connie Ryan, who held the

Dennis Leonard

fort until permanent replacement Billy Hunter took over.

California's Nolan Ryan was the strikeout leader with 341, the fifth time he had topped the 300 mark in whiffs.

Three no-hitters were pitched in the league this year: on May 14 Kansas City's Colborn no-hit the Rangers, 6–0; on May 30 Cleveland's Dennis Eckersley no-hit the Angels, 1–0; and on September 22 the Angels were embarassed again, this time by Texas's Bert Blyleven, 6–0.

The All-Star Game was played at Yankee Stadium on July 19, with the National League winning again, 7–5.

The New York-Kansas City rematch in the pennant playoff again went five games and for the second year in a row New York won it in the ninth inning of the finale, scoring three runs for a 5–3 win.

In the National League East, the Phillies were repeaters, Danny Ozark's team finishing five games ahead of the Pirates. Steve Carlton won his second Cy Young Award, going 23–10, followed by Larry Christenson's 19–6. Ozark again received explosive years from Mike Schmidt (38 home runs, 101 RBIs) and Greg Luzinski (39 homers, 130 RBIs), but the biggest hitting in the league this year came from Cincinnati's MVP-winning George Foster, who led with 52 homers and 149 RBIs.

Second-place Pittsburgh received stellar years from batting champion Dave Parker (.338), Rennie Stennett (.336), and left-hander John Candelaria, who led in winning percentage with .800, based on his 20–5 record, and also led in ERA with 2.34.

On August 29 the Cardinals' Lou Brock rubbed yet another Ty Cobb record from the books when he stole his 893rd career base. Cobb's record of 892 had stood for nearly 40 years.

Montreal had the Rookie of the Year in young outfielder Andre Dawson, who batted .282.

In the West, the Dodgers and Reds continued to play ping-pong with the title, with the honors going this year to the Dodgers by ten games. It was a satisfying victory for first-year manager Tom Lasorda, who had replaced Walter Alston, who had retired after twenty-three years. (Only Connie Mack and John McGraw had managed one team longer.)

The Dodgers were the first team to have four men with 30 or more home runs in the same season: Steve Garvey (33), Reggie Smith (32), and Dusty Baker and Ron Cey (30 each). Tommy John, two years after having his left elbow reconstructed in surgery, was Lasorda's ace with a 20–7 record.

Cincinnati finished second despite the June 15 acquisition of Tom Seaver from the Mets, where the great pitcher had been sniping at management over contract renegotiations. Seaver was 14–3 with the Reds and had a combined 21–6 season. The Reds' Pete Rose had 204 hits, the ninth season of 200 or more for him, tying another Cobb record.

Other 20-game winners in the league were Chicago's Rick Reuschel (20–10) and St. Louis's Bob Forsch (20–7).

On August 1, the Giants' Willie McCovey hit the 18th (and last) grand slam of his career, the league record for jackpot shots. (Lou Gehrig's 23 remain the major league mark.)

The Phillies won the opener of the playoffs against the Dodgers, but Lasorda's men came back to take the next three, with Don Sutton and Tommy John turning in some impressive pitching.

In the World Series, the Yankees took the Dodgers in six, with Torrez winning twice, including the wrap-up sixth game. The star of this particular October pageant, however, was Reggie Jackson, who capped a spectacular Series by hitting three home runs in the finale, giving him a World Series record total of five. The Dodgers' Reggie Smith hit three home runs, but, as one writer put it, "was out-Reggied."

Jackson's sixth-game detonations were a fitting climax to the entire season, in which a record 3,644 home runs were hit.

Dusty Baker

Tom Lasorda

BASEBALL

1978

Unlike the 1980s, when no division winner seemed able to repeat, the 1978 season saw the four 1977 winners back in the playoffs, although it took a herculean Yankees stretch drive to complete the quartet. Trailing Boston by 14 games on July 17, the Yankees followed the breathtaking pitching of Ron Guidry (25–3), survived what was becoming their annual currents of turmoil, and caught the stumbling Red Sox. Along the way they lost their tempestuous skipper Billy Martin, replaced on July 24 with the more placid Bob Lemon, and kept winning.

The key series of the season was played at Fenway Park on September 7–10. Trailing by four, the New Yorkers swept the Sox to tie for first place, which was where both clubs were when the regular season ended, locked together with 99–63 records. In a one-game tie-breaker played at Fenway, the Yankees won, 5–4, on the strength of a three-run homer by Bucky Dent (just his fifth of the year) and a solo shot by Reggie Jackson, beating Mike Torrez, who had free-agented himself to Boston.

Guidry's 25–3 record gave him the highest winning percentage ever for a 20-game winner, .893, making him an easy Cy Young Award winner. The slim, hard-throwing lefty also led with a 1.74 ERA and nine shutouts. The Yankees also had a 20–9 season from Ed Figueroa, 12–6 from Catfish Hunter (most of those wins coming in the second half), and superb relief work from Sparky Lyle and free-agent signee Goose Gossage. Lou Piniella's .314 led the team.

Top, left to right: Billy Martin, George Steinbrenner. Bottom, left to right: Thurman Munson, Reggie Jackson.

Don Zimmer's Red Sox had the consolation of having the player of the year in MVP Jim Rice, who tore the league apart with leading totals in home runs (46), triples (15), slugging (.600), hits (213), RBIs (139), and total bases (406, most in the league since Joe DiMaggio's 418 in 1937). Zimmer's ace was Dennis Eckersley (20–8), while reliever Bob Stanley was 15–2.

Minnesota's Rod Carew won his seventh and last batting title with a .333 average, while Detroit had the Rookie of the Year in second baseman Lou Whitaker, who batted .285. It was an all-rookie keystone combo for the Tigers, with shortstop Alan Trammell also breaking in this year. Other 20-game winners included Milwaukee's Mike Caldwell (22–9), Baltimore's Jim Palmer, for the eighth time (21–12), and Kansas City's Dennis Leonard (21–17).

Whitey Herzog's Kansas City Royals made it three straight in the West with a five-game margin over California and Texas. Along with Leonard, the K. C. staff had lefties Paul Splittorff (19–13) and Larry Gura (16–4), and effective relief work from another left-hander, Al Hrabosky.

Second-place California was devastated when on September 23 their good-hitting outfielder Lyman Bostock was shot to death in Gary, Indiana, in a case of mistaken identity. Formerly of the Minnesota Twins, Bostock had been signed that year as a free agent. The twenty-seven-year-old Bostock played four years in the major leagues and had a .311 lifetime batting average.

The National League won its seventh straight All-Star game and 15th of the last 16, defeating the American League, 7–3, in the game played at San Diego Stadium on July 11.

For the third year in a row the Yankees defeated the Royals in the playoffs, three games to one. George Brett hit three home runs for the Royals in a losing cause in game 3.

The Phillies won their third straight National League East title by just 1½ games over Pittsburgh. Danny Ozark's club had its biggest winner in Steve Carlton (16–13). Greg Luzinski had another sizable year for the Phillies, hitting 35 home runs and driving in 101 runs.

Pittsburgh's Dave Parker repeated as batting champion (.334) and was voted MVP. Cincinnati's George Foster was also a repeater—as home run (40) and RBI (120) leader. It was Foster's third straight year as RBI leader, tying a major league record coheld by such elite names as Ruth, Cobb, Wagner, Hornsby, and Medwick.

In the West, the Dodgers made Tom Lasorda two-for-two, winning over Cincinnati by 2½ games. The Dodgers' "happy family" image was marred by an August clubhouse brawl between Steve Garvey and Don Sutton, but the club seemed to cohere after that and played some of its best ball of the year. Burt Hooton (19–10) led a deep

Tommy John

starting rotation that included Tommy John, Doug Rau, Sutton, and Rick Rhoden, with young Bob Welch joining the staff late in the season. Garvey was the team's top hitter with a .316 average and 113 runs batted in. This talented championship club attracted enough fans to make the Dodgers the first team in baseball history to pass the three-million mark in paid attendance.

The pennant may have gone to the Dodgers, but the headlines went to Pete Rose. Cincinnati's thirty-seven-year-old third baseman and hit machine mesmerized the universe of baseball by putting on a 44-game hitting streak, from June 14 to August 1, when he was finally stopped in Atlanta by left-hander Larry McWilliams and Gene Garber. Rose's streak set a new modern National League record, eclipsing by seven Tommy Holmes's 1945 standard. Earlier in the season, on May 5, Rose rapped out his 3,000th career hit.

Another milestone hit came on June 30 when the Giants' Willie McCovey became the 12th player in major league history to connect for 500 home runs. The National League's Rookie of the Year was Atlanta third baseman Bob Horner, who hit 23 home runs in 89 games and batted .266. The Cy Young Award went to San Diego's Gaylord Perry, who was 21–6. Having won the award with Cleveland in 1972, Perry was the first to win it in both leagues. Houston's J. R. Richard, 18–11 on the year, had 303 strikeouts, setting a new record for National League right-handers.

There were two no-hitters in the league this year: the Cardinals' Bob Forsch pitched the first on April 16,

stopping the Phillies, 5–0; and on June 16 the Reds' Tom Seaver pitched the only no-hitter of his glittering career, a 4–0 handcuffing of the Cardinals.

The Dodgers defeated the Phillies (losers for the third straight time) in the pennant playoffs, three games to one, with Steve Garvey hitting four home runs for the Dodgers. The final game was settled in the bottom of the 10th inning on Bill Russell's game-winning single.

The World Series saw the Yankees again beat the Dodgers in six. After losing the first two games, the New Yorkers swept the next four. While Davey Lopes hit three home runs for the Dodgers, the Yankees had heroes aplenty in Bucky Dent (10 hits), Brian Doyle, filling in for the injured Willie Randolph (.438 batting average), and Graig Nettles, whose spectacular play around third base was reminiscent of Brooks Robinson at his best.

Willie McCovey

1979

Four new division champions were crowned this year. In the American League East, Earl Weaver's Orioles were back on top, finishing eight games ahead of Milwaukee. With Jim Palmer sliding to 10–6 after eight 20-win seasons in nine years, the O's found a new ace in Cy Young Award–winning left-hander Mike Flanagan, who was 23–9. Young first baseman Eddie Murray contributed 25 home runs and 99 RBIs, while the club's top slugger was Ken Singleton with 35 homers and 111 RBIs.

Second-place Milwaukee put together one of the league's strongest lineups, with four .300 hitters—Cecil Cooper, Paul Molitor, Sixto Lezcano, and Charlie Moore. The club also hit with power—Gorman Thomas led the league with 45 home runs, while Ben Oglivie hit 29, Lezcano 28, and Cooper 24.

The third-place Red Sox smashed the ball even harder than the Brewers, with Fred Lynn and Jim Rice doing a large share of it. Lynn led the league with a .333 average, hit 39 home runs, and drove in 122 runs, while Rice batted .325, with 39 home runs and 130 RBIs. Three other Red Sox players had over 20 home runs: Butch Hobson (28) and Carl Yastrzemski and Dwight Evans (21 each). Boston had 194 homers to Milwaukee's 185.

Generally, it was a heavy-hitting year in the league (the collective average was .270). California's Don Baylor was the MVP on the strength of a resounding season: 36 home runs, a league-leading 139 RBIs, and a .296 batting average. Boston's Yastrzemski observed a personal milestone by getting his 3,000th career hit on September 12.

The Yankees, who had signed free agent Tommy John, were taken out of the race when teammates Goose Gossage and Cliff Johnson had a swing-out in the clubhouse in April in which the irreplaceable Gossage suffered a thumb injury that sidelined him for nearly half the season. John was 21–9 with his new club, while Guidry followed his super 1978 year with an 18–8 record.

The last-place Toronto Blue Jays continued playing like an expansion club, losing 109 games. After three years their record was 166–318.

In the West, Jim Fregosi's California Angels moved Kansas City out of the top spot after three years. One of the most active signers of free agents, the Angels had added Rod Carew to an already star-filled lineup that included Bobby Grich, Baylor, Carney Lansford, Brian Downing, and Joe Rudi. Dave Frost (16–10) and Nolan Ryan (16–14) were Fregosi's top winners.

While California, finishing three games on top, had six regulars at .290 or better, second-place Kansas City had five, topped by George Brett's .329 and Willie Wilson's .315. Wilson led with 83 stolen bases, most in the league since Ty Cobb's 96 in 1915.

Pitching for Minnesota now, Mike Marshall put his special talents on display for the American League, setting a new league record by appearing in 90 games, winning 10 and saving 32.

Along with Flanagan and John, Minnesota's Jerry Koosman was also a 20-game winner (20–13). Toronto shortstop Alfredo Griffin (.287) and Minnesota third baseman John Castino (.285) shared Rookie of the Year honors.

The National League continued to dominate the All-Star Game, beating the American, 7–6, in the game played at Seattle's Kingdome on July 17. It was now eight in a row and 16 of 17 for the Nationals.

In the pennant playoffs, it was Baltimore over California, three games to one, with Scott McGregor pitching a classy six-hit shutout in the final game.

Pete Rose free-agented himself out of Cincinnati after 16 years and signed a lucrative five-year contract with the Phillies. A first baseman now, Pete batted .331 and, by collecting 208 hits, broke the record he coheld with Cobb for 200 hits in a season—Pete had now done it ten times. Nevertheless, the Phillies finished fourth, despite the efforts of Rose and of Mike Schmidt, who blasted 45 home runs and drove in 114 runs.

The eastern division winners, for the sixth time since 1970, were Chuck Tanner's Pirates, despite their most successful pitcher (John Candelaria) having just 14 victories. The power hitting of co-MVP Willie Stargell, Dave Parker, and Bill Robinson, combined with Bill Madlock's .328 average (after his midseason acquisition from the Giants) helped thrust the Pirates to a narrow two-game margin over the second-place Montreal Expos. Another big factor in the Pirates' success was the relief pitching of Kent Tekulve, who appeared in 94 games, winning 10 and saving 31.

Third-place St. Louis had the batting champion in first baseman Keith Hernandez (.344), who shared the MVP award with Stargell, in the first tie vote for the distinction. In addition to Hernandez, the Cards had four other .300 hitters: Ken Oberkfell, Garry Templeton, George Hendrick, and Lou Brock. Playing his final season, Brock had his 3,000th career hit on August 13. He retired as the all-time stolen base leader with 938.

Chicago's Dave Kingman led in home runs with 48 and San Diego's Dave Winfield had the most RBIs, 118. A pair of brothers were the league's only 20-game winners: Atlanta's Phil Niekro (21–20) and Houston's Joe Niekro (21–11). Houston's J. R. Richard broke his own National League strikeout record for right-handers by fanning 313, exactly 100 more than runner-up Steve Carlton. The Cy Young Award went to Cubs relief pitcher Bruce Sutter, who appeared in 62 games, winning 6 and saving 37. In 101 innings, Sutter fanned 110 and allowed just 67 hits.

The Rookie of the Year was Dodgers right-hander

Rick Sutcliffe, who broke in with a 17–10 record.

The only no-hitter of the major league season was pitched by Houston's Ken Forsch (joining his brother Bob as the only no-hit brother act), who stopped Atlanta on April 7, 6–0, in what was the second game of the year for both clubs.

In the West, Cincinnati (managed now by John Mc-Namara) was back on top, by a scant 1½ games over Houston. Surviving the loss of Rose, the Reds got .300 seasons from Pete's third-base successor Ray Knight, Ken Griffey, and George Foster. Tom Seaver at 16–6 led a rather shaky pitching staff.

Houston had strong pitching from Joe Niekro, Richard, and bullpen ace Joe Sambito, but handicapped by its spacious Astrodome hit just 49 home runs all season (as opposed to Cincinnati's 132); it was the lowest total for a National League team since the Boston Braves hit 44 in 1946.

In the playoffs, the Pirates charged through the Reds in three straight.

The World Series saw the Pirates make another charge. Down three games to one to Baltimore, they stunned the Orioles by winning the next three, led by the lusty hitting of Stargell, Omar Moreno, Tim Foli, Dave Parker, and Phil Garner, each of whom had 10 or more hits. The Pirates averaged 12 hits per game and had a team average of .323 for the Series. Stargell hit all three of his club's home runs.

Don Baylor

J. R. Richard

RIGHT: Mike Cuellar, Baltimore's four-time 20-game winner. He was with five clubs during his 15-year career, winning 185 and losing 130.

BELOW: The multitalented Bobby Bonds. He came up with the Giants in 1968 and subsequently played for seven other clubs. For his 14-year career he batted .268.

The Yankees' Bobby Murcer is clearly in disagreement with umpire Frank Umont's call. Bobby was trying to steal second, but the peg to Orioles second baseman Bobby Grich (left) nipped him. The action occurred at Yankee Stadium on September 1, 1970.

Danny Frisella (left) and Tug McGraw, Mets relievers. Frisella worked for five clubs in a 10-year career, with a 34-40 record. McGraw split his 19-year career between the Mets and Phillies, retiring in 1984 with a 96-92 record.

Dave Giusti. Giusti came to the majors with Houston in 1962 as a starter, but it was as a relief pitcher for the Pirates in the 1970s that he had his greatest success. He was 100–93 for his 15-year career.

Rico Carty, National League batting champion with Atlanta in 1970. Carty played for six clubs in both leagues during his 15-year career, batting .299.

RIGHT: Manny Sanguillen, Pittsburgh's good-hitting catcher. He played for 13 years, compiling a .296 batting average.

Pete Rose (left) is being hugged by the Giants' Dick Dietz after Pete scored the winning run in the bottom of the 12th inning of the 1970 All-Star Game, bowling over Indians catcher Ray Fosse. Coach Leo Durocher is at the right.

The demolition of Pittsburgh's Forbes Field in 1970.

Houston's Don Wilson, who pitched from 1966–74, logging a 104–92 record. He died accidentally in January 1975, from carbon monoxide poisoning, a month before his thirtieth birthday.

Brooks Robinson rapping out an RBI single in the second inning of the second game of the 1971 World Series. The on-deck batter is Dave Johnson.

The pitching star of the 1971 World Series, Steve Blass spent his entire ten-year career with the Pirates, winning 103 and losing 76.

Larry Dierker, who pitched for Houston from 1964–76, finishing up with the Cardinals a year later. Lifetime record: 139–123.

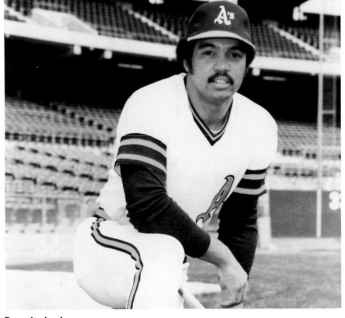

Reggie Jackson

Brooks Robinson knocking down a line drive, recovering, and throwing the runner out during the 1971 World Series.

RIGHT: Joe Rudi, 16-year outfielder with the Athletics and two other clubs. Lifetime average: .264.

LEFT: Shortstop Bert Campaneris, one of the key men on the Oakland championship teams of the early 1970s. Bert played for four clubs during his 19-year career, retiring in 1983 with a lifetime average of .259. He led in stolen bases six times.

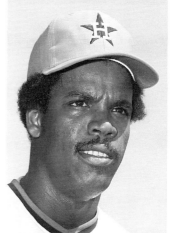

Seventeen-year major league veteran Cesar Cedeno, who had his best years with Houston in the 1970s. Playing for four clubs, he mounted a .284 career average.

Three-time 20-game-winner Vida Blue. He pitched for the A's, Royals, and Giants from 1969–86, winning 209 and losing 161.

BELOW: A couple of aces frolicking on a motorbike before the start of the 1972 American League pennant playoffs between their clubs. Detroit's Mickey Lolich (left) and Oakland's Catfish Hunter.

Rollie Fingers, bullpen ace of the Oakland championship teams and one of the great relievers of all time. Pitching for the A's, Padres, and Brewers from 1968–85, he was 114–118 with a record 341 saves.

Longtime National League outfielder Gary Matthews, who finished up a 16-year career with Seattle in 1987. He also played for the Giants, Braves, Phillies, and Cubs, batting .281.

Wilbur Wood, hardworking knuckleballer of the White Sox in the 1970s. A 17-year major-leaguer, Wood, a four-time 20-game winner, was 164–156 lifetime.

Kansas City Royals southpaw Paul Splittorff. He pitched from 1970–84. Lifetime record: 166–143.

Pete Rose and Pete Jr. Pete Sr.'s pensive mood can be attributed to the 3–2 loss his team just absorbed at the hands of Oakland in the seventh game of the 1972 World Series.

The story is on the scoreboard. Nolan Ryan is facing Amos Otis, the last batter in Ryan's May 13, 1973, no-hitting of the Royals.

Right-hander Steve Busby, whose fine career was cut short by a sore arm. He pitched from 1972–80, winning 70 and losing 54.

Mets catcher Jerry Grote, one of the outstanding defensive catchers of his time. He played in the majors for 16 years, 11 with the Mets. He batted .252 lifetime.

Fred Lynn, the only man to win both Rookie of the Year and MVP honors in the same year.

Phillies third baseman Mike Schmidt in 1973, his first full season in the majors.

Tom Seaver

The Mets' Jon Matlack checking the mail. The left-hander pitched for the Mets and Rangers from 1971–83, winning 125 and losing 126.

BELOW: Shea Stadium, home of the New York Mets.

A little farther and Mets shortstop Bud Harrelson would go right through the wickets. The catcher is the Giants' Dave Rader.

In the big leagues the better part of two decades, Manny Mota's lifetime 150 pinch hits are the major league record. He played for the Pirates, Giants, Expos, and Dodgers, for whom he delivered most of his pinch hits in the 1970s. He retired in 1982 with a .304 batting average.

A 23-year veteran, Rusty Staub played for five clubs in both leagues, batting .279.

Houston's Lee May (left) and the Mets' Cleon Jones. May was a long-ball—hitting first baseman for the Reds and three other clubs from 1965—82, retiring with 354 home runs and a .267 batting average.

Nicknamed "The Mad Hungarian," lefty Al Hrabosky was a top-flight reliever for the Cardinals, Royals, and Braves from 1970—82. Lifetime record: 64—35.

Rod Carew, the most successful hitter of his era. Playing with the Twins and Angels from 1967—85, he won seven batting titles, batted over .300 for 15 consecutive seasons, collected 3,053 career hits, and retired with a .328 batting average.

Ron Cey, third baseman on the Dodgers' durable infield of the 1970s. After a decade with the Dodgers, he played for the Cubs and finished up with Oakland in 1987. He batted .261 for his 17-year career.

Garry Maddox, who played the outfield for the Giants and the Phillies from 1972–86, batting .285.

A 22-year major leaguer, most of it spent with the Giants, Willie McCovey hit 521 home runs and batted .270.

One of the top third baseman of his era, Buddy Bell came to the big leagues with Cleveland, later playing for Texas and Cincinnati. He's the son of former Cincinnati slugger Gus Bell.

One of the great pitchers of all time, Jim Palmer spent his entire 19-year career (1965–84) with Baltimore. Eight times a 20-game winner, his bottom line stands at 268–152.

Don Sutton with the Dodgers in 1970s. His steady efficiency finally carried him into the elite 300-victory class.

Steve Garvey, first baseman with the Dodgers and Padres from 1969–87. He had 200 or more hits in a season six times. Lifetime average: .294.

Shortstop Bill Russell. He spent his entire career (1969–86) with the Dodgers, batting .263.

Left to right: Boston's Doug Griffin, Luis Tiant, and Carl Yastrzemski. They are exchanging some banter with Milwaukee first baseman George Scott, a former teammate.

Luis Tiant pitched for six clubs in his 19-year career (1964–82), having his best years with the Red Sox in the 1970s. A four-time 20-game winner, he was 229–172 lifetime.

Second baseman and speedster Davey Lopes, who played in the big leagues for 16 years, most of them with the Dodgers. He retired in 1987 with a .263 average.

Eighteen major league seasons produced a .297 lifetime average for Joe Torre. The National League batting champion and MVP in 1971, Joe played for the Braves, Cardinals, and Mets.

Jeff Burroughs, the American League's MVP in 1974 while playing for the Texas Rangers. He played for four other clubs, retiring in 1985 with a .261 average.

The indefatigable Mike Marshall. He pitched in the majors for 14 years for nine different clubs in both leagues, retiring in 1981 with a 97–112 record.

Pittsburgh's two-time batting champion, Dave Parker.

BELOW: St. Louis's Busch Stadium

Jim Rice

Catcher Carlton Fisk (left) and left-hander Bill Lee. Fisk joined the Red Sox in 1969 and signed with the White Sox in 1981. Lee pitched with the Red Sox and Expos from 1969–82, compiling a lifetime record of 119–90.

Minnesota's Lyman Bostock bearing down on home plate as Kansas City's Buck Martinez prepares to make the play.

Frank Tanana, who came to the majors with California in 1973 and later pitched for Boston, Texas, and Detroit.

Pete Rose doing it his way.

Johnny Bench

George Brett, who batted .390 in 1980.

BELOW: The Mets' Felix Millan laying down a bunt.

John Candelaria, Pittsburgh ace in the 1970s. He was a 20-game winner in 1977.

BELOW: The Mets' Dave Kingman scoring as Cardinals catcher Ted Simmons awaits the ball.

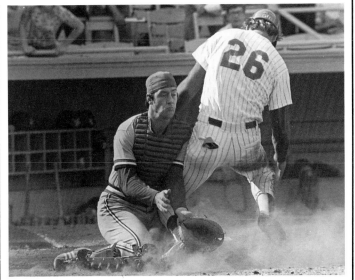

It's the first inning of game 3 of the 1976 American League pennant playoffs at Yankee Stadium, and Kansas City's George Brett is scoring on a sacrifice fly. The catcher is Thurman Munson.

Chris Chambliss hitting the home run in the bottom of the ninth inning of game 5 of the 1976 American League playoffs that gave the Yankees the pennant.

Dave Concepcion, shortstop on Cincinnati's "Big Red Machine." He began his long big-league career in 1970.

Ken Griffey, .300-hitting outfielder on Cincinnati's championship clubs of 1975–76.

A bad arm curtailed the career of gifted left-hander Don Gullett. He played from 1970–78 for the Reds and Yankees. Lifetime record: 109–50.

In a career covering more than two decades, Graig Nettles played for six clubs in both leagues, spending 11 years with the Yankees.

Thurman Munson, Yankees catcher and team leader. He played from 1969–79, when he lost his life in a plane crash at the age of 32. Five times a .300 hitter, his career average is .292.

Joe Morgan, a 22-year major leaguer, playing for the Astros, Reds (for whom he had his best years), Giants, Phillies, and A's. He retired in 1984 with a .271 batting average.

The Mets let Amos Otis get away to Kansas City in 1970 and Otis starred for the Royals for the next 14 years. He retired with Pittsburgh in 1984, batting .277 for his career.

BELOW: Mark "The Bird" Fidrych posing with friend. Fidrych was 29–19 for his injury-shortened career.

Three-time National League RBI leader George Foster. He came to the big leagues with the Giants in 1969 and had his greatest years for the Reds in the 1970s. He later played for the Mets. He hit 348 home runs and batted .274.

Hal McRae. He came to the big leagues with the Reds in 1968, went to Kansas City in 1973, and played until 1987. He was the RBI leader in 1982. The 19-year veteran batted .290.

Baltimore shortstop Mark Belanger making the play on Jim Rice at second base. One of baseball's finest-fielding shortstops, Belanger was with Baltimore from 1965–81, finishing up with the Dodgers in 1982. Lifetime average: .228.

The Phillies' Dave Cash about to make a play on the sliding Joe Morgan. A 12-year second baseman with four National League clubs from 1969–80, Cash was a lifetime .283 hitter.

Greg Luzinski was a big blaster for the Phillies and White Sox from 1970–84, ringing up a .276 career average.

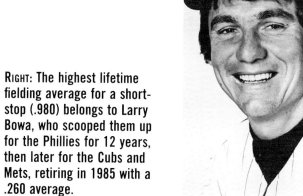

RIGHT: The highest lifetime fielding average for a shortstop (.980) belongs to Larry Bowa, who scooped them up for the Phillies for 12 years, then later for the Cubs and Mets, retiring in 1985 with a .260 average.

A quartet of dynamos that helped "The Big Red Machine" roar along. Left to right: Tony Perez, Johnny Bench, Joe Morgan, and Pete Rose.

LEFT: Texas right-hander Bert Blyleven showing off his no-hit baseball. He no-hit California on September 22, 1977.

Rick Reuschel. He was a 20-game winner for the Cubs in 1977.

Outfielder Richie Zisk, a hard hitter for the Pirates, White Sox, Rangers, and Mariners. He played from 1971–83, batting .287.

Lou Piniella, who spent most of his 18-year major league career with the Yankees. He batted .291 lifetime.

Lou Brock

Steve Rogers, Montreal ace of the 1970s and early 1980s. Lifetime record: 158–152.

Willie Randolph, second baseman on the powerful Yankees teams of the late 1970s.

Champagne in hand, the Giants' John Montefusco is ready to celebrate his September 30, 1976, no-hitter over the Braves.

Ron Guidry, whose 1978 season was one of the finest any pitcher has ever had.

Mike Schmidt

Butch Hobson gave the Red Sox some hard-hitting years at third base in the late 1970s. He later played briefly for the Angels and Yankees, retiring in 1982 with a .248 average.

Reggie Jackson watching the flight of his record fifth home run of the 1977 World Series and his third of game 6. The pitcher is the Dodgers' Charlie Hough, the catcher Steve Yeager, the umpire John McSherry.

Bucky Dent coming home after his crushing three-run homer against the Red Sox in the one-game playoff for the American League East division title between Boston and New York in 1978. Welcoming Dent are Roy White (number 6) and Chris Chambliss.

BELOW: Red Sox pitcher Mike Torrez, who gave up the Dent home run, in the dugout after the inning was over.

Tom Seaver in the Cincinnati dugout. Manager Sparky Anderson is at the far left.

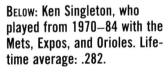

BELOW: Ken Singleton, who played from 1970–84 with the Mets, Expos, and Orioles. Lifetime average: .282.

Frank White, long-time second baseman of the Kansas City Royals.

Keith Hernandez with the Cardinals in 1977.

BELOW: Jim Palmer (left) and Mike Flanagan, longtime bulwarks of the Orioles' pitching staff.

Baltimore skipper Earl Weaver, one of the most successful of all managers.

Red Sox shortstop Rick Burleson firing on to first to complete a double play. The man on the ground is Oakland's Rickey Henderson.

Philadelphia's Veterans Stadium

Cleveland's Bobby Bonds is trying to steal second, but Boston's Jerry Remy has the ball waiting for him.

Willie Stargell

California second baseman Bobby Grich is avoiding the spikes of Cleveland's Mike Hargrove. A top performer for the Orioles and Angels from 1970–86, Grich batted .266.

Kent Tekulve, a workhorse reliever for the Pirates and Phillies.

Pitcher Bert Blyleven (center) is being mobbed by jubilant teammates after Pittsburgh defeated Cincinnati in the 1979 National League pennant playoffs. The airborne man on the right is Mike Easler.

Don Mattingly, American
League batting champion
in 1984.

1980

The Yankees were the eastern division champs for the fourth time in five years in 1980. The club, under manager Dick Howser (as well as under owner George Steinbrenner, the game's most volatile chief executive), finished three games ahead of Baltimore.

Yankees pitching was an oddity this year—the club's top four winners were all left-handers: Tommy John (22–9), Ron Guidry (17–10), Rudy May (15–5), and Tom Underwood (13–9). Backing up this southpaw quartet were a pair of highly effective hard-throwing right-handed relievers—set-up man Ron Davis and closer Goose Gossage.

Reggie Jackson had his best year as a Yankee and one of the best of his career. Tying Milwaukee's Ben Oglivie for the home run lead at 41, Jackson drove in 111 runs, and for the first and only time batted .300, ending the season with precisely that figure.

The most devastating hitting of the year came from Kansas City's George Brett, whose smoking bat signaled a summer of immense proportions. After sparring with .400 late into the season, the Royals' third baseman settled for a magisterial .390, major league baseball's highest average since Ted Williams's .406 in 1941. In leading the Royals to their own fourth division title in five years, Brett (the runaway MVP) drove in 118 runs in 117 games. Many of those runs were scored by leadoff man Willie Wilson, who stitched together his own superb season, leading with 230 hits, 133 runs scored (most in the league since 1949), and batting .326. Wilson also established a new major league record for official at-bats with 705. Willie included 79 stolen bases in his season, but was outdone in this department by Oakland's Rickey Henderson, who stole 100, breaking Ty Cobb's American League record by four.

Baltimore, second in the East, had a couple of 20-game winners, including the Cy Young Award honoree in Steve Stone (25–7) and left-hander Scott McGregor (20–8). The Orioles had now had five of the last eight Cy Young Award designees.

The Rookie of the Year was Cleveland outfielder Joe Charboneau, a colorful character who hit 23 home runs and batted .289. The RBI leader was Cecil Cooper with 122. The Milwaukee first baseman put together his own brilliant year, batting .352 and collecting 219 hits, but was overshadowed by Brett. In addition to Cooper, two other Brewers, Oglivie and Gorman Thomas, also drove in over 100 runs. A rumbling volcano of a team, the Brewers clubbed 203 home runs.

1980–
New Pinnacles of Success
1988

Willie Wilson

Bill Buckner

Jim Frey's Royals, who easily beat out Billy Martin's Oakland A's by 14 games in the West, had Dennis Leonard at the top of their mound corps with a 20–11 record, while the A's had Mike Norris at 22–9. The Royals received the league's best relief work from submariner Dan Quisenberry, who relieved 75 times, winning 12 and saving 33.

The All-Star Game was played on July 8 at Dodger Stadium in Los Angeles, with the National League, following a familiar script, winning 4–2 for their ninth consecutive victory.

The Yankees and Royals met in the pennant playoffs for the fourth time in five years, and this time the outcome was different, the Royals stunning their three-time tormentors in three straight. The highlight came in game 3 at Yankee Stadium. Trailing 2–1 in the top of the seventh, the Royals had two men on and two out with Brett facing Gossage. It was a classic confrontation—the great fastballer reliever versus the notorious fastball hitter. The victor was Brett, with a titanic home run into the Stadium's third deck. The Royals were on their way to their first World Series.

Emulating the Yankees and Royals, the Philadelphia Phillies were division winners for the fourth time in five years, edging Montreal by a single game, with Mike Schmidt's game-winning home run on the next-to-last day providing the clincher. For Schmidt it was a stellar MVP season, the great third baseman leading in home runs (48) and RBIs (121). Manager Dallas Green's club also had the Cy Young Award winner, Steve Carlton winning for the third time on the basis of a 24–9 record.

Second-place Montreal had a pair of .300 hitters in outfielders Ellis Valentine and Andre Dawson, while their third outfielder, Ron LeFlore, stole 97 bases, third-highest total in National League history.

The batting title went to Chicago first baseman Bill Buckner, who batted .324, beating out Keith Hernandez's bid for a second straight title by three points.

One no-hitter was pitched in the big leagues this year, by the Dodgers' Jerry Reuss, who stopped the Giants on June 27, 8–0. Reuss lost a perfect game on a first-inning throwing error by shortstop Bill Russell.

In the West, the Houston Astros won their first division title, though not without some anxious moments. Leading the second-place Dodgers by three games, the Astros went into Los Angeles to close out the season with a three-game series, needing just one win to clinch. The Dodgers, however, swept a weekend of pulsating baseball by scores of 3–2, 2–1, and 4–3, forcing a one-game playoff for the division title. With knuckleballer Joe Niekro on the mound, the Astros rescued themselves from total humiliation with an easy 7–1 win, the victory making Niekro 20–12 for the season. The Astros had suffered a grievous midseason loss when their ace pitcher, J. R. Richard (10–4 at the time), suffered a near-fatal stroke that ended his career.

Second-place Los Angeles had the compensation of having the Rookie of the Year in left-handed reliever Steve Howe, who was 7–9 with 17 saves.

The 1980 National League pennant playoffs were easily the most exciting in the history of these World Series preambles. The Phillies won in five, with the games going this way:

Game 1: Philadelphia 3, Houston 1.
Game 2: Houston 7, Philadelphia 4 (10 innings).
Game 3: Houston 1, Philadelphia 0 (11 innings).
Game 4: Philadelphia 5, Houston 3 (10 innings).
Game 5: Philadelphia 8, Houston 7 (10 innings).

Having won their first pennant in 30 years, the Phillies then went on to win their first world championship ever, defeating Kansas City in six games, despite four home runs by the Royals' Willie Aikens and three by Amos Otis. Reliever Tug McGraw appeared four times for the Phillies, striking out 10 in seven innings, winning one, losing one, and saving two.

1981

The 1981 major league season has a Grand Canyon right in the heart of it—a tremendous gouged-out hole caused by the players' strike that ran from June 12 through August 9, erasing 713 games from the schedule and costing an estimated $100,000,000 in player salaries and franchise revenues.

The strike, which was called by the players, was provoked by the owners, who were trying to reclaim some of their bargaining-table and courtroom losses. The owners were asking for compensation for the loss of a player to free agency in the form of a player in return from the signing club (after fifteen men on that club's roster had been protected). The players saw this concept as inhibiting to free agency. Armed with strike insurance purchased from Lloyd's of London, the owners stood their ground and let the players walk, and for the first time since 1876, the heart of an American summer passed without big-league baseball being played.

The strike was finally settled, with a modest compromise on the thorniest issue—compensation. The clubs would create a pool of players to be made available to teams who lost players to free agency (this meant every team, whether they had signed a free agent or not). Ironically, this compromise agreement which ended the strike of 1981 was quietly dispensed with by mutual agreement several years later.

When agreement was reached in early August, it was decided to split the season into two distinct halves. Those clubs who were leading their divisions on June 12 were declared winners of the first half and would play the second-half winners for the division title. This created double-tiered playoffs before pennant winners could be decided—divisional and then league. If the same team happened to win both halves, they would play the second-half runner-up for the title. It was all a patently nonsensical scheme, as crack-brained as anything in major league history, and in fact caused three teams with the best combined records in their respective divisions to miss the pennant playoffs —Milwaukee in the American League East, St. Louis in the National League East, and Cincinnati in the National League West.

The first-half winners in the American League were Gene Michael's Yankees in the East, by two games over Baltimore, and Billy Martin's A's in the West, by 1½ games over Texas. Martin's club got off to a fast start, setting a league record by winning their first 11 games.

The second-half winners were Buck Rodgers's Milwaukee Brewers in the East and Jim Frey's Kansas City Royals in the West. (Frey was replaced late in the season by Dick Howser.) Kansas City's qualifying for the divisional playoffs pointed up the absurdity of the entire split-season concept, for the Royals' full-season winning

Eddie Murray

percentage of .485 was fourth-best in the division.

The Yankees beat the Brewers in five games to win the East, while the A's ran over the Royals in three straight to win the West. In the pennant playoffs the Yankees (now managed by Bob Lemon) rubbed out the A's in three straight, with Graig Nettles driving in nine runs. Over the full season, the Yankees' .551 winning percentage was bettered by both Milwaukee and Baltimore; nevertheless, the New Yorkers were the American League pennant winners.

Boston's Carney Lansford was the league's leading batter with a .336 average. Other leading statistics reflected the loss of one-third of the season: there was a four-way tie for the home run crown between Baltimore's Eddie Murray, California's Bobby Grich, Boston's Dwight Evans, and Oakland's Tony Armas at 22 each; while Murray was the RBI leader with 78. Four pitchers tied for the lead in games won with 14: Milwaukee's Pete Vukovich, Baltimore's Dennis Martinez, Oakland's Steve McCatty, and Detroit's Jack Morris.

Milwaukee's Rollie Fingers was both MVP and Cy Young Award winner. The premier reliever won 6, saved 28, and had a 1.04 ERA. New York's Dave Righetti, 8–4, was Rookie of the Year.

Ironically, in major league baseball's most imperfect season, a perfect game was pitched. It came from the strong right arm of Cleveland's Len Barker, who on May 15 completely shut down Toronto, 3–0. It was the ninth perfect game of the century and first in 13 years.

The All-Star Game, with which the season was resumed after the strike, was played at Cleveland's Municipal Stadium on August 9, with the National League winning for the 10th straight time, 5–4.

BASEBALL

In the National League East, Dallas Green's Phillies won the first half, by 1½ games over the Cardinals, and Jim Fanning's Expos the second half, by a half-game over the Cardinals. Fanning was a late-season replacement for Dick Williams. In the divisional playoffs it was Montreal in five games, with Steve Rogers brilliant in two winning efforts, including a shutout in the finale.

In the West, Tom Lasorda's Dodgers won the first half, a half-game over the Reds, with Bill Virdon's Astros winning the second half, 1½ games over the Reds. (John McNamara's Reds, with the best winning percentage in the league—.611—watched both sets of playoffs on television.) In the western divisional playoffs, the Dodgers came from two games down to beat the Astros in five, behind the solid pitching of Burt Hooton, Fernando Valenzuela, and Jerry Reuss, who pitched a shutout in the finale.

The pennant playoffs saw the Dodgers beat the Expos in five games. The winning blow was a pinch-hit home run by Rick Monday in the top of the ninth inning of the fifth game, giving the Dodgers a 2–1 pennant-clinching victory.

As in the American League, National League statistics reflected the truncated season. Pittsburgh's Bill Madlock won his third batting title with a .341 average, Mike Schmidt was the home run leader (for the fifth time) with 31, and also led in RBIs with 91, earning his second straight MVP Award. Montreal's speed-demon rookie Tim Raines led with a remarkable 71 stolen bases in just 88 games.

The reason Raines did not get the Rookie of the Year Award was named Fernando Valenzuela. The Dodgers' screwballing left-hander started off in truly spectacular fashion. Baseball's most unlikely looking hero since Yogi Berra, the plump, twenty-year-old Mexican opened the season with eight straight wins, five of them shutouts. For the two-thirds of a season, Valenzuela was 13–7 with league-leading totals in strikeouts (180) and shutouts (8). Along with Rookie of the Year honors, he was also the Cy Young Award winner. The biggest winner of the year, however, was Cincinnati's Tom Seaver, who posted a 14–2 record.

There were a few landmark achievements in the league during this sundered season. On April 29, the Phillies' Steve Carlton became the first left-hander to strike out 3,000 batters and later, on September 21, Carlton's 3,118th career strikeout eclipsed Bob Gibson's National League record total. On June 10, the Phillies' Pete Rose rapped out his 3,630th lifetime hit, tying him with Stan Musial at the top of the league for career hits. (Pete had to wait 50 days for the strike to end before drilling hit number 3,631 on August 10.)

Two no-hitters were pitched this year. The first was by Montreal's Charlie Lea, 4–0, over the Giants on May 10. And then on September 26, Houston's Nolan Ryan went into the record books all by himself when he pitched his fifth no-hitter, stifling the Dodgers, 5–0. Ryan and Sandy Koufax had been tied with four no-hitters each.

The World Series, which didn't start until October 20, was won by the Dodgers over the Yankees in six games, after the Yankees had taken the first two. Yankees reliever George Frazier tied an unwanted Series record by losing three games. (The only other pitcher to lose three games in a single Series was Lefty Williams, of the tainted 1919 White Sox, when Lefty wasn't trying very hard.) It was the 11th time the Yankees and Dodgers had met in the World Series, with the Dodgers winning for only the third time. The Series brought a merciful end to baseball's most farcical and forgettable season.

Nolan Ryan

Bill Madlock

1982

The Milwaukee Brewers had been growing stronger each year and were expected to contend in 1982. When the club got off to a slow start, manager Buck Rodgers was replaced in early June by Harvey Kuenn, who told the boys to "relax and have fun." The boys did just that, at the expense of American League pitchers. Nicknamed "Harvey's Wallbangers" for their long-ball propensities, the Brewers slugged their way to a narrow one-game division title over the Orioles, whose long-time manager Earl Weaver had announced his retirement with the close of the season. (Like many announced retirements, as opposed to forced ones, this proved to be temporary.)

Holding a three-game lead over Baltimore, the Brewers came to town for a season-ending four-game series. Weaver's club suddenly arched its back and took the first three games, deadlocking the race with one last game to play. But Kuenn's team, behind the clutch pitching of the recently acquired Don Sutton, tore into the Orioles for a 10–2 victory and won the division title.

The Brewers received good pitching from Cy Young Award winner Pete Vukovich (18–6) and Mike Caldwell (17–13) and some more top-drawer relief work from Rollie Fingers, who won 5 and saved 29 before arm miseries put him out of action in early September. But it was hitting that gave the Brewers their identity. Shortstop Robin Yount turned in an MVP year, batting .331, hitting 29 homers, and driving in 114 runs. Cecil Cooper had 32 homers, 121 RBIs, a .313 average; Paul Molitor batted .302; Gorman Thomas led the league with 39 home runs and drove in 112 runs; Ben Oglivie hit 34 homers and drove in 102 runs; and Ted Simmons hit 23 homers and drove in 97 runs. Overall, the Brewers hit 216 home runs, had four 100-RBI men, and three with over 200 hits—Cooper, Yount, and Molitor.

Second-place Baltimore received good years from Eddie Murray and Rookie of the Year Cal Ripken, who split his time between third base and shortstop, batting .264 and driving in 93 runs.

In the West, the California Angels employed some heavy hitting of their own to take the division, winning by three over the Royals. Manager Gene Mauch's club had five men with over 20 home runs—Doug DeCinces (30), Fred Lynn (21), Brian Downing (28), Don Baylor (24), and Reggie Jackson (39). Reggie had left the Yankees and signed with the Angels as a free agent, delivering a big season for Mauch. Jackson tied Thomas for the league home run lead and drove in 101 runs. With free-agent signee Rod Carew on first base, the Angels had four former MVPs in the lineup; Carew, Lynn, Baylor, and Jackson. The club's big winner was junk-balling left-hander Geoff Zahn, 18–8.

Second-place Kansas City had the batting champion

Cecil Cooper

Cal Ripken

in Willie Wilson (.332, one point better than Yount), and the RBI leader in Hal McRae, who had a hefty total of 133.

Oakland's flashy Rickey Henderson set an all-time one-season base-stealing record with 130, which was immediately hailed as baseball's latest "unbreakable" record. (Rickey set another, less heralded record: he was caught 42 times.) Chicago's LaMarr Hoyt was the top winner with 19 in a season that saw no American League pitcher win 20. Seattle's Gaylord Perry became the eighth pitcher in modern times to accumulate 300 wins when he beat the Yankees on May 6. (Later in the season, in August, Perry was ejected from a game and suspended for 10 days for allegedly throwing a spitball.)

The American League playoffs saw the Brewers come from an 0–2 deficit to take three straight and win the pennant, despite Fred Lynn's 11-for-18 performance (.611) for the Angels and Don Baylor's 10 RBIs. The big hit was a two-run single by Cecil Cooper in the bottom of the seventh of the final game, which won it for the Brewers, 4–3.

The All-Star Game was played at Montreal's Olympic Stadium on July 13, with the National League winning for the 11th straight time, 4–1.

In the National League West, Joe Torre's Atlanta Braves jumped off to a record 13–0 start, slumped badly in midseason (at one point losing eight straight to the Dodgers over two horrendous weekends), but hung on to scratch out the division title by one game over the Dodgers and two over the Giants.

With two games to go, the Braves led the Dodgers by one and the Giants by two. On Saturday, the Dodgers eliminated the Giants with a 15–2 drubbing while the Braves were beating San Diego. Then on the final day, the Giants avenged themselves upon the Dodgers with a 5–3 victory (on veteran Joe Morgan's home run), insuring an Atlanta division title.

The Braves had the MVP in outfielder Dale Murphy, who hit 36 home runs and tied Montreal's Al Oliver for the RBI lead with 109. Bob Horner hit 32 homers and drove in 97 runs, as he and Murphy powered the club all season. Forty-three-year-old knuckleballer Phil Niekro was the ace of a rather shallow staff with a 17–4 record, though the Braves got some powerful relief pitching from right-handers Steve Bedrosian and Gene Garber.

The Dodgers' Fernando Valenzuela followed up his sensational rookie season with a 19–13 record, and Pedro Guerrero turned in a slugging summer with 32 home runs and 100 RBIs. In addition, the team had the Rookie of the Year for the fourth time in a row in second baseman Steve Sax, who batted .282 and brought to an end the long-time infield quartet of Steve Garvey, Davey Lopes, Bill Russell, and Ron Cey, which had been intact since June 1973.

In the East, Whitey Herzog's Cardinals beat out the

Dale Murphy

Phillies by three games. The Cards, who hit just 67 home runs, were glued together by shortstop Ozzie Smith, acquired from San Diego the previous winter. Outfielder George Hendrick was the team's only long-baller, with 19 homers and 104 RBIs. Bob Forsch and Joaquin Andujar, with 15 wins apiece, were Herzog's top pitchers, with the key man on the staff being relief pitcher Bruce Sutter, who appeared 70 times, winning 9 and saving 36.

Philadelphia's Steve Carlton won 23 and lost 11 (he was the major league's only 20-game winner this year) and was voted an unprecedented fourth Cy Young Award. Montreal's Al Oliver was the batting champion with a .331 average. The home run leader was New York's Dave Kingman with 37, despite a puny .204 batting average that was freighted with 156 strikeouts.

On June 22, Philadelphia's Pete Rose moved into second place on the all-time hit list with his 3,772nd safe rap, passing Henry Aaron. Only Ty Cobb with 4,191 remained ahead of Rose.

The playoffs were a cakewalk for the Cardinals as they swept the Braves in three.

The World Series went the full seven, with the Cardinals outlasting the Brewers, despite some sharp Milwaukee hitting by Yount (12 hits) and Molitor (11 hits). In the opening game the two got nine hits between them, with Molitor becoming the first ever to rap five hits in a World Series game. In the end, however, the suffocating relief pitching of Sutter (one win, two saves) tipped the balance in favor of St. Louis.

Steve Carlton

Whitey Herzog

1983

After 16 years the Baltimore Orioles had a new manager. His name was Joe Altobelli and all he did in his first year in Baltimore was win the East (by six games over Detroit), the playoffs, and the World Series. Despite injuries during the season to ace starters Mike Flanagan and Jim Palmer and reliever Tippy Martinez and the ineffectiveness of Dennis Martinez (7–16), the O's still managed to win 98 games and come out on top, thanks to Altobelli's skillful manipulating of his platoon players and the winning seasons of Scott McGregor (18–7) and Mike Boddicker (16–8). Eddie Murray turned in the by now standard Eddie Murray year (33 home runs, 111 RBIs, .306 batting average), while shortstop Cal Ripken batted .318, hit 27 homers, had 102 RBIs, led the league with 47 doubles and 211 hits, and was voted MVP.

The Tigers had a rare .300-hitting double-play combination in Alan Trammell (.319) and Lou Whitaker (.320), a 20-game winner in Jack Morris (20–13), and another ace in Dan Petry (19–11).

The Yankees, being managed for the third time by Billy Martin, had Ron Guidry turn in his best record since his sensational 1978 season with a 21–9 mark. The year's highlight for Yankees fans came on July 4 at Yankee Stadium when Dave Righetti pitched a 4–0 no-hitter over the Red Sox. Righetti's final out of the game was a strikeout of Wade Boggs, who in his first full season led the league with a .361 batting average, drilling 210 hits. Boggs's Red Sox teammate Jim Rice was the home run king with 39 and tied Milwaukee's Cecil Cooper for the RBI leadership with 126. Oakland's Rickey Henderson became the first player to go over 100 steals in a season twice, stealing 108 bases for Oakland.

It was a banner year for the Chicago White Sox, who won the American League West by a sumptuous 20 games. The Sox had a pair of 20-game winners in Cy Young Award honoree LaMarr Hoyt (24–10) and Richard Dotson (22–7), the Rookie of the Year in outfielder Ron Kittle (35 home runs, 100 RBIs), and some muscular hitting from Carlton Fisk (26 homers) and DH Greg Luzinski (32 homers).

Kansas City's Dan Quisenberry set a new major league record for saves with 45. On September 29, Oakland's rookie right-hander Mike Warren tossed a 3–0 no-hitter against the White Sox.

On July 24 the celebrated Pine Tar Game took place at Yankee Stadium. After George Brett had homered off Goose Gossage in the top of the ninth to give the Kansas City Royals a 5–4 lead, a Yankees protest that the pine tar on Brett's bat exceeded the legal limit was upheld by the umpires, who ruled Brett out and gave the Yankees a 4–3 victory. The ensuing Kansas City protest to league president Lee MacPhail, however, resulted in the umpires being overruled and the game ordered resumed from the point of Brett's home run. The game was completed on August 18, with the Royals holding their lead and winning, 5–4.

The American League finally broke their All-Star Game losing streak at 11, beating the Nationals, 13–3, the game being played at Chicago's Comiskey Park on July 6. The highlight was the first grand slam homer in All-Star history, struck by California's Fred Lynn in a seven-run third inning.

The White Sox won the first game of the pennant playoffs, but Baltimore regrouped and took the next three. Orioles pitching allowed just one run in those three games.

On July 18 the Phillies fired manager Pat Corrales, and the man who did the firing, general manager Paul Owens, replaced him. Under Owens, the club caught fire and rode a 22–7 September tailwind into a first-place finish, six games ahead of the Pirates. The Phillies again had the Cy Young Award winner, though this time it wasn't Steve Carlton but John Denny, at 19–6 the league's top winner, marking the first time since 1931 the league was without a 20-game winner (forgetting the 1981 strike year). The Phillies had some vintage players in Pete Rose at first base and Joe Morgan at second (both well past their primes), while the star of the team was Mike Schmidt, whose 40 home runs gave him the leadership for the sixth time. The Phillies also had a superb bullpen with Ron Reed and left-handers Al Holland and Willie Hernandez.

Second-place Pittsburgh had the batting champion, as Bill Madlock's .323 average made him a four-time winner. (It was the Pittsburgh club's 23rd batting title, most in the major leagues. Detroit was second with 22.) Atlanta's Dale Murphy, for the second straight year the MVP, led with 121 RBIs, while Montreal's Tim Raines tore up the basepaths with 90 steals.

Yet another monumental old record was retired this year. On April 23, Houston's Nolan Ryan surpassed Walter Johnson as the all-time strikeout leader with his 3,509th career strikeout. Johnson's record had stood for 56 years. By season's end, however, Carlton had passed both Johnson and Ryan with 3,709 whiffs to Ryan's 3,677. On September 23, Carlton chalked up his 300th big-league victory, ending the year with the well-rounded lifetime record of 300–200.

On July 29, a dislocated thumb ended Steve Garvey's National League endurance record of 1,207 consecutive games, 923 games (or 5½ seasons) less than Lou Gehrig's major league mark. Garvey was now with the San Diego Padres, having left Los Angeles as a free agent after 14 years.

In the National League West, Tom Lasorda's Dodgers finished first, three games ahead of the defending

champion Braves. With Fernando Valenzuela and Bob Welch the top winners at 15 apiece, the Dodgers used the solid slugging of Pedro Guerrero (32 homers, 103 RBIs) as their main springboard to the top.

The league's Rookie of the Year was the Mets' multitalented outfielder Darryl Strawberry, who broke in with 26 home runs and a .257 batting average.

On September 26, the Cardinals' Bob Forsch pitched his second career no-hitter, stopping Montreal, 3–0.

With Gary Matthews hitting three home runs and driving in eight runs, the Phillies beat the Dodgers in the playoffs in four games. Steve Carlton was outstanding in two winning performances for the Phillies.

The Phillies won the opening game of the World Series, but after that it was a Baltimore runaway, the O's sweeping the next four. The Orioles got some surprising extra-base power from their normally light-hitting catcher Rick Dempsey, who slammed four doubles and a home run.

Bob Welch

1984

One of the charms of baseball is its system of checks and balances. The strongest teams still lose around 60 games every year, just as the weakest will win 60 or 70. So what the Detroit Tigers did in the opening months of the 1984 season was so statistically out of proportion it was stunning. Sparky Anderson's team came charging out of the starting gate with a velocity that soon left them a mere blur in the eyes of the rest of the league, winning 10 of their first 11 and 35 of their first 40. (When Sparky titled his book about the 1984 season *Bless You, Boys,* it was understandable.)

Winning by 15 games over a talented Toronto team, the Tigers were a nicely balanced club. Sparky's three strong starters were led by Jack Morris (who no-hit the White Sox on April 7, 4–0), who was 19–11, Dan Petry, 18–8, and Milt Wilcox, 17–8. In addition, the Tigers had two superb relievers in Aurelio Lopez, who was 10–1 with 14 saves, and left-hander Willie Hernandez, acquired from the Phillies in a spring trade. The screwballing Hernandez turned in one of the great relief-pitching seasons of all time, with a 9–3 record and 32 saves in 33 opportunities. He was so consistently effective all summer that he won both the MVP and Cy Young Awards.

The Tigers got power hitting from catcher Lance Parrish (33 homers, 98 RBIs) and outfielder Kirk Gibson (27 homers), and great keystone play from Alan Trammell (.314) and Lou Whitaker (.289), in addition to near-flawless center fielding from Chet Lemon.

Jack Morris

A new young star emerged in the league this year in the Yankees' Don Mattingly. The twenty-three-year-old first baseman batted .343 and won the batting crown, beating out teammate Dave Winfield (.340) on the last day of the season. Mattingly also drove in 110 runs and led with 207 hits and 44 doubles.

The home run and RBI leader was Boston outfielder Tony Armas, with 43 and 123, respectively. Baltimore's Mike Boddicker, with a 20–11 record, was the league's only 20-game winner. The Rookie of the Year was Seattle's Alvin Davis, who hit 27 home runs and drove in 116 runs. The game of the year was pitched by California's tall right-hander Mike Witt on the last day of the season. On September 30 Witt pitched a perfect game against the California Angels, winning 1–0 on an unearned run.

The Kansas City Royals under Dick Howser edged out the California Angels for the western division title by three games. Left-hander Bud Black topped the staff with a 17–12 record, but Dan Quisenberry was never far away. The tireless underhanded reliever appeared 72 times, winning six and saving 44, figuring in more than half of the club's 84 wins. With Willie Wilson missing the first six weeks of the season due to a suspension stemming from a drug possession conviction, and a knee injury limiting George Brett to 104 games, the Royals were surprise winners.

In addition to Alvin Davis (who got his chance only because of an early-season injury to regular first baseman Ken Phelps), Seattle introduced another rookie star in left-hander Mark Langston, who was 17–10 with a league-leading 204 strikeouts.

On September 17, California's Reggie Jackson hit his 500th career homer, becoming the 13th player in history to attain 500 in bingo shots.

The National League won the All-Star Game by a 3–1 score. The game was played at San Francisco's Candlestick Park on July 10.

Detroit stayed hot right on through the playoffs, rubbing out the Royals in three straight, with Wilcox and Hernandez collaborating on a three-hit, 1–0 shutout in the finale, nullifying a brilliant three-hit effort by K.C.'s Charlie Leibrandt.

The New York Mets unveiled the most exciting young pitcher seen in years in nineteen-year-old right-hander Dwight Gooden. Poised and savvy, with a high-rising fastball and savagely arcing curve, the youngster was 17–9, with a terrific strikeout pitch—276 in 218 innings, including back-to-back games of 16 whiffs each on September 12 and 17, tying the major league two-game record. His 276 strikeouts not only led the league but broke Herb Score's 29-year-old rookie record.

Gooden's superlative pitching, however, was not enough, and the Mets finished 6½ behind Jim Frey's Chicago Cubs, who finished on top for the first time since 1945. The key move for the Cubs was the June acquisition of right-hander Rick Sutcliffe from the Indians. Sutcliffe went on to win the Cy Young Award with a near-perfect 16–1 record. The Cubs also had the league's Most Valuable Player in second baseman Ryne Sandberg, who batted .314, joining with Leon Durham, Ron Cey, Keith Moreland, Gary Matthews, and Jody Davis to give Chicago one of its most potent attacks in years. In the bullpen Frey had the intimidating Lee Smith, who fastballed his way to 9 wins and 33 saves.

The third-place Cardinals had the league's only 20-game winner in Joaquin Andujar (20–14) and got a record-tying 45 saves from Bruce Sutter.

In the National League West, Dick Williams led his San Diego Padres to their first division title, winning by 12 games over the Braves. Eric Show led a so-so staff with 15 wins. Like all championship teams, the Padres had a big gun in the bullpen—Goose Gossage, weaned away via free agency from the Yankees. Gossage won 10 and saved 25. The Padres had only one .300 hitter, but he was the league's best—outfielder Tony Gwynn, with a .351 average, built on a foundation of 213 hits. Padres first baseman Steve Garvey fielded to a perfect 1.000 percentage (the first time in history it had been done over the full season

at the position), handling 1,319 chances.

Atlanta's Dale Murphy and Philadelphia's Mike Schmidt tied for the home run lead with 36, while Schmidt also tied for the RBI lead with Montreal's Gary Carter at 106.

Early in the season, on April 13, Montreal's Pete Rose tagged his 4,000th career hit and began the countdown to Ty Cobb in earnest. On August 16, Rose was dealt back to Cincinnati where he assumed a player-manager role, closing the season with 4,097 hits—94 away from equaling Cobb's record.

In the ongoing duel for most lifetime strikeouts, Houston's Nolan Ryan closed out the season with 3,874 to Steve Carlton's 3,872.

In the pennant playoff, San Diego came from an 0–2 deficit in games to win in five. The Padres won game 4, 7–5, on Garvey's two-run homer in the bottom of the ninth.

Detroit proved in the World Series that it was their year, from opening day to the final putout. The Tigers easily defeated the Padres in five, on the pitching of Jack Morris (2–0) and the strong hitting of Trammell and Gibson, each of whom homered twice.

On October 1, Peter Ueberroth replaced Bowie Kuhn as baseball's sixth commissioner.

Ryne Sandberg

Dale Murphy

1985

There was a momentary blip in the season in early August when the players, dissatisfied with the progress (or lack of it) of talks for a new basic agreement between them and the owners threatened to strike and did indeed walk off the job for two days. But both sides quickly came to the jarring reality that this might be one strike too many and the walkout came to a halt.

The American League East had its fifth different division winner in five years as the Toronto Blue Jays, managed by Bobby Cox, made their debut in the winner's circle. Toronto's top pitcher was the much-traveled veteran right-hander Doyle Alexander, 17–10. The Blue Jays had some fine young players, among them shortstop Tony Fernandez and a trio of twenty-five-year-old outfielders: George Bell, Lloyd Moseby, and Jesse Barfield, with Bell the club's top hitter with 28 home runs and 95 RBIs.

The Yankees finished second, two games out, due mainly to an eight-game losing streak in September. The club had undergone its usual managerial whirligig, with Billy Martin (for the fourth time) replacing Yogi Berra after 16 games. It was the club's 12th managerial change since the advent of George Steinbrenner in 1973. The Yankees had dealt for Oakland's Rickey Henderson, an impending free agent whom the A's felt they would be unable to sign. Henderson received a hefty contract and

then went out and earned it, batting .314, scoring 146 runs (most in the league since Ted Williams's 150 in 1949), and stealing a league-high 80 bases. The man who more often than not was driving Henderson home was first baseman Don Mattingly, who turned in one of the most devastating all-around offensive seasons since the heyday of Williams. The MVP batted .324, hit 35 home runs, collected 211 hits, and led with 48 doubles and a resounding 145 runs batted in, most in the league since Al Rosen had the same total in 1953. Ron Guidry pitched to a 22–6 season and the forty-six-year-old knuckleballer Phil Niekro was 16–12, including his 300th major league victory on the last day of the season.

Last year's runaway division winners, Detroit, came in third, 15 games out, despite having the home run leader in Darrell Evans, who hit 40. Boston's Wade Boggs drilled a prodigious 240 hits (most in the league since 1928) as he won his second batting title with a .368 average. Those 240 hits included a league record 187 singles.

In the West, Dick Howser's Kansas City Royals won their sixth division title in 11 years, finishing one game up on the Angels. Young right-hander Bret Saberhagen was 20–6, winning the Cy Young Award, while left-hander Charlie Leibrandt was 17–9 and Dan Quisenberry remained the bullpen star with eight wins and 37 saves, appearing in 84 games. The Royals got some big punch from first baseman Steve Balboni, who hit 36 home runs, and from George Brett, who hit 30 homers, drove in 112 runs, and batted .335. Willie Wilson's 21 triples were the most in the league since Dale Mitchell's 23 in 1949.

The White Sox had the Rookie of the Year in shortstop Ozzie Guillen, who batted .273 and flashed a snappy glove. Two years before, the Sox had lassoed Tom Seaver from the Mets as a compensation selection, and so it was in a White Sox uniform that the veteran National League star won his 300th game, beating the Yankees in New York on August 4. On the same day, California's Rod Carew delivered his 3,000th big-league hit, becoming the 15th man in modern history to reach this rarefied summit.

The National League won the All-Star Game, played at Minnesota's Hubert H. Humphrey Metrodome on July 16, by a score of 6–1.

The pennant playoffs had been extended to a best-of-seven format now, putting them on a par with the World Series. This expansion favored Kansas City in 1985, for the Royals lost three of the first four, but then came back to sweep the last three and head for the World Series. George Brett, always a murderous hitter in crucial situations, homered three times for the Royals.

The most avidly anticipated hit of the 1985 season was delivered by Pete Rose in Cincinnati on September 11. It was a single off San Diego's Eric Show and it was the 4,192nd of Rose's career, enabling him to finally surpass

Lloyd Moseby

Ty Cobb as baseball's most prolific compiler of base hits.

In the National League East, it was a summer-long battle between the Cardinals and Mets, with Whitey Herzog's Redbirds not clinching until the season's final weekend, ending up three games ahead. The Cardinals had the MVP in center fielder Willie McGee, who had 216 hits and won the batting title with a .353 average. The club also had the Rookie of the Year in outfielder Vince Coleman, who stole 110 bases. The Cardinals' heavy hitter was first baseman Jack Clark with 22 home runs, while second baseman Tommy Herr drove in 110 runs and Ozzie Smith continued to set new standards for playing shortstop.

Cardinals pitching saw one of the most remarkable form reversals in major-league history. After starting the season with a 1–7 record, left-hander John Tudor won 20 of his next 21 decisions to finish with a 21–8 record, including ten shutouts. Joaquin Andujar was 21–12 and Danny Cox 18–9.

The most sensational pitching of the year was done by the Mets' Dwight Gooden. In winning the Cy Young Award, Gooden rang up a 24–4 record, 268 strikeouts, and a 1.53 ERA, leading the league in wins, whiffs, and ERA. Atlanta's Dale Murphy was the home run leader with 37 and Cincinnati's Dave Parker was tops with 125 RBIs.

In the West, Tom Lasorda's Dodgers beat out the Reds by 5½ games. The Dodgers' main strength lay in their four starters—Orel Hershiser (19–3), Fernando

Joaquin Andujar

Valenzuela (17–10), Bob Welch (14–4), and Jerry Reuss (14–10). The club's decisive hitting was done by Pedro Guerrero, with 33 home runs and a .320 batting average, and Mike Marshall, who had 28 homers and 95 RBIs.

Pete Rose's second-place Reds had the first 20-game winning rookie since 1954 in left-hander Tom Browning (20–9) as well as a strong young reliever in southpaw John Franco, who was 12–3 with 12 saves.

Houston's Nolan Ryan recorded his 4,000th career strikeout during the season, and his 209 whiffs were the tenth time he had passed the 200 mark in the category that he had made uniquely his own, tying Tom Seaver's major league record. At the end of the season the race for the all-time strikeout leadership between Ryan and Steve Carlton read like this: Ryan 4,083, Carlton 3,920, with Carlton steadily losing ground to the erosions of arm miseries, which this season held him to a 1–8 record and put him on the disabled list for the first time in his career.

In the National League playoffs, the Cardinals staged a memorable comeback; after losing the first two games to the Dodgers, the Cards took the next four, with the help of a distinctly non-Cardinal weapon—the home run. Ozzie Smith won game 5 for St. Louis in the bottom of the ninth inning with a home run off Dodger reliever Tom Niedenfuer—the first home run the switch-hitting Smith had ever hit from the left side. In game 6, the Dodgers were leading, 5–4, in the top of the ninth when Clark came to bat with runners on second and third and two out. Electing to pitch to the dangerous Clark, Lasorda saw Niedenfuer give up yet another game-winning home run, a tremendous three-run shot that proved to be the pennant winner.

As they had done in the playoffs, so did Kansas City do in the World Series—turn a 1–3 deficit in games to a world championship. The key to the Series was game 6. Trailing 1–0 in the bottom of the ninth, the Royals loaded the bases with one out, helped by a missed call at first base by umpire Don Denkinger, and pinch-hitter Dane Iorg singled to right to score two runs. Game 7 was an 11–0 Kansas City blowout, marked by disputes that saw the ejections of Andujar and Herzog. Bret Saberhagen won twice for the Royals, including the game 7 shutout.

1986

The Red Sox took the early lead in the American League East and all summer the skeptics waited for what they assumed would be the inevitable collapse. There was a bit of a stumble in August, but then quick recovery and John McNamara's men went on to win by 5½ games over the Yankees.

The Red Sox had their usual array of good hitters, but this time the critical element was the overpowering pitching of Cy Young Award winner Roger Clemens, whose 24–4 record assured the team of going through the season without any crippling losing streaks. Clemens, who was also the MVP, led with a 2.48 ERA and had 238 strikeouts, among them an exciting record-setting performance on April 29, when he fanned 20 Seattle Mariners (helping the Mariners along to a new league record for strikeouts by a club in one season—1,148). The Red Sox also received winning pitching from Dennis "Oil Can" Boyd (16–10) and left-hander Bruce Hurst (13–8).

Boston's Wade Boggs won his second batting crown in a row and third overall, with a .357 average. Jim Rice drove in 110 runs and batted .324. DH Don Baylor, obtained in a spring swap with the Yankees, hit 31 home runs and knocked in 94 runs.

The Yankees got an unexpected 18–6 record from left-hander Dennis Rasmussen, as well as another season of bulging production from Don Mattingly (by now generally acclaimed as the game's best all-around player). Mattingly batted .352, hit 31 homers, drove in 113 runs, and led in hits (238) and doubles (53). Rickey Henderson's 87 stolen bases gave him the lead for the seventh straight year. Left-hander Dave Righetti, switched from the starting rotation to the bullpen a few years before, set a new record with 46 saves.

Detroit tied a record with six men hitting 20 or more home runs, including their entire infield of Darrell Evans, Lou Whitaker, Alan Trammell, and Darnell Coles, who were joined by Lance Parrish and Kirk Gibson. Jack Morris continued on as the biggest winner of the 1980s, with a 21–8 record. Milwaukee's left-handed Teddy Higuera was the league's other 20-game winner with a 20–11 mark. Toronto's Jesse Barfield was the home run leader with 40 and Cleveland's Joe Carter led in RBIs with 121.

In the West, Gene Mauch's California Angels came in first, five games ahead of Texas. California pitching was guided by two young right-handers and one veteran righty. Mike Witt (18–10) and Kirk McCaskill (17–10) were the top winners, just ahead of forty-one-year-old Don Sutton, who was 15–11, including his 300th career victory on June 18. Making a big difference in the Angels lineup was Wally Joyner, a baby-faced rookie first baseman, who hit 22 homers, drove in 100 runs, and batted .290.

Joyner was one of several impressive rookies to hit the league this year, including Texas's Pete Incaviglia, who hit 30 home runs and drove in 88 runs (though his record was marred by 185 strikeouts); Seattle's Danny Tartabull, with 25 homers and 96 RBIs (he fanned 157 times); Cleveland's Cory Snyder, who in two-thirds of a season hit 24 homers; and the Rookie of the Year, Oakland's Jose Canseco, who hit 33 homers and drove in 117 runs (he struck out 175 times).

Minnesota's Kirby Puckett took some advice from batting coach Tony Oliva, adjusted his swing slightly and went from four home runs, 74 RBIs, and a .288 batting average in 1985 to 31, 96, and .328 in 1986. Puckett was joined by Gary Gaetti, Kent Hrbek, and Tom Brunansky in giving the Twins their most potent lineup in years.

Between August 6 and 20, Texas Rangers reliever Dale Mohorcic worked in 13 consecutive games, tying Mike Marshall's iron-man record (Mohorcic pitched 14 innings throughout this stretch).

There was one no-hitter in the league this year, delivered by Chicago's Joe Cowley, 7–1, over the Angels on September 19.

The American League won the All-Star Game, 3–2. It was played on July 15 at Houston's Astrodome.

In the pennant playoffs, it looked like California's Gene Mauch was going to win his first pennant after 25 years of managing. He was, in fact, one strike away. The Angels had taken a three-to-one lead in games and were leading the Red Sox, 5–2, in the top of the ninth of game

Wade Boggs

5. A Don Baylor home run made it 5–4, and then with two out, Dave Henderson hit a stunning two-run homer to put the Red Sox up by a run. The Angels tied it in a tension-soaked last of the ninth, but Boston finally won it in 11, 7–6. The series then went back to Fenway Park, where the Sox rolled over a seemingly demoralized Angels club by scores of 10–4 and 8–1 to take the pennant.

In the National League East, it was the New York Mets all the way, winning 108 games, playing such efficient ball throughout the season that as early as June Cardinals manager Whitey Herzog conceded that the New Yorkers would not be caught. Davey Johnson's club ended up 21½ games ahead of second-place Philadelphia.

The Mets' pitching was strong and deep, with left-hander Bob Ojeda at 18–5 the big winner, followed by Dwight Gooden (17–6), Sid Fernandez (16–6), and Ron Darling (15–6). The Mets also had a stellar righty-lefty bullpen tandem in Roger McDowell (14–9 with 22 saves) and Jesse Orosco (8–6, 21 saves).

Second baseman Wally Backman topped the Mets hitters with a .320 batting average, followed by Keith Hernandez, baseball's best defensive first baseman, who batted .310. Gary Carter drove in 105 runs and Darryl Strawberry 93.

The second-place Phillies had Mike Schmidt put together his third MVP season. By now ranked by many as the greatest third baseman in history, Schmidt led in home runs for the eighth time (a National League record) with 37 and in RBIs for the fourth time with 119.

Montreal's Tim Raines was the batting leader with a .334 average, edging the Dodgers' Steve Sax by two points, and the Cardinals' nonstop Vince Coleman led with 107 stolen bases. The Cards had the Rookie of the Year in fireballing reliever Todd Worrell, who won 9 and saved 36.

In the West, Hal Lanier's Houston Astros were easy winners over Cincinnati, by 10 games. Houston's driving force was right-hander Mike Scott, whose mastery of the split-fingered fastball (known to old-timers as the fork ball) earned him an 18–10 record, a league-leading 306 strike-outs, and 2.22 ERA, the Cy Young Award, and the crowning achievement of a September 25 2–0 no-hitting of the Giants, which had the added fillip of being the Astros' division-clinching victory.

Houston had a couple of .300 stickers in third baseman Denny Walling and outfielder Kevin Bass, a gifted second baseman in Bill Doran, and one genuine thunder-maker in first baseman Glenn Davis, who hit 31 home runs and drove in 101 runs. On September 23, Houston left-hander Jim Deshaies established a new major league record by striking out the first eight men he faced. Deshaies went on to fan only two more for a game total of ten as he two-hit the Dodgers, 2–0.

The league's top winning pitchers were Los Angeles' Fernando Valenzuela (21–11) and San Francisco's Mike Krukow (20–9).

On July 6, Atlanta's Bob Horner became just the fourth player in National League history to homer four times in a nine-inning game, feasting on Montreal pitching. (Horner's heroics notwithstanding, Montreal won the game, 11–8.)

Sid Fernandez

Mike Scott

On August 11, Cincinnati's forty-five-year-old player-manager Pete Rose set a National League record with the 10th five-hit game of his career. A few days later Rose, without formal announcement, ceased inserting himself in the lineup. He never batted again, ending his career with 4,256 lifetime hits, most in baseball history.

The National League playoffs matched the American League's in tension and drama. With Scott virtually untouchable in winning 1–0 in the opener and 3–1 in game 4, the series was tied two games apiece. The Mets had won game 2 easily behind Ojeda and then taken a dramatic 6–5 win in game 3 on Len Dykstra's two-run homer in the bottom of the 9th. Game 5 went to the Mets, 2–1, in 12 innings, on Gary Carter's single, after a blistering pitching duel between Gooden and Nolan Ryan. Game 6 was one of baseball's all-time heart-stoppers. Losing 3–0 in the top of the 9th, the Mets spoiled a marvelous effort by lefty Bob Knepper by scoring three runs and tying the score. Each team scored in the 14th, Houston on a stunning game-tying home run by Billy Hatcher. The Mets then scored three times in the top of the 16th, only to see the Astros come charging back with two and have the winning runs on base when Orosco finally whipped the game-ending, pennant-clinching strikeout past Kevin Bass. Orosco won three games in the playoffs.

The Red Sox–Mets World Series went unexcitingly through five games with the Sox winning three of them. Boston was now one game away from their first world title since 1918. After nine innings, game 6 was tied at 3-all. Boston scored two in the top of the 10th. Now they were a half-inning from that long-elusive title. Then two outs. Then one out. Then one strike. At that point the 1986 World Series became indelibly memorable. Singles by Carter, Ray Knight, and Kevin Mitchell scored one run, a wild pitch by reliever Bob Stanley allowed the tying run home, and then, most incredibly of all, a routine grounder by Mookie Wilson went through the legs of first baseman Bill Buckner, allowing Knight to score with the winning run. The Mets won it all in game 7, coming from a 3–0 deficit to an 8–5 victory and the world championship.

Kevin Mitchell

1987

It was a year of booming home runs—a record year, in fact, with 4,458 of the crowd pleasers being hit, a 17 percent increase over 1986; and crowd pleasers they were, as major league attendance reached a new high, 52,029,664. There were grumblings—from pitchers and certain purists—about a livelier ball and the corking of bats turning respectable singles hitters into menacing brutes, but the baseball establishment preferred looking at the bottom line.

In the American League East, the leading Toronto Blue Jays took a sudden, fatal nosedive in the last week of the season when they lost seven straight, allowing a 3½-game lead to melt away, and ended two games behind Sparky Anderson's Tigers. (True, the Jays were without their gifted shortstop Tony Fernandez during the capsize and without catcher Ernie Whitt for part of it, but history usually prefers the dramatic to the detailed.)

The Tigers were led by their reliable ace Jack Morris, who was 18–11, and they got an unexpected 32 home runs from catcher Matt Nokes, replacing Lance Parrish, who had taken the free-agency route to Philadelphia. The Tigers also got a high-caliber all-around season from shortstop Alan Trammell, who hit 28 home runs, drove in 105 runs, and batted .343. Darrell Evans hit 34 homers and late-season pickup Doyle Alexander spun out a 9–0 record.

Toronto had the MVP in George Bell, who put together a tremendous year with 47 home runs and a league-high 134 RBIs, while Fernandez batted .322. Southpaw Jimmy Key was 17–8, and fastballing bullpen ace Tom Henke proved that in the age of the relief pitcher won-lost records meant little, going 0–6 while notching 34 saves. Toronto enjoyed the single most explosive team outburst of the season, hitting a record 10 home runs in one game on September 14 at the expense of a shell-shocked Baltimore pitching staff.

Boston's Wade Boggs's .363 batting average gave him his fourth silver bat and third in a row. Boggs also accumulated 200 hits for the fifth straight year, tying a major league record coheld by Al Simmons, Charlie Gehringer, and Chuck Klein. New York's Don Mattingly set a new big-league standard with six grand slam homers (he had never hit any until this season) and also tied Dale Long's record by hitting home runs in eight consecutive games.

Milwaukee, which started the season with a rush of 12 straight wins, had the year's only no-hitter, pitched by left-hander Juan Nieves against Baltimore on April 15, a 7–0 win. The Brewers also had Paul Molitor put on an exciting 39-game hitting streak. A .353 hitter for the season, Molitor's streak was the fifth longest in modern times, topped only by Joe DiMaggio (56), Pete Rose (44),

Alan Trammel

George Sisler (41), and Ty Cobb (40).

In the West, the Minnesota Twins under freshman skipper Tom Kelly won 85 games and with them the division, two games better than Kansas City. With Frank Viola (17–10) and Jeff Reardon (31 saves) keying the pitching staff, the Twins shot a lot of missiles out of their Hubert H. Humphrey "Homerdome." Gary Gaetti hit 31, Kent Hrbek 34, Tom Brunansky 32, and Kirby Puckett 28.

Oakland, which had the 1986 Rookie of the Year in long-balling Jose Canseco, culled the honors again in long-balling young first baseman Mark McGwire, who left all rookie home run records in tatters. McGwire led the league with 49 long-distance belts, breaking the freshman record of 38 held by Wally Berger and Frank Robinson. McGwire was the first rookie home run king since Al Rosen in 1950. The chief beneficiary of the young first baseman's booming bat was right-hander Dave Stewart, who posted a surprise 20–13 record for the A's.

As young McGwire was starting his career, an old favorite was ending his. Finishing his career in Oakland, where he had starred years before, Reggie Jackson called it quits after 21 years and 563 home runs, the latter figure sixth best on the career list.

After missing spring training because of a holdout and then getting off to a sluggish 4–6 start, Boston's Roger Clemens returned to his 1986 form and finished with a 20–9 record, good enough for a second straight Cy Young Award.

The All-Star Game, played at Oakland's Alameda County Stadium on July 14, went to the National League, 2–0, in 13 innings.

In the pennant playoffs, a fired-up Minnesota team downed Detroit in five games.

The New York Mets were heavily favored to repeat in the National League East, but then an almost diabolic series of misfortunes befell their pitching staff, beginning with Dwight Gooden's two-month loss to drug rehabilitation. At one time or another, pitchers Sid Fernandez, Rick Aguilera, David Cone, Roger McDowell, and Ron Darling were on the disabled list, and 1986's ace, southpaw Bob Ojeda, was out for most of the season with arm miseries. Nevertheless, helped by the heavy sticking of Darryl Strawberry (39 home runs) and Howard Johnson (36 homers), the Mets made a race of it, losing out to Whitey Herzog's Cardinals by three games.

The Cardinals were not without their own injury-related pitching problems, most notably the loss of left-hander John Tudor for much of the season due to a broken leg suffered in a freak dugout accident. The Cards won despite having three 11-game winners heading their staff, but a bullpen deep and strong helped compensate. Todd Worrell (33 saves) and left-handers Ken Dayley and Ricky Horton pitched effectively out of the St. Louis pen all season. Despite a September injury that all but eliminated him from postseason play, first baseman Jack Clark blasted 35 homers and drove in 106 runs as the Cardinals' number one slugger. Willie McGee knocked in 105 runs and Ozzie Smith continued to write the book at shortstop, while also contributing a .303 batting average. Vince Coleman was again the most successful base stealer with 109.

The biggest offensive noise in the league was made by the Cubs' Andre Dawson. Dawson, a free agent who was being shunned by the allegedly colluding major league teams, came to the Cubs and offered to sign a blank contract. The Cubs accepted, filled in a $500,000 salary figure (less than half of Dawson's market value), and watched Andre go to work. With 49 home runs and 137 runs batted in, Dawson spiced the season for the last-place Cubs and was voted the league's Most Valuable Player.

The Phillies' Steve Bedrosian was the Cy Young Award winner for his 40 saves. San Diego had both the batting champion in Tony Gwynn and the Rookie of the

Jack Clark

314

Will Clark

Year in catcher Benny Santiago. Gwynn's .370, which earned him his second batting title, made him the league's first .370 hitter since Stan Musial in 1948, while Santiago caught everyone's attention with a 34-game hitting streak late in the season.

The Phillies' Mike Schmidt achieved a personal milestone by hitting his 500th career homer on April 18. For Houston's Nolan Ryan it was a most curious year. Still pouring in his fast one at over 90 mph, the forty-year-old Ryan finished with an 8–16 record despite 270 strikeouts (a record 11th time over 200) and league-leading 2.76 ERA. Ryan ended the season with 4,547 career strikeouts, far ahead now of the 4,131 of runner-up Steve Carlton, who was struggling to keep a faltering career going. (After leaving the Phillies, Carlton had pitched for the Giants, White Sox, and Indians before catching on with the Twins, the shadow of his former self growing increasingly fainter.)

Roger Craig's San Francisco Giants were the winners in the West, by six games over Cincinnati (who finished second for the third year in a row). Like Herzog's Cardinals, Craig's Giants had no aces—a 13-game winner was the class of the staff—but, again like the Cardinals, the Giants were well-stocked in the bullpen, with Scott Garrelts, Don Robinson, and left-hander Craig Lefferts. First baseman Will Clark was the team's main siege gun with 35 homers and 91 RBIs. Part-timer Mike Aldrete (.325) and Candy Maldonado supplemented Clark's good hitting.

To many, Craig's performance was a job of managerial wizardry, having led to a division title a team that just two years before had finished dead last, losing 100 games.

The Giants, however, couldn't finish off the Cardinals in the playoffs after holding a 3–2 edge in games, finally losing in seven.

The World Series also went the full seven, but this time the Cardinals came up a dollar short, losing to the Twins, who backed Frank Viola's two wins and Jeff Reardon's strong relief pitching with solid hitting.

1988

After two successive years of record home run hitting, the majors saw a 29 percent drop in long-ball production in 1988. Most people attributed the fall-off to a less lively ball as well as a slightly enlarged strike zone. The drop-off did not affect Oakland's Jose Canseco, however, who increased his home run total from 31 to 42 in leading the American League. The Mets' Darryl Strawberry repeated his 1987 total of 39 and this time they were good enough to top the National League.

Right after the All-Star break, the Red Sox changed managers, John McNamara leaving and third-base coach Joe Morgan taking over. The change produced "Morgan's Miracle": 12 straight wins, 19 of 20, an American League record 24 straight wins at home, and a second East Division title in three years for Boston.

Boston's mechanical hitter Wade Boggs batted .366 and won his fourth straight batting title and fifth overall, building his average on 214 hits, establishing a new record with six straight seasons of 200 or more hits. Mike Greenwell batted .325 and drove in 119 runs, Dwight Evans was a .293 hitter with 111 RBIs, and young center fielder Ellis Burks rounded off a superb outfield with a .294 average and 92 RBIs. Left-hander Bruce Hurst (who free-agented himself to San Diego after the season) was 18–6 and Roger Clemens was 18–12, leading the league with 291 strikeouts and 8 shutouts. Lee Smith, obtained from the Cubs, anchored the bullpen with 29 saves. Boston's margin over second-place Detroit was just one game.

A mere 3½ games separated first-place Boston and fifth-place New York in the East. In New York, the managerial whirl continued, with Billy Martin's fifth tenure as Yankee manager ending on June 23, when he was replaced by the man he had replaced, Lou Piniella, who in turn was replaced by Dallas Green after the season. New York's Rickey Henderson's 93 stolen bases gave him the lead for the eighth time.

The one Eastern team that was never in contention was Baltimore. The Orioles opened the season by shattering all records for futility by losing their first 21 games.

Toronto's Dave Stieb finished the season with a pair of one-hitters, in each case losing his no-hit bid with two out in the ninth inning. In all, Stieb pitched a record three one-hitters in 1988.

In the West it was all Oakland. With Canseco hitting 42 home runs and leading with 124 RBIs (he also stole 40 bases, becoming the first member of the 40–40 club) and Mark McGwire hitting 32, the Athletics won 104 games and ran away to an easy 13-game lead over second-place Minnesota. Center fielder Dave Henderson added 24 home runs to the Oakland output. Dave Stewart was again a 20-game winner for the A's (21–12), followed by Bob Welch (17–9) and Storm Davis (16–7), and an exception-

Walter Weiss

ally strong bullpen headed by Dennis Eckersley (45 saves).

Canseco was the league MVP, although some people felt Minnesota's Kirby Puckett might have won the award. The Twins slugger led with 234 hits, banged out 24 homers, drove in 121 runs, and batted .356, highest by an American League right-handed hitter since Joe DiMaggio's .357 in 1940. Minnesota left-hander Frank Viola was the Cy Young Award winner with a 24–7 record, while Oakland's shortstop Walter Weiss was Rookie of the Year, giving the A's the honor for the third year in a row, following McGwire and Canseco.

The league's other 20-game winner was Kansas City's Mark Gubicza (20–8).

The All-Star Game, played July 12 at Cincinnati, went to the American League by a 2–1 score.

It was all Oakland in the pennant playoffs, as Tony LaRussa's team swept Boston in four straight, with Eckersley getting a save in all four games.

The Mets were expected to win in the National League East and they did, despite a midsummer doldrum that saw them leading Pittsburgh by just a half game on July 21. The club's strong pitching then showed the way and they finished up with 100 wins and a 15-game bulge over the second-place Pirates.

Davey Johnson's team got a surprise 20–3 season from right-hander David Cone, 18–9 from Dwight Gooden, and 17–9 from Ron Darling, plus strong relief work from Roger McDowell and newcomer Randy Myers, a fireballing lefty. Strawberry's 39 homers and 101 RBIs led the team, with Kevin McReynolds driving in 99 runs.

Pittsburgh's strength came primarily from the all-around play of center fielder Andy Van Slyke, third baseman Bobby Bonilla (each with 100 RBIs), outfielder Barry Bonds, and second baseman Jose Lind.

Following some truly spectacular pitching by Orel Hershiser, Tom Lasorda's Dodgers won the West by a comfortable seven games over the Reds (who finished second for the fourth straight year). Hershiser, whose 23–8 record earned him the Cy Young Award, finished the season with five straight shutouts, ten shutout innings of a no-decision game and a record 59 consecutive scoreless innings, breaking by one-third the record set by Don Drysdale in 1968. Tim Leary (17–11) helped pick up the slack left by an injury-riddled 5–8 season suffered by erstwhile ace Fernando Valenzuela.

The Dodger attack was led by the spirited Kirk Gibson, signed as a free agent. Voted the MVP Award, the ex-Tiger batted .290 and hit 25 home runs. Mike Marshall's 82 RBIs led the team.

Cincinnati had the league's top southpaw in Danny Jackson (23–8), obtained in a trade with Kansas City; lefty John Franco's 39 saves; and the Rookie of the Year in third baseman Chris Sabo. On September 16, lefty Tom Browning (18–5) delivered the league's third perfect game of the modern era, stifling the Dodgers 1–0. Earlier in the season, Browning's teammate Rob Robinson had come within a strike of pitching a perfect game against Montreal.

San Diego's Tony Gwynn won his third batting title with a .313 average, lowest in league history. The league RBI leader was San Francisco's burgeoning superstar first baseman Will Clark, who had 109 to go with his 29 home runs. The Giants' thirty-nine-year-old ace Rick Reuschel was 19–11, while another senior mound ace, Houston's forty-one-year-old Nolan Ryan, led with 228 strikeouts. While not as inept as Baltimore, the Atlanta Braves began the season by losing their first ten games, a new league record.

Pete Rose was suspended for 30 days by league president Bart Giamatti for shoving umpire Dave Pallone during an argument on April 30. And in a break with tradition, the Chicago Cubs finally installed lights in Wrigley Field and began a limited schedule of night ball on August 9.

During the regular season, the Mets had beaten the Dodgers 11 times in 12 games, but in the playoffs the Dodgers upset the New Yorkers in seven games, with Hershiser pitching a shutout in the finale.

David Cone

Right-hander Steve Stone, an 11-year major leaguer who pitched for four clubs. He won 25 games and the Cy Young Award with the Orioles in 1980. Lifetime record: 107–93.

BELOW: Andre Dawson. He came to the major leagues with the Expos in 1974; in 1987, playing for the Cubs, he was the league's MVP.

The World Series featured a moment of pure theatrics. In the bottom of the ninth inning of the opener an injured Kirk Gibson made his only appearance of the Series. Summoned from the trainer's room with his team losing 4–3, Gibson, barely able to swing or run, delivered a pinch–home run to give the Dodgers a stunning 5–4 victory. From there, Dodger pitching went on to tame the bruising Oakland bats (Canseco was 1-for-19 and McGwire 1-for-17) and win the Series in five games. Hershiser pitched a three-hit, 6–0 shutout in Game 2 and a 5–2 four-hitter in the fifth and final game.

Len Barker, twice the American League's strikeout leader.

Tony Armas, the American League's RBI leader in 1984.

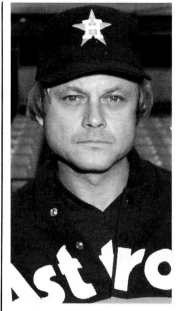

Joe Niekro. Like his brother Phil, Joe spent more than two decades in the major leagues, winning over 200 games.

Dave Winfield, the National League's RBI leader in 1979 with San Diego, and later a consistent 100-RBI man for the Yankees.

The Dodgers' Davey Lopes is trying to make a play on the Pirates' Omar Moreno, but without that ball he doesn't have much chance.

BELOW: Fernando Valenzuela early in his spectacular 1981 rookie season, icing his left arm after another victory.

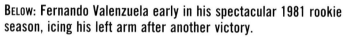

Three mainstays of Milwaukee's 1982 American League pennant winners. Left to right: catcher Ted Simmons, pitcher Rollie Fingers, and shortstop Robin Yount.

Cincinnati's Riverfront Stadium

A two-time American League home run leader for Milwaukee, Gorman Thomas was a free-swinger for three clubs from 1973–86, batting .225.

Paul Molitor

RIGHT: Ben Oglivie played for the Red Sox and Tigers, but had his best years with Milwaukee in the early 1980s. He played from 1971–86, batting .273.

Steve Kemp, twice a 100-RBI man for the Tigers.

319

Toronto's Dave Stieb, the American League ERA leader in 1985.

Two-time National League MVP Dale Murphy of the Atlanta Braves.

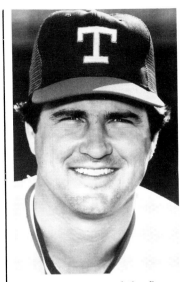

Jim Sundberg, one of the fine defensive catchers of his time.

Pirates second baseman Johnny Ray.

Master of the split-fingered fastball and one of the greatest of all relief pitchers: Bruce Sutter. He had his top years with the Cubs and Cardinals.

One of the American League's top third basemen for 15 years, Doug DeCinces played for the Orioles and Angels, batting .259.

Houston infielders Phil Garner (left) and Ray Knight.

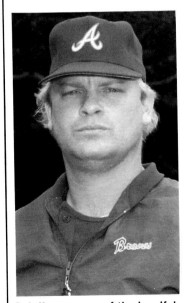

Bob Horner, one of the handful of major leaguers to hit four home runs in a single game.

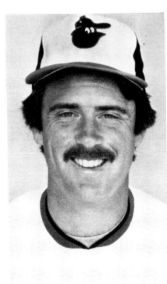

Baltimore southpaw Scott McGregor, a 20-game winner in 1980.

Right-hander Mike Boddicker, a 20-game winner for Baltimore in 1984.

Harold Baines, for years one of the solid men in the Chicago White Sox lineup.

Al Bumbry, hustling outfielder for the Orioles from 1972–84. He finished with San Diego in 1985. Lifetime average: .281.

Charlie Hough, a longtime reliever for the Dodgers who was converted into a successful starter by the Texas Rangers.

BELOW: Jerry Reuss, who came to the majors with the Cardinals in 1969 and later had his best years for the Pirates and Dodgers.

Mario Soto, Cincinnati's hard-throwing right-hander.

Don Mattingly, by consensus the best ballplayer of his time.

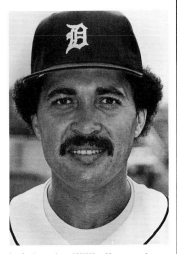

The heavy-hitting Pedro Guerrero of the Los Angeles Dodgers.

Left-hander Willie Hernandez, whose sensational relief work in 1984 helped the Tigers to the pennant.

Lou Whitaker, Detroit's best second baseman since the heyday of Charlie Gehringer.

Kirk Gibson, Detroit star who took the free agency route to the Dodgers in 1988.

Lance Parrish, a bulwark behind the plate for the Tigers. He joined the Phillies as a free agent in 1987.

Dan Petry, one of the aces of the 1984 world-champion Tigers.

Detroit's Chet Lemon, one of the top defensive center fielders of the 1980s.

Alvin Davis, Seattle's Rookie of the Year first baseman in 1984.

LEFT: Darrell Evans, a 20-year major leaguer with the Braves, Giants, and Tigers. He was the American League home run leader in 1985.

Seattle left-hander Mark Langston, who led the league in strikeouts three of his first four years.

Chicago Cubs catcher Jody Davis.

Formerly with the Dodgers and Indians, Rick Sutcliffe won a Cy Young Award with the Cubs in 1984.

Lee Smith, fastballing reliever of the Cubs, who was traded to the Red Sox in 1987.

BELOW: Yankees relief ace Dave Righetti.

Dickie Thon, Houston's talented shortstop, whose big-league career was wrecked when he was hit in the face with a pitched ball in 1984.

Toronto's George Bell, the American League's MVP in 1987.

Tony Fernandez, Toronto shortstop.

RIGHT: Rickey Henderson. He came to the majors with Oakland in 1979 and joined the Yankees in 1985. He led the American League in stolen bases seven straight years.

Jesse Barfield of the Toronto Blue Jays, the American League home run leader in 1986.

BELOW: Tony Gwynn, who won batting championships with the San Diego Padres in 1984, 1987 and 1988.

Wade Boggs (left) and George Brett.

Bret Saberhagen, a 20-game winner in 1985.

The Cardinals' Willie McGee, the National League MVP in 1985.

Milwaukee's Teddy Higuera, a 20-game winner in 1986.

Montreal's Tim Raines, the National League batting champion in 1986.

Vince Coleman of the Cardinals, one of baseball's most electrifying baserunners.

LEFT: Todd Worrell, ace reliever of the 1985 and 1987 Cardinals pennant winners.

RIGHT: John Tudor pitched for the Red Sox and Pirates before attaining stardom with the Cardinals.

Montreal third baseman Tim Wallach.

Kansas City reliever Dan Quisenberry.

Boston's Roger Clemens, American League Cy Young Award winner in 1986 and 1987.

Darryl Strawberry, the multitalented outfielder of the New York Mets.

Pete Rose rapping out career base hit 4,192, setting a new major league record.

The infield for the 1985 and 1987 St. Louis Cardinals pennant winners. (Left to right): third baseman Terry Pendleton, shortstop Ozzie Smith, second baseman Tommy Herr, and first baseman Jack Clark.

Orel Hershiser, who was 19–3 for the Dodgers in 1985.

Dave Winfield (left) and Don Mattingly.

Cleveland's Joe Carter, the American League RBI leader in 1986.

Bruce Hurst

BELOW: Mike Witt, California Angels ace, who pitched a perfect game in 1984.

Pete Incaviglia, long-ball hitter of the Texas Rangers.

RIGHT: Bob Boone came up with the Phillies in 1972, joined the Angels in 1982, and went on to catch more games than anyone in major league history.

Dwight Evans, longtime outfield star of the Red Sox.

The New York Mets' Dwight Gooden, who was 24–4 in 1985.

Outfielders Len Dykstra (left) and Darryl Strawberry of the Mets.

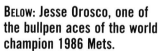

BELOW: Jesse Orosco, one of the bullpen aces of the world champion 1986 Mets.

California's Wally Joyner, one of the hard-hitting young rookies that came into the American League in 1986.

Pete Rose (left) and Mike Schmidt.

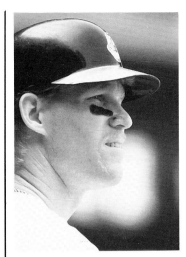

Cory Snyder of the Cleveland Indians.

Keith Hernandez

Nolan Ryan

Bob Ojeda, who came to the Mets from the Red Sox and helped pitch the New Yorkers to the world championship in 1986.

BELOW: Houston's hard-hitting first baseman Glenn Davis.

Bill Doran of the Houston Astros.

RIGHT: Frank Viola, southpaw ace of the 1987 world champion Minnesota Twins.

Ron Darling, one of the aces of the 1986 New York Mets.

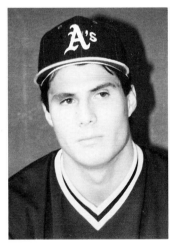

Oakland's Jose Canseco, Rookie of the Year in the American League in 1986.

Catcher Gary Carter. He came to the majors with Montreal in 1974 and joined the Mets in 1985.

The Mets' Mookie Wilson avoiding the Bob Stanley wild pitch that allowed the Mets to score the tying run in the bottom of the 10th inning of game 6 of the 1986 World Series.

The Metrodome, home of the Minnesota Twins.

A trio of hard hitters who helped bring the 1987 championship to Minnesota. Left to right: outfielders Tom Brunansky and Kirby Puckett and first baseman Kent Hrbek.

Twins third baseman Gary Gaetti.

Danny Tartabull, long-distance hitter for Kansas City.

329

Carney Lansford. He came to the majors with the Angels in 1978, won a batting champion-ship with the Red Sox in 1981, and joined Oakland in 1983.

BELOW: Kansas City's Kevin Seitzer, a .323 hitter in his first full season (1987).

Oakland's Mark McGwire, whose 49 home runs in 1987 established a new record for rookies.

Cincinnati outfielder Eric Davis.

Cardinals shortstop Ozzie Smith.

BELOW: Catcher Benny Santiago of the San Diego Padres, the National League Rookie of the Year in 1987.

A trio of American League batting champions. Left to right: Don Mattingly, George Brett, and Wade Boggs.

I N D E X

INDEX

INDEX

INDEX

INDEX

I N D E X